T0248527

PATHS TO PRISON:
ON THE ARCHITECTURES OF CARCERALITY

COLUMBIA BOOKS ON
ARCHITECTURE AND THE CITY

The path that emerges from the Olympic Motel offers a way to describe contemporary carcerality, which entangles the devouring tendencies of privatization and the sanctioned punitive policies of the racial state.

i am asking us to consider how white supremacy is fully engaged in the organization of systemic violence and the social subjection of white civil society's historical racial antagonists, even and especially as its institutional forms—including its political and intellectual leadership—convene a (relative) diversity of nonwhite bodies.

The rent party offered black tenants a space to revel in the joy of being housed while also forsaking the conservative imperative to worship the "cult of the home."

The wealth built by the C&O, which in turn was built by those explicitly understood as "slaves of the state," was coal wealth, and Ruffin's "vicinage" was the territory marked by coal's extraction.

...the act of riding the bus constitutes the work of social reproduction in a very literal sense—it is the work of keeping people alive.

...the change of the Library of Congress subject heading from "illegal aliens" to "noncitizens" reflects a more accurate summation of the penal logic: much like citizens must be made, so too must non-citizens.

Disappearing insurgent and rebellious people was a way to efface and erase the new ways of knowing, feeling, and sensing created by the many social movements of the period.

Scale and infrastructure are sometimes weapons. And language is both.

Indigenous peoples reject the idea that the way of life supported by pipeline infrastructure should be accelerated or intensified and instead step into the vulnerable and volatile space between the proposal and potential completion of pipelines to protect the land, water, air, plant, and animal relations.

This era of data
is an intensification of capitalist exploitation, but it is
simultaneously and through identical means an intensification of the state's capacity for bodily domination.

The racial became discursively productive of concepts and representations of human difference, ones that established hierarchies of mental and physical fitness affirming why Europeans were the most capable of advancing world civilization; in other words, why they were most capable of being modern.

It is a
sonic and visual mode of refusal—a student can't be transformed into the "wayward" without accompanying data—
which works to reject the supposed knowledge of the state
that pathologizes blackness into something to be reformed
or subdued.

The
spaces we inhabit seem to leave little room for imagining
what alternatives exist to the hoarding, hunting, and fencing tendencies of settler colonial homemaking that mark
the American Dream with so much violence.

459   JASMINE SYEDULLAH

PATHS TO PRISON:
ON THE ARCHITECTURES OF CARCERALITY

Edited by
Isabelle Kirkham-Lewitt

Contributions by
Dylan Rodríguez
Adrienne Brown
James Graham
Brett Story
Jarrett M. Drake
Stephen Dillon
Sable Elyse Smith
Anne Spice
Wendy L. Wright
Mabel O. Wilson
Leslie Lodwick
Jasmine Syedullah

COLUMBIA BOOKS ON
ARCHITECTURE AND THE CITY

EXTENDED STAY:
I.E. "THE MORE THINGS CHANGE, THE MORE
THINGS STAY THE SAME"

ISABELLE KIRKHAM-LEWITT

Behind the Houston Processing Center, there is a motel, a prison farm, a plantation, a Supreme Court case, a tax exemption, a landlord, and a developer. To echo Stephen Dillon in this book, it could go "on and on and on and on and on and on and on." (269–291)

> About $25 a night can get you a single room, a bathroom down the hall, and three meals in a Houston hostelry, which seems pretty reasonable at today's prices. In fact, it isn't even the "guests" who pay. But there's a drawback. They can't check out at will...
> —Marjorie Anders, describing the Houston Processing Center in *Clovis News Journal*, August 4, 1985[1]

In November 1983, the Corrections Corporation of America (CCA) received its first federal contract from the Immigration and Naturalization Service (INS) to build an immigrant detention center in Houston, Texas. The following April, it opened the Houston Processing Center, designed to accommodate roughly 350 individuals. It took just five months for the CCA to finance, design, build, and open the Houston center—though still not fast enough for the INS, which had already begun to enforce the more punitive policies of the early Reagan administration and to carry out a mode of governance that conflated criminal and immigration procedures.[2] These policies had spatial consequences,

1   Marjorie Anders, "Counties Turning to Privately Operated Jails," *Clovis News Journal*, August 4, 1985.

taking shape in new architectural devices meant to support a broader and enduring carceral system that instrumentalizes and weaponizes the built environment.

On January 22, 1984, with the construction for the Houston Processing Center underway, the CCA opened an interim facility at the Olympic Motel along Interstate 45. The motel's short-lived role as detainer is preserved only in a horrifyingly hokey video of CCA co-founders T. Don Hutto and Tom Beasley recounting the early days of their company.[3] The INS had "very unrealistic expectations," says Hutto. "They gave us ninety days." The two arrived in Houston on New Year's Eve to begin searching for their surrogate detention site: "We were both getting pretty weary. We had found a lot of places, but nothing seemed quite to work, nothing you could secure in a short period of time. Then we saw this big 'ole sign: the 'Olympic Motel.'"[4] They made an offer to lease the place.

Once rented, the CCA installed a 12-foot cyclone fence around the perimeter of the motel, "laced with bamboo to thwart the curious" and topped with coiled barbed wire.[5] The pool was drained and filled in with sand. The rooms

2   For a more in-depth history of the origins of "crimmigration," see César Cuauhtémoc García Hernández, "Creating Crimmigration," *Brigham Young Law Review* 2013, no. 6 (February 2014): 1457–1515, https://digitalcommons. law.byu.edu/lawreview/vol2013/iss6/4; and Jonathan Simon, "Refugees in a Carceral Age: The Rebirth of Immigration Prisons in the United States," *Public Culture* 10, no. 3 (Spring 1998): 577–607.

3   The Nation, "Corrections Corporation of America's Founders Tom Beasley and Don Hutto," video, 2:47, February 27, 2013, originally published on CCA's website, https://www.youtube.com/watch?v=DAvdMe4KdGU.

4   A noteworthy coincidence: more than a decade later, in 1997, CCA bought another Olympic—the Olympic Hotel and Spa in Fallsburg, New York—for $470,000, in the hopes of expanding its operations to the Northeast. For more on this, see Lauren Brooke-Eisen's *Inside Private Prisons* (New York: Columbia University Press, 2017), 103; and Steven Donziger, "The Hard Cell," *New York Magazine*, June 9, 1997, 26–28.

5   Wayne King, "Contracts for Detention Raise Legal Questions," *New York Times*, March 6, 1984, https://www.nytimes.com/1984/03/06/us/contracts-for-detention-raise-legal-questions.html.

were secured, windows outfitted with iron bars, and doors
with exterior locks. Promising to return the motel in "three
times as good a condition" and to leave all the "improvements in place," not much else was done to the existing
building. Signs were left untouched: "Olympic Motel,"
"Color TV, Radio, Telephone," and "Day Rates Available"
were still advertised to the highway. The renovation was
an exercise in DIY securitization that included Hutto,
American Express card in hand, running to a Houston
hardware store for supplies and a Walmart for toiletries;
the CCA hiring the landlord's family as staff; and the motel
employing additional guards from ABM Security Services.
On Super Bowl Sunday of 1984, Hutto produced ad-hoc
photo ID cards and fingerprinted individuals himself
while other company leaders "distributed sandwiches and
helped security staff escort detainees to their living quarters."[6] The architectural sleights of hand carried out at the
Olympic Motel modeled the ease with which motel slipped
into detention site, living quarters into cells, and hostelry
into (site of) captivity.

This slippage is at the heart of the CCA's founding. Describing the company's premise, co-founder Tom
Beasley once said you could "sell prisons 'just like you were
selling cars, real estate, or hamburgers.'"[7] Or, considering
that CCA obtained its initial funding from serial entrepre-
neur Jack Massey—famed eventual owner of Kentucky
Fried Chicken and founder of the Hospital Corporation
of America (HCA)—it was just like selling fried chicken

6   Damon Hininger, "T. Don Hutto—The Mettle of the Man Behind Our
     Proud Facility," Employee Insights, CCA, January 19, 2010, https://perma.cc/
     G9ZZ-KVAJ.

7   Holly Kirby et al., *The Dirty Thirty: Nothing to Celebrate about 30 Years of
     Corrections Corporation of America* (Austin: Grassroots Leadership, 2013),
     1. For more about the founding of the company, see Winthrop Knowlton's
     case study *Corrections Corporation of America* (Cambridge, MA: Harvard
     Kennedy School of Government Case Program, 1985).

An intertitle from the CCA video of co-founders T. Don Hutto and Tom Beasley discussing how they secured the first of many contracts for housing detained undocumented immigrants. Courtesy of *The Nation* and posted to YouTube, February 27, 2013, https://www.youtube.com/watch?v=DA vdMe4KdGU.

oh no! where
we gonna'
put 'em?

or hospitals. The forced equivalence underwriting CCA's corporate model prefigured its speculative and opportunistic development model, which registered the built environment through spatial analogs.

That the Olympic Motel came to house 140 asylum seekers and undocumented immigrants awaiting deportation over the course of four months ultimately faded into obscurity once the official Houston Processing Center opened. Hutto and Beasley's use of the motel is now a self-professed scrappy origin of one of today's largest for-profit prison corporations—CCA "was a start-up before start-ups were fashionable. We met the deadline, the detainees arrived, and a new relationship was forged between government and the private sector."[8] This privately run detention facility speaks to a particular spatial tendency within the larger neoliberal project: "enterprise zones" that privatize the usual functions of the state. The company found an untapped site of possibility in the space behind bars, a space cleared by the social engineering, deregulation, and financialization of the 1970s and 80s, which converted government, corporations, and citizens into opportunities for investment and capitalization.[9]

8   Hininger, "T. Don Hutto."
9   The corporate globalization and deindustrialization of this period—exacerbated in the 1990s with free trade agreements like NAFTA—was a force of impoverishment. The spaces of concentrated poverty, disinvestment, and joblessness left in the wake of America's development path were met with attacks on welfare and social programs, with the War on Drugs, with "tough on crime," with more police, and more prisons. Angela Y. Davis has described the racialized social crisis that emerged from this pattern of economic development and globalized capital: "In fleeing organized labor in the US to avoid paying higher wages and benefits, [corporations] leave entire communities in shambles, consigning huge numbers of people to joblessness, leaving them prey to the drug trade, destroying the economic base of these communities and thus affecting the education system, social welfare and turning the people who live in those communities into perfect candidates for prison. At the same time, they create an economic demand for prisons, which stimulates the economy, providing jobs in the correctional

I.E. "THE MORE THINGS CHANGE, THE MORE THINGS STAY THE SAME"

The CCA positioned itself as the answer to two interrelated problems: corrections bureaucracies—"the most entrenched bureaucracies of all"—and the growing demand for detention space.[10] The company sold a more "efficient" and "economical" delivery system of detention from construction to operation. Its ability to open the Houston Processing Center in roughly five months and at a cost of $14,000 per bed—opposed to the two years and $26,000 per bed it would have taken the INS—was celebrated by proponents of privatization.[11] Today, the company claims that it delivers cost savings up to 25 percent and cuts the construction time of new facilities by 40 percent. Unencumbered by red-tape (like public approval), the company could "act faster than public agencies in everything from [attaining funding to choosing a site] to construction to buying shampoo."[12] CCA's operational efficiencies, no matter how small, are a part of the company's larger cost-saving efforts to reduce the labor of managing its facilities through design. In fact, the provisional "design elements"—cyclone fence, barbed wire, bamboo, sand, exterior locks, iron bars—working to turn the Olympic Motel into a site of captivity also worked to undermine the conventional image of corrections.[13]

industry for people who often come from the very populations that are criminalized by this process. It is a horrifying and self-reproducing cycle." See Angela Y. Davis, "Globalism and the Prison Industrial Complex: An Interview with Angela Y. Davis," by Avery F. Gordon, *Keeping Good Time: Reflections on Knowledge, Power, and People* (Abingdon, UK: Routledge, 2016), 48–49.

10 Erik Larsen, "Captive Company," *Inc.*, June 1, 1988, https://www.inc.com/magazine/19880601/803.html.

11 James Austin and Garry Coventry, *Emerging Issues on Privatized Prisons* (Washington, DC: Bureau of Justice Assistance, 2001), 15, https://www.ncjrs.gov/pdffiles1/bja/181249.pdf.

12 Larsen, "Captive Company."

13 CCA rebranded as CoreCivic in October 2016. According to the company today, "Many of the once iconic symbols of correctional facilities that required substantial staffing, such as high concrete perimeter walls and

In 1967, Jack Massey, then owner of KFC, wrote a letter to persuade family friend Tommy Frist Jr., who was struggling to decide whether to pursue a career in business or medicine, to join the company: "Chicken, beef, or medicine. Make your decision soon." The note inspired Frist Jr. to choose a hybrid of the three. In 1968, Massey and Frist Jr. founded HCA, a "new kind of hospital company." Courtesy of HCA.

Jimmy, I hope this will be of interest to you

Jack

The World's No. 1 Chicken Salesman Goes

Beef & Ham

Chicken Beef or Medicine

Make your decision soon

The Olympic Motel modeled the private-prison product CCA would ultimately become known for. It gave built form to the fiscal conservatism and tough-on-crime policies of the time that also recast asylum seekers and refugees, primarily from Latin America, as criminals. On the heels of the Mariel boatlift and in the midst of a raging civil war in El Salvador, the INS saw detaining large numbers of asylum seekers and refugees as a form of deterrence. By 1982 "all aliens without proper travel documents [were to be] detained pending a determination of their status."[14] Not only did the INS's budget for detention grow exponentially throughout the 80s (from $15.7 million to over $149 million) but so did its capacity to hold individuals and the average length of detention (from approximately 7 days in 1984 to 23 days in 1990).[15] As the INS intensified its policing and detaining efforts in the border region, US senator Lloyd Bentsen aired that it seemed the entirety of South Texas had become a "massive detention camp."[16]

even higher guard towers, have been rendered obsolete by modern technologies. Yet, such structures still exist at many government-owned correctional facilities across the country. CoreCivic's design elements can create meaningful short- and long-term savings, while improving facility safety and security." See CoreCivic, *ESG Report: Environmental, Social and Governance* (2018), 17.

14 Codified in 8 C.F.R. SS 212.5, 235.3. See Michael Welsh, "The Immigration Crisis: Detention as an Emerging Mechanism of Social Control," in "Immigration: A Civil Rights Issue for the Americas in the 21st Century," ed. Susanne Jonas and Suzie Dod Thomas, special issue, *Social Justice* 23, no. 3 (Fall 1996): 170.

15 According to a report produced by the US General Accounting Office in 1992: "INS can detain about 99,000 aliens a year at its current facilities. However… about 489,000 aliens were subject to detention between 1988 and 1990 because they were criminal, deportable, or excludable. INS has released criminal aliens and not pursued illegal aliens because it did not have the detention space to hold them." United States General Accounting Office, *Immigration Control: Immigration Policies Affect INS Detention Efforts*, report to the Chairman of the United States Senate Committee on Judiciary Subcommittee on International Law, Immigration, and Refugees (Washington, DC, 1992), 3. See also Welsh, "The Immigration Crisis," 170.

16 César Cuauhtémoc García Hernández, *Migrating to Prison: America's*

In the context of this hostile territory and to the desperate eye of the CCA, the Olympic Motel offered 12,466 square feet of latent detention space. While this particular narrative of corporate annexation fell in line with a longer history of recycling and reusing sites of internment, it also marked the beginnings of an increasingly pervasive model that propagates the need it intends to fulfill. It is a model in which architecture is both the promise and the guarantor of carceral expansion. The fast and cheap delivery of beds at the Olympic Motel satisfied the current demand and also incentivized a future demand. It was proof for the CCA that they had not only devised an iterable scheme for the privatized service of carceral detention, which presupposed its continuance on a new market, but also that they had innovated a system of delivery through the built environment.

Between Use and Misuse

The case of the Olympic Motel shows how the late-capitalist carceral system might be less about producing new architectural forms than constructing new uses out of an otherwise familiar spatial environment. It is a story that recounts both the situated origins of a particular model of carceral production and the pervasive workings of neoliberalism. Sara Ahmed writes that "use offers a way of telling stories about things," that "what has been used in the past can just as easily point us toward the future," and that "if use records where we have been, use can also direct us along certain paths."[17] That the Olympic Motel was taken up, put to use, or misused by the CCA on behalf of the INS is not intended to overly "direct" attention to the

Obsession with Locking up Immigrants (New York: New Press, 2019), 63.

17 Sara Ahmed, *What's the Use?* (Durham, NC: Duke University Press, 2019), 22–23.

Olympic Motel at 5714 Werner Street, along the North Freeway, Houston, TX 77079, pictured here with a billboard advertisement from Texas Christian University that reads "Opportunity is Waiting." © Google Street View 2015.

prominence of private corporations in the prison-industrial complex, nor is it intended to perpetuate the misconception that private prisons are the "corrupt heart" of this system of incarceration.[18] Rather, it is a story of urban-carceral transformation that evidences *how* the state—in this case through its corporate appendages—moves, restructures, and expands itself across the built environment according to its coercive functions. This is a narrative, then, that traces the sites of production, buildings, legal proceedings, rhetorical arguments, and financial instruments it *uses* to do so. The path that emerges from the Olympic Motel offers a way to describe contemporary carcerality, which entangles the devouring tendencies of privatization and the sanctioned punitive policies of the racial state. In other words, the short-lived fate of the Olympic Motel helps to tell the story of the status quo. "What is the status quo?" asks and answers Ruth Wilson Gilmore: "Put simply, capitalism requires inequality and racism enshrines it."[19]

Use is contingent on the form it is given by practice, ideology, and policy. That the Olympic Motel could be "secured in a short period of time" speaks not only to its architectural characteristics but also to longstanding and widespread social beliefs about what kinds of places contain, support, enable, or are needed by certain ways of life. Take, for instance, Justice Antonin Scalia's dissent in the 2015 Supreme Court case *City of Los Angeles v. Patel*:

> Motels not only provide housing to vulnerable transient populations, they are also a particularly attractive site for criminal activity ranging from drug

18   Over 90 percent of individuals are held in public prisons. See Wendy Sawyer and Peter Wagner, "Mass Incarceration: The Whole Pie 2020," Prison Policy Initiative, press release, March 24, 2020, https://www.prisonpolicy.org/reports/pie2020.html.

19   Ruth Wilson Gilmore, "The Worrying State of the Anti-Prison Movement," *Social Justice*, February 23, 2015, http://www.socialjusticejournal.org/the-worrying-state-of-the-anti-prison-movement.

dealing and prostitution to human trafficking... Motels provide an obvious haven for those who trade in human misery.[20]

This vision of how crime and poverty are distributed in space directs how the motel is legislated, policed, and circumscribed along racial lines—"insofar as geography," as Jackie Wang observes in *Carceral Capitalism*, "is a proxy for race."[21] Scalia's statement evinces the biases that enlist the motel as a mechanism of racial enclosure. The degree to which crime is inherent at motels, and thus the degree to which those who use, live, or reside in them are criminalized, deprived, and immobilized, is also determined through a partisan push and pull. In the majority opinion, Justice Sonia Sotomayor articulates her own argument about the intended and non-intended function of architectural objects: "Hotels—like practically all commercial premises or services—can be put to use for nefarious ends. But unlike the industries that the court has found to be closely regulated, hotels are not intrinsically dangerous."[22] While this juxtaposition may in some ways reproduce an all-too-easy dichotomy between conservative and liberal agendas, it also demonstrates the way in which judicial and political arguments proscribe and prescribe legitimate uses of state force in the built environment. At

20   City of Los Angeles v. Patel, 576 US__(2015), dissent, 1, https://www.supremecourt.gov/opinions/14pdf/13-1175_k537.pdf.

21   Wang writes this specifically about the supposed "race neutrality" of PredPol, a predictive policing software that focuses its crime data on time and location rather than on personal demographics. Though "PredPol is a spatialized form of predictive policing that does not target individuals or generate heat lists, spatial algorithmic policing, even when it does not use race to make predictions, can facilitate racial profiling by calculating proxies for race, such as neighborhood and location." Typology can be added to this list of proxies. See Jackie Wang, *Carceral Capitalism* (South Pasadena: Semiotext(e), 2018), 249.

22   *Patel*, 576 US__, opinion of the court, at 14.

the very least, these contrary opinions insert the motel and the manifold vulnerabilities, itinerancies, and possibilities that it supports into the struggle over how and where carceral state power is expanded and justified.

"We can ask about objects by following them about," Ahmed writes.[23] This call to attend to the "strange temporalities of use" unsettles certain assumptions about the built environment's relationship to and participation in the carceral state. It offers a way to unfix the prison as a place and also as a set of political, pedagogical, and theoretical concerns. This implies eschewing the often all-too-stable concept of "site" and "place" within the discipline of architecture. It is a specifically architectural misprision to understand incarceration as a solid architecture that one is "put into" or "let out of," an isolated and neatly packaged typological envelope of discipline and control. *Paths to Prison: On the Architectures of Carcerality* is instead premised on an understanding of the prison as a diffuse, porous, and mobile entity that coordinates the tactics, materials, and bodies that circulate beyond and through it. It is concerned with the "both/and" of the prison, where "the physical instantiation of the carceral is at once everywhere and also very specifically somewhere," as Wendy L. Wright writes. (363–384) That is, this book attempts to register the *mobility* of carcerality—which casts the prison as a machinery of oppression, a social and political economy of confinement that extends well beyond the institution's walls.

The prison pervades, with various degrees of intensity and duration, the everyday terrain between distinct spaces of containment: typologies and histories and lived experiences assumed to be "outside" of the sphere of incarceration. As Brett Story offers, "to consider 'ordinary space' is therefore to contend with how the prison system etches its violence into the social fabric in ways as diverse and

23   Ahmed, *What's the Use?*, 23.

complex as they are quiet and mundane." (211–237) To bring this idea back to the history of the Olympic Motel, it is perhaps the motel's ordinariness that obscures the extraordinary circumstances that have come to mark and mobilize it.

To understand the prison today, one must pursue, as Jarrett M. Drake powerfully proposes, "not a cultural *biography of things* but rather an *ethnography of exchange*." (241–265) This book aims to trace the contours of such an exchange. It follows the objects and ideologies that underwrite the prison, how they ebb and flow across the carceral continuum in the present, tracking how these objects and ideologies mutate in their historical course. The Olympic Motel models a very discrete exchange—a single site that moves "through hands, contexts, and uses" with enormous consequences for the lives within it—while also demanding that we look elsewhere, in time and in place, to see how such spatial fungibility is made possible. To tell the story of the state's insatiable custodial appetite, one must pursue various protagonists (human and otherwise), slip between past and present, and move across both discursive and material sites. It requires a narrative that is not set spatially or historically but that, in its movement, pieces together a layered geography of carcerality. Drawing on the struggle, imagination, and potential of Black women's geographies to reframe and undo traditional geographic "arrangements," Katherine McKittrick writes in *Demonic Grounds* "that our engagement with place, and with three-dimensionality, can inspire a different spatial story, one that is unresolved but also caught up in the flexible, sometimes disturbing, demands of geography, which some people 'wouldn't think was so sane.'"[24] *Paths to Prison* is deeply indebted to McKittrick's work and seeks to engage

24   Here McKittrick is writing about, and quoting from, Octavia Butler's
      Kindred—about how Dana Franklin, the young Black narrator and

the long tradition of thinking, living, and writing oppositional discourses that resist and find ways *out* of dominant spatial patterns that actively try to block the possibility of holding various places, practices, and oppressions in mutual relation.

Accounting for architecture's participation in the carceral state means leaning into inconclusiveness. This book thus also emerges from an invitation put forth by Avery Gordon in *Ghostly Matters* to "make contact with what is without doubt often painful, difficult, and unsettling" and to write new stories about "what happens when we admit the *ghost*—that special instance of the merging of the visible and the invisible, the dead and the living, the past and the present—into the making of worldly relations and into the making of our accounts of the world."[25] Gordon's ghost—like McKittrick's unresolved story and Ahmed's proposal to follow—offers new epistemologies, methodologies, and ways of writing for the field of architecture. It insists that current accounts of the built world carry the full presence or weight of the past and insists on registering how the supposedly "over-and-done-with" is materialized in "new" forms and "new" structures. *Paths to Prison* proposes that we look behind and across carceral sites to see how historical forms of racial violence and dispossession are inherited, learned, determined, naturalized, and

protagonist of *Kindred*, moves rather inexplicably between 1976 Los Angeles and antebellum Maryland, between her apartment and a plantation, between her present life and the life of her forebears. See Katherine McKittrick, *Demonic Grounds: Black Women and the Cartographies of Struggle* (Minneapolis: University of Minnesota Press, 2006), 2. Butler elsewhere has said that time travel was "just a device for getting the character back to confront where she came from." And yet, this device produces a new unstable and uneven terrain—a different "spatial story" that "hooks" and "stacks" spatially and temporally distinct sites into one. See Octavia Butler, "An Interview with Octavia Butler," by Randall Kenan, *Callaloo* 14, no. 2 (Spring 1991): 496.

25   Avery F. Gordon, *Ghostly Matters: Haunting and the Sociological Imagination* (Minneapolis: University of Minnesota Press, 2008), 23, 24.

struggled over in the present—how incarceration manifests or reenacts racial, economic, and social hierarchies.

As Dylan Rodríguez poignantly states, the term "mass incarceration" has "canonized a relatively coherent narrative structure, based on a generalized assumption that such juridically sanctioned, culturally normalized state violence is a betrayal of American values as well as a violation of the mystified egalitarian ethos that constitutes US national formation." (97–128) Taking Rodríguez's diagnosis as a challenge, this book aims to counter the apparent stability of that narrative with non-linear and mobile accounts of the seemingly disparate institutions, ideologies, practices, and spaces that enforce and perpetuate carceral power. It picks up the argument that this work is constitutive of and faithful to the foundations and values of the United States of America—that what we have come to call "mass incarceration" is not an aberration among American values but representative of them.

> When I get out of Cummins
> I'm goin' up to Little Rock.
> I'm gonna walk right up those Capitol steps,
> And I ain't gonna even knock.
> And if the legislature's in session,
> There's some things I'm gonna say.
> And I'm gonna say, gentleman…
> You say you're tryin' to rehabilitate us,
> Then show us you are…
> —Johnny Cash, "When I Get Out of Cummins,"
> performed at Cummins Prison Farm, April 1969.

On April 17, 1969, prisoners of the Cummins Prison Farm at the Arkansas State Penitentiary filed a suit in the District Court for the Eastern District of Arkansas to challenge the conditions of their confinement. They argued in *Holt v. Sarver* that the prison's isolation unit constituted "cruel and unusual punishment" in violation of the Eighth and Fourteenth Amendments.[26] Two months later, Judge Jesse Smith Henley agreed with the prisoners, concluding that their prolonged confinement in the unit was not only "mentally and emotionally traumatic" but "physically uncomfortable," "hazardous to health," and "degrading and debasing."[27] Judge Henley ordered injunctive relief and required Arkansas's Commissioner of Corrections—Robert Sarver, the named defendant in the case—to report the progress being made at Cummins.[28] This case sparked an almost decade-long series of litigations against the Arkansas Department of Corrections (ADC), which culminated in the 1978 United States Supreme Court case *Hutto v. Finney*. The petitioner in this final litigation was Terrell Don Hutto, the head of the ADC between 1971 and 1976—and the future cofounder of CCA.

On February 18, 1970, prisoners of Cummins and the adjacent Tucker Intermediate Reformatory filed additional claims against the ADC in *Holt v. Sarver II*—citing that the entire system, not just the specific practice of isolation, amounted to "cruel and unusual punishment." Judge Henley ruled again, this time more vociferously, against the entire state penal system: "For the ordinary convict a sentence to the Arkansas Penitentiary today amounts to a banishment from civilized society to a dark and evil world completely alien to the free world, a world that is

26 Holt v. Sarver, 300 F. Supp. 825 (E.D. Ark. 1969), https://www.clearinghouse. net/chDocs/public/PC-AR-0004-0006.pdf.

27 Holt v. Sarver, 300 F. Supp. 833.

28 Robert Sarver was ordered to report to the court within 30 days about the steps being taken the resolve the problems (i.e. unsanitary and inhumane isolation cells, no medical attention, and a total lack of protection and precaution against prisoner assault). The court did not find his report and progress adequate.

administered by criminals under unwritten rules and customs completely foreign to free world culture."[29]

To the petitioners of *Holt v. Sarver II*, Cummins extended a familiar political-economic system of power, violence, and exploitation, with "rules and customs" rooted in the nation's history of slavery. Unfreedom at Cummins was anything but "alien" to them, as Judge Henley would have it. The prison farm reeked of the plantation. Their claims expressed a lived historical consciousness, not a departure from some body of civilized norms. Cummins enshrined a set of practices and forced labor that was not "foreign to free world culture" but integral to it. Despite his denunciation of the system, Judge Henley rejected the petitioners' additional assertion that forced, uncompensated prisoner labor violates the Thirteenth Amendment, which states that "neither slavery nor involuntary servitude" shall exist "except as a punishment for crime."

While much has been written about how the Thirteenth Amendment rearticulated a model of labor exploitation based on racial subjugation—forced upon those made unfree by criminalization rather than by bondage—the legal arguments in *Holt v. Sarver II* are evidence of another transition. The case documents not only how the state of Arkansas exchanged the plantation for the prison farm in the twentieth century (swapping one form of incarceration for another) but also how legal rhetoric and language obscures this particular typological fungibility in the present. The question of how slavery endures is a question of how it metamorphosed in its abolition; it is a question that offers a framework to excavate the legal, economic, and social regimes that shape—with various degrees of consistency/inconsistency, continuity/discontinuity—the spaces and practices of captivity rationalized by "crime" and those

29   Holt v. Sarver, 309 F. Supp. 362 (E.D. Ark. 1970), https://law.justia.com/cases/federal/district-courts/FSupp/309/362/2096340.

rationalized by "race." In other words, in what ways does *Holt v. Sarver II* continue (or not continue) the work of the criminal justice system post-Emancipation more broadly, which, as Angela Y. Davis has said before, "played a significant role in constructing the new social status of former slaves as human beings, whose citizenship status was acknowledged precisely in order to be denied"?[30]

Cummins Prison Farm, today called Cummins Unit, is a 16,600-acre maximum security prison and working farm that houses up to 1,876 individuals. It is the oldest prison in Arkansas alongside the Tucker Unit. In 1897, as the state took an outsized role in determining labor relations with the land following Reconstruction, the Arkansas General Assembly authorized public "purchase with funds at its disposal [of] any lands, buildings, machinery, livestock, and tools necessary for the use, preservation, and operation of the penitentiary."[31] A few years later in 1902, the state purchased the Cummins and Maple Grove plantations from Edmond Urquhart, one of the "oldest cotton oil men in the country," for $140,000.[32] In 1916—three years

---

30   See her conversation with Avery F. Gordon, "Globalism and the Prison Industrial Complex: An Interview with Angela Y. Davis," 52. I am also thinking of Nikhil Pal Singh's description of "exceptional zones of armed appropriation": "The latter are domains not only for enacting plunder, that is, primitive accumulation (or accumulation by dispossession), but also for *developing cutting-edge procedures, logics of calculation, circulation, abstraction, and infrastructure*—the slaver's management of human cargo, the camp, the prison, the forward military base—*innovations that can proceed insofar as they are unfettered by legally protected human beings advancing new prejudices, built upon the old.*" Emphasis added. In Singh, "On Race, Violence, and So-Called Primitive Accumulation," *Social Text* 34, no. 3 (September 2016): 41.

31   Jane Zimmerman, "The Convict Lease System in Arkansas and the Fight for Abolition," *The Arkansas Historical Quarterly* 8, no. 3 (Autumn 1949): 177.

32   See Edmond Urquhart's entry in Henry Hall, ed., *America's Successful Men of Affairs: An Encyclopedia of Contemporaneous Biography*, vol. 1 (New York: The New York Tribune, 1895), 667. For sale of land, see Jobe v. Urquhart, 102 Ark. 470 (1912).

after the state abolished convict leasing and turned more fully to penal farms—it gobbled up the nearby Tucker plantation in Jefferson County too. That Cummins Prison used to be Cummins Plantation—and that Arkansas's prison system consolidated the acreage of a planter class— was not unique. There was "Ramsay" in Texas, "Angola" in Louisiana. These names signaled the exchangeability, inextricability, and slippage between sites of labor: one under (and governed by) slavery, and one apparently not.

Descriptions of prison life at Cummins and of the economic system circumscribing it reproduce this metonymic link.[33] Judge Henley's 1970 opinion quoted extensively from a report prepared by the Penitentiary Study Commission of 1967 on the fertility of Cummins's land and the profits reaped by the state from the prisoners' labor.[34] According to the report, there were 9,070 acres of land in cultivation at Cummins; the principal crops were cotton, soybeans, vegetables, and fruit; and prisoners tended to 2,070 cattle, 800 hogs, 40 horses, 160 mules, and 1,600 poultry. In 1966, the prison made $1,415,419.43 from the sale of crops alone. Rational and capitalistic, Cummins was representative of the "ideal goal for southern penology" in the early twentieth century.[35] While the self-supporting prison farm was dressed in reformist and agrarian rhetoric—not only claiming to "make a man out of Ishmael" or "good" laboring citizens out of criminals but

33   Amy Cluckey and Jeremy Wells, introduction to "Plantation Modernity," ed.
      Cluckey and Wells, special issue, *The Global South* 10, no. 2 (Fall 2016): 1–10.
34   It should be said that the Arkansas prison system had by this time been
      under intense scrutiny for years. The so-called reform era of 1967–1968 was
      driven by Governor Winthrop Rockefeller under Thomas O. Murton, who
      found hundreds of skeletons buried on Cummins Prison Farm. See Thomas
      O. Murton and Joseph Hyams, *Accomplices to the Crime: The Arkansas
      Prison Scandal* (New York: Grove Press, 1969).
35   For more on the "ideal goals for southern penology," see Blake McKelvey,
      "A Half a Century of Southern Penal Exploitation," *Social Forces* 13, no. 1
      (October 1934–May 1935): 114.

also requiring the warden to "be an experienced farmer of known executive ability"—it maintained a brutal economic form underneath.[36]

> Men assigned to the fields are required to work long hours six days a week, except for a few holidays, if weather permits. They are worked regardless of heat... The men are not supplied by the State with particularly warm clothing for winter work, nor are they furnished any bad weather gear. There is evidence that at times men have been sent to the fields without shoes or with inadequate shoes. The field work is arduous and is particularly onerous in the case of men who have had no previous experience in chopping and picking cotton or in harvesting vegetables, fruits, and berries. What skills they may acquire in connection with their field work are of very little, if any, value to them when they return to the free world.[37]

The court's verdict that the carceral machine in Arkansas was *not* slavery, the prison farm *not* the plantation, is indicative of the way formal law eclipses lived experience.[38] The analogic reasoning of *Holt v. Sarver II* reifies social and spatial boundaries. These legal distinctions follow strictly semantic definitions that prohibit the judicial system from coming to terms with embodied realities on the ground, which reproduce similar systems of

---

36   "Convicts Who Are in Demand after Serving Terms," *New York Times*, June 4, 1911, https://timesmachine.nytimes.com/timesmachine/1911/06/04/106783727.pdf.

37   Holt v. Sarver, 309 F. Supp. 370.

38   For a prolonged legal parsing of the Thirteenth Amendment, see Michele Goodwin, "The Thirteenth Amendment: Modern Slavery, Capitalism, and Mass Incarceration," *Cornell Law Review* 104, no. 899 (2019): 900–975, https://www.lawschool.cornell.edu/research/cornell-law-review/Print-Edition/upload/Goodwin-final.pdf.

production marked by a racial-colonial-capitalist matrix of exploitation, accumulation, and dispossession. At the same time, from a contemporary perspective, it is crucial to take stock of all the ways that prison labor today is *different* from slave labor; all the ways that logics of exploitability co-exist with logics of disposability in carceral labor relations; all the ways that the mechanisms of dehumanization, which shape the laboring body under these regimes, emphasize different devalued identities and subjectivities.[39] However, the legal emphasis on how the prison farm and the plantation are categorically *not* the same—especially when, in the case of Cummins, it is the same land, the same soil, being tilled over and over again—forecloses the possibility of seeing how they might be interlocked, or at least tethered to one another, in a shifting and drifting narrative of institutional evolution that exists in unfinished and inexorable ways, across space and time.

To determine whether the ADC as a whole constituted "cruel and unusual punishment" required evaluating it against other prevailing (and constitutional) systems, practices, and conditions. It required extending analogical models across time and across status quos. Judge Henley's

39   In regards to this string of "differences": Many scholars, including Ruth Wilson Gilmore and James Kilgore, have written extensively on the myth of the contemporary prison as a site of labor exploitation—reframing the prison's relation to labor according to incapacitation, idleness, underwork, and boredom, which in turn has prompted analyses of the prison as a warehouse for dealing with surplus populations. For an incredibly clear and succinct discussion between the two on captive labor forces today, see Ruth Wilson Gilmore and James Kilgore, "Some Reflections on Prison Labor," *The Brooklyn Rail*, June 2019, https://brooklynrail.org/2019/06/field-notes/Some-Reflections-on-Prison-Labor; and James Kilgore, "The Myth of Prison Slave Labor Camps in the US," *CounterPunch*, August 9, 2013, https://www.counterpunch.org/2013/08/09/the-myth-of-prison-slave-labor-camps-in-the-u-s. For more on the hermeneutic of racial capitalism and on the racial dimensions of dispossession (body) and expropriation (land), see the "Gratuitous Violence" section in the introduction of Wang, *Carceral Capitalism*, 85–95, as well as pages 99–126.

Cummins Prison Farm, 1973. Photograph by Bruce Jackson.

Cummins Prison Farm, 1974. Photograph by Bruce Jackson.

Cummins Prison Farm, 1975. Photograph by Bruce Jackson.

Cummins Prison Farm, 1975. Photograph by Bruce Jackson.

Cummins Prison Farm, 1975. Photograph by Bruce Jackson.

opinion was inextricably linked to what is, or what was at the time, considered "modern."[40] His interpretation of "cruel and unusual punishment" was contingent upon this modernness too: "The term cannot be defined with specificity. It is flexible and tends to broaden as society tends to pay more regard to human decency and dignity and becomes, or likes to think that it becomes, more humane."[41] In addition to declare what the institution was *not*—"We are not dealing with free world housing; we are not dealing with theatres, restaurants, or hotels"—the court had to establish a comparative model to assess how "bad" or how different the ADC was from other acceptable, or more palatable, correctional administrations elsewhere. These statements about typology contain implicit judgements about who deserves certain protections and who does not, which in turn determine the quality of life of those subject to the law: again, "we're not dealing with children... but with criminals."[42]

Prompted by Henley's ruling, what change would come over the next decade would be piecemeal and super-

40 It should not go unsaid that an important justification for the prison farm was its supposed innovation, not necessarily of penal techniques but of agriculture. The famed Parchman Prison in Mississippi modeled the profitability and sustainability of state penitentiary farms, which were championed as sites of agricultural modernization: "The warden is making an experiment also on this farm... he has 200 acres in cotton, and is trying five of the best weevil-resisting varieties of cotton, cultivating under the Federal Department of Agriculture directions, and with ample labor... The result of his work is being watched with interest by the farmers of the surrounding country, for the test means so much to them." See "Convicts Who Are in Demand After Serving Terms."

41 Holt v. Sarver, 309 F. Supp. 380. This analogic model extended even to the court's preemptive statement about ameliorating unconstitutional prison conditions: "Where an unconstitutional situation is found to exist in a given prison, the prison authorities cannot escape responsibility for it by merely pointing to the existence of the same situation in other prisons, or by establishing that conditions in their prison are 'better' or 'no worse than' conditions prevailing elsewhere." See Holt v. Sarver, 300 F. Supp. 828.

42 Holt v. Sarver, 309 F. Supp. 381.

ficial. In 1971, Sarver would be replaced by CCA's T. Don
Hutto, who was then warden of the W.F. Ramsey Unit, a
notoriously brutal prison farm in southeastern Texas. As
the new commissioner of the ADC, Hutto would, among
other things, attempt to modernize and streamline certain
conditions at Cummins, building new facilities to alleviate
overcrowding and converting the manual farming operation to a more mechanized one.[43] In 1973, Judge Henley
would release the ADC from the court's jurisdiction, writing, "the Court is convinced that today it is dealing not
so much with an unconstitutional prison system as with
a poorly administered one."[44] This ruling-cum-warning
would continue to play out in the court. In 1976, Judge
Henley would rule again that specific aspects of the ADC
were indeed unconstitutional, citing, in particular, two of
Hutto's innovations: the punitive wing of the new East
Building and the "grue" disciplinary diet (which he had
brought and introduced to Cummins from Ramsay).[45]

Writing in the *New York Times* on February 17, 1978,
only four days before the case would be argued in the
United States Supreme Court as *Hutto v. Finney*, Thomas O.
Murton—the superintendent of Arkansas's penal system
before Robert Sarver—summed up the "Arkansas effect:"

43   "During Hutto's first year in Arkansas, farm operations brought in almost
      $1.7 million in revenue." See Shane Bauer, "Today It Locks Up Immigrants.
      But CoreCivic's Roots Lie in the Brutal Past of America's Prisons,"
      Mother Jones, September/October 2018, https://www.motherjones.com/
      crime-justice/2018/09/corecivic-private-prison-shane-bauer-book.

44   The ruling continues: "However, unconstitutionality can arise from poor
      administration of valid policies as well as from policies that are constitution-
      ally invalid themselves." See Holt v. Hutto, 363 F. Supp. 202 (E.D. Ark. 1973),
      https://law.justia.com/cases/federal/district-courts/FSupp/363/194/2254773.

45   "Grue" at Cummins was a 4-inch-square "substance created by mashing
      meat, potatoes, oleo, syrup, vegetables, eggs, and seasoning into a paste and
      baking the mixture in a pan." See the full Supreme Court ruling, Hutto v.
      Finney, 437 US 678 (1978), https://supreme.justia.com/cases/federal/us/437/
      678.

"The hearings have come and gone, four commissioners of correction have come and gone, paid staff guards have replaced the former inmate guards, new buildings have been erected. But the more things change, the more they apparently remain the same."[46]

On June 23, 1978, delivering the majority decision for the Supreme Court, Justice John Paul Stevens affirmed that *certain* conditions of confinement in Arkansas's prisons were unconstitutional. While the legal question had been diluted to whether punitive isolation for more than thirty days violated the Eighth and Fourteenth Amendments (the answer was an equivocal yes), the case also revisited the routine abuses suffered by incarcerated people in Arkansas. That the question of forced labor at Cummins was only a footnote in this final decision—and that the Thirteenth Amendment was absent—is not surprising. Rather it speaks to the ways that contesting an entire social institution, "from the fields to the hole," on the basis that it reenacts the brutalities (and racial control) of another is continually thwarted by the court. The law serves to entrench social and racial hierarchies: it only offers remedies when claims against those hierarchies are non-intersectional and non-systemic. The persistence of the plantation model short-circuits questions of constitutionality. It should not be minimized: the long legal arc of *Holt v. Sarver* marked the first successful lawsuit filed by incarcerated people against a correctional institution—and no matter how incremental the change was, it represented, in the words of Judge Henley a decade earlier, the first large-scale "attack on the System itself."[47] Yet to rule against the cumulative damages, harms, and effects of the penal system would mean to admit or rule against forms of violence that are foundational to US jurisprudence—and

---

46   Thomas O. Murton, "The Arkansas Effect," *New York Times,* February 17, 1978, https://www.nytimes.com/1978/02/17/archives/the-arkansas-effect.html.

47   Holt v. Sarver, 309 F. Supp. 365.

to acknowledge that normalizing systems of power tread through and across supposedly "over and done with" historical antecedents into the present.

Between Freedom and Unfreedom

Paths to Prison: On the Architectures of Carcerality invites the discipline of architecture to think about typology diachronically—to extend the geography of architectural inquiry to encompass "plantation futures," which, as Katherine McKittrick writes, offer a "conceptualization of time-space that tracks the plantation toward the prison and the impoverished and destroyed city."[48] Rather than recapitulate the neoslavery narrative, this book asks: How is the logic of the plantation reconfigured in post-slave contexts, and how might these logics undergird or pass through socio-spatial life, organization, development, and expropriation in the present?

The warning, however cliché, from Thomas O. Murton about the supposed reforms of the Arkansas Department of Corrections—"the more things change, the more they apparently remain the same"—resonates with legal scholar Reva Siegal's description of a mode of "preservation through transformation." Siegal's term offers a framework for understanding the way basic forms of racial, class, and gender domination remain intact even when the legal rules and rhetoric governing those hierarchies change as the status quo, and what can be socially stomached, changes.[49] It also offers a way to evaluate to what degree white supremacy relies on the typological continuity of repressive mechanisms. This book thus asks:

48   Katherine McKittrick, "Plantation Futures," *Small Axe: A Caribbean Platform for Criticism* 17, no. 3 (November 2013): 2. Also see McKittrick, "On Plantations, Prisons, and a Black Sense of Place," *Social & Cultural Geography* 12, no. 8 (2011): 956.

Which discursive formations and physical sites preserve white supremacy and maintain the blueprints for today's racial carceral state while claiming they don't? What other supposedly distinct typologies are entangled in this exchange?

Siegal's proposal to hold continuity and change together can also be reframed: Notions of "freedom" are always shadowed by the ways we are made unfree by design. Jasmine Syedullah asks, "What if the spaces where we have been taught to feel most at home are holding us captive?" (459–484). She argues that all imaginations of freedom should be rooted in the *practice* of inhabiting spaces of confinement.[50] Beyond the loophole of the Thirteenth Amendment, this book aims to puncture languages of liberation and bring together architectural narratives that practice this kind of inhabitation—that

---

49   An important disclaimer on the neoslavery narrative: For every account of continuity, there must also be an account of discontinuity. Michelle Alexander has put it very clearly: "Since the nation's founding, African Americans repeatedly have been controlled through institutions such as slavery and Jim Crow, which appear to die, but then are reborn in new form, tailored to the news and constraints of the time." See Michelle Alexander, "The Rebirth of Caste," in *The New Jim Crow: Mass Incarceration in the Age of Colorblindness* (New York: New Press, 2012), 21. So, too, has Loïc Wacquant outlined a historical sequence that inevitably moves from one "peculiar institution" to another, linking chattel slavery, Jim Crow, the ghetto, and the hyperghetto/prison. See Loïc Wacquant, "From Slavery to Mass Incarceration: Rethinking the 'Race Question' in the US," *New Left Review* 13 (January–Feburary 2002): 41–60, https://newleftreview.org/II/13/loic-wacquant-from-slavery-to-mass-incarceration. However, this book intends to disrupt the inevitability of Wacquant's "path." In this way, I am indebted to Jordan T. Camp for his counternarrative to Wacquant in *Incarcerating the Crisis: Freedom Struggles and the Rise of the Neoliberal State* (Berkeley: University of California Press, 2016) and thus, of course, to Stuart Hall's notion of contradiction and crisis: "As I see it, history moves from one conjuncture to another rather than being an evolutionary flow. And what drives it forward is usually a crisis, when the contradictions that are always at play in any historical moment are condensed, or, as Althusser said, 'fuse in a ruptural unity.'" See Stuart Hall and Doreen Massey, "Interpreting the Crisis," *Soundings* 44 (Spring 2010): 57, https://www.lwbooks.co.uk/sites/default/files/s44_06hall_massey.pdf.

in addition to looking at the ways architecture impris-
ons, looks at the ways it apparently does not. What other
loopholes—legal, spatial, financial, or otherwise—blur
the distinction between freedom and unfreedom? This is
another method of shifting the frame away from the prison
as such and towards the promises and spaces of liberal-
ism, as a way to see all other conditions of civil existence
knotted into and connected to the prison. In this way, this
book aims to describe the "double bind of freedom," which,
as Saidiya Hartman has written, intertwines the "emancipated and subordinated, self-possessed and indebted,
equal and inferior, liberated and encumbered, sovereign
and dominated, citizen and subject."[51]

Maintaining this "bind" takes routine ideological,
rhetorical, economic, legal *work*—which determines and
distributes forms of citizenship unevenly across the built
environment and renders those inequities as "normal."
The work of carceral normalization is not always overt; it
is not simply carried out by extreme acts of authority or
blatant criminalization but by what Naomi Murakawa and
Katherine Beckett have called the "shadow" carceral state,
which "operates in opaque, entangling ways, ensnaring an
ever-larger share of the population through civil injunctions, legal financial obligations, and violations of administrative law."[52] It operates through "liminal," "fuzzy," "fungible," and "serpentine" mechanisms that reproduce and

50   Syedullah writes that "we need fugitives to find loopholes in our language
     of liberation." These words have guided me in life and in work, ever
     since encountering them in her piece "What the World Needs Now," in
     angel Kyodo williams, Lama Rod Owens, and Jasmine Syedullah, *Radical
     Dharma: Talking Race, Love, and Liberation* (Berkeley, CA: North Atlantic
     Books, 2016), 184.
51   Saidiya V Hartman, *Scenes of Subjection: Terror, Slavery, and Self-Making in
     Nineteenth-Century America* (New York: Oxford University Press, 1997), 117.
52   Katherine Beckett and Naomi Murakawa, "Mapping the Shadow Carceral
     State: Toward an Institutionally Capacious Approach to Punishment,"
     Theoretical Criminology 16, no. 2 (2012): 222.

"mimic" punishment under terms that declare themselves "not-punishment." This book hopes to surface how the carceral state annexes that which is supposedly free from its grips and to make visible the effort exerted by this entity's many tentacles to normalize the production and maintenance of penal power.

> Where processes of racialization arise, the shadow of property generally looms.
> —Adrienne Brown and Valerie Smith[53]

Thirty-five years after its first detention facility opened in Houston, Corrections Corporation of America, now called CoreCivic, owns and operates forty-three correctional and detention facilities and manages an additional seven federally owned facilities—which altogether span 14.5 million square feet and hold 73,000 beds across the United States. The company has also expanded its portfolio to include twenty-nine residential reentry facilities and an additional twenty-eight properties that it leases to third parties or government agencies. The company's rebranding and its expanding real estate portfolio are two sides of the same coin: the corporation's "new view of corrections" that increasingly relies on the acquisition and transformation of the built environment. Not only does the company pride itself on controlling approximately 59 percent of all privately owned prison beds in the United States, but it also believes itself to be, more generally, "the largest private owner of real estate used by US government agencies."[54]

The cover of CCA's 2009 annual letter to shareholders encapsulates this relation. Titled *Partnership Prisons: The*

---

53   Adrienne Brown and Valerie Smith, eds., *Race and Real Estate* (New York: Oxford University Press, 2016), 3.

I.E. "THE MORE THINGS CHANGE, THE MORE THINGS STAY THE SAME"

Best of Both Worlds, the document juxtaposes two equally generic images: a white corrections officer and an exterior view of an unspecified facility somewhere in the desert. Save for the blurry perimeter fence in the background, the property looks like any other office park. The "best of both worlds" refers to CCA's public-private partnerships: "the essential oversight and accountability of government" coupled with "the flexibility, efficiency, and cost effectiveness of private business." No matter how trite, this image captures a corporation in transition—a corporation that, for political expediency, future viability, and risk transference, has managed to move seamlessly from detainer to landlord and back.

This movement is possible because of a particular financial mechanism: the Real Estate Investment Trust (REIT). Created by Congress in 1960, REITs were designed to give investors the opportunity to pool capital for income-producing real estate—entirely free from federal corporate taxes. Operating like a mutual fund, the trust structure offers stockholders the chance to invest in large-scale commercial real estate assets and earn a share of the profit without having to actually buy, manage, or finance property themselves. For a company to qualify for REIT designation, it has to derive at least 75 percent of its gross income from real estate (rents from real property) and 95 percent from "passive" financial instruments (as opposed to "active" business activities).[55] This distinction between "passive" and "active" investment is crucial to understanding what passes the REIT income test—and what kind of

54   See CoreCivic, Form 10-K for the fiscal year ended December 31, 2019 (February 20, 2020), http://ir.corecivic.com/static-files/acc01462-f138-4e80-a699-10db834fec73.

55   There are, of course, many rules governing the REIT designation (like a company must also distribute 90 percent of its taxable income to shareholders annually). But because REITs do not have to pay taxes, they have grown increasingly controversial—as more and more companies, including

Partnership Prisons: The Best of Both Worlds. Cover of CCA's 2009 annual letter to shareholders, http://ir.corecivic.com/static-files/31ae442b-741e-482a-8125-bd8cdaa60209.

Partnership Prisons:
The Best of Both Worlds

CCA.
America's Leader in Partnership Corrections

bureaucratic maneuvering was undertaken by the CCA. REITs are restricted by the types of activities and services they can provide to their real estate assets, but the passage of the REIT Modernization Act in 2001 produced a loophole that allows companies to reap the benefits of massive tax breaks by breaking apart their active business activities (the operational side of, for example, private prison management) from their passive real estate investment (such as the ownership of correctional and detention facilities) through subsidiaries.[56]

And that's exactly what CCA did. In 2013, the company (still CCA at the time) successfully converted its corporate structure to an REIT.[57] This meant that it had convinced the IRS of two things: first, that its facilities are *not* "lodging" or "healthcare," and second, that the money it receives from government tenants is "rents from real property."[58] Declaring what the company (and thus what corrections) was *not* (neither site of care or housing) allowed CCA to claim that their property was held for investment, not operation. There is a similar denial in its

tech companies, claim the core of their business to be real estate. By 2011, the total market value of REITs had surged to $451 billion from $9 billion in 1990, bringing with it a whole slew of questions as to what constitutes real estate and "rents from real property." For a more detailed history of REITs, see Peter E. Boos, "Runaway REIT Train? Impact of Recent IRS Rulings," *Tax Notes*, September 15, 2014, http://www.taxhistory.org/www/features.nsf/Articles/FFF8F863CF33DB1E85257E1B004BAD8F.

56   The act made the passive/active distinction even harder to parse as it gave a trust the opportunity to form and own Taxable REIT Subsidiaries (TRS), which would allow that trust to carry out non-customary services without jeopardizing its REIT status. For more on this, see "Summary of the REIT Modernization Proposal," Nareit, https://www.reit.com/nareit/advocacy/policy/federal-tax-legislation/reit-modernization-act-rma/summary-reit-modernization.

57   CCA's transition was not unique. The other major US-based for-profit prison corporation, GEO Group, restructured as an REIT in 2013 as well.

58   See what appears to be CCA's private letter ruling from the IRS: Jonathan D. Silver, Letter no. 201320007 to Company A, May 17, 2013, https://www.irs.gov/pub/irs-wd/1320007.pdf.

second request: to consider money paid by federal agencies
to incarcerate and house people as rent meant fundamentally bypassing the actual tenants of CCA's facilities. The
IRS's determination opened up a redefinition of carceral
space—labeling the state as the tenant and not the individuals sanctioned there.

The REIT regime incentivizes building and leasing,
not managing or operating. While the Houston Processing
Center was the CCA's first model of privatization (financed,
owned, and operated by CCA), the company has since
shifted toward other models: privately financed and owned
but publicly operated; privately financed and owned but
eventually transferred to the public sector (i.e. rent-to-
own); and publicly owned but privately financed, designed,
constructed, and maintained.[59] Speaking at the 2017
National Association of REITs conference, CoreCivic CEO
Damon Hininger described these new arrangements as "a
really meaningful catalyst for growth for the company and
a great way... to diversify the company moving forward."
This diversification was also a new distribution of risk—
as Hininger continues, "the operational risk and the head-
line risk is with the government jurisdiction—*we're just the
owner of the real estate.*"[60]

In CCA's 2012 annual letter to shareholders announcing its new tax status, the company put forth a markedly different image of the company: as $3.6 billion in
fixed assets. Alongside the narrative of REIT-generated
double-digit growth, the company doubled down on its
commitment to real estate with sterile and glossy aerial

59   For an extensive report on contract agreements, see *In the Public Interest,
      An Examination of Private Financing for Correctional and Immigration
      Detention Facilities*, June 2018, https://www.inthepublicinterest.org/wp-
      content/uploads/ITPI_PrivatePrisonP3s_June2018FINAL.pdf.
60   Emphasis added. See CoreCivic, company presentation, June 7, 2017,
      REITWeek 2017: NAREIT's Investor Forum, New York, webcast, https://
      reitstream.com/webcasts/reitweek2017.

photographs of its properties—described not according to function but to acreage, square footage, number of beds, and age. These specifications were part of a new language aimed at repackaging CCA's facilities as attractive investment opportunities.[61] The company's ability to build shareholder value was thus intimately connected to its ability to build a stable real estate portfolio. CCA's portfolio was sold as a "just-in-time inventory" of leasable space—one that was integral to the growth model of the company. The inventory was intended to accommodate the immediate and future needs of government partners and policy makers, thereby linking what the company offers (and what the company is) to whatever political, economic, and cultural climate it faces.

CCA's tactical sprawl picked up speed between 2013 and 2016. In response to dips in national prison populations and increasing criminal sentencing reforms, CCA letters to shareholders began to cite "America's recidivism crisis," emphasizing "alternatives" to incarceration and an increased interest in reentry programming. In three years, it acquired three "community" corrections companies. These acquisitions enabled CCA to be a "better" service provider to its government "tenants," but they also enabled the company to consolidate its increasingly dispersed (and diverse) footprint. The groundwork was laid for an emerging "treatment industrial complex."[62] If this was "the link between prison and the community," then CCA, according

---

61   What is attractive? The company touted, in particular, the number of
      "bought-and-paid-for" available beds; the ability to offer expanded
      correctional "capacity" (immediate leasable relief); the seventy-five-year
      economic lifespan of its facilities due to concrete and steel construction
      (and their overall newness with a median age of seventeen years); the
      flexibility of its lease agreements; the investment-grade credit rating of its
      government partners; and the 90 percent contract renewal rate. See John
      D. Ferguson and Damon T. Hininger, *A New View of Corrections: 2012
      Annual Letter to Shareholders* (Nashville: CCA, 2012), http://ir.corecivic.
      com/static-files/56582057-2c3f-42df-9f63-b768e6d73872.

to Hininger, was poised to supplant that connection as it continued to "develop a robust pipeline of acquisition opportunities in this fragmented market."[63]

In October 2016, CCA became CoreCivic. With a solid REIT backbone and the foundation already laid for a pipeline to the community, the company underwent another round of rhetorical sanitization, corporate renovation, and targeted acquisition.[64] Everything about the way CoreCivic presents itself today is designed to be benign. Alongside the tagline "Better the public good," the company adopted

62   For more on this, see Caroline Isaacs, *Treatment Industrial Complex: How For-Profit Prison Corporations are Undermining Efforts to Treat and Rehabilitate Prisoners for Corporate Gain* (Austin: Grassroots Leadership, 2014), https://grassrootsleadership.org/sites/default/files/reports/TIC_report_online.pdf; and Liliana Segura, "The First Step Act Could be a Big Gift to Core Civic and the Private Prison Industry," *The Intercept*, December 22, 2018, https://theintercept.com/2018/12/22/first-step-act-corecivic-private-prisons.

63   Speaking at a town hall meeting in 2014 on the importance of capitalizing on reentry and on the emerging market for community alternatives, Hininger ranked the company's allegiances: "It's a responsibility to our government partners, to our shareholders, to the communities we live in and help protect, to victims of crime and to the inmates entrusted in our care." See Damon Hininger, remarks prepared for CCA's 2014 Third Quarter Town Hall, CCA Headquarters, Nashville, August 22, 2014, script, https://ccamericastorage.blob.core.windows.net/media/Default/documents/Social-Responsibility/Providing-Proven-Re-Entry-Programs/Hininger-Reentry-Speech-Transcript.pdf. For the second quote see Hininger, remarks during CCA's 2015 Third Quarter Earnings Call, November 5, 2015, transcript, Seeking Alpha, November 6, 2015, https://seekingalpha.com/article/3659136-corrections-corporation-americas-cxw-ceo-damon-hininger-q3-2015-results-earnings-call.

64   Its chosen new name, rid of all corrections connotations, did not come without controversy. The nonprofit Community Initiatives for Visiting Immigrants in Confinement (CIVIC)—now Freedom for Immigrants—alleged that CoreCivic violated its common-law trademark rights. Dedicated to abolishing US immigration detention, the organization saw the new visual identity "as a [deliberate] effort to create undue confusion for immigrants in detention and exploit the goodwill associated with our name." Perhaps confusion was the intention. See Freedom for Immigrants, "Our Founding," https://www.freedomforimmigrants.org/our-founding. For more on

The first page of CCA's 2012 annual letter to shareholders, titled *A New View of Corrections,* http://ir.corecivic.com/ static-files/56582057-2c3f-42df-9f63-b768e6d73872. The CCA also showcased Jenkins Correctional Center, Millen, GA: 105 acres, 233,000 square feet, 1,124 beds, one year old; Nevada Southern Detention Center, Pahrump, NV: 120 acres, 189,000 square feet, 1,074 beds, three years old; and Saguaro Correctional Facility, Elroy, Arizona: 34 acres, 352,000 square feet, 1,896 beds, six years old (this last facility is, in fact, the unnamed facility on the cover of the 2009 report).

ON THE COVER:
**ADAMS COUNTY
CORRECTIONAL CENTER**
NATCHEZ, MS

2,232 | **143**
BEDS | ACRES

464,000 SQ.FT.
AGE: 5 YEARS

**LAKE ERIE CORRECTIONAL
INSTITUTION**
CONNEAUT, OH

1,798 | **119**
BEDS | ACRES

310,000 SQ.FT.
AGE: 14 YEARS

a "bolder, sleeker and more modern" typeface and a color palette intended to invoke "safety, strength, passion, stability, integrity and seriousness." Its new logo? A 13-stripe American flag extruded to symbolize a building.

Business offerings like "Inmate Services" and "Security" were replaced with "Safety," "Community," and "Properties"—new umbrella terms for an expanding inventory of diverse carceral products. Today, CoreCivic Community encompasses a vast network of residential reentry centers and non-residential services. In 2018, the company acquired Rocky Mountain Offender Management Systems (RMOMS) and Recovery Monitoring Solutions, adding to its portfolio new programs like probation supervision, electronic monitoring and GPS tracking, remote electronic alcohol monitoring, random urine screening, and cognitive behavioral therapy. Perhaps not unlike the early prison-farm experiments in agricultural techniques, CoreCivic's "community" and those in it have become the test site (and subjects) for a technological-social apparatus of governance—the gears of which have already been and will continue to be loosened for general use.

The company has continued to metastasize with CoreCivic Properties. In the last few years, it has moved further into "non-corrections" space—acquiring and constructing a 261,000-square-foot Capital Commerce Center in Tallahassee, Florida, that is leased mostly to the Florida Department of Business and Professional Regulation; a 541,000-square-foot office building in Baltimore, Maryland, that is under a 20-year lease with the Social Security Administration; and a 217,000-square-foot built-to-suit building in Dayton, Ohio, for the National Archives and

CoreCivic's new visual identity, see "Corrections Corporation of America Rebrands as CoreCivic," News, CoreCivic, October 28, 2016, https://www.corecivic.com/news/corrections-corporation-of-america-rebrands-as-corecivic; and also "Logos and Color Palette," CoreCivic, https://www.corecivic.com/logos.

I.E. "THE MORE THINGS CHANGE, THE MORE THINGS STAY THE SAME"

Records Administration, which includes 1.2 million cubic feet of storage space (90 percent of which is dedicated to the archives of the IRS).[65] CoreCivic now declares itself a "diversified government solutions company"—detainer, landlord, and developer. Still, according to their 2018 SEC filing, CoreCivic Safety made up 87 percent of the company's total net operating income—compared to only 4.8 percent from CoreCivic Community—and of that, ICE accounted for 25 percent of the company's total revenue.[66] The company may now be painted True Navy, Smoked Crimson, and Soft Gray, but, as the adage says, uttered this time by Tony Grande, Executive Vice President and Chief Development Officer of CoreCivic, "the more things change, the more they stay the same.'"[67]

Between Continuity and Discontinuity

The REIT regime is a regime of ownership, and regimes of ownership are racially constructed. CoreCivic's sprawl manifests the long legacy of state-sanctioned white possession—its external reach both a product and productive of settler colonial dynamics. The company's ambition is infrastructural. Its "robust pipeline of acquisition opportunities" serves to lay claim to an even greater territory that spans

---

65   See CoreCivic, *2018 Annual Report*, http://ir.corecivic.com/static-files/3cc 197ff-e1a0-495a-b1fc-1c347733d320; and John Egan, "How One Private Prison REIT Is Trying to Diversify," *National Real Estate Investor*, March 22, 2019, https://www.nreionline.com/reits/how-one-private-prison-reit-trying-diversify.

66   Further, the US Marshals Service accounted for 17 percent, and the Federal Bureau of Prisons accounted for 6 percent. See CoreCivic, Form 10-K for the fiscal year ended December 31, 2018 (February 25, 2019), http://ir.corecivic.com/static-files/f289bea9-086c-4540-82b2-114dbfb95e4e.

67   Tony Grande, "In Times of Change, a Constant Purpose," *CoreCivic Magazine*, Winter 2017, 7, https://ccamericastorage.blob.core.windows.net/media/Default/documents/InsideCCA/CCMagazine-2017-Winter-FINAL_Digital.pdf.

corrections and non-corrections spaces, the prison and the community, already-cornered markets and new markets. In January 2020, CoreCivic announced that it had acquired an additional twenty-eight properties, which it would lease exclusively to the General Services Administration. Distributed throughout the mid-South, this additional 445,000 square feet is intended to house numerous federal agencies, including the Social Security Administration, the Department of Homeland Security, and the Office of Hearings Operations.[68] By catering itself to federal and state bureaucracies through property relations, the company aims to become even more "critical" to the functioning of government—perhaps even a "critical infrastructure," to use the federal government's own parlance. And it is through this criticality, through its role as landlord to the state's "non-coercive" business, that CoreCivic manages to reinscribe the punishing and criminalizing functions of the carceral state anew. For as a discursive and legal categorization, "critical infrastructure" assigns national value and security to supply chains of capital—supply chains that "make daily life possible"—and criminalizes efforts to disrupt and upend those chains.[69] As a technique of settler colonial governance—of invasion, expropriation, accumulation, and dispossession—these projects, writes Anne Spice, anticipate "the circulation of certain materials, the proliferation of certain worlds, the reproduction of certain

68 According to CoreCivic, the transaction "elevates" the company's ranking to "a top-15 owner of GSA-leased assets." See CoreCivic, "CoreCivic Acquires 28 Property, 445,000 SF Portfolio of GSA Leased Assets," press release, January 6, 2020, http://ir.corecivic.com/node/20826/pdf.

69 "Critical infrastructure" encompasses that which "provides the essential services that underpin American society," that "serves as the backbone of our nation's economy, security, and health," and that is "so vital to the United States that [its] incapacity or destruction would have a debilitating impact on [the country's] physical or economic security or public health or safety." See Cybersecurity and Infrastructure Security Agency, "Sector-Specific Agencies," last modified August 22, 2018, https://www.cisa.gov/sector-specific-agencies.

subjects" and disavow the rights and jurisdictions of other subjects, worlds, and materials. (307–358) What values, beliefs, and ways of living are foreclosed or peripheral or antagonistic or dangerous to the state's epistemology of critical infrastructure?

Paths to Prison: On the Architectures of Carcerality parses the ideological backbone of American society in order to reveal how it criminalizes any subjectivity that opts out or does not fit within the consolidating "we" of the nation— but also how this backbone is entirely dependent on and supported by the continued exploitation of these communities. As outgrowths of the state, these "invasive infrastructures" might make daily life possible, but they only do so for some, and the futures they aim to structure are *settler* futures.[70] Perhaps the Olympic Motel was early evidence of this colonial futurity—for "colonialism is justified as using what is unused," reminds Ahmed.[71] *Paths to Prison* attempts to account for these Janus-faced constructions. As James Graham warns, the "double rhetoric of plight and opportunity is the cleared and leveled site on which a long string of government-backed dispossessions—of native lands, of mineral rights, of labor power, of unfree bodies—takes place." (159–206)

This book interrogates how the groundwork is laid for this more invasive understanding of carceral infrastructure—one that folds the punishing regime (and

---

70 Every press release, SEC filing, and annual report by CoreCivic includes a boilerplate "forward-looking statement": something that declares the company's "beliefs and expectations of the outcome of future events." This kind of disclaimer is a standard business practice, intended to hedge against social, political, economic risks and uncertainties that might make such corporate expansions difficult. The company writes: "All statements, other than statements of historical fact, are statements that could be deemed forward-looking." These futures are signaled by words like "'anticipate,' 'believe,' 'continue,' 'could,' 'estimate,' 'expect,' 'intend,' 'may,' 'plan,' 'projects,' 'will.'"

71 Ahmed, *What's the Use?*, 47.

thus the prison) into "other" regimes (ownership, knowledge, martial, and so on). It helps to elucidate that "savage encroachments of power take place through notions of reform, consent, and protection," or through Property, Community, and Safety.[72] The aim here is to complicate the metaphor of "pipelines" to prison, which so disproportionately affect communities of color and which are most acutely guided by the conditions of daily life.[73] While the book aims to describe various spaces, institutions, and practices that enact or reflect the structural violence of the prison, it does not intend to create hard-and-fast linkages between those sites, nor does it intend to suggest that these connections, as modes of conveyance, are smooth, easy, and without friction. The book engages "pipelines" only insofar as they can be disrupted—not a relentless or unchanging explanation for the way things are but an intersectional account that helps widen the frame used to understand architecture's relationship to the carceral state.

If pipelines aim to guarantee a certain future and fate, then this book is assembled against these projections: "Permanence is not the goal here," writes Adrienne Brown. (133–155) Pipelines clog and leak; they can be rerouted, subverted, blocked by official and unofficial means. Instead of confirming straight lines or tracks, *Paths to Prison* elucidates the physical and social contraptions that attempt to circumscribe or enclose certain lives, places, and communities, and the insurgent "social relations" that emerge "in excess of" (again, Brown) and against these invasive incursions.

---

72   Hartman, *Scenes of Subjection*, 5.
73   Angela Y. Davis, "Political Prisoners, Prisons, and Black Liberation," May 1971, History Is a Weapon, https://www.historyisaweapon.com/defcon1/davispoprprblli.html.

I.E. "THE MORE THINGS CHANGE, THE MORE THINGS STAY THE SAME"

> What is it about blackness and Latinidad that turns one's house (roof, protection, and aspiration) and shelter into a death trap?
> —Paula Chakravartty and Denise Ferreira da Silva[74]

The Olympic Motel may no longer be in use, but it is still valuable as a model and a caution for the way the racial logics of occupation, terror, and exception are injected into the built environment. "Racial difference," writes Mabel O. Wilson, "became productive of the material conditions of modern life, fueling the unequal distribution of the resources—food and shelter—that sustain it." (389–409) Perhaps the Olympic Motel testifies to a moment of redistribution, in which resources have been usurped, transformed, and reapportioned to serve a carceral machinery that relies on racial difference being maintained. As Naomi Murakawa reminds us, policy "produces social effects that reinforce their own stability."[75] The word "spatial" could be added to that sentence: Policy, immigration or criminal, produces social and spatial effects that promise and guarantee the continuation of this expansion. Amidst the now sprawling landscape of immigrant detention, the motel has resurfaced over and over again.[76] It is a site that not only

74 Paula Chakravartty and Denise Ferreira da Silva, "Accumulation, Dispossession, and Debt: The Racial Logic of Global Capitalism—An Introduction," *American Quarterly* 64, no. 3 (September 2012): 367.

75 This is Murakawa citing Paul Pierson, "The Study of Policy Development," in "New Directions in Policy History," ed. Julian E. Zelizer, special issue, *Journal of Policy Development* 17, no. 1 (2005): 37, in Naomi Murakawa, *The First Civil Right: How Liberals Built Prison America* (Oxford: Oxford University Press, 2014), 16.

76 Today, ICE detains more than twenty times more people than the INS did in the 1980s. This increase has been supported by a spatial mobilization that marshals, to various degrees and temporalities, "ordinary" sites across the built environment. In 2019, ICE reported detaining 486,190 individuals

captures the militarization against and dehumanization of asylum seekers, refugees, and undocumented people but also evidences this violence.

In 2018 the Trump Administration sought to end the twenty-two-year-old Flores Settlement Agreement. Settled in 1997, Flores was the result of a class action lawsuit filed on behalf of two young girls, Alma Yanira Cruz and Jenny Lisette Flores, who had come to the US fleeing the civil war in El Salvador in the 1980s and who were instead met with the punitive and procedural brutality of the INS. The agreement set protections and standards for the treatment of minors in detention. As the world confronted the brutal conditions at immigration facilities along the US southern border in 2019, Flores emerged again in the mainstream media—revealing that at the origin of Flores, there too was a motel.

For weeks after entering the US, Cruz and Flores were locked in over-crowded rooms at a makeshift detention center in Pasadena, CA. "The facility was a 1950s-style hotel shaped like a U," recounts Carlos Holquin, the lawyer who eventually brought the case to court. "The INS

and holding individuals on average for thirty-three days. It held nearly 70,000 migrant children in custody—a 42 percent increase from 2018. See Emily Kassie, "Detained: How the United States Created the Largest Immigrant Detention System in the World," *Marshall Project*, September 24, 2019, table "Growth of Detention: Fiscal Years 1979–2019," https://www.themarshallproject.org/2019/09/24/detained; Christopher Sherman, Martha Mendoza, and Garance Burke, "US Held Record Number of Migrant Children in Custody in 2019," *Associated Press*, November 12, 2019, https://apnews.com/015702afdb4d4fbf85cf5070cd2c6824; and Shannon Najmabadi, "Across the Country, Basements, Offices, and Hotels Play Short-Term Host to People in ICE Custody," *Texas Tribune*, August 29, 2018, https://www.texastribune.org/2018/08/29/heres-ice-network-basements-offices-and-hotels-hold-immigrants. CoreCivic maintains in its immigration detention factsheet that "CoreCivic does not operate temporary shelters or even contract with federal agencies that do." See CoreCivic, "Myth vs. Fact: Core-Civic's Valued but Limited Role In the Immigration System," https://www.corecivic.com/hubfs/_files/Myth%20Versus%20Fact%20CoreCivic%20Private-%20Detention.pdf.

I.E. "THE MORE THINGS CHANGE, THE MORE THINGS STAY THE SAME"

essentially put a chain-link fence in front of it with a sally port and concertina wire on top." Behavioral Systems Southwest, who had been contracted by the INS to operate the facility, drained the swimming pool. The children had no access to visitation, no recreation, no education: "The kids would essentially just hang around by the drained pool or on the balconies for days—or weeks or months—until it was determined what to do with them."[77]

As Sara Ahmed writes, "We learn a lot about form when a change in function does not require a change in form."[78] In both Flores and the Olympic Motel, the perimeter fence, the concertina wire, the iron bars, and the drained pool all signal that the motel has ceased to be a motel as we know it. They are provisional signs of a change in function, which does not compromise the existing form but communicates that guests "cannot check out at will." Or, that, perhaps, guests are not "guests" at all. That this exchange is possible testifies to certain ideas that have coalesced around the motel already. In these stories, it is possible to glimpse how the motel is reinforced and consolidated at the level of enclosure *and* also rendered typologically and spatially expansive at the level of an urban system of circulation and capture.

This duality is depicted in a cartoon by Lalo Alcaraz of a "Motel 6 Immigration Detention Camp." In it, a sign that reads "Immigration Detention Camp" has been affixed to the company's recognizable "6" sign, and the motel's

77   Listen to Carlos Holguin on "The History of the Flores Settlement and Its Effects on Immigration," *All Things Considered*, NPR, June 22, 2018, MP3 Audio, 7:33, https://www.npr.org/2018/06/22/622678753/the-history-of-the-flores-settlement-and-its-effects-on-immigration; and Lorelei Laird, "Meet the Father of the Landmark Lawsuit that Secured Basic Rights for Immigrant Minors," *ABA Journal*, February 1, 2016, http://www.abajournal.com/magazine/article/meet_the_father_of_the_landmark_lawsuit_that_secured_basic_rights_for_immig.
78   Ahmed, *What's the Use?*, 34.

otherwise generic little buildings surrounded by a perimeter fence with barbed wire. The sketch makes visible the
character of carcerality in the US, which is as much about
mobility as immobility. The irony of this image, though, is
that a motel doesn't even need a fence around it in order to
carry out the custodial practices of the state. The cartoon,
which went viral alongside the hashtag #BoycottMotel6,
was drawn in response to the allegations against Motel
6 for its role in collaborating with ICE to arrest guests.
According to the suit:

> Since at least 2015, Motel 6 has had a policy or prac-
> tice of providing to ICE agents, upon their request,
> the list of guests staying at Motel 6 the day of the
> agents' visit… Lists included some or all of the fol-
> lowing information for each guest: room number,
> name, names of additional guests, guest identifica-
> tion number, date of birth, driver's license number,
> and license plate number… The ICE agent would
> review the guest list and identify individuals of in-
> terest to ICE. Motel 6 staff observed ICE identify
> guests of interest to ICE, including by circling guests
> with Latino-sounding names.[79]

Over two and a half years, 80,000 names were
disclosed and countless individuals arrested, detained, and
deported as a result of warrantless searches, often in the
form of "knock and talks." These enforcement tactics represent a particular regime of policing that asserts state force
in everyday life through the cooperation and consent of the
private sector. Motel 6 shared its guest data by choice—a

[79]   The case dealt specifically with Motel 6 locations across Arizona and Washington State. The company has since agreed to pay $12 million to settle the
claims. See State of Washington v. Motel 6 Operating LP et al., King County
Sup. Ct. No. 18-2-00283-4 SEA (2019), http://agportal-s3bucket.s3.amazona
ws.com/uploadedfiles/Another/News/Press_Releases/Complaint.Scan2.pdf.

choice made possible by the previously cited *City of Los Angeles v. Patel*, which declared that hotel/motel operators are not obligated to turn their guest data over to police without a warrant—turning the supposedly protected "bed space" of the motel room into the captive bed space of another. This cooperation finagles apparent if illusory thresholds between the right to be secure in one's room (not to mention one's body, home, and life) and the interests of the state (which has a monopoly on violence). Given that Motel 6 owns and operates 12,000 motels and 105,000 rooms across the US and Canada, its disperse geography of "places of public resort, accommodation, assemblage, or amusement" expresses the pervasive tyranny of possible coercion or probable cooperation: "for every wall that provides shelter is one that confines."[80]

This potentiality, the fine line between two radically different embodied conditions, and the *degree* to which the motel is used by the state as a force of immobility rely on a set of assumptions and biases that are constructed along racial, political, and class lines. Take for instance ICE spokesperson Yasmeen Pitts O'Keefe's defense of the agency's specific targeting at motels: "Hotels and motels have frequently been exploited by criminal organizations engaged in highly dangerous illegal enterprises, including human trafficking and human smuggling."[81] O'Keefe's statement does a lot of work: it defines the motel as a place of deviancy, it criminalizes individuals who frequent it, and it ultimately legitimizes the agency's strategic, racially motivated violence and excessive surveillance at Motel

80   "Control Systems," *The Avery Review,* http://averyreview.com/topics/control-systems.

81   Alicia A. Caldwell and Chris Kirkham, "Washington Attorney General Sues Motel 6 for Sharing Guest Info with Feds," *Wall Street Journal,* January 3, 2018, https://www.wsj.com/articles/washington-attorney-general-sues-motel-6-for-sharing-guest-info-with-feds-1515016334.

6 locations across the south- and northwest. All of these fabricated conditions naturalize a continuum of punishment and a distributed form of governance organized around a building typology, enforced and carried out by cooperating institutions, organizations, and corporations. As Angela Y. Davis has famously argued, the "institution of the prison and its discursive deployment produce the kind of prisoners that in turn justify the expansion of prisons."[82] The motel is thus a spatial opportunity for ICE, as it was for T. Don Hutto.

The motel has always accommodated mobility. It, too, must be considered unstable as a site that moves between these determined oppositions. It offers a way of attending to carcerality in the built environment that is both local and general, fixed and fluid, concerned with citizenship and noncitizenship, freedom and unfreedom, legality and illegality, who deserves the state's incursion and who does not. It is a site where rights are never just asserted but contested. What is a death trap for some is a lifeline to others, and endlessly vice versa. While the motel has been a useful agent of social death for CoreCivic and its corporate peers, for ICE, and for the Supreme Court, it has also been a space for asserting collective life. Other motels across the southwest are being repurposed as migrant shelters—as way stations on longer paths toward asylum.[83] But even across Motel 6s, individuals are demonstrating how "it is always possible to create space for opposition within the hold of structural violence and domination, to move closer to freedom while still within the borders of hostile territory," as Syedullah writes again. And this opposition is crucially not always expressed in loud acts of resistance

82   Angela Y. Davis and Gina Dent, "Prison as a Border: A Conversation on Gender, Globalization, and Punishment," *Signs* 26, no. 4 (2001): 1238.

83   Miriam Jordan, "A New Surge at the Border Is Forcing Migrant Families into Motel Rooms," *New York Times*, October 18, 2018, https://www.nytimes.com/2018/10/18/us/migrant-families-arizona-ice-motels.html.

but through the quiet persistence of seeking out ways to survive, to access resources not otherwise available, and to live fully. Individuals detained at Motel 6 reported being there for many reasons: some relied on the chain to escape sweltering heat, to access an air-conditioner, to find space away from their families to wrap Christmas presents.[84] These examples are not intended to reproduce a hierarchy of "innocent" need or behavior. For need—"nefarious" (to use Sotomayor's phrase) or not—should never be criminalized. Full stop. These examples instead point to all the ways one finds sanctuary, shelter, and freedom not necessarily via routes leading somewhere else supposedly free or totally different but via practices that carve out new space for mobility within even the most restricted environments and circumstances.

Between Mobility and Immobility

How the institution of the prison has been and continues to be represented is a political project. Just as the prison is discursively called on to legitimize its own expansion, it is also visually deployed to make a reality without it seem impossible. It is worth repeating Gina Dent's often-cited statement on the grip that images of prison hold on our imagination: "The history of visuality linked to the prison is also a main reinforcement of the institution of the prison

---

84   For the original exposé of Motel 6's practices, see Antonia Noori Farzan and Joseph Flaherty, "Attorneys Suspect Motel 6 Calling ICE on Undocumented Guests," *Phoenix New Times*, September 13, 2017, https://www.phoenix newtimes.com/news/motel-6-calling-ice-undocumented-guests-phoenix-immigration-lawyers-9683244; also see Francesca Paris, "Motel 6 to Pay $12 Million After Improperly Giving Guest Lists to ICE," *NPR*, April 5, 2019, https://www.npr.org/2019/04/05/710137783/motel-6-to-pay-12-million-after-improperly-giving-guest-lists-to-ice; and Joseph Flaherty, "Motel 6 to Settle Class-Action Discrimination Lawsuit Over Collusion with ICE," *Phoenix New Times*, July 9, 2018, https://www.phoenixnewtimes.com/news/phoenix-civilian-review-board-defund-the-police-11474245.

as a naturalized part of our social landscape."[85] The task of this book then is to make the familiar unfamiliar, to uncongeal the congealed, to denaturalize all that has been naturalized for us—shifting the epistemological frame away from the prison as such (or, in certain moments, zooming so far into the center of it) that we lose sight of it altogether, and recording what comes into view in its stead. *Paths to Prison* picks up and echoes a provocation from Brett Story: "Prisons are spaces of disappearance."[86] She means this in many ways: Prisons disappear bodies; they disappear the social crises they are tasked to solve; they are built in increasingly distant sites meant to disappear the violence, pain, and grief that they inflict and leave behind. But when directed at the field of architecture—a field that prides itself on its capacity to envision worlds totally different than our own—this proposition demands we rethink what it even means to visualize, to see or to not see, a space that actively holds itself out of view. The discursive underwrites the visual. The intelligibility of our language structures the coherence of our images. Sable Elyse Smith repeats that "scale and infrastructure are sometimes weapons. And language is both." (293) By changing or by disappearing and decreasing the opacity of the vocabularies, narratives, myths, and pedagogies that confirm the prison at the center of our field of vision—and that block out all of the other architectures that prop up the social functions of the prison as it courses through daily life—perhaps the

85   Gina Dent, "Stranger Inside and Out: Black Subjectivity in the Women-in-Prison Film," in *Black Cultural Traffic: Crossroads in Black Performance and Black Popular Culture*, ed. Harry Elam and Kennel Jackson (Ann Arbor: University of Michigan Press, 2003), quoted in Angela Y. Davis, *Are Prisons Obsolete?* (New York: Seven Stories Press, 2003), 17–18.

86   Brett Story, Jack Norton, Jordan T. Camp, Annie Spencer, Christina Heatherton, and Kanishka Goonewardena, "Brett Story, The Prison in Twelve Landscapes (documentary, 87 Min., 2016)," in "Neoliberal Confinements: Social Suffering in the Carceral State," ed. Alessandro De Giorgi and Benjamin Fleury-Steiner, special issue, *Social Justice* 44, nos. 2–3 (2017): 163–176.

discipline can start to un-circumscribe how it imagines, understands, and rejects its own complicity in the carceral state.

The "paths" of *Paths to Prison* offer not a fixed or inexorable account of how things are but a set of starting points and methodologies for re-seeing the architecture of carceral society and for undoing it altogether. As paths, they let us sidestep, arrive, bypass, and look back at the prison differently—carrying us through other sites, past and present, that serve "to establish a spatial distinction between the dispossessed and the free, the expendable and the nonexpendable, the abnormal and the normal, and to manifest the ongoing production of racial boundaries of this transitional space," as Leslie Lodwick writes. (413–454) By locating architecture along other disciplinary paths too, we can better see its impact and be more critical about how it participates and exerts (or refuses to exert) this power. *Paths to Prison* intends to write new paths to prison into histories of architecture—histories that, by extending both what constitutes the carceral and what is ensnared in it, reveal more possibilities for rejecting it altogether. This is a book then that moves to see the prison anew, that shifts the frame in order to yield a different picture:

Not of concrete walls but of highways, archives, the control unit, FamilySearch, Sensorvault, Church of Jesus Christ of Latter-Day Saints, the plantation, White Reconstruction, the Chesapeake and Ohio Railroad Company, fire camps, Appalachian coal mines, the Los Angeles Police Department, clinical psychology, critical infrastructure, a north Harlem apartment, the Thirteenth Amendment, alternative charter schools, private telecommunication networks, chain-link fences…

Not of crime but of oppression, redlining, debt, counter-insurgency, domestic warfare, wage theft, anti-

EXTENDED STAY

Blackness, residential apartheid, extraction, White Geology, pathology, racial difference, surveillance, racial-colonial state violence, data colonialism, unemployment, home-ownership, imperialism, gentrification, invasion, home contracts, Otherness, stigma...

Not of only the racial state but also of liberal multiculturalism, the American Dream, popular consent, cooperation, diversity, reform, "something akin to freedom," the post-racial state...

Not of social death but of rent parties, eviction resistance, human and other-than-human relations, homefulness, poverty scholarship, captive maternals, liberation, repair, rebellious affects, anti- and ante-ownership, lines of flight, sitting with what is, writing, touching, dancing, kinship, care, self-determination, waywardness...

Sable Elyse Smith, *Coloring Book 24*, 2018. Screen printing ink and oil stick on paper, 60 x 50 inches. Courtesy of the artist; JTT, New York; and Carlos/Ishikawa, London.

CARCERAL ARCHITECTURES OF POLICING: FROM "MASS INCARCERATION" TO DOMESTIC WARFARE

DYLAN RODRÍGUEZ

The Fallacy of "Mass Incarceration"

The ascendance of a national discourse on "mass incarceration" during the first two decades of the twentieth century calls for rigorous critical attention. In addition to its wide circulation as a rhetoric of coalescence—for academic, activist, nonprofit, journalistic, public policy, popular-cultural, and state mobilizations—the phrase has canonized a relatively coherent *narrative* structure, based on a generalized assumption that such juridically sanctioned, culturally normalized state violence is a *betrayal* of American values as well as a violation of the mystified egalitarian ethos that constitutes US national formation.[1] In his 2015 address to the National Forum on Criminal Justice, legal scholar and former president of the John Jay College of Criminal Justice Jeremy Travis resonates this durable reformist *bildungsroman*:

> The unifying theme that we must keep in mind is this: we live in an era of mass incarceration because we have chosen, through policy choices, to dramatically expand the use of prison as a response to crime. There is a corollary to this finding: If our democracy

---

1   For some of the most rigorously researched and well-argued examples of this reformist narrative, see Peter K. Enns, *Incarceration Nation: How the United States Became the Most Punitive Democracy in the World* (New York: Cambridge University Press, 2016), 157; Glenn C. Loury, *Race, Incarceration, and American Values* (Cambridge, MA: MIT Press, 2008), 28; and John F. Pfaff, *Locked In: The True Causes of Mass Incarceration— and How to Achieve Real Reform* (New York: Basic Books, 2017), 162.

got us here, it is our democracy that must get us out of here.[2]

Here, it is the tyranny of the (white/multiculturalist) "we" that animates the subject of patriotic outrage and asserts a universalized American accountability, bypassing the long historical facts of particular peoples' alienation from the nation-building project.

"Mass incarceration" evidences an ideological formation that shapes the language and policy of the contemporary (abortively "post-racial") racist state while expanding the conceptual and political scope of a punitive and racist approach to policing, criminalization, and human capture. Craig Willse offers a critical method that illuminates how the racially criminalized condition of "homelessness" is not only a systemic *outcome* of economic, cultural, and juridical relations of dominance, but also a violently normative discursive regime that assembles institutional power by rigorously obfuscating the *modalities of life* produced by such systemic dominance:

The construction of "homelessness" as a problem has in fact obscured the material conditions that produce housing deprivation, proliferating expertise and management techniques while allowing housing insecurity to expand... In fact housing systems and their inhabitants are conformed through relations of capital and sociolegal regulation. In other words, the life organized by systems of housing insecurity and deprivation does not precede those systems. Rather, housing systems produce the lives contained within, shaping, for example, vulnerability to living without shelter as an expression and experience of racialized subordination in labor market and consumer economies.[3]

FROM "MASS INCARCERATION" TO DOMESTIC WARFARE

Following Willse's analytical and theoretical app-roach, i am concerned with how "mass incarceration" has become a strangely *generic* term of twenty-first-century liberal-progressive coalescence. The rhetoric of "mass incarceration" hails a broadly reformist consensus that selectively displaces, appropriates, obscures, and/or overtly dismisses *radical and abolitionist* approaches to carceral state violence, gendered racial criminalization, and anti-Black social liquidation. How, then, does the discourse of "mass incarceration" spread the subtle absurdities of a multiculturalist, post-racial liberal agenda by subsuming the targeted casualties of the racial-colonial carceral state under the terms of a "mass"? What are the extended consequences of a "mass incarceration" reform narrative that rests on the premise that the criminal justice regime is *not* functioning as its founders and most fair-minded admin-istrators intend it to function? The narrative structure of mass incarceration misapprehends the cultural-political fallout of *carceral domestic warfare.* The long historical consequences of the dynamic, carceral marshaling of police power, criminal justice policy, and racialized national culture are transgenerational, and they have fundamen-tally deformed the capacities of targeted communities to reproduce within a sociality that is constituted by the logics and juridical-policing protocols of gendered racist state violence.

Recent grassroots formations like Chicago's We Charge Genocide, for example, demystify the *targeted* (hence not "mass") casualties of carceral domestic war and demonstrate why it may be necessary to depart from

2   See Jeremy Travis, "Reducing Mass Incarceration: Exploring the Value of Values," opening address, 2015 National Forum on Criminal Justice, Atlanta, Georgia, August 3, 2015.
3   Craig Willse, *The Value of Homelessness: Managing Surplus Life in the United States* (Minneapolis: University of Minnesota Press, 2015), 54.

DYLAN RODRÍGUEZ

mass incarceration discourse and its implicit reliance on false equivalences, fraudulent (white/multiculturalist) humanist universalisms, and generalized erasure of anti-Blackness as the structuring formation of dominance and violence that animates the modern regimes of policing and criminalization in the US and elsewhere.[4] Here, i am following João Costa Vargas and Moon-Kie Jung's definition of anti-Blackness as "structured, ubiquitous, and perduring disadvantages for Black people and structured advantages for nonblacks. Such articulated disadvantages and advantages take place in the realms of ontology (how individuals constitute and define themselves as such), sociability (lived social experience), and access to resources... The likelihood of social and physical death is a direct function of antiblackness."[5]

Anti-Blackness, in this conceptualization, is the epistemic, aesthetic, ontological, and political condition of colonial, chattel, and modern socialities and not merely a secondary expression or consequence of otherwise non-anti-Black social formations. To the extent that anti-Blackness constitutes sociality as such, it permeates the insti-

4   See We Charge Genocide, *Police Violence Against Chicago's Youth of Color*, report submitted to United Nations Committee against Torture on the occasion of its review of the United States of America's Third Periodic Report to the Committee Against Torture (Chicago, 2014), 4, accessed February 14, 2015, http://report.wechargegenocide.org.

5   On anti-Blackness, João Costa Vargas and Moon-Kie Jung also offer: "Antiblackness helps us grasp the types of symbolic and actual forms of violence one is subjected to." For more on their heuristic conception, see João Costa Vargas and Moon-Kie Jung, introduction to *Antiblackness*, eds. Vargas and Jung (Durham, NC: Duke University Press, forthcoming 2021). Calvin Warren's philosophical conceptualization provides a complementary framing: "*antiblackness*: an accretion of practices, knowledge systems, and institutions designed to impose nothing onto blackness and the unending domination/eradication of black presence *as* nothing incarnated. Put differently, antiblackness *is* anti-nothing. What is hated about blacks is this nothing, the ontological terror, they must embody for the metaphysical world." See Calvin Warren, *Ontological Terror: Blackness, Nihilism, and Emancipation* (Durham, NC: Duke University Press, 2018), 9.

tutionalizations of private property, criminal justice, law enforcement, and post-emancipation approaches to incarceration. A radical recognition of the long *carceral* genealogy of anti-Blackness structured We Charge Genocide's grassroots work between 2014–2016, which authored a story of the historical present tense that exemplifies a critical, abolitionist, Black radical departure from the political *telos* of mass incarceration narrativity.[6] Defined as "an intergenerational effort to center the voices of the young people most impacted by police violence," We Charge Genocide articulated its mission through a Black radical and Black feminist radical tradition that drew on the legacies of Ida B. Wells and the Civil Rights Congress.[7] Typical of its narrative praxis, We Charge Genocide excoriated the American Civil Liberties Union in 2015 for its weak, uninformed negotiations with the Chicago Police Department over its notoriously racist "stop-and-frisk" policies.[8] We Charge Genocide confronted and re-scripted the ACLU's reductive understanding of Chicago policing:

> We understand police violence to be rooted in historical and systemic anti-Blackness that seeks to control,

6   See We Charge Genocide, *Police Violence Against Chicago's Youth of Color.*
7   See Ida B. Wells-Barnett, "Southern Horrors: Lynch Law in All Its Phases" (1892), in *Selected Works of Ida B. Wells-Barnett*, ed. Trudier Harris (New York: Oxford University Press, 1991), 14–45; and William L. Patterson, ed., *We Charge Genocide: The Historic Petition to the United Nations for Relief from a Crime of the United States Government against the Negro People* (New York: Civil Rights Congress, 1951).
8   Regarding the larger context of stop-and-frisk policing, see Michael D. White and Henry F. Fradella, *Stop and Frisk: The Use and Abuse of a Controversial Policing Tactic* (New York: New York University Press, 2016); Kami Chavis Simmons, "The Legacy of Stop and Frisk: Addressing the Vestiges of a Violent Police Culture," *Wake Forest Law Review* 49 (2014): 849–871; Andrew Gelman, Jeffrey Fagan, and Alex Kiss, "An Analysis of the New York City Police Department's 'Stop-and-Frisk' Policy in the Context of Claims of Racial Bias," *Journal of the American Statistical Association* 102 (2007): 813–823.

contain, and repress Black bodies through acts of repeated violence. Stop and frisk should be understood as a tool police use to punish Black people just for *being*. Police violence is always state-sanctioned violence, and further strengthening narrow supervision of police action by elites will never address that. This is why any legislative or law-based campaign to address police violence requires not just policy change, but an actual transformation of power relations between communities of color and the police.[9]

We Charge Genocide's narrative praxis exemplifies a form of creative, collective critique that disrupts and transforms the common lexicon of "police brutality" while bringing urgent, incisive attention to the historical present tense of ordinary peoples' normalized encounters with state-facilitated and state-condoned social evisceration. This radical genius emanates from a shared, complex comprehension of the United States as an accumulation of multiple generations of institutionalized dehumanization. Following We Charge Genocide's narrative logic: before there was "mass incarceration," there was already *incarceration*, structured in the logics, geographies, and architectures of anti-Black policing and chattel genocide.

The (anti-)social formations of militarization, criminalization, and patrolling are historically central to the construction, reproduction, and institutional coherence of the white Civilizational project's most classical iterations in racial plantation slavery, racial colonialism, land occupation, genocidal conquest, and post-emancipation apartheid. It is dangerous, however, to conflate the martial *institutionalization* of such relations of dominance with a transhistorical *dependence on* white bodily monopoly (or even

9   We Charge Genocide, "An Open Letter to the ACLU of Illinois Regarding Stop and Frisk," online letter, August 12, 2015, http://wechargegenocide.org/an-open-letter-to-the-aclu-of-illinois-regarding-stop-frisk.

majority) within the institutional geographies of personnel, administrative leadership, and bureaucratic management.

"Join LAPD" as Warfare/Diversity Mandate: The Carcerality of White Reconstruction

The notion of "White Reconstruction" names a historically persistent, continuous, and periodically acute logic of reform, rearticulation, adaptation, and revitalization that constitutes worldmaking and white social and ontological self-making within the changing humanist (and modern) projects of Civilization/Manifest Destiny/Progress, etc.[10] While its logics of (anti-)social formation are inseparable from a chronic global white supremacist modernity, it is nonetheless possible to identify when its projects unfold with an intensity that is period-specific: like the long half century that followed the formal juridical abolition of the US apartheid order, often called the "post–civil rights period."

The most recent, ongoing period of White Reconstruction encompasses a racial-political *complex*—a dynamic interaction of institutional protocols, jurisprudence, policy, popular and state cultural productions, and public discourses—of liberal reform, *prima facie* institutional inclusion (and the accommodation of disfranchised identity claims, like diversity, multiculturalism, etc.), capital accumulation, hetero-patriarchal dominance, industrialized ecological expropriation, territorial occupation, and criminalization of profiled bodies and targeted geographies. This complex, which is relatively symbiotic (though sometimes apparently chaotic and contentious), includes the unfolding, quaking, and convulsive reactions against the liberationist rebellions and social-political transformations

10   See Dylan Rodríguez, *White Reconstruction* (New York: Fordham University Press, forthcoming 2020).

that defined the mid-to-late-twentieth-century Western racial-colonial order: from the US-based Black freedom and anti-apartheid Civil Rights movements to revolutionary anti-colonialist struggles and feminist insurgencies worldwide. The crystallization of this ensemble of transformation, reform, and reaction raises epochal questions: How do the terror of gendered white supremacy, the violence of anti-Black sociality, and the Civilizational order of conquest, colonialism, and militarized white occupation (e.g. gentrification, Zionism, settler nationalism) outlive the formal abolition of specific racist state and social regimes? How do the living, collective, accumulated experiences of this terror, violence, and colonial occupation toxify *and constitute* once-excluded peoples' access to rights, civil subjectivity, and other forms of political recognition within the reconstructing Civilizational order?

What if the sociality of the "post–civil rights" United States is *constituted* by the carceral displacement, systemic damaging, and degradation of targeted bodies? What if these are the conditions through which social totality is rendered "whole"—as nation, community, people? While there are many ways to illuminate the force of White Reconstruction across intimate and macrosocial scales, it may be useful to engage in a genealogy of the *pluralist* inhabitations of historical white supremacist social logics and political technologies within contemporary institutionalizations of diversity, inclusion, and multiculturalism. At face value, such institutionalizations appear to significantly reform or substantively transform regimes of racist state violence that are historically characterized by white bodily monopolizations of personnel/leadership/administration as well as generally aggressive white supremacist ideological animus. Yet, on deeper analysis, such systemic rearticulations extend and complicate rather than disrupt or abolish historical ensembles of racial-colonial state violence.

FROM "MASS INCARCERATION" TO DOMESTIC WARFARE

White Reconstruction encompasses a period-specific mobilization of institutional rhetorics, cultural and discursive regimes, political-juridical strategies, and (militarized) racial statecraft that 1) sustain anti-Black and racial-colonial (domestic) war as the condition of the social formation of the United States, while 2) constituting struggles for political and cultural hegemony that are strategically, unevenly, and inconsistently inclusionist, diversity directed, and/or multiculturalist in form. These diversity-directed struggles for hegemony are significant in their relative newness. This is in part because they are waged on or in proximity to the normative racial statecraft of liberal/desegregated racial-colonial "recognition," in which people historically targeted by formalized protocols of categorical alienation and exclusion from the racialized chattel settler state are non-consensually subjected to the novel and constantly changing mandates, processes, and compulsory rituals of pluralist inclusion and accommodation into proper national personhood (citizenship). Glen Coulthard (Yellowknives Dene) crystallizes the centrality of liberal recognition to Indigenous peoples' exposure to the post-1980s iterations of the Canadian nation-state:

> Instead of ushering in an era of peaceful coexistence grounded on the ideal of *reciprocity* or *mutual* recognition, the politics of recognition in its contemporary liberal form promises to reproduce the very configurations of colonialist, racist, patriarchal state power that Indigenous peoples' demands for recognition have historically sought to transcend.[11]

---

11   Glen Sean Coulthard, *Red Skin, White Masks: Rejecting the Colonial Politics of Recognition* (Minneapolis: University of Minnesota Press, 2014), 3. Emphasis in the original.

For Coulthard, the pageantry and public exercises of liberal recognition (e.g. voting rights, formal equality under the law, citizenship status, compulsory multiculturalism and "diversity" mandates, state apologies and/or piecemeal financial redress for past atrocities) extend rather than replace, repair, or even mitigate the ensemble of state and cultural practices that sustain colonial occupation and war as Canada's condition of national coherence and sovereignty. The implications of this critique are vast: the invasive premises of the liberal extension of politicality (and full sociality) permanently delineate, disrupt, and redefine the structures and discursive regimes of citizenship, freedom, bodily integrity, and personhood as they are contingently accessed by the non-normative (non-)subjects and targets of the anti-Black, racial-colonial settler state. In this context, criminal law, policing, electoral politics, border militarization, corporate media, carceral schools, foundation- and think-tank-funded academic research agendas, prisons, jails, reservations, detention centers, and other such institutions signify the relations of *coercive power* that overdetermine White Reconstruction's struggles over hegemony (as the mediated, *non*-coercive power of consent). Put differently, the cultural-political terrain of White Reconstruction's particular moment of hegemonic struggle is distinctive because the conditions of anti-Blackness, racial-coloniality, and domestic war are the necessary precedents and foundations on which a logic of *white/multiculturalist solicitation* anticipates the bodily presence and delimited inclusion of human groups previously marginalized or excluded from the domain of political coalitions, historical blocs, and social subjectivities within the modern (post-conquest, post-emancipation) US nation-building project.[12]

12   See Sara Ahmed, *On Being Included: Racism and Diversity in Institutional Life* (Durham, NC: Duke University Press, 2012).

Consider the Los Angeles Police Department's conspicuous efforts to augment and publicly signify the demographic diversity of its officers during the first two decades of the twentieth century. Responding to the far-reaching, systemic corruption of the LAPD's Rampart Division throughout the 1990s, a June 2001 federal consent decree forced the City of Los Angeles and the LAPD to remediate what US Attorney General Janet Reno and the Civil Rights Division of the Department of Justice called "a pattern or practice of unconstitutional or otherwise unlawful conduct that has been made possible by the failure of the City defendants [City of Los Angeles, Board of Police Commissioners of the City of Los Angeles, and the LAPD] to adopt and implement proper management practices and procedures."[13] (The terms of the decree allowed the city, the Board, and the LAPD to admit no culpability.) In the wake of this liberal racial state intervention, the LAPD engaged in a series of piecemeal internal reforms and public relations pageantry that included sponsoring the 2005 Gay Games Sports and Cultural Festival (part of a national initiative to increase the numbers of out gay cadets), co-sponsoring the 2006 Tenth Annual International Criminal Justice Diversity Symposium under the leadership of LAPD Chief William Bratton (the former New York Police Department commissioner who famously authorized city-wide police harassment of Black and Latinx residents under the rubric of "broken windows" policing), and the ongoing "Join LAPD" recruitment initiative.[14]

13   US v. City of Los Angeles, 2:00-cv-11769-GAF-RC, at 1 (consent decree) (CD Cal. June 5, 2001).
14   See "Los Angeles Police Department Sponsors Gay Games," Gay Games VII: Chicago 2006, press release, December 23, 2005, accessed December 2008, http://www.gaygameschicago.org/media/article.php?aid=123; "10th Annual International Criminal Justice Diversity Symposium: Beyond Tolerance," Los Angeles Law Enforcement Gays and Lesbians (LEGAL) archived March 29, 2009, https://web.archive.org/web/20090329113605/http://

Enacting a public-facing mission of domestic militarist inclusivity, the LAPD has been guided by the recommendations of a 2009 study by the RAND Center on Quality Policing (funded by the Ralph M. Parsons Foundation), which included both a directive to "identify ways to streamline and prioritize applicants in the recruiting process that can meet both recruiting and diversity goals"[15] and a summary recommendation to "tailor media mix to attract diversity target groups."[16] The LAPD's diversity recruitment efforts are animated by the pedantic cultural and visual production of a reforming racial state, relying on vernacular and visual exhibitions of bodily difference and non-normative subjectivities as their primary vehicles of popular outreach. Headlined by its "Join LAPD" campaign, the state's aspirational notion of a refurbished, reconstituted police demographic flows through highway billboards, internet advertisements, and multiple social media venues, including a widely visited Facebook page, constantly updated "@joinlapd" Twitter and Instagram accounts, a devoted YouTube channel, and a self-standing "Join LAPD" website (joinlapd.com) that is distinct in substance and design from the LAPD's official site (lapdonline.org).

www.losangeleslegal.org/pages/symposium/symposium1-cover.shtml; and William Bratton and George Kelling, "There Are No Cracks in the Broken Windows: Ideological Academics Are Trying to Undermine a Perfectly Good Idea," *National Review Online*, February 28, 2006, https://www.nationalreview.com/2006/02/there-are-no-cracks-broken-windows-william-bratton-george-kelling. For an overview of the contemporary history of "zero tolerance" and "broken windows" policing, see Christian Parenti, *Lockdown America: Police and Prisons in the Age of Crisis* (London and New York: Verso, 2000).

15   Nelson Lim, Carl Matthies, Greg Ridgeway, and Brian Gifford, *To Protect and Serve: Enhancing the Efficiency of LAPD* (Santa Monica, CA: RAND Corporation, 2009), 4.

16   Lim, Matthies, Ridgeway, and Gifford, "Summary," in *To Protect and Serve*, xix.

FROM "MASS INCARCERATION" TO DOMESTIC WARFARE

Stuart Hall's versatile and durable reconceptualization of "hegemony" helps contextualize "Join LAPD" as an exemplary articulation of the pedagogical and cultural technologies of the racial-carceral state. For Hall, the contemporary state is a complex arrangement of institutions, interests, and political blocs that is actively engaged in struggles to build consensus-based—that is, hegemonic—social rule across different gendered racial constituencies. While the racial state remains the central apparatus for the expression of coercive rule (that is, legitimated state-sanctioned violence), Hall argues that its primary expression of power in the post–World War II context increasingly takes the form of institutional mobilizations that attempt to cultivate some version of popular consent across a dominant ensemble of authorities, ideological assumptions, and institutional protocols. He writes,

> The state is no longer conceived as simply an administrative and coercive apparatus—it is also "educative and formative." It is the point from which hegemony over society as a whole is ultimately exercised (though it is not the only place where hegemony is constructed). It... condenses a variety of different relations and practices into a definite "system of rule"... The modern state exercises moral and educative leadership... It is where the bloc of social forces which dominates over it not only justifies and maintains its domination but wins by leadership and authority the active consent of those over whom it rules.[17]

Following Hall, the pedagogical racial state actively *produces* and *participates in* a discursive terrain that encompasses visual culture, the built environment, official

17   Stuart Hall, "Gramsci's Relevance for the Study of Race and Ethnicity," *Journal of Communication Inquiry* 10, no. 2 (1986): 18–19.

The first image featured on "LAPD: Diversity" alongside the tagline "Diversity in Our City and Department," https://www.joinlapd.com/diversity-our-city-and-department.

vernaculars and slogans, and other material texts that form the cultural conditions through which White Reconstruction coheres *as a particular ensemble of consensus-building regimes*, even and especially as it imagines, marshals, and coordinates the reform *and periodic expansion* of gendered racist domestic warfare. The uneven (though significant) implementation of diversity mandates, compulsory tolerance and sensitivity protocols, and other "post–civil rights" multiculturalisms signify the (perhaps momentary) obsolescence of classical white supremacy as a model of power and socially-ordering violence that is based primarily or even predominantly on the vesting of hegemonic institutional power in the exclusionary collectivity of the white social body.

The critical challenge, in such a moment, is to consider the political and cultural implications of a multiculturalist white supremacy that actively releases—or is forced to release—its stranglehold on apartheid forms of institutionality at the same time that it reproduces the ascendancy of White Being. Guided by Sylvia Wynter's radical critique of European and Euroamerican humanism and "Man," i understand White Being as the militarized, normative paradigm of *human* being that inhabitants of the ongoing half-millennial Civilizational project have involuntarily inherited as a violent universal. Wynter's durable contribution to Black Studies and the critical humanities enables a conceptualization of White Being as a narrative, ceremonial, ritualized practice of human being that pivots on relations of dominance with other beings (human and otherwise) and aspirational mastery over the wildness and unknowability of nature and the physical universe.[18]

18   Among her many contributions, see Sylvia Wynter and Katherine McKittrick, "Unparalleled Catastrophe for Our Species? Or, to Give Humanness a Different Future: Conversations," in Katherine McKittrick, ed., *Sylvia Wynter: On Being Human as Praxis* (Durham, NC: Duke University Press, 2015), 9–89.

FROM "MASS INCARCERATION" TO DOMESTIC WARFARE

White Being's *ascendancy*, in turn, requires perpetual mobilizations of (legitimated state and extra-state) violence and colonial-chattel power that form the premises of the degrading, negating, and deadly differentiations. Post-racial, multiculturalist, diversity-valorizing Americanism is the racial narrative *telos* of the twenty-first century US, even and especially amidst white supremacist and "white nationalist" reaction.[19] While the phenotypes of white supremacy expand and multiply—a reordering of bodies necessary to the reproduction of White Being's ascendancy in changing historical conditions—the internal coherence of white supremacy *as a logic of social formation* is sustained, complicated, redeemed, and enhanced.

Thus, between the subtle rainbow flag overlay on the windshield of an LAPD squad car and the Instagram commemoration of 2019 International Women's Day, the "Join LAPD" initiative offers a dynamic, living archive of liberal multiculturalism as a political and pedagogical tactic of racial state rearticulation that expands as it reforms the logics and protocols of racial-colonial domestic (carceral) war. Here, the imperatives of militarized, gendered racial policing are intensified by the rhetorical and ideological turn toward demographic, identity-based inclusivity in the hiring and mobilization of domestic militarism's on-the-ground personnel. In this context, "Join LAPD" cannot be reduced to a pandering public relations campaign or short-lived pseudo–affirmative action drive. Rather, it is part of a sustained, reformist diversity

19 Here, i am invoking the rhetoric of a post–civil rights United States in its popular cultural and public intellectual renditions. This notion is animated by a (not exclusively white or white supremacist) nationalist political desire to transcend—hence decisively obscure, displace, and/or neglect—the political antagonisms and social crises that are inscribed by "race" as a determination and mediation of institutionalized relations of dominance and human hierarchy. The primary arguments of this chapter suggest a fuller rebuttal of the "post–civil rights" and "post-racial" rubrics.

joinlapd ✓ • Follow
LAPD Ahmanson Recruit Training Center

joinlapd ✓ @joinlapd believes in the International Women's Day theme #iwd2019, "Balance for Better". Join us at our Hiring Seminar tomorrow to hear from Women in our Command Staff: Assistant Chief Beatrice Girmala, Commander Beverly Lewis, and Commander Ruby Flores. Hear the story behind their rise through the ranks, and why Balance truly is Better in LAPD. Start your journey tomorrow! For more info visit www.JoinLAPD.com #ChooseYourPurpose

548 likes

MARCH 6, 2019

Add a comment...

mandate that has resulted in the percentage of "Latino" LAPD officers more than doubling and the proportion of "Asian" officers tripling between 1990 and 2015. Notably, these augmentations have been paralleled by a *decrease* in the ratio of Black LAPD personnel during the same period. While rigorous explanations for the latter trend exceed our purposes here, it is worth questioning whether domestic militarism's multiculturalist rearticulation rests on the continued police violence against Black communities, bodies, and profiles, and whether this structure of continuity produces a culture of virulent alienation between police forces and their prospective Black cadets.[20]

Read within the logics of White Reconstruction, "Join LAPD" is simultaneously a recruitment device and *pedagogical racist state regime* that attempts to displace, deflect, and abandon the LAPD's place in this twentieth-century ensemble of modern US racial-colonial state power. Max Felker-Kantor's critical interdisciplinary history of the LAPD in the years between the 1965 Watts rebellion and 1992 LA uprising concisely frames the longer precedents of this multiculturalist rearticulation:

> Racial targeting was central to the LAPD's expansion of police power and efforts to control the streets at all costs. Residents of color, because the police viewed them as disorderly and lawless, had long been the subjects of the LAPD's police power. As African American and Mexican migrants reshaped Los Angeles's racial geography during the postwar era, they confronted a police force intent on maintaining Los Angeles's reputation as the nation's "white spot." As part of a system of racialized punishment that was rooted in Los Angeles's history of settler colonialism

---

20   On domestic militarism, see Ruth Wilson Gilmore, "Globalization and US Prison Growth: From Military Keynesianism to Post-Keynesian Militarism," *Race & Class* 40, no. 2–3 (1999): 171–188.

and racism, the growth of police power in the decades after the 1960s was organized around the aim of controlling the city's black and brown populations. Intensified police power and racially targeted policing were not incidental but mutually constitutive.[21]

Understood in the context of the 2001 consent decree and the longer, post-war history of establishing and violently enforcing geographies of criminalization and racial dominance in Los Angeles,[22] the LAPD's twenty-first-century diversity recruitment efforts must be differentiated from two implicit possibilities: first, the sudden overhaul of the LAPD's on-the-ground-policing methods (e.g. use of gang "task forces" and databases, SWAT, gendered racial profiling, and juridically sanctioned killing of Black and Latinx civilians);[23] and second, the institutionalized

---

21 Max Felker-Kantor, "Introduction: The Police Power," *Policing Los Angeles: Race, Resistance, and the Rise of the LAPD* (Chapel Hill: University of North Carolina Press, 2018).

22 On the racial, class, and gender relations of power and state violence that have shaped the historical geographies of Los Angeles, see Mike Davis, *City of Quartz: Excavating the Future in Los Angeles*, 6th ed. (London and New York: Verso, 2006); Scott Kurashige, *The Shifting Grounds of Race: Black and Japanese Americans in the Making of Multiethnic Los Angeles* (Princeton, NJ: Princeton University Press, 2008); Daniel Widener, *Black Arts West: Culture and Struggle in Postwar Los Angeles* (Durham, NC: Duke University Press, 2010); Laura Pulido, Laura R. Barraclough, and Wendy Cheng, eds., *A People's Guide to Los Angeles* (Berkeley: University of California Press, 2012); Laura Pulido and Josh Kun, eds., *Black and Brown in Los Angeles: Beyond Conflict and Coalition* (Berkeley: University of California Press, 2014); and Laura Pulido, *Black, Brown, Yellow, and Left: Radical Activism in Southern California* (Berkeley: University of California Press, 2006).

23 While journalistic accounts of LAPD violence and "brutality" are widely available, a recent article in the respected international periodical the *Guardian* provides a symptomatic overview: see Sam Levin, "Hundreds Dead, No One Charged: The Uphill Battle Against Los Angeles Police Killings," *The Guardian*, August 24, 2018, https://www.theguardian.com/us-news/2018/aug/24/los-angeles-police-violence-shootings-african-american.

antiracist commitment to ending focused and strategic militarizations against (queer and transgender) sex workers, homeless people, undocumented communities, and criminalized Black and Brown youth. Rather than aborting its long historical role in the Southern California theater of domestic war making, the LAPD seems to be offering an institutional concession that "classical" white supremacist policing must undergo substantive reform to remain politically and institutionally viable. This process, rendered compulsory by federal state intervention as well as ongoing grassroots resistance, rebellion, and periodic retaliation from people and communities most vulnerable to police violence, entails a dismantling of the white supremacist policing regime's most *evidently* classical elements—including (but not limited to) the optics and nationalist theater of white (male) police officers patrolling, detaining, humiliating, intimidating, harassing, abusing, torturing, and assassinating city residents targeted by racialized, sexualized, and gendered criminal/suspect/gang profiles.

Qualitative, anecdotal, and statistical evidence indicate that initiatives like "Join LAPD" do not retract or even reduce the asymmetrical policing of racially criminalized populations. Instead, diversity mandates signify revisions of the *white supremacist institutional phenotype*, a model of racial reform that has become increasingly widespread since the successful mid-1990s neoconservative attacks on affirmative action.[24] The LAPD has, in this way, become a state platform for a form of public theater that performs the obsolescence of old-school white supremacist policing while retaining a paradigmatic commitment to juridically sanctioned, culturally legitimated racial domestic warfare.

24   On the neoconservative movement to end affirmative action and progressive attempts to resist its abolition, see Paul M. Ong, ed., *Impacts of Affirmative Action: Policies and Consequences in California* (Walnut Creek, CA: AltaMira Press, 1999); Lydia Chávez, *The Color Bind: California's Battle to End Affirmative Action* (Berkeley: University of California Press, 1998).

FROM "MASS INCARCERATION" TO DOMESTIC WARFARE

As the multiculturalist approach to officer recruitment gains discursive and bureaucratic traction, the white supremacist substructure of policing remains a primary determination of the LAPD's on-the-ground operations. Damien Sojoyner's study of the symbiotic continuities between policing, criminal justice, and public schools in Los Angeles County suggests that the widely shared liberal-progressive rhetoric of the "school-to-prison pipeline" is not only a fatally flawed metaphor, but also drastically underestimates how (poor, Black, and Latinx predominant) schools must themselves be conceptualized as criminalized, actively policed carceral sites ("enclosures"). By conceptualizing schools as enclosures, Sojoyner draws on Clyde Woods's historical geography of the Black South to create an analytical framework through which to comprehend the normalization of carceral domestic war—policing, criminalization, and incarceration—in the continuous flow of staff, jurisprudence, state/law enforcement officials, administrators, and discursive structures (languages of Black student and family pathology, criminalizing representations of "at-risk" youth, etc.) *across* schools, courts, jails, prisons, and youth detention facilities.[25] Sojoyner contextualizes the ramping up of the LAPD's militarized repressive capacities in the latter decades of the twentieth century as the precursor for the symbolic, ideological, and political maneuvers of "Join LAPD" and other such publicity/recruitment campaigns:

Although the presence of police and representatives of the criminal justice system have had a sordid past in the lives of Black people, the type of repression that was ushered in during the late 1960s and early 1970s and enhanced during the 1980s and 1990s was

---

25   Clyde Adrian Woods, *Development Arrested: The Blues and Plantation Power in the Mississippi Delta* (London and New York: Verso, 1998).

formerly relegated only for moments deemed "states of emergency" (that is, riots, massive political demonstrations). Yet, in this new epoch, the extreme and excess became normalized as a continual presence within Black communities.[26]

Prior to and since the issuance of the 2001 consent decree, the LAPD's identification with high-profile, scandalous incidents and institutionalizations of racist state violence have rendered the notions of both "scandal" and "incident" insufficient. Los Angeles has long boasted the largest jail system in the United States (and, according to the ACLU, "the world")—a carceral toll overwhelmingly borne by poor Black and Latinx people (including youth, undocumented migrants, and those jailed while awaiting trial).[27] Throughout the late 1990s, the LAPD's Rampart Division was involved in multiple conspiracies to fabricate and steal evidence (including over $1 million of cocaine) used to frame hundreds of innocent people (more than 100 of whom have since been released from prison and jail after courts overturned their convictions). The Rampart Division was engaged in numerous incidents of civilian shootings, in-station beatings, and street tortures. Crucially,

26   Damien M. Sojoyner, *First Strike: Educational Enclosures in Black Los Angeles* (Minneapolis: University of Minnesota Press, 2016), 72.

27   The ACLU asserts, "Los Angeles County Jails, with an average daily population nearing 22,000, is the biggest jail system in the world." See "LA County Jails," ACLU, https://www.aclu.org/issues/prisoners-rights/cruel-in-human-and-degrading-conditions/la-county-jails. On Los Angeles jails, see Amanda Petteruti and Nastassia Walsh, *Jailing Communities: The Impact of Jail Expansion and Effective Public Safety Strategies, A Justice Policy Institute Report* (Washington, DC: Justice Policy Institute, 2008), especially page 23 and 26; "Los Angeles County Jail System By the Numbers," Los Angeles Almanac, http://www.laalmanac.com/crime/cr25b.php; James Austin et al., *Evaluation of the Current and Future Los Angeles County Jail Population* (Denver: JFA Institute, 2012); and Breeanna Hare and Lisa Rose, "Pop. 17,049: Welcome to America's Largest Jail," *CNN*, September 26, 2016, https://www.cnn.com/2016/09/22/us/lisa-ling-this-is-life-la-county-jail-by-the-numbers/index.html.

a prevalence of Black and Latinx officers were exposed as
central figures and implicated as co-conspirators in the
investigation and criminal proceedings that revealed the
depth and scope of the "Rampart scandal."[28] In continuity, the widely broadcast police violence of the 2007 May
Day repression, in which LAPD riot control officers—many
of them Latinx—attacked immigrant rights activists and
other civilians during a peaceful gathering at MacArthur
Park, further demonstrates that the institutional logics
and inhabitations of racist state violence are not reducible
to the uniformed, reactionary white cop.[29]

Political scientist and Black Lives Matter Los Angeles
(BLMLA) chapter co-founder Melina Abdullah illustrates
the diversified LAPD's continued (post–consent decree)
complicity in patterns of fatal racist state violence. In a
September 2017 radio interview with KPFK (90.7 FM, Los
Angeles), Abdullah asserts:

> There is no shortage of police killings here. LAPD
> leads the nation in killing its residents. Out of the last
> five years, it's led the nation in killings every single
> year except for when Los Angeles County Sheriff's
> Department surpasses it. So when we talk about LA
> County, it's the most deadly place, in terms of police
> killings, in the entire nation.[30]

---

28 *Frontline*, season 19, episode 10, "LAPD Blues," directed by Michael Kirk,
    written by Kirk and Michael J. Boyer, aired May 15, 2001, on PBS. For
    historical context, see Kristian Williams, *Our Enemies in Blue: Police and
    Power in America* (Boston: South End Press, 2007).

29 Joel Rubin, "11 LAPD Officers Face Discipline in May Day Melee," *Los
    Angeles Times*, September 17, 2008, http://articles.latimes.com/2008/sep/17/
    local/me-mayday17.

30 Melina Abdullah, "Why LA's DA Refuses to Prosecute Killer Cops,"
    interview by Sonali Kolhatkar, September 29, 2017, in *Rising Up with
    Sonali*, Los Angeles, CA, KPFK 90.7, https://www.risingupwithsonali.com/
    why-las-da-refuses-to-prosecute-killer-cops.

BLMLA's public discourse obliterates the ideological pretensions of "Join LAPD" in a widely circulated 2017 petition addressed to LA County District Attorney Jackie Lacey. Titled "Prosecute Police Who Kill Our People," the campaign holds Lacey accountable for reproducing the fatal consequences of police impunity, sparing her no criticism as the first African American to hold this particular public office.

> During her terms in office, nearly 300 Los Angeles County residents have been killed by police, including #EzellFord, #KendrecMcDade, #JohnHorton, #NephiArreguin, #MichelleShirley, #RedelJones, #WakieshaWilson, #JRThomas, #KeithBursey, #JesseRomero, #EdwinRodriguez, #KennyWatkins, #BrendonGlenn, #BrotherAfrica, #ZelalemEwnetu, #CarnellSnell and literally hundreds of others. In the case of Brendon Glenn, the officer was actually recommended for charges by the Los Angeles Police Department. NO OFFICER HAS EVER BEEN CHARGED FOR THE KILLING OF A RESIDENT BY LACEY.
>
> Los Angeles Police Department, Los Angeles County Sheriffs, and the policing units throughout the County lead the nation in the killing of community residents. For at least the last five years, LAPD and LA County Sheriff have led the nation in police killings. Yet, the District Attorney has not charged a single officer in any of these killings. The message sent to Los Angeles County law enforcement units is that they can kill residents and get away with it. Police cannot be relied on to hold themselves accountable, this is the work of the District Attorney.[31]

As it continues to kill Black and Brown civilians with effective juridical sanction, the LAPD's assimilation into a

FROM "MASS INCARCERATION" TO DOMESTIC WARFARE

post–Proposition 209, post–affirmative action statecraft of diversity reflects two mutually reinforcing institutional logics. On the one hand, "Join LAPD" is indisputably an *externally* (federal consent decree) coerced departure from a densely white male heteronormative officer profile that became a political and tactical liability in the long aftermath of the 1992 LA rebellion. Put another way, the *policing phenotype*—the *signifying body* of law enforcement—became increasingly incompatible with the changing form of the racial state in its various scales of iteration (local, state, regional, and national). On the other hand, the LAPD's turn toward personnel inclusivity is inseparable from a long-held juridical and cultural mandate to facilitate, sustain, and enhance the systemic, everyday processes of racist criminalization and domestic war as a matter of cohering and reproducing a condition of urban social (dis)order.

Wakiesha Wilson's Ashes

As a period-specific racial state strategy, "Join LAPD" reembodies as it reproduces a climate of fatal hostility, in which moments of Black insurgency consistently reveal the distressing *abnormality* of this normalized condition of war. At times, such rebellion creates instructive and inspirational lessons for those seeking liberation from the (multiculturalist) institutional and cultural structures of subjection that permeate the relations of dominance, occupation, and violence between police and criminalized

31 Black Lives Matter Los Angeles, "Prosecute Police Who Kill Our People," public petition, September 11, 2017, https://campaigns.organizefor.org/petitions/los-angeles-county-da-prosecute-police-who-kill-our-people. See also Black Lives Matter Los Angeles, "Sign BLMLA's Petition to Prosecute Police Who Kill Our People," Black Lives Matter, October 17, 2017, https://blacklivesmatter.com/sign-blmlas-petition-to-prosecute-police-who-kill-our-people. Emphasis in the original.

peoples. By way of example: Sheila Hines-Brim, aunt of Wakiesha Wilson, did not accept the LAPD's explanation that there was "no evidence any force was used" when her 36-year-old niece died in police custody on Easter Sunday 2016. As BLMLA members mobilized around Wilson's case in support of Hines-Brim and Wilson's mother Lisa Hines, the LA City Council voted unanimously in December 2017 to pay up to $298,000 to settle the case brought against the city. In contrast, the Los Angeles Police Commission denied any LAPD culpability in Wilson's death and, as noted above, no criminal charges were filed by LA County District Attorney Jackie Lacey.[32] Hines-Brim, whose unrelenting demand for accountability remained unquenched by the settlement and undeterred by the LAPD's denials, radically altered the normalized/abnormal relations of gendered racial bodily integrity, racist state–induced death, and white supremacist governance at the Police Commission's regularly scheduled public meeting in May 2018. Enacting a disruption of the racist state's procedural ceremony of engagement with the (Black) community and Wakiesha Wilson's survivors, Hines-Brim recast her niece's murder as a forever curse on the police chief:

> Wakiesha Wilson's aunt, Sheila Hines-Brim attended the meeting with Wilson's mother, Lisa Hines. Throughout the meeting, some attendees were directed to leave due to multiple interruptions. Hines-Brim proceeded towards Los Angeles Police Chief Charlie Beck and threw a white, powder-like substance at him.
>
> "That's Wakiesha," Hines-Brim exclaimed as she walked away, "That's Wakiesha! She's going to stay with you!"
>
> The meeting quickly ended. Police officers pro-

32   Kate Mather, "LA Agrees to Pay Nearly $300,000 to Settle Case of Woman Who Died in LAPD Jail Cell," *Los Angeles Times*, December 13, 2017,

ceeded to arrest Hines-Brim. Fire crews were urgently called to identify the substance and whether it was dangerous. Joshua Rubenstein, the police department's spokesman, shared that although it doesn't seem hazardous, the department has not confirmed what it was.

Hines-Brim was arrested on charges of suspicion of battery on an officer. She shared after her release, "I used her ashes so they can be with him, so he can feel her, because he murdered her. They covered it up."[33]

A more rigorous conception of the systemic logic of white supremacy—*which is not reducible to the white body itself*—might help delink white supremacy's "substructure" (its logics of violence and ordering) from reductive notions of the white supremacist "phenotype" (the exclusive or otherwise overwhelming presence of white bodies). Put differently, i am asking us to consider how white supremacy is fully engaged in the organization of systemic violence and the social subjection of white civil society's historical racial antagonists, even and especially as its institutional forms—including its political and intellectual leadership—convene a (relative) diversity of nonwhite bodies. What new political languages, organizing strategies, and conceptual frameworks can enable an adequately critical,

https://www.latimes.com/local/lanow/la-me-ln-lapd-settlements-20171213-story.html.

33   Isra Ibrahim, "Woman Throws Ashes of Niece Who Died in Police Custody at LAPD Chief," *The Black Youth Project*, May 11, 2018, http://blackyouth project.com/woman-throws-ashes-of-niece-who-died-in-police-custody-at-lapd-chief. See also Kristine Phillips, "'That's Wakiesha!' a Woman Said as She Threw Her Niece's Ashes at the Los Angeles Police Chief," *The Washington Post*, May 9, 2018, https://www.washingtonpost.com/news/post-nation/wp/2018/05/09/thats-wakiesha-a-woman-said-as-she-threw-her-nieces-ashes-at-the-los-angeles-police-chief.

ambitiously transformative response to multiculturalist white supremacy?

"Join LAPD" indicates a constitutive tension in White Reconstruction's struggle to reconstitute hegemony while retaining the militarized protocols and methods of the racist state: the reconstruction simultaneously *solicits* the historical targets of white supremacist, patriarchal, heteronormative racial-colonial violence, while *refurbishing* (and thus *reproducing*) the relations of dominance that constitute the primary terms of the modern racial order. To consider the multiculturalist "turn" in the demographic composition of certain bureaucratic, professional, and administrative spaces within historically white supremacist social and state formations, then, is to apprehend how Sylvia Wynter's "Man" attempts to sustain and galvanize a global order of power by selectively revising the bureaucratic pathways and discursive terms of piecemeal (that is, contingent and non-comprehensive) access for historically excluded others to participate in an ensemble of hegemonic institutions (schools/colleges/universities, police, military, electoral politics, and state-funded service professions, to name a few). Wynter's "Man" references the peculiar "genre" of the human that is forcibly imposed on the rest of humanity as the universalized template for proper species-being. The New World slave plantation is, she writes,

> a dominant *logic*, and it's a specific *cultural* logic, but it is also an ethical logic, a paradoxical realpolitik and a secular one that is in the process of emerging. It is this reasons-of-state ethic/logic that is going to bring in the modern world, what I call the millennium of Man. *We have lived the millennium of Man in the last five hundred years* [emphasis added]; and as the West is inventing Man, the slave-plantation is a central part of the entire mechanism by means of which that logic

is working its way out. But that logic is total now, because to be not-Man is to be not-quite-human. Yet that plot, that slave plot on which the slave grew food for his/her subsistence, carried over a millennially *other* conception of the human to that of Man's.[34]

Following Wynter, multiculturalist white supremacy is Man's solicitation and incorporation of "nonwhite" and counter-normative/queer/trans subjects and bodies into a *millennial* order of white power/ascendancy. These processes of bodily exhibition, institutional expansion, and symbolic-ideological rearticulation attempt to *discipline, selectively assimilate, and otherwise dissipate* insurgent modalities of human being that persist within and against the violent and violating ascendancy of Man—including and especially Wynter's particular logic of the plantation, a relation of dominance against Afro-descended Black people that shapes and influences other Civilizational racial-colonial power formations.

Here, it is necessary to consider again how White Reconstruction raises a structuring racial-colonial contradiction: there is a struggle for hegemony as a system of social order and dominance; the notion of "hegemonic" power is premised on the primacy of consensual rather than coercive/violent relations of power; yet, because anti-Blackness and racial-colonial relations of dominance *constitute and cohere sociality as such*, the struggle for hegemony is already confounded by the conditions of carceral state and extrastate violence (domestic war). In order to fully appreciate the LAPD's response to the 2001 consent decree as a symptomatic indication of the *speculative cultural algorithms* of White Reconstruction, it is also necessary to consider how the "Join LAPD" campaign is more than a cynical,

34 Sylvia Wynter, "The Re-Enchantment of Humanism: An Interview with Sylvia Wynter," by David Scott, *Small Axe* 8 (September 2000): 165.

superficial ploy to quell federal governmental criticism and the decree's implicit threat of receivership. Rather, such efforts reflect a dynamic, dialogical relation between state agencies and institutional geographies that expand the capacities of the racial/racist state as a *pedagogical* (and not merely coercive) political, juridical, *and culturally productive* totality. Here, the notion of a speculative cultural algorithm suggests that the historical field of White Reconstruction involves an interplay between the *actuarial* (predictive and anticipatory) routines of institutional protocol, discursive rationalization (of reform, repression, contradiction, etc.), and disciplinary-to-punitive statecraft (jurisprudence, policing, criminalization, etc.), and the *aspirational and experimental* (hence speculative) dimensions of a period-specific statecraft, which constantly coordinates and rearticulates domestic warfare and gendered racial reform as a complex and simultaneous *totality* rather than an irreconcilable or explosive internal contradiction.

The scholarly activist obligation, in the contemporary moment, is to consider the political and cultural implications of a multiculturalist white supremacy that actively releases—or is forced to release—its stranglehold on apartheid forms of institutionality at the very same time that it reproduces the ascendancy of White Being. As the planners, organic intellectuals, administrators, and armed officers of the pedagogical state continually test, revise, and institutionalize the cultural algorithms of White Reconstruction, there is neither respite nor security from the recalibrations of domestic racial-colonial warfare. How are we to conceptualize, confront, oppose, creatively disrupt, and/or transform this multiculturalist renaissance of the white supremacist form? How does the recasting and redistribution of bodies, subjects, and identities within the formally desegregated geographies of white supremacy compel a reframing of antiracist, abolitionist, antigenocide, decolonizing, and radical liberationist work?

Sable Elyse Smith, *Coloring Book 6*, 2018. Screen printing ink and oil stick on paper, 60 x 56 inches. Courtesy of the artist; JTT, New York; and Carlos/Ishikawa, London.

Together, Pat and Judge Friendly ride the elevator upstairs to a room with benches. Lots and lots of people are waiting.

"It is hard to wait," says Judge Friendly.

"There are many families here, so we hope you don't mind waiting. We have quiet puzzles to work on."

What 10 things don't belong in this picture?

WORKING TO GET FREE AT THE RENT PARTY

ADRIENNE BROWN

> After the slave ship and the plantation, the third revolution of black intimate life unfolded in the city. The hallway, bedroom, stoop, rooftop, airshaft, and kitchenette provided the space of experiment.
> —Saidiya Hartman, *Wayward Lives, Beautiful Experiments*

A 2019 report by the Samuel DuBois Cook Center on Social Equity at Duke University estimates that predatory home contract sales extracted between $3 billion and $4 billion from black Chicagoans in the 1950s and 1960s.[1] Unable to receive fair mortgage rates on the regulated market, many black residents of the redlined city turned to the exploitative secondary market of home contracts to pursue their dreams of home ownership. Offering the "illusion of a mortgage" with none of its protections, home contracts stipulated that buyers pay high-interest monthly payments to sellers for homes they could not own outright until the contract was paid in full. In addition to footing the bill for any repairs to the home—a home they had no way of knowing the true condition and thus true value of given the lack of procedures like inspection or appraisal—buyers lost the entirety of their investment if they moved before the contract was complete and could be evicted for as much as a single late payment. Between 75 and 95 percent of the homes sold to black families in this period were on

---

1   Sharon McCloskey and Bruce Orenstein, eds., *The Plunder of Black Wealth in Chicago: New Findings on the Lasting Toll of Predatory Housing Contracts* (Durham, NC: The Samuel Du Bois Cook Center on Social Equity at Duke University, 2019), https://socialequity.duke.edu/wp-content/uploads/2019/10/Plunder-of-Black-Wealth-in-Chicago.pdf.

contracts marked up by an average of 84 percent.

While previous scholars have studied the predatory nature of contract buying, the Cook Center's report is the first to quantify the scope of wealth extracted by these predatory instruments during the decades of their most frequent use. But these contracts were merely one regional instance within the much broader history of race-based exclusion and expropriation perpetuated through housing. Just imagine how staggering the amount would be if one calculated the total wealth either lost or redistributed from Emancipation to the present through the systemic limiting of black access to property and its attendant protections. Contract buying joins the land seizures authorized by Jim Crow, the discriminatory housing policies administered by the New Deal state, lending and insurance redlining, and the more recent targeting of black borrowers for subprime mortgages on a long list of property inequities that have significantly widened the wealth gap between whites and blacks in the United States to this day.[2] The extent of these housing-related thefts and obstructions in the postbellum period is one reason why scholars and activists have increasingly framed the demand for reparations as redressing not only slavery but the multitude of injuries and injustices blacks continued to be subject to after Emancipation.[3]

Even as blacks encountered systemic obstruction and theft while pursuing the stabilities associated with prop-

2   Lest we think that increasing minority access to markets is the solution for inequality, in her book *Carceral Capitalism*, Jackie Wang describes the "expropriation through financial inclusion" faced by minority buyers in relation to the 2008 housing market crash in particular as black and Latinx borrowers were targeted for subprime mortgage loans. See Jackie Wang, *Carceral Capitalism* (South Pasadena: Semiotext(e), 2018), 134. Moreover, this tally of lost black wealth in relation to the land must also be weighed in relation to native dispossession from the land.

3   For more on the recent trajectory of reparations see Katherine Franke's *Repair: Redeeming the Promise of Abolition* (Chicago: Haymarket Books, 2019).

erty ownership in the US, they also experienced dispro-
portionate policing and prosecution for remaining mobile. States and municipalities have long used vagrancy
statutes to criminalize the homeless and the jobless, those
untethered to civil society by property or wage, for centuries. In the US, one key purpose of vagrancy laws after
Emancipation was to regulate black movement. Vagrancy
statutes, as Saidiya Hartman writes, became "the legal
means to master the newly masterless."[4] Vagrancy was
not treated as something one did but was instead used to
describe one's status as a person. "Status offenses" such
as vagrancy, Hartman argues "were critical to the remaking of a racist order in the aftermath of Emancipation."[5]
Contributing to the notion that criminality was inherent
to specific populations, vagrancy laws framed black bodies
deemed "out of place" as inherently unlawful.

Caught between the carceral logics of the emerging Jim Crow regime in the South and vagrancy statutes nationwide, African Americans in the late nineteenth
and early twentieth centuries found themselves squeezed
financially and spatially.[6] Impeded in their efforts to own
property and at risk of being criminalized for moving too
far out of their "place," blacks were left no option but the
predatory renting practices in segregated areas. Such
conditions helped to consolidate black urban communities into ghettoes, cultivating a reliable racialized surplus
population furnishing the economy with both disposable
labor and, eventually, vulnerable consumers primed for
further extraction through debt.[7] Black urban residents

4   Saidiya V Hartman, *Wayward Lives, Beautiful Experiments: Intimate Histo-
     ries of Social Upheaval* (New York: W.W. Norton & Company, 2019), 242.
5   Hartman, *Wayward Lives, Beautiful Experiments*, 243.
6   Though this essay is primarily interested in the early twentieth century, this
     is not to say that this squeeze is not in operation today. See, for instance,
     Matthew Desmond's *Evicted: Poverty and Profit in the American City* (New
     York: Crown, 2016); and the disproportionate number of black women
     evicted in the US dealing with the very costly afterlife of these restrictions.

who migrated North as part of the Great Migration were not only generally restricted to overcrowded parts of the city but paid extraordinarily high rents for the privilege— sometimes paying double what white tenants had either previously been charged or were currently being charged elsewhere.[8] A vast exploitative rental regime emerged in the urban North in the early twentieth century to profit from black residential containment, a situation enforced by redlining policies that limited where blacks could live as well as their ability to access fair mortgages.[9] With black residents paying disproportionately expensive rents with disproportionately low and often unstable wages, housing segregation functioned not only as a mechanism of exclusion but also as a tool for expropriation through black enclosure.

The correlated constrictions of space and income that residents faced in urban black belts helps us to better situate the motivations of desperate home contract buyers. Already accustomed to paying dearly for substandard housing, black renters were willing to risk entering into home contracts in order to better, if only slightly, the physical and financial conditions in which they dwelled. For many of these tenants, contract buying was the next best option to outright home ownership. If "owning property

7   See Michael Dawson and Megan Ming Francis, "Black Politics and the Neoliberal Racial Order," *Public Culture* 28, no. 1 (January 2016): 23–62.

8   For instance, as Shannon King notes, "blacks in West Harlem earned approximately 17 percent less than the typical family in the entire city, but paid three dollars more per room per month." King also notes that blacks even paid more than whites, moreover, when they occupied the same buildings. Shannon King, *Whose Harlem Is This, Anyway?: Community Politics and Grassroots Activism During the New Negro Era* (New York: New York University Press, 2015), 96.

9   It is important to note, as N.D.B. Connolly has argued in detail, that Americans of all colors—including African Americans—profited from exploitative regimes of property ownership. See N.D.B. Connolly, *A World More Concrete: Real Estate and the Remaking of Jim Crow South Florida* (Chicago: University of Chicago Press, 2014).

and having those rights of ownership respected by others is a necessary predicate to freedom and citizenship," as legal scholar Katherine Franke argues, pursuing ownership through home contracts was, for many black renters, a risk worth taking despite the high cost and the scant consumer protections.[10]

But while some black tenants sought to get as close to home ownership as possible through home contracts, others—either out of necessity or out of choice—pursued alternative ways of staying housed outside the margins of respectability. Contrary to the well-oiled propaganda machine of the American Dream in the early twentieth century, home ownership was not the aspiration for all. Whereas both the state and the private housing market aggressively promoted the link between ownership and citizenship, particularly after the 1917 Russian Revolution, we find black tenants during this period managing the ghetto's financial and spatial squeeze in ways that did not require them to invest in the promises or the increasingly linked ideals of property and citizenship. Those struggling to afford their marked-up rents tended to live closely with others, often sharing space with boarders whom they did not previously know. These living situations were an affront to social reformers who warned against the ills of ghetto living—blaming its close and cramped quarters for destabilizing the family unit and cultivating criminality—and who, alongside boosters for the real estate industry, valorized the owned home for its alleged capacity to stabilize the state, keep workers rooted in one place, and promote heterosexual families integral to propagating so-called "good populations."[11]

10   Franke, *Repair*, 17.
11   This was the term of twentieth-century land economist and leader of the Progressive movement Richard Ely. See Richard Ely, "Private and Public Colonization," *The National Real Estate Journal* 26, no. 6 (1923): 46–49.

WORKING TO GET FREE AT THE RENT PARTY

When taking in boarders did not cover the rent, some black residents opened their homes to neighbors and strangers for raucous house parties to make up the difference. While the rent party, as it was called, has its roots in Southern church socials and fish fries, it took on its most distinctive form in the Northern cities blacks migrated to en masse in the early twentieth century. Peaking in popularity in the 1920s and 1930s, rent parties helped working-class residents afford the inflated rents in crowded black enclaves.[12] Tenants advertised the gatherings on printed cards, inviting locals and passersby to eat, dance, and drink the night away for a small entry fee, which would go towards the occupants' rent. Alongside their practical function of keeping residents housed, rent parties also facilitated the sensory dispossession of their guests in crowded spaces where "bedlam reigned," as one attendee described. Known for good music, hearty food, bad liquor, low lights, close dancing, late nights, and the occasional violent incident, rent parties were places for attendees to let loose and rub up against just about anybody while assisting their neighbors in avoiding dispossession for another month.

At a time when realtors and the state were framing home ownership as a civic duty and a moral benefit, the rent party reframed housing as a mere necessity around which social relations in excess of ownership and its narrow rights could emerge. The rent party offered black tenants a space to revel in the joy of being housed while also forsaking the conservative imperative to worship the "cult of the home." Teeming with sound, food, and people, the rent party was a source of social life as well as an instrumental response to social death administered through residential apartheid. They served as places where black residents could rehearse other ways of occupying and enjoying

12   See King, *Whose Harlem Is This, Anyway?*; and Mark D. Naison, *Communists in Harlem During the Depression* (New York: Grove, 1985), 23.

residential space beyond the limited notion of freedom the liberal state yoked to home ownership. To follow Fred Moten, "It could be called the house party but don't let that mislead you into thinking that house implies ownership."[13] Rather, as Moten suggests, we find the rent party's attendees to be "preoccupied with disowning, with unowning, with homeless anti- and ante-ownership, and this is their party because they're always trying to give it away, like a bird in hand, hand in hand, hand to hand."[14]

The Problem of Negro Housing

The Northern rent party emerged in response to the conditions circumscribing black dwelling. While realtors and bureaucrats deemed shortages in the housing market after the First World War a temporary crisis, blacks largely experienced crises of housing as an ongoing norm. Crowded quarters, aging housing, and the impending threat of dispossession characterized not only the living conditions of blacks who migrated North at the turn of the century, but African Americans more broadly post-Emancipation.[15] Although blacks owned property in both the North and the South before and after slavery, their sovereignty over that property could be challenged at any moment. For Southern black landowners, the Jim Crow regime made it difficult to

13   Fred Moten, "Air Shaft, Rent Party," in *Stolen Life* (Durham, NC: Duke University Press, 2018), 188.

14   Moten, "Air Shaft, Rent Party," 188.

15   As David Madden and Peter Marcuse note, while "the idea of crisis implies that inadequate or unaffordable housing is abnormal, a temporary departure from a well-functioning standard," "for working-class and poor communities, housing crisis is the norm." See David Madden and Peter Marcuse, *In Defense of Housing* (London and New York: Verso, 2016), 9. They cite Engels as identifying this point in his 1872 *The Housing Question* in which he notes that housing has always been a question for the oppressed. For more on the connection between the plantation economies of the South and the emergence of the urban ghetto in the North, see Hartman, *Wayward Lives, Beautiful Experiments*.

enforce their ownership in the face of state-sanctioned white terrorism. The profits whites incurred from share-cropping further incentivized black peonage via land, conditions that made Northern migration all the more appealing.

The dwelling conditions migrants found in the North, however, were not materially much better than what they had endured in the South. Sometimes they were far worse. While before the nineteenth century, blacks residing in the urban North may have lived alongside whites and immi-grants in mixed neighborhoods, this changed drastically with the onset of the Great Migration in the 1910s. As black populations nearly doubled in metropolitan areas between 1915 and 1920, and as Eastern and Southern European immigrants who had arrived in the US in the late nine-teenth century began to be assimilated into whiteness in the early twentieth, the creation of the black ghetto began in earnest—restricting blacks to dwelling in districts whites had largely abandoned. While whites treated black and immigrant dwellers similarly in the late nineteenth century, "the very consciousness of whites in the North," as one scholar notes, "seemed to change during the few years from 1917 to 1920 from an 'ethnic' view of urban diversity to one more centered on race."[16] Whites in this period increas-ingly feared blackness as an absolute threat to residential order and, most significantly, to residential value.

Municipal governments and private realtors deployed a number of tactics to consolidate and contain the rising number of blacks moving to the North. When the use of public zoning to bar blacks from residential areas failed to pass legal muster, extralegal tactics for enforcing black containment followed. These tactics included the adop-tion of ethics pledges barring realtors from actively inte-grating neighborhoods, lenders agreeing to not lend to

16   Richard Sander, *Moving Towards Integration: The Past and Future of Fair Housing* (Cambridge, MA: Harvard University Press, 2018), 53.

blacks seeking to buy in white neighborhoods, the emergence of neighborhood improvement associations designed to maintain the residential color line, and the normalization of racial covenants in housing deeds. Collectively, these efforts amounted to a fairly comprehensive system of private zoning, which intervened when state-mandated forms of racial segregation failed.[17]

Except for some concerned reformers and members of the slumming white avant-garde who viewed black housing as a lurid site of fascination, black housing in the North received little sustained attention in the white public sphere.[18] It is a bit surprising, then, to find the housing conditions of African Americans identified as a specific area of concern in Herbert Hoover's 1931 President's Conference on Home Building and Home Ownership. Although President Hoover ignored this particular housing matter in his own speeches, the organizers dedicated one of the conference's eleven subcommittees to studying Negro Housing.[19] Headed by black educator and civil rights activist Nannie Burroughs, the committee issued a report not only detailing the specific housing issues faced by African Americans but also formulating some solutions.

Though the state and the private housing industry largely ignored its findings, the Negro Housing report offered a clear-eyed assessment of the racism and inequality largely responsible for the poor state and scant availability of Negro housing. "The racial factors in the problem of housing," the report asserts, "are very largely those

17   Sander, *Moving Towards Integration*, 61.
18   One key exception was in the wake of riots like those in Chicago in 1919. The Chicago Commission on Race Relations focused extensively on black housing in its 1922 report, *The Negro in Chicago: A Study of Race Relations and a Race Riot* (Chicago: University of Chicago Press, 1922).
19   See Herbert Hoover, "Address to the White House Conference on Home Building and Home Ownership, December 2, 1931," in *Public Papers of the Presidents: Herbert Hoover, 1929–1933*, 4 vols. (Washington, DC: Government Publishing Office, 1976), 3:572–3:577.

prompted by whites in an attempt to limit the areas in which Negroes may live."[20] But despite its condemnation of the policies and practices facilitating residential segregation, the committee agreed with bureaucrats and realtors on one crucial point: that home ownership was the key to solving the housing problems of blacks and whites alike. Confirming the fears of reformers and realtors, Burroughs's committee warned against the dangers of overcrowded apartments and tenements: "The extent to which morals and health are jeopardized by the promiscuous taking in of roomers has been well established by many studies." Boarders, the report declared, are "one of the principal evils in Negro housing."[21] According to the committee, the antidote to this residential promiscuity was to make home ownership—described as an "index to social stability and good citizenship"—more affordable across the color line.[22]

The Committee on Negro Housing's decision to render the path to civil rights as coterminous with the path to home ownership would find continued support in the decades to come. But its embrace of ownership as an index of social stability and superior citizenship signaled their tacit acceptance of the notion that it inherently made for better citizens and neighbors. Advocating for increased black access to home ownership and its alleged graces meant the committee did not question whether the form of citizenship it allegedly fortified was worth pursuing. Yet while the largely middle-class black and white members of the Committee on Negro Housing imagined ownership paving the way to civil rights, rent party revelers across town were experimenting with other modes of being at home.

20   Nannie H. Burroughs and Charles S. Johnson, *Negro Housing: Physical Aspects, Social and Economic Factors, Home Ownership and Financing*, ed. John M. Gries and James Ford (Washington, DC: President's Conference on Home Building and Home Ownership, 1932), 73.

21   Burroughs and Johnson, *Negro Housing*, 72.

The Rent Party as Problem and Solution

The rent party's archive is scant. Too dark to film or photograph and too noisy (and sweaty, perhaps) to record, the early rent party largely escaped technological capture. What we know about these gatherings comes from oral histories and memoirs, police reports, sensational newspaper accounts, and a handful of literary representations. As an improvisational social form, the rent party has been most studied by scholars of black performance. In one of the rent party's starkest assessments, dance scholar Katrina Hazzard-Gordon insists that these functions "remained essentially an individual response to a large-scale problem" that "could not galvanize the community into a political unit."[23] "Had a political organization or strong tenants' movement addressed housing needs," she concludes, "the rent party might not have developed such support."[24] For Hazzard-Gordon, the rent party was the result of a political vacuum. It marked the absence of black organization rather than its expression.

Hazzard-Gordon frames the rent strike and the rent party as oppositional forms. And yet, the fact that they both punctuated Harlem's residential scene in the 1920s and 1930s suggests that one did not negate the possibility of the other. The first rent strike of black Harlem tenants in 1916 was led by women and followed by the formation of several other local tenant organizations—the most famous being the Harlem Tenants League led by communist Richard B. Moore between 1928 and 1930.[25] Rent strikes typically elicited few concessions from landlords, and not because rent

22   Burroughs and Johnson, *Negro Housing*, 79.
23   Katrina Hazzard-Gordon, *Jookin': The Rise of Social Dance Formations in African American Culture* (Philadelphia: Temple University Press, 1990), 115.
24   Hazzard-Gordon, *Jookin'*, 97.
25   See King, *Whose Harlem Is This, Anyway?*, 98–103.

parties distracted tenants from "real" politics. Rather, as historian Mark Naison notes, rent strikes proved challenging for Harlem's most vulnerable residents because of how saturated the housing market was for blacks who were barred from residing beyond Harlem's heaving borders.[26] Given the difficulty of acquiring housing in Harlem, working-class black tenants in particular risked worse accommodations or even homelessness should strikes fail. Black tenants were thus at the mercy of landlords who knew they had nowhere else to go.[27]

Unable to afford strikes or court battles, Harlem's working-class tenants initiated other types of housing actions. In fact, the rent party shares similarities with perhaps the most widespread tactic for combatting rental exploitation in Harlem and other black enclaves: eviction resistance. Eviction actions entailed groups of people moving furniture back into dispossessed units and obstructing police efforts to see evictions through in the hopes of buying precious time for evicted tenants. Like the rent party, these actions coalesced with little notice or planning and relied on the involvement of strangers and passersby. Participants rarely knew the dispossessed personally as they generally joined in on the spot to help resist.[28]

26   Mark D. Naison, "From Eviction Resistance to Rent Control: Tenant Activism in the Great Depression," in *The Tenant Movement in New York City, 1904–1984*, ed. Mark D. Naison and Ronald Lawson (New Brunswick, NJ: Rutgers University Press, 1986), http://www.tenant.net/Community/history/hist-toc.html.

27   The period's most successful rent strikes took place in Harlem's wealthy enclave of Sugar Hill. The Sugar Hill strikes began in 1934 when black professionals residing at 281 Edgecombe Avenue learned they were paying nearly double the rent of its previous white tenants. Residents collectively withheld rent and hired lawyers to fight their landlords in municipal court. In contrast to the earlier efforts of working-class Harlem strikers, Sugar Hill tenants could afford both the money and the time it took to pursue their claims in court. For more on the Sugar Hill rent strikes, see Naison, "From Eviction Resistance to Rent Control."

28   Naison argues that eviction resistance proved a far more powerful tool than rent strikes, which were often difficult to organize. As he notes, "eviction

The spontaneous and temporary collectivities nurtured by the rent party align most strongly not with the strike, then, but with the riot—a form that, like the rent party, is often "understood to have no politics at all, a spasmodic irruption to be read symptomatically and perhaps granted a paternalistic dollop of sympathy" as Joshua Clover writes.[29] "The riot, as is broadly agreed even among its partisans," Clover continues, "is a great disorder," a diagnosis often assigned to the rent party as well.[30]

The rent party's social and political contours have garnered more sympathetic examination in recent work by James Wilson, Martin Summers, Stephen Robertson, Fred Moten, and Shane Vogel.[31] Moten and Vogel, though in different ways, most explicitly challenge Hazzard-Gordon's insistence on the rent party's apoliticism. For Vogel, rent parties are sites for rethinking the very terrain of the political itself. He considers the Harlem Renaissance at large and the rent party in particular as manifestations of a

resistance did not require active support from the population or even the political sympathy of the victim. Given the overextended schedules of marshals and police, a handful of Party cadre could move the furniture back, provided the rest of the neighborhood was sympathetic or indifferent." Naison, "From Eviction Resistance to Rent Control," 14.

29   Joshua Clover, *Riot. Strike. Riot: The New Era of Uprisings* (London and New York: Verso, 2016), 3. While the strike is generally associated with properly "organized" Marxist action, Clover notes that "those who have accorded the riot the potential for an insurrectionary opening onto a social rupture come generally from intellectual and political traditions indifferent or even antithetical to the command of state and economy, most famously (but not exclusively) those of some strands of anarchism."

30   Clover, *Riot. Strike. Riot*, 4.

31   See James F. Wilson, *Bulldaggers, Pansies, and Chocolate Babies: Performance, Race, and Sexuality in the Harlem Renaissance* (Ann Arbor: University of Michigan Press, 2010); Martin A. Summers, *Manliness and Its Discontents: The Black Middle Class and the Transformation of Masculinity, 1900–1930* (Chapel Hill: University of North Carolina Press, 2004); and Stephen Robertson, Shane White, Stephen Garton, and Graham White, "Disorderly Houses: Residences, Privacy, and the Surveillance of Sexuality in 1920s Harlem," *Journal of the History of Sexuality* 21, no. 3 (September 2012): 443–466.

"different kind of politics: a sensate politics that figured prominently in the Harlem Renaissance's cultures of sexual dissidence."[32] To recapture the "radical experimentations with sexual subjectivity and dissident form," Vogel turns to descriptions of the rent party performing, what he terms, "critical sensuousness"—a mode in which the senses "expand the boundaries of the known world," queering one's "spatial orientation" within the intimate and domestic spaces of the rent party.[33]

While Vogel claims the rent party to incubate a "sensate politics," Moten sees the rent party as political, extra-political, and apolitical simultaneously. Occurring or slipping between the manifold meanings of "party," Moten insists that "this new political party is not a political party." Instead he describes the rent party as "the old-new, extrapolitical party of the ones who are none" as well as "the violent birth or birth announcement of the last political party."[34] It is the indeterminability of the party that makes the rent party difficult to demarcate from the riot. Creating not quite a genealogy between the rent party and the riot, Moten instead posits the multiple relational possibilities between the two as synonymous, yoked, and coeval.

How the rent party causes one to feel in their body—challenging attendees to reconsider whether one has *a* body at all as opposed to an "everybody," "anybody," and a "no-body" all at once, as Moten insists—is critical to both Vogel and Moten's conception of the rent party's potentialities. This potential becomes even crisper when juxtaposed with home ownership discourse from the period promoting ownership as the pinnacle of individual sovereignty—a capacity also often associated with white racial identity.

32   Shane Vogel, "The Sensuous Harlem Renaissance: Sexuality and Queer
      Culture," in *A Companion to the Harlem Renaissance*, ed. Cherene
      Sherrard-Johnson (Chichester: Wiley-Blackwell, 2015), 268.
33   Vogel, "The Sensuous Harlem Renaissance," 277.
34   Moten, "Air Shaft, Rent Party," 188.

Realtor discourse alleged home ownership could transform revolutionaries into patriots, (some) immigrants into whites, and men into *real* men, primarily through property's capacity to allow one to feel more sovereign over their persons and property. It was a way of buying the right to exclude others from private space. By contrast, the rent party's disruptive sensorium muddled subjects' perception of both each other and of themselves *as* selves as they attached to a temporary scene created by its participants rather than a permanently owned space. What Moten and Vogel seem to be naming in the rent party's political possibility is its refusal of a politics organized around the liberal investment in American individualism, increasingly anchored to home ownership. If home ownership was touted as the ideal apparatus for reproducing the social and racial status quo, tenants at the rent party maintained and extended their home in the short term without pledging long-term allegiance to the physical and economic structures propping up their continued exploitation.

This is not to deny that tenants living in the crowded and crumbling conditions of many Harlem residences would have likely leaped at the opportunity to buy or rent elsewhere. Joshua Clover's observation that rioters "make structured and improvisational use of the *given* terrain"—"neither made nor chosen"—also applies to the rent party.[35] But in the course of fulfilling the base economic need of shelter, rent parties made space for hosts and attendees to treat private property as *merely* a necessity rather than as a calling, a civic duty, or a "universal yearning." Instead they suggested the vital sociality and even plural forms of subjectivity to be found beyond ownership.

Mrs. Bailey's Dispossessive Futurities

35   Clover, *Riot. Strike. Riot*, 46.

While Nannie Burroughs was endorsing home ownership as the best antidote to the "promiscuous taking in of roomers," other women were testing out the productive and liberatory possibilities of embracing this promiscuousness in housing. Black women were active in rent parties not just as attendees but as hosts and entertainers. Rent party advertisements from the period list names such as Elivra, Barbara, and Mrs. Kelly as official hosts. These functions were often held on Thursday and Saturday nights, evenings that black domestics most regularly had off.[36] In the early twentieth century, black women in the North were largely employed by the white families that the state and the private housing market most actively encouraged to purchase homes. Perhaps it was their inclusion in white residential spaces as workers coupled with their exclusion from these same spaces as tenants that well positioned black women domestics to assess the racialized injustices of the housing market and seek other ways of claiming space.[37] While the rent party was certainly an economic necessity for tenants—and a way to avoid being put out—it also enabled a provisional lifestyle in which women could elude the entrapment or containment of either marriage or property. It provided a space to socially, sexually, sensorially, *and* financially wander.

36   Women also helped to invent and refine the social dances popularized at rent parties, including the Charleston, Black Bottom, Bump, Mess Around, and the Fish Tail, later coopted by Broadway and the cabaret scene.

37   Saidiya Hartman has exhaustively described the limited economic opportunities and the exacting legal and social regimes of discipline and punishment black women faced upon migrating North while also attending to their experiments in daring to pursue their desires despite these conditions. Echoing Vogel's focus on the "radical experimentations with sexual subjectivity and dissident form" undertaken by black and queer Harlemites, Hartman reclaims the innovative radicalism of the young black women whose "transformations of sexuality, intimacy, affiliation, and kinship taking place in the black quarter of northern cities," she writes, "might be labeled the revolution before Gatsby." See Hartman, *Wayward Lives, Beautiful Experiments*, 61.

The rent party thrown by the central protagonist of journalist Ira Reid's 1927 account "Mrs. Bailey Pays the Rent" is such a space.[38] The title derives from the piece's lyrical epigraph, the jazz standard "Bill Bailey, Won't You Please Come Home" in which the fictional Mrs. Bailey implores her husband to return home, promising "I'll do the cookin' honey, I'll pay the rent." This figure serves as the basis for the composite Mrs. Bailey, the host of the rent party at the center of Reid's essay. Although Reid was employed by the National Urban League at the time, his account of Mrs. Bailey's party eschews empirical evidence.[39] Outside of newspaper reports, "Mrs. Bailey Pays the Rent" is one of the few works documenting the rent party during their peak popularity. Foregoing sociological dissection, however, Reid's account reads more like a lyrical sketch than gritty urban reportage. While Mrs. Bailey in the song is driven by her desire for her husband to come home—defined by traditional virtues such as marriage and cooking—Reid's host seems uninterested in this vision of domestic life. His Mrs. Bailey is too busy choreographing the complex movement of bodies temporarily occupying her space. She doesn't yearn for the attributes persistently attached to home ownership in this period—there is no mention of marriage, no reproductive futurity through children, no democracy, no strictly defined moral virtue. Maybe she wants these things, maybe she doesn't; maybe she is too busy or too overworked to entertain these desires; maybe she would abandon her current home and her current company at the prospect of owning elsewhere; or maybe the burden of an owned home makes

38   Ira D. Reid, "Mrs. Bailey Pays the Rent," in *Ebony and Topaz: A Collectanea*, ed. Charles S. Johnson (New York: Opportunity and National Urban League, 1927), 144–148.

39   For more on Reid's style as a sociologist, see Francille Rusan Wilson, "Mapping the Great Migration," in *The Segregated Scholars: Black Social Scientists and the Creation of Black Labor Studies, 1890–1950* (Charlottesville: University of Virginia Press, 2006), 115–172.

her shudder. All we know is that Mrs. Bailey wants to pay her rent this month and that throwing a good party is integral to that mission.

Instead of offering motivations for Mrs. Bailey's actions, Reid inundates us with the practical tasks of readying the party, from renting chairs to setting up the live band. We are introduced to the party's saxophonist who "quit the stage to play for the parties because he wanted to stay in New York."[40] The rent party thus not only helped people stay put but it is itself part of what made staying in Harlem worthwhile. For this saxophonist, it is New York at large rather than privately owned domestic space that accrues the status of home. From the start of Reid's narration, a different teleology of home starts to emerge— one that frames the rent party as a financial necessity for enduring Harlem's harsh conditions as well as part of what make Harlem worth enduring at all. Permanence is not the goal here nor is ownership the catalyst for belonging— Mrs. Bailey's apartment is instead a temporary frame for a social vibrancy that will dissipate in a few hours' time. Reid underscores the tension between the rent party's base financial function, enabling Mrs. Bailey and the musicians she hires to pay their rents and stay put, and the party's social function of encouraging fleeting collectivities that make remaining in the city even desirable.

In this vein, Reid's account presents the rent party as a mixture of subjects and events that seem to add up to everything and nothing simultaneously. A nameless woman deals poker in a back room. A girl remarks that "this party's getting right." Mrs. Bailey announces the evening's menu of pig feet and chili. There is a fevered rush to the kitchen. A fight breaks out between two men over a woman. The muscle paid to keep the peace intervenes on the dance floor. The musicians continue to "exhort" fifteen

40   Reid, "Mrs. Bailey Pays the Rent," 147.

or twenty dancing couples. The party encourages temporary forms of sociality that crescendo and dissipate just as quickly. Reid's narration has a blasé quality, capturing the everydayness of the rent party and undermining the broader public's fascination with Harlem as both a site of primitivist fantasy and moral deviance. While social reformers and white thrill seekers from downtown both underscored Harlem's "promiscuous" and chaotic living conditions, the reformers aimed to restructure these conditions. Chic white "slummers"—referred to in Reid's piece as the "Harlem copyists of Greenwich Village"—instead celebrated the pure bacchanalia they believed was innate to black living. By narrating the rent party as a genre with conventions, including violence, Reid disturbs its reputation as a purely chaotic space—highlighting the ways the rent party attendees, to again cite Joshua Clover, made "structured and improvisational use of the given terrain." Though appearing random and chaotic, the specific kind of social and sensorial disorientation one seeks on the rent party's dance floors, kitchens, or backrooms, Reid suggests, is carefully cultivated and controlled by the Mrs. Baileys who make it possible.

The function finally wraps at two in the morning, at which point Mrs. Bailey "calmly surveyed a disarranged apartment, and counted her proceeds."[41] While the story details all of the rent party's notable customs—its rich food, sultry sounds, fervent dancing, backroom gambling, and envy-driven violence—Reid refuses to offer a verdict regarding its value. There's no moral to impart here about this financial and social form. Reid avoids adjudicating what he describes as the rent party's "by-products both legal or otherwise" as virtues or vices. He instead floats along the surface of its various vignettes, privileging the limning of its atmosphere over determining its worth.

41   Reid, "Mrs. Bailey Pays the Rent," 147.

Refusing to collapse domestic space into interior subjectivity, Reid adopts a kinetic form of narration that sketches events and movements amidst the rent party to depict a space that is private yet public, contained yet overflowing, circumscribed but porous.

Reid does acknowledge the violence that occasionally erupts at rent parties. "Not always is it a safe and sane affair," he laments, since "you are seldom certain of your patrons." Given such risks, "there may be tragedies." Reid cites an article from the *New York Age* reporting on an incident at a rent party where "one jealous woman cut the throat of another, because the two were rivals for the affections of a third woman."[42] The *Age* sensationalizes this violence, comparing it to a "recent Broadway play," and decries the rent party as "dangerous to the health of all concerned." Reid on the other hand provides no commentary on this anecdote beyond including it. He does not deny the rent party's occasional violence but neither does he dwell on it nor the queer desire that fueled it. Just like the outburst at Mrs. Bailey's party, this violence is derived from a person's attempt to possess the object of their affection. No matter the source of the desire, to seek permanent possession at the rent party is to produce its greatest tragedy. By including the *Age* report, Reid offers readers a subtle but urgent repudiation of ownership—one that echoes Fred Moten's later understanding of the house party as something that gathers those "preoccupied with disowning." The eruption of the desire to own another during the party not only causes physical harm; it also disrupts the possibility for sensorial and bodily dispossession central to the party's ethos.

Like Moten and Vogel, Reid stops short of vesting the rent party with a specific political valence. Yet Reid does hint at its potential to incubate enduring coalitions. He

42   Reid, "Mrs. Bailey Pays the Rent," 147.

first notes the recent difficulty of determining "whether or not one is attending a bonafide rent party" given the increasing number of organized conglomerates throwing them. As opposed to cash-strapped tenants hosting more improvised affairs, "the party today may be fostered by the Tenants Protective Association," Reid explains, "or the Imperial Scale of Itinerant Musicians, or the Society for the Relief of Ostracized Bootleggers."[43] But per his treatment of other aspects of the rent party, Reid does not condemn this organized cooption. Rather, he makes space for this evolution, acknowledging that "musicians and bootleggers have to live as well as the average tenant, and if they can combine their efforts on a business proposition, the status of both may be improved." Reid frames the rent party as a vehicle for any number of social and political configurations, spanning from noble collectivists to the lumpenproletariat of smugglers. He welcomes the formalization of the rent party as a strategic tool for bettering the lives of the itinerant at different scales. Reid once more dwells in the tensions of the rent party's capacity to inaugurate temporary socialities that may or may not beget more enduring social formations, to encourage social itineracy while providing some financial stasis, and to afford residents the ability to stay put without ownership.

With the concluding anecdote of "Mrs. Bailey Pays the Rent," we find Reid still inhabiting the ambivalent position he seems to most relish. His final words underscore what he describes as the "very close margin both socially and economically" under which the rent party operates. The final vignette begins with a nine-year-old boy gazing up from the street to his apartment in the middle of the night. When the music coming from the apartment dies down, the boy shouts up to his mother that he's tired and wishes to come home. A man sticks his head out of

43   Reid, "Mrs. Bailey Pays the Rent," 148.

the window to relay a message: "Your ma says to go to the Midnight Show, and she'll come after you. Here's four bits. She says the party's just got going good."[44]

This encounter is recounted neither to lament nor celebrate this young boy's plight. It is instead left to stand as a self-explanatory illustration of the rent party's complex demands. The mother is absent from this scene, her wishes ventriloquized by a nameless man who may or may not speak for her. As the author of this piece, Reid could be said to occupy a similar position as message-giver. Like this deliverer, he, too, is the vessel for telling a woman's story in light of her corporeal absence. We might read this last line as Reid's acknowledgement of the women who drive the rent party while underscoring his inability to access or fully represent their subjectivity.

Whereas the song that opens Reid's piece is about a husband and wife, the piece leaves us wondering about the fate of a different dyad: that of mother and son. Given the boy's expulsion from one rented space to take up refuge in another, it's hard to know if his exile is one of salvation or of neglect, whether the collectivity he might find at the midnight show is markedly better or worse than what might be found at the party. But there is no third option granting him protected rest. The boy must leave home to have a home to return to. This ending foregrounds several competing futurities, with the boy's immediate future and perhaps his longer-term prospects placed next to the potential futurity of a party that "just got going good." The situation of this mother and son epitomizes the rent party's dichotomous identity as an improvised form that displaces even as it facilitates (residential) stability, a function encouraging the sensorial and social dispossession of attendees while allowing tenants to remain in possession of their space, a celebration of itineracy in the name of staying housed. There is no conclusive ending imagined for the different tenants, partygoers, neighbors, and strangers the rent party both unites and displaces. Reid's piece merely frames the divergent desires of this young boy who wants to stop and his mother who needs to keep going. The rent party cannot reconcile their aims—only set them in relation to one another. Whereas reformers of the day would have us hear the boy's cries as a moral shame, Reid, Vogel, and Hartman urge us to attend to his mother's utterances just as closely. What might the party that has "just got going good" make possible for the one, the son, and the many? What modes of dwelling and living can she glimpse therein?

"In constantly telling us that there's a party going on," critic Fred Moten writes, "the party is constantly showing us that there's a riot going on, which is how it gets itself smiling, like an antinuclear family affair."[45] Reid's disinterest in rebutting or reigning in the rent party's more riotous aspects seems to anticipate Moten's later appraisal. "Mrs. Bailey Pays the Rent" continually probes the rent party's potential for creative destruction, weighing whether this phenomenon is merely a regrettable symptom of capitalist exploitation or a seed leading to its disruption if not destruction. In collecting tenants, musicians, bootleggers, and the various unassociated into relation and fostering an atmosphere where possessiveness is the ultimate agent of tragedy, Reid's vision of the rent party helmed by the stoic Mrs. Bailey mirrors the social scene of the eviction riot fomenting across Harlem. Both formations challenge the dichotomies of inside and outside, stranger and kin, owning and dwelling. Whereas Reid's story opens with the Mrs. Bailey of song repeatedly crooning for her husband to please come home, we close with this nameless woman biding her time, waiting for the good times to start with the strangers with whom she is in the moment making home.

44   Reid, "Mrs. Bailey Pays the Rent," 148.
45   Moten, "Air Shaft, Rent Party," 188.

Sable Elyse Smith, *Coloring Book 8*, 2018. Screen printing ink and oil stick on paper, 60 x 56 inches. Courtesy of the artist; JTT, New York; and Carlos/Ishikawa, London.

Together, Pat and Judge Friendly ride the elevator upstairs to a big room with benches. Lots and lots of people are waiting.

"It is hard to wait," says Judge Friendly.

"There are many families here, so we hope that everyone brings something to read or quiet puzzles to work on."

What 10 things don't belong in this picture?

BRUSHY MOUNTAIN AND THE ARCHITECTURE OF CARCERAL EXTRACTION

JAMES GRAHAM

The past quarter century has seen the United States' population of federal and state prisoners more than double.[1] During this period, a third of the prisons built to accommodate this carceral inflation were located in four rural regions—west Texas, south-central Georgia, the Mississippi Delta, and the coalfields of Appalachia—even as their prisoners were primarily supplied by cities and towns elsewhere.[2] The same decades-long conditions that ravaged cities (deindustrialization, automation, disenfranchisement, finance capital, and so on) also decimated rural sites of industry, coal extraction among them, leaving such areas eager for available vectors of state funding.[3] The Appalachian prison boom has offered a particularly vivid window into the seductive double narrative of socioeconomic deterioration and opportunity, as the carceral state, the argument goes, arrives in the form of job-producing outposts that fill the voids left by coal's ongoing decline.

1   Department of Justice figures put the combined federal and state prison
    population at 771,243 in 1990 and 1,489,363 in 2017, down from a peak of
    over 1,600,000 in 2009.
2   Robert Todd Perdue and Kenneth Sanchagrin, "Imprisoning Appalachia:
    The Socio-Economic Impacts of Prison Development," *Journal of
    Appalachian Studies* 22, no. 2 (Fall 2016): 212.
3   On the particular racialization of carcerality from the 1970s onward, see
    among many other sources Loïs Wacquant, "From Slavery to Mass
    Incarceration," *New Left Review*, no. 13 (January–February 2002): 41–60;
    Jackie Wang, *Carceral Capitalism* (South Pasadena: Semiotext(e), 2018). On
    the supposed economic benefits of prisons, see Perdue and Sanchagrin,
    "Imprisoning Appalachia"; Judah Schept and Jordan E. Mazurek, "Layers
    of Violence: Coal Mining, Convict Leasing, and Carceral Tourism in Central
    Appalachia," in *The Palgrave Handbook of Prison Tourism*, ed. Jacqueline
    Z. Wilson et al. (London: Palgrave Macmillan, 2017), 171–190; Brett
    Story, *Prison Land: Mapping Carceral Power across Neoliberal America*
    (Minneapolis: University of Minnesota Press, 2019).

Critical accounts of the Appalachian prison industry tend to frame its growth as the exchange of one exploitation for another, from the extraction of carbon to the warehousing of individuals, from the settler colonial seizure of native lands for trapping, foresting, and eventually mining to the late-capitalist carceral economy. This perspective is a valuable one, offering certain continuities in Appalachia's ongoing role within national and state imaginaries as a margin of sorts to be opportunistically drawn on. Its implication of transition (from coal to prison) is a rhetorical tendency belonging both to critics and boosters, albeit with different terminologies and valences. It is framed as a dynamic turn from one kind of work to another, from the exploitation of resources to the financialization of inequality, from the leveling of mountaintops to construction on these freshly manufactured plateaus, from a twentieth-century industrial economy insatiably stoked by anthracite and other unearthed materials to a twenty-first-century neoliberalism powered by "the state's capacities of containment, displacement, and dispossession," as Brett Story puts it.[4] Just as "coal" is not simply a material that produces heat but an assemblage of infrastructures, economies, and environmental effects that are coextensive with capitalism itself, "the carceral" is a geography that spreads wider than the perimeters of its institutions.[5]

This essay pulls on a different but hopefully complementary thread by seeking out historical sites that might

4   Story, *Prison Land*, 6.
5   There is an increasingly ample literature that helps expand our understanding of the breadth of carceral geographies and their ties to globalization, finance capital, and urban management; three that have been crucial for my own work are Angela Y. Davis, *Are Prisons Obsolete?* (New York: Seven Stories, 2003); Ruth Wilson Gilmore, *Golden Gulag* (Berkeley: University of California Press, 2007); Wang, *Carceral Capitalism*. For a recent review of relevant literature see Sara M. Benson, *The Prison of Democracy: Race, Leavenworth, and the Culture of Law* (Berkeley: University of California Press, 2019), 5–10.

help us think about longer-standing entanglements of coal and the carceral, pointing to the ongoing presence of the prison as a participant in Appalachia's development—or, more precisely, Appalachia's capitalization-by-extraction in both the registers of material and labor. Mining, particularly but not only that of coal, is as demonstrative as any industry of the many complicities between the extractive and carceral aspects of industrial development, in the United States as elsewhere. (Enslaved Scottish coal miners, for example, were at work in Great Britain until 1775; the twentieth century's gulags and labor camps often featured forced resource extraction in comparatively remote environments.) In looking at the coal-turned-prison landscapes of Appalachia, the research that follows situates itself within the overlaps between resource territory—in this case the Cumberland Plateau, the southernmost section of the Appalachians—and carceral labor, particularly the convict-leasing practices of the Reconstruction-era South and their aftereffects. This entanglement culminates in the Brushy Mountain State Penitentiary in eastern Tennessee, colloquially just "Brushy," a site in which the governmental prerogatives of extractive incarceration became acutely visible as the nineteenth century turned to the twentieth.

While convict leasing and other forms of prison labor were practiced across the United States (dating even before the American Revolution), they took on a particular texture in the deep South, where states often ceded full control of the management of select convict populations to private contractors who paid for their services.[6] This specific experiment in the total corporate financialization

6   Alex Lichtenstein, *Twice the Work of Free Labor: The Political Economy of Convict Labor in the New South* (London and New York: Verso, 1996), 3. On the politics of Reconstruction and its disastrous effects for black Southerners in particular, see Eric Foner, *Reconstruction: America's Unfinished Revolution, 1863–1877* (New York: Harper & Row, 1988).

of incarcerated bodies and withdrawal of governmental responsibility had largely waned by the 1900s (with state-run chain gangs, prison farms, and prison workshops becoming preferred models), and was eventually replaced in the 1930s with a formalized system of inmate labor at the federal level. Carceral outsourcing would not be seen again in the United States to this extent until the 1980s with the rise of the private prison industry—a comparatively minor part of the larger prison system, as Ruth Wilson Gilmore has observed, but a revealing one in its economic model. Whether private or state-run, the late-twentieth-century prison has seen its finances reversed—the body of the convict no longer seen as a labor-bearing commodity to be leased (though convict labor is still often used to offset some of the costs of imprisonment) but rather marked as a kind of surplus, to use Gilmore's terms again. The prison, or rather the body of the prisoner, becomes a vector for payments from a government interested in devolving its carceral industry into corporate hands or legitimizing the state's control over an increasingly unnecessary labor force.[7]

Considering coal and convict labor as a post-Emancipation "slavery by other means" also allows us to explore the on-the-ground implications of what Kathryn Yusoff has termed White Geology. "Geology is a mode of accumulation, on one hand, and of dispossession, on the other, depending on which side of the geologic color line you end up on," Yusoff observes, marking a fundamental "carceral geo-logics" at stake in the exploitation of carbon to begin with.[8] Just as "slavery weaponized the redistribution of energy around the globe" in terms of human labor,

7   Ruth Wilson Gilmore, "Prisons and Class Warfare," interview by Clément Petitjean, Verso (blog), August 2, 2018, https://www.versobooks.com/blogs/3954-prisons-and-class-warfare-an-interview-with-ruth-wilson-gilmore.

8   Kathryn Yusoff, *A Billion Black Anthropocenes or None* (Minneapolis: University of Minnesota Press, 2018), 3, xiv.

so did the mobility of coal (typically mined under exploitative conditions), a twinned process that "renders matter as property" whether that matter be human or fossil.[9] The two meet in the geological threshold of the mineshaft, and crucially, for Yusoff, though "Blackness is the energy and flesh of the Anthropocene, it is excluded from the wealth of its accumulation."[10] This essay follows Yusoff in exploring the affects and operations of a particular genre of mine, which might be understood as something of a microcosm of twentieth-century racial capitalism writ large. While the South's shift from chattel slavery to state-sanctioned prison labor meant that whites, Native Americans, and others were also caught up in the carceral-extractive apparatus of prison mining (one of several modes of incarceration devised in this period), its purpose was to maintain an antebellum racial subjugation of labor—a fact that asks us to reckon again with the methods of extraction that powered the industrializing South and to trouble the still-prevalent narrative that the Appalachian citizen, and the Appalachian coal miner in particular, is and was characteristically white.[11]

The sites this essay considers were in some ways marginal to the development of coal in the United States. Even in their prime these were not coal deposits as productive as those in West Virginia or Pennsylvania when seen on the national scale (let alone the western coalfields of Wyoming and other states that now supply more than half of US coal). But they were nonetheless crucial in the regional industrialization of the formerly agrarian South, which in turn congealed a dynamic of labor, race, and

9   Yusoff, *A Billion Black Anthropocenes or None*, 15, 4.
10   Yusoff, *A Billion Black Anthropocenes or None*, 82.
11   Alongside a good bit of recent journalism on the notion of "Affrilachia," coined in the 1990s by the writer Frank X Walker, see Joe William Trotter Jr., *Coal, Class, and Color: Blacks in Southern West Virginia, 1915–1932* (Urbana: University of Illinois Press, 1990).

environmental exploitation that distinctly continued the logics of the plantation economy, one supported by Thirteenth Amendment labor.[12] In reading the twenty-first century's rural prison boom against late-nineteenth-century forms of carceral extraction, I hope to draw out certain historical differences alongside an enduring trope of Appalachian "underdevelopment," whether according to the dictums of industrial or post-industrial capitalism. This double rhetoric of plight and opportunity is the cleared and leveled site on which a long string of government-backed dispossessions—of native lands, of mineral rights, of labor power, of unfree bodies—takes place.[13]

Newgate of Connecticut

A pre-Revolutionary detour: the jail that eventually became the first state prison in the United States got its start as a copper mine. The Simsbury mines, as they were known in the early eighteenth century, were worked at various moments under the auspices of various corporate structures by free labor, slave labor, and British miners—who, as one nineteenth-century historian noted, would have been surprised to find that "they were actually hewing out prison cells, for the lodgment of their friends."[14] The Colony of Connecticut acquired the mines in 1773 for roughly sixty pounds and converted them into a prison for

---

12   See Katherine McKittrick's theorization of the plantation as a central geographical device in how "the relational violences of modernity produce a condition of being black in the Americas that is predicated on struggle." Katherine McKittrick, "On Plantations, Prisons, and a Black Sense of Place," *Social & Cultural Geography* 12, no. 8 (2011): 947–963; Katherine McKittrick, "Plantation Futures," *Small Axe: A Caribbean Platform for Criticism* 17, no. 3 (November 2013): 1–15.

13   See Story, *Prison Land*, 83.

14   Richard H. Phelps, *A History of Newgate of Connecticut, at Simsbury, Now East Granby: Its Insurrections and Massacres, the Imprisonment of the Tories in the Revolution, and the Working of Its Mines* (Albany, NY: J. Munsell, 1860), 26.

British loyalists on the grounds that a cavern would be impossible to escape from, a bit of hubris that was immediately tested when its first prisoner escaped by being hoisted out of a secondary air shaft after only eighteen days in confinement.[15] The prison became known as Newgate, a reference to the London prison by the same name. Early prisoner records list the Tories kept there while later ones document a preponderance of burglars, horse stealers, and forgers.[16]

Though this mine-turned-jail is in many ways a peculiar and unrepresentative example of the penal techniques of the early United States, it evinces a series of assumptions that undergirded a great deal of American carceral thought across the long nineteenth century—notably that conviction was a two-fold imprisonment that required serving one's sentence as well as repaying the state for it with their labor. "A typical inmate, sentenced to five years' imprisonment, would find that his financial obligation was about $375," notes Denis R. Caron. "At the stated rate, he would have to remain in Newgate an additional six years to work off the debt."[17] In its earliest days, Tories held at Newgate were expected to work at the extraction of copper alongside skilled, freely laboring miners. The drawbacks to having prisoners performing this kind of underground labor were quickly discovered—not only were unskilled miners inefficient, the work also afforded them precisely the kinds of tools that would abet their escape.[18] After several jailbreaks and the repeated arson of the guard-house, the prisoners were moved to Hartford in 1777, end-

15   Phelps, *A History of Newgate of Connecticut*, 37.
16   A registry of the prisoners over the years is housed on the Connecticut Department of Economic and Community Development's website, https://portal.ct.gov/-/media/DECD/Historic-Preservation/04_State_Museums/Old-New-Gate-Prison-and-Copper-Mine/Old-New-Gate-Prisoner-List.pdf.
17   Denis R. Caron, *A Century in Captivity: The Life and Trials of Prince Mortimer, a Connecticut Slave* (Durham: University of New Hampshire Press, 2006), 82–83.

"A View of the Guard-House and Simsbury Mines, Now Called Newgate, A Prison for the Confinement of Loyalists in Connecticut," 1781. Courtesy of the Connecticut Historical Society.

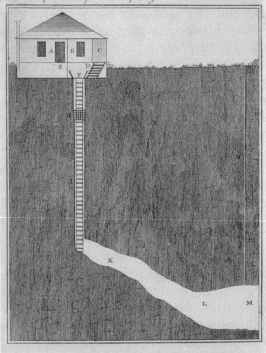

A View of the GUARD-HOUSE and SIMSBURY-MINES now called Newgate, A Prison for the Confinement of Loyalists in Connecticut.

ing the site's operations as a prison mine. After the facilities were reconstructed in 1780, individuals at Newgate worked primarily aboveground—summoned out of the cavern at 4 am and sent back below twelve hours later. Prisoners mostly manufactured nails until 1815, when the prison began to diversify its industries (including a novel treadmill-like machine for the tortuous human-powered grinding of grain).[19]

A record of the layout of Newgate was engraved around 1799 by Richard Brunton, who had received a two-year term for the crime of counterfeiting. (This was a common enough sentence; records point to more than fifty prisoners engaged in passing or making counterfeit bills, and another twenty-some for forgery.) An itinerant portrait engraver by trade, Brunton was accused in 1795 of counterfeiting bank bills but was released for lack of evidence. He was arrested again in 1799 for minting coins, and this time the charge stuck.[20] In Newgate he continued to practice his craft by mining his own copper, forming it into plates, and making painstaking engravings. One depicted the superintendent at the time, Maj. Reuben Humphreys, and another captured the prison grounds and its occupants. The guardhouse (with its access to the caverns below) occupies the center of the image, while a flattened rendition of the wooden barricade that surrounded the yard until 1802, when it was replaced by stone, forms its frame. A well-worn path traces the route from the guardhouse to the workshop, walked on a daily basis by the prisoners. It is a

18   Noah A. Phelps, *A History of the Copper Mines and Newgate Prison, at Granby, Connecticut: Also, of the Captivity of Daniel Hayes, of Granby, by the Indians, in 1707* (Hartford, CT: Press of Case, Tiffany, and Burnham, 1845), 13–14.

19   Caron, *A Century in Captivity*, 78–86.

20   Deborah M. Child, "Richard Brunton: An Artist of No Ordinary Character," *Journal of the American Revolution*, May 7, 2015, https://all thingsliberty.com/2015/05/richard-brunton-an-artist-of-no-ordinary-character.

strange scene, populated by an in-progress flogging along-side a sense of quotidian daily life that might resemble a small town as much as it does a prison.

In its industriousness, Newgate was an early if imperfect illustration of how "the essence, the motive power, of the nineteenth-century American prison," as the criminologist Martin Miller puts it, "was the profitable utilization of convict labor."[21] None other than Gustave de Beaumont and Alexis de Tocqueville took note of this on their famed 1831 tour of American prisons, when they visited Newgate's successor, Wethersfield State Prison, terming it "one of the good prisons, if not the best."[22] The resulting book was a tract *On the Penitentiary System of the United States, and Its Application in France*, which extolled the "Auburn system," so named because of its development at the prison in Auburn, New York—the first to turn a profit from the labor of its prisoners.[23] They would be expected to work by day and spend their nights in solitary confinement, maintaining silence (enforced by floggings) throughout. For Beaumont and Tocqueville, the indiscriminate use of full-time solitary confinement was "ruinous to the public treasury"—the fact that it "never effected the reformation of the prisoners" was only a secondary shortcoming, showing the extent to which economic imperatives

21 Martin B. Miller, "At Hard Labor: Rediscovering the Nineteenth-Century Prison," *Issues in Criminology* 9, no. 1 (Spring 1974): 91–114.

22 Gustave de Beaumont and Alexis de Tocqueville, *On the Penitentiary System in the United States, and Its Application in France*, trans. Francis Lieber (Philadelphia: Carey, Lea & Blanchard, 1833), 29.

23 *On the Penitentiary System in the United States* was published alongside Tocqueville's *Democracy in America* and Beaumont's novel *Marie, or Slavery in the United States* (both 1835). On the complex relationships between these three books by Tocqueville and the lesser-known Beaumont, including the centrality of race in understanding their interpretations of the US penitentiary system as well as Tocqueville's thoughts on democracy's "tyranny of the majority," see Sara M. Benson, "Democracy and Unfreedom: Revisiting Tocqueville and Beaumont in America," *Political Theory* 45, no. 4 (August 2017): 466–494.

Richard Brunton, "A Prospective View of Newgate, Connecticut's State Prison," ca. 1799. Courtesy of the Connecticut Historical Society.

A PROSPECTIVE VIEW OF OLD NEWGATE Connecticut's STATE PRISON.

The subterraneous Vault, over which this place is built was wrought about the middle of the 17.th Century for the purpose of obtaining Copper Ore, the opening into those Gloomy Caverns is a Descent of 25 feet, from thence Descending in various Serpentine Directions 70 Yards, opens to the Well, is in depth 74 feet from the surface to the Water.

1 The Commandants apartment. 2. the Guard Room. 3. the work shop. 4 the store for Nails. 5 the Bake house 6 the Cole house. 7 the Smiths shop. 8 the Well 9 the gate for Entrance. 10 the Picket's inclosure, of the Prison 11 the path leading from the work shop to the Caverns.

shaped the spaces and the practices of nineteenth-century incarceration.[24]

Further, as the first jail in the United States to be designated a "state prison," Newgate was likewise the first to demonstrate the possibility that the state's carceral capacities could be used to continue slavery under the banner of public institutions rather than personal property. (Slavery was not fully abolished in Connecticut until 1848, though the import of slaves was outlawed in 1774 and "gradual abolition" was passed in 1784.)[25] When Beaumont and Tocqueville visited Wethersfield, no mention is made as to whether they met a 107-year-old prisoner named Prince, who had been transferred there four years prior after already serving eighteen years at Newgate. But it is not hard to imagine Prince's obliged role in Wethersfield's scenographic "display of mastery," to borrow a term from Saidiya Hartman, that was as critical as the prison's other functions of power in maintaining the line between free and unfree—encountering this centenarian convict was surely a part of Beaumont and Tocqueville's curious form of witness.[26] Enslaved around 1730 at the age of six or seven, Prince was taken to Connecticut where he spent many of his years laboring in a rope factory.[27] In the mid-1790s he witnessed legal machinations that posthumously overturned his owner's last will and testament which included Prince's freedom. Still enslaved two decades later, he was accused and convicted in 1811 of mixing arsenic into his

24 Beaumont and Tocqueville, *On the Penitentiary System in the United States*, 3.

25 "Gradual abolition" legislated the freeing of children born into Connecticut slavery at the age of 25.

26 Saidiya V Hartman, *Scenes of Subjection: Terror, Slavery, and Self-Making in Nineteenth-Century America* (Oxford: Oxford University Press, 1997), 7.

27 Prince later received the last name Mortimer, that of a former owner, from the courts upon imprisonment. My account of his story here is drawn from the very detailed attempt at piecing together his scantly documented life found in Caron, *A Century in Captivity*.

new owner's chocolate and was sent to the caverns at Newgate, where labor was expected of the inmates even if mining had ceased. He died in Wethersfield in 1834 at the age of 110 (fifty years after the state's passage of "gradual abolition"), having never seen freedom in the United States. Prince's century-long deprivation may have been unique in its immediate context, as only around 300 slaves remained in Connecticut at the time of his imprisonment and still fewer at his death (Brunton's engraving speaks to the racial composition of Newgate at the turn of the nineteenth century), but it speaks to the ways in which Emancipation was "less the grand event of liberation," as Hartman puts it, "than a point of transition between modes of servitude and racial subjugation."[28]

Newgate was also an early American example of the touristic curiosity aroused by carceral extraction, as the prison received visitors (whatever their motivations) seeking a view into the sublime spaces of mining and to encounter the unfree labor confined therein. 5,000 people came to Newgate in 1810 alone to visit its aboveground facilities as well as its caverns—"the relief of a perfumed handkerchief always at the ready," one historian speculated.[29] In that sense, Beaumont and Tocqueville's prison visits decades later were not so remarkable—the staged spectacle of incarceration was amply open to both domestic and international audiences, and it was of a piece with the rise of carceral museology and criminological institution-building in the nineteenth century.[30] In the twenty-first, penal tourism is now a common strategy for the revitalization of decommissioned sites, and today Newgate and its caverns

28   Hartman, *Scenes of Subjection*, 6. The figure for the number of slaves in Connecticut is drawn from aggregated US Census data at https://userpages. umbc.edu/~bouton/History407/SlaveStats.htm.

29   Caron, *A Century in Captivity*, 91.

30   Jennifer Turner and Kimberly Peters, "Unlocking Carceral Atmospheres: Designing Visual/Material Encounters at the Prison Museum," *Visual Communication* 14, no. 3 (August 2015): 311.

are accessible to the public in summer months, even including reenactments of prisoner life and escape—a commingling of the blunt materiality of imprisonment, the equally but differently blunt materiality of extraction, and the social infrastructures of touristic experience.[31]

"Slaves of the State"

In the aftermath of the Civil War, the racial demography of Southern prisons effectively inverted. As has often been noted, the Thirteenth Amendment's abolition of slavery and involuntary servitude included an explicit provision for maintaining the practice "as a punishment for crime whereof the party shall have been duly convicted," and the prisons were filled to suit.[32] Even the Juneteenth degree, ostensibly emancipating the slaves of Texas, added that "the freedmen are advised to remain quietly at their present homes and work for wages"—a statement that, in Jackie Wang's words, "recoded the master-slave relation (between owner and owned) as an employer-worker relation, albeit completely on the terms of the (former) slave owners."[33] In Georgia, to take another example, virtually none of the state's prisoners at Milledgeville,

---

31 For a compendious overview of penal tourism, see Jacqueline Z. Wilson et al., eds., *The Palgrave Handbook of Prison Tourism* (London: Palgrave Macmillan, 2017).

32 The debates around the Thirteenth Amendment—whose ultimate wording had been proposed by a slaveholding senator from Missouri—are concisely and forcefully retold in Lee Wood and Barbara Esposito, *Prison Slavery in the Thirteenth Amendment* (Washington, DC: Committee to Abolish Prison Slavery, 1978). Among many other sources, see Edward L. Ayers, *Vengeance and Justice: Crime and Punishment in the Nineteenth-Century American South* (New York: Oxford University Press, 1984); Douglas A. Blackmon, *Slavery by Another Name: The Re-Enslavement of Black People in America from the Civil War to World War II* (New York: Doubleday, 2008); Dennis Childs, *Slaves of the State: Black Incarceration from the Chain Gang to the Penitentiary* (Minneapolis: University of Minnesota Press, 2015); Lichtenstein, *Twice the Work of Free Labor*.

33 Wang, *Carceral Capitalism*, 87.

its only penitentiary, were black in 1864—"discipline" and "punishment" had been remanded to the plantation rather than the auspices of the state.[34] By 1880, however, more than 90 percent of Georgia's prisoners were classified as non-white (specifically, "black," "yellow," or "colored") with similar shifts happening across the other Southern states.[35] The continued capture of the labor and personhood of the carcerally dispossessed—the vast majority of whom, after 1865, were black, though white Southerners, Native Americans, and others were in the mix—and the creation of convict-leasing programs allowed both the state and the leaseholder to profit from that labor while transferring the responsibility of housing and maintaining its captives to private interests.[36]

If later political rhetoric often sought to obscure the directness of convict leasing's line from plantation to prison, at least one judge of the period was clear on the point. In a famous passage from the 1871 ruling *Ruffin v. Commonwealth*, Judge J. Christian of the Supreme Court of the Commonwealth of Virginia opines that the incarceration-state dynamic was precisely that of slave and owner. "He has, as a consequence of his crime, not only forfeited his liberty," the ruling argues, "but all his personal rights

34 Milledgeville burned down in 1864 as the Union Army swept across Georgia; it remains uncertain whether it burned at Sherman's hands or those of the prisoners who had been pardoned by Governor Joseph E. Brown in the hopes that they would help defend the city. See *New Georgia Encyclopedia*, "Georgia Penitentiary at Milledgeville," by Nicole Mitchell, last modified December 9, 2013, https://georgiaencyclopedia.org/articles/history-archaeology/georgia-penitentiary-milledgeville.

35 Christopher Muller, "Freedom and Convict Leasing in the Postbellum South," *American Journal of Sociology* 124, no. 2 (September 2018): 368.

36 "From a purely penological point of view, the convict lease was a fiscally conservative means of coping with a new burden: the ex-slaves who were emancipated from the dominion of the slaveholder only to be subject to the authority of the state. But from a broader perspective, the lease was much more than a convenient fiscal and penal stopgap; it stood as a system of forced labor in an age of emancipation." Lichtenstein, *Twice the Work of Free Labor*, 3.

except those which the law in its humanity accords to him. He is for the time being a slave of the State. He is *civiliter mortus*."[37] Both the language and the legal philosophy of the ruling were unusual even for the late nineteenth century—the historian Matthew J. Mancini makes note of many judicial opinions of the era that began from the assumption that prisoners maintained all rights *except* those explicitly denied by states, and that the "civil death" of imprisonment was an extreme interpretation even in 1870—but the fact remained (and remains) that the effect of incarceration was to enable the same total alienation of labor and the techniques of bodily control that also defined the plantation system.[38]

The "slaves of the state" passage is well-known in the legal history of the Thirteenth Amendment; the facts of the case are less commonly told. Woody Ruffin was a black prisoner of the Commonwealth of Virginia who was convicted of a felony and had been housed in the Virginia State Penitentiary in Richmond.[39] The penitentiary had opened in 1800 and stemmed from the penal enthusiasms of Thomas Jefferson, who had returned from his ambassadorship in France with an interest in the panopticon as a penal form and the alternation of daily labor and nightly solitude as a penal technique (the early stirrings of what would become the Auburn system). Advocating during his brief governorship of Virginia for a state prison to be built on those lines, and in fact supplying his own design that was never built, the institution of the prison was an ongoing interest on Jefferson's part, as an architect as well as

---

37   Ruffin v. Commonwealth, 62 Va. 796 (1871).

38   Matthew J. Mancini, *One Dies, Get Another: Convict Leasing in the American South, 1866–1928* (Columbia: University of South Carolina Press, 1996), 26–28.

39   Ruffin's race went unremarked on in the court's opinion. However, his race was noted in brief news writeups that appeared after his initial conviction. See for example "Richmond Items," *New Orleans Times-Picayune*, January 15, 1871, 16.

a state administrator.[40] The project would in later years be given to Benjamin Latrobe, the first professional architect in the United States, who would spend the following decades at work on the nation's capital. If Newgate was the nation's first state prison, the penitentiary in Richmond was supposed to be its first *modern* prison, in its architecture and in its penal philosophy. This supposed modernity notwithstanding, it was inadequate from its very opening, with poor ventilation and a complete lack of heat, and became still more so after the Civil War due to overcrowding. In 1866 Virginia passed a "Vagrancy Act" (of a type then pervasive in the North and South alike) that stipulated up to three months of forced labor for the unemployed or homeless, with little doubt as to who, after Emancipation, that newly unemployed and homeless population might largely be.

The 1870 Constitution of Virginia authorized penal servitude in its Bill of Rights, using the same phrasing that the federal government did to describe the Thirteenth Amendment, and on April 23, 1870, Virginia's General Assembly approved legislation "to hire out... such able-bodied convicts in the penitentiary... as can be spared from the workshops therein, to responsible persons, to work in stone quarries, or upon any railroad or canal in this State, or any other suitable labor."[41] Shortly thereafter, Ruffin, among others at the Virginia State Penitentiary, was leased to what would become known as the Chesapeake and Ohio Railroad Company (C&O) and sent to Bath County. (This was right around the time that another black Virginia inmate by the name of John Williams Henry was leased to the C&O—who, it has recently been suggested, might

---

40   Jefferson's later 1823 plans for a prison built in Nelson County, Virginia, are discussed by Mabel O. Wilson in this volume, see "Design of the Self and the Racial Other," 389–409.

41   The relevant passage of this legislation is recorded in *Ruffin v. Commonwealth.*

Benjamin Henry Latrobe, drawings for the Virginia "Penitentiary House," 1797. Courtesy of the Library of Virginia.

Internal Elevation of the Infirmary in the West Wing.

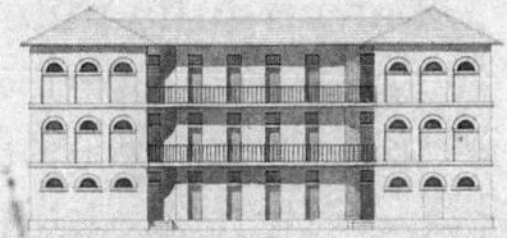

Internal Elevation of the Women's Court, or of the East Wing.

View in perspective of the Gate of the Penitentiary House.

B. H. Latrobe Architect 1797

have been the folk hero John Henry, immortalized in song for tunneling faster than a steam-powered machine he was racing, though the race cost him his life.)[42] In an attempted escape, Ruffin killed one of the railroad's guards, Louis F. Swats, and was returned to Richmond where he was tried and sentenced to be hung. Ruffin appealed this initial ruling on the basis of his location at the time of his escape, since the Constitution of Virginia guarantees the accused the right "to a speedy and public trial, by an impartial jury of his vicinage." For all of the force of its rhetoric, *Ruffin v. Commonwealth* was a technical ruling—against Ruffin's claim that he had the right to be tried in Bath County rather than Richmond, the court deployed the notion that a prisoner is a "slave of the state," or *civiliter mortus*, simply to excuse Virginia from that particular notion ("vicinage") in its Bill of Rights.

What emerges most forcefully in *Ruffin v. Commonwealth*, beyond its oft-repeated turn of phrase that articulated the removal of the prisoner's legal rights, is an apt description of the carceral state's spatialities of power. "Where is the vicinage of a convict in the penitentiary? What county can be said to be his vicinage?" it asks. "Not in his case the county in which the offence is committed; because in the eye of the law he is *always in the penitentiary.*"

42   John Henry is the subject of many myths, with other accounts suggesting he was from Alabama, if he existed at all. The heroism of his death is the common denominator in all variants on the song as well as an assumption that undergirds historical reconstructions of who he might have been: "John Henry he hammered in the mountains / His hammer was striking fire / But he worked so hard, it broke his heart / John Henry laid down his hammer and died, Lord, Lord / John Henry laid down his hammer and died." Scott Reynolds Nelson's research (disputed by some John Henry aficionados) suggests that John Williams Henry was a black inmate of the Virginia Penitentiary, having been convicted for burglary, and that the contest likely took place during the construction of the C&O's Lewis Tunnel, a county over from Woody Ruffin's assignment. Scott Reynolds Nelson, *Steel Drivin' Man: John Henry, The Untold Story of an American Legend* (New York: Oxford University Press, 2006).

THE ARCHITECTURE OF CARCERAL EXTRACTION

This is as clear a statement as any of the existential geographies of imprisonment: "Wherever he may be, until he has served out to the last moment, the term fixed by the sentence of the law, or has been pardoned, he is still a convict in the penitentiary... If he can be said to have a vicinage at all"—this "if" again implying the civil death of the incarcerated's personhood—"that vicinage as to him is within the walls of the penitentiary, which (if not literally and actually) yet in the eye of the law surround him wherever he may go."[43]

To read the ruling architecturally, what would the site of Woody Ruffin's incarceration be, if the walls of the penitentiary in Richmond were not its extents? It is Latrobe's dysfunctional panopticon, but it is also the railroad tracks through the Appalachian foothills, spatially coincident with Ruffin's indenture to the C&O, run by Collis P. Huntington. Connecting West Virginia to the Atlantic port of Hampton Roads, the C&O never did much passenger business, focusing instead on the movement of mined coal—a crucial moment in the industrial development of the region and the flow of Appalachian commodities to port cities and industrialists elsewhere. West Virginia's second-largest city, a crucial transfer point between the C&O and the barges of the Ohio River, bears Huntington's name. If Ruffin's imprisonment was only ever inside the Virginia State Penitentiary, then its spatial reach extended across this infrastructure that opened up routes for the movement of Appalachian anthracite. The wealth built by the C&O, which in turn was built by those explicitly understood as "slaves of the state," was coal wealth, and Ruffin's "vicinage" was the territory marked by coal's extraction.

Exhausted Sites of Convict-Lease Mining

43   *Ruffin v. Commonwealth.* Emphasis added.

BRUSHY MOUNTAIN

Ruffin v. Commonwealth's juridical terminology may not have been widely shared, but its vision of an expanded carceral space in the name of resource development was certainly found elsewhere. "There are two classes of persons who go to Dade County coal mines," wrote a journalist for the *Atlanta Weekly Constitution* in 1886—"members of the legislature and long-term, able-bodied convicts."[44] Georgia's small but consequential coal mining industry was among the sectors of development that benefited from the convict-lease system, holding 45 percent of Georgia's convict leases in the early 1890s. As Alex Lichtenstein has noted, the more skilled aspects of coke production were often handled by free white labor, meaning that the revaluation of coal mining as a form of unskilled labor justified the introduction of leased convicts (90 percent of whom, as previously mentioned, were black) into what had previously been understood to be a site for free labor.[45] This was not a color line enforced by racial classification so much as a subtler but no less effective encoding of exploitation (on principally but not exclusively racial grounds) within the division of extractive labor.

In the case of the Dade County mines, the legislators arrived in a variety of capacities. A special committee of the Georgia legislature visited the mines among other sites of convict leasing in 1881, finding that the practice "contains nothing that tends to the reformation of the criminal," though little effort was made to reform or end it.[46] Moreover, the Dade Coal Company was *owned* by a legislator—Joseph E. Brown, Georgia's secessionist governor throughout the Civil War and, from 1880–1891, one of the state's US senators, whose postwar millions were built almost entirely on profits from convict labor leased on favorable terms from the state. "Would to God Governor

44   "Dade County Coal Mines," *Atlanta Weekly Constitution*, July 20, 1886.
45   Lichtenstein, *Twice the Work of Free Labor*, 113–116.
46   "The Leased Convicts of Georgia," *New York Times*, July 26, 1881.

Brown had every convict in Georgia under his wise and humane control," opined a visitor from 1879, though the conditions at Coal City, as the mines were also known, were anything but.[47] The *Weekly Constitution*'s 1886 visit came on the heels of a labor strike calling for the abolition of corporal punishment, the dismissal of foremen, and better food; the Dade Coal Company's response was to starve them into submission.[48] Little changed in the following decades, despite a wide array of critical voices, since the state and its taxpayers had grown accustomed to the substantial revenues generated by what was effectively post-abolition enslavement. In 1897 Georgia established a prison commission that effected some reforms (even briefly exploring the idea of buying the Dade County Coal Mines to operate as a state industry), though convict leasing continued until 1909—after which the state monopolized the labor of its prisoners in road camps.[49]

In Alabama, where like other Southern states over 90 percent of state and county prisoners were black toward the end of the nineteenth century, carceral labor provided a longstanding and substantial portion of the state's revenues after the state warden, John G. Bass, began leasing convicts in 1875—a moment of fiscal crisis for the state but also a moment when industrialists began redeveloping coal mines that had been largely dormant since the end of the Civil War. The practice began in a piecemeal fashion, but by 1888 both the coal-mining and convict-leasing industries had consolidated to the point that the Tennessee Coal, Iron, and Railroad Company, which had two years earlier acquired the Pratt Mines in Birmingham, controlled the

47   "A Striking Scene: The Exchange of Prisoners at the Dade County Coal Mines," *The Atlanta Daily Constitution*, April 9, 1879.

48   "Senator Brown's Convicts: An Attempt Being Made to Starve Them into Submission," *New York Times*, July 14, 1886; Lichtenstein, *Twice the Work of Free Labor*, 126.

49   On this see the chapter "Bad Boys Make Good Roads," in Lichtenstein, *Twice the Work of Free Labor*, 152–185.

rights to every able-bodied inmate in Alabama at a rate of $9 to $18.50 per month, depending on the prisoner's level of skill.[50] Even a group committed to the abolition of the convict-lease system published a pamphlet that "heartily endorses the theory that the convict should be made to work at some gainful occupation and maintain himself, with, if possible, a margin of profit for the state and his family, if it is destitute," adding only that "it is *cheaper*... to correct him as to restore him as a useful member of society"—again showing how pervasive the idea was that imprisonment could and should produce economic gains for the state.[51]

Pratt Mines is one among many examples of how the architecture of extractive incarceration was typically designed under the mantle of progress, codifying the very thing (the appropriation of unfree labor) being contested—an example of what Hartman describes as "the savage encroachments of power that take place through notions of reform."[52] In 1883, the state instituted a board of inspectors to mediate the relationship between prisoners and coal companies. The board was ineffectual in its first years, but under the direction of Reginald H. Dawson and state physicians (notably Russell Cunningham, who would later serve for a year as governor of Alabama), the board began to play a role in shaping the form of these carceral-extractive environments. Required by prison-reform legislation to reside where the greatest number of prisoners did, Cunningham moved to Pratt Mines to become the onsite physician and

50   Figures drawn from *Encyclopedia of Alabama*, "Convict-Lease System," by
       Mary Ellen Curtin, last modified May 13, 2019, http://www.encyclopedia
       ofalabama.org/article/h-1346.
51   William E. Fort et al., *Let's Get Rid of Alabama's Shame: The Convict
       Lease or Contract System: Facts, Figures, Possible Remedies* (Birmingham,
       AL: Statewide Campaign Committee for the Abolishment of the Convict
       Contract System, 1923), https://cdm16044.contentdm.oclc.org/digital/
       collection/p4017coll8/id/13001. Emphasis in the original.
52   Hartman, *Scenes of Subjection*, 5.

surgeon, and through his interventions in the housing and medical care of the prisoners, he effectively designed a complex that would be taken as the model for a "modern" and "hygienic" convict-lease mining operation.[53] A Sanborn Fire Insurance Map drawn in April 1888 documents an orthogonally ordered complex with a full complement of outbuildings needed to run the operations of both mine and prison. Stables, sheds, workshops, and a coal tipple gather around the access to the mine to the northeast of the site, while a hospital, dining room, kitchen, bathhouse, commissary, and the kettles used to boil the convicts' clothes flank the prison itself.[54] A state commission visiting Pratt City in 1897 judged the buildings to be "well located, of proper architecture, and of good appointment," and the hospital "splendid."[55]

The same report, however, also admitted that the "mortality for convicts is so far in excess of that for the general population and for free miners… that it at once challenges the attention," and it admonished the prison system for selecting convicts unsuited for the work. To do so, the report decried, was a "great inhumanity," one "not only resulting in unusual and cruel punishment, but also in death."[56] Convict mining would last another thirty years in Alabama, with still less discrimination in prisoners' ability to endure its conditions of labor. After the exhaustion of

53   *Encyclopedia of Alabama*, "Russell M. Cunningham," by Marlene Hunt Rikard, last modified September 30, 2014, http://www.encyclopediaof alabama.org/article/h-1620.

54   Sanborn Map Company, *Sanborn Fire Insurance Map from Birmingham, Jefferson County, Alabama*, map 27 of 29, April 1888, https://loc.gov/item/ sanborn00015_002.

55   Georgia General Assembly, *Report of the Committee Appointed by the General Assembly to Investigate the Convict Lease System* (Montgomery, 1897), 626.

56   Georgia General Assembly, *Report of the Committee Appointed by the General Assembly to Investigate the Convict Lease System*, 628, 630. Mortality rates for convict leases were ten times greater than for free white miners, and four times greater than for free black miners.

Sanborn Fire Insurance Map showing the facilities at Pratt's Slope No. 2, 1888.

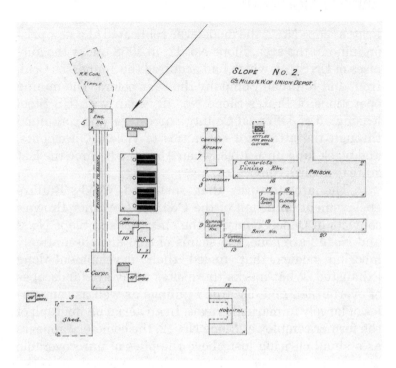

SLOPE No. 2.
6½ MILES N.W. OF UNION DEPOT.

R.R. COAL TIPPLE

5 ENG. HO.

W. TANKS.

6

4 CARPR.

3 SHED.

AIR SHAFT

BLACKSMITH

AIR SHAFT

AIR COMPRESSOR.

10

B.SM.

11

CONVICTS KITCHEN

7

COMMISSARY

8

KETTLES FOR BOILG CLOTHES.

CONVICTS DINING RM

PRISON.

1

2

16

17

TAILOR SHOP

18

CLOTHING RM.

GUARDS SLEEPING RM.

9

GUARDS KITCH.

BATH HO.

19

13

20

HOSPITAL.

12

Pratt's Slope No. 2, the model was replicated at a new prison mine in the area, Slope No. 12, in 1908 under the auspices of US Steel, which had acquired the Tennessee Coal, Iron, and Railroad Company the year before. The mining operations of Pratt's Slope No. 12 began with US Steel leasing all of Jefferson County's arrestees, and continued through the attendant casualties of violence, accidents, and black lung until 1928, when Alabama became the last state to abolish convict leasing.[57]

The architectures that sustained Woody Ruffin's enslavement on behalf of the C&O, or Governor Brown's convicts in Dade County, or the operations at Slope No. 2 and No. 12 are gone, the seams of coal and the unfreely laboring bodies that fueled their development long exhausted. What marks these sites today are landscapes of overburden and discarded tailings as well as cemeteries of largely unmarked graves. In an aerial photograph of the former complex at Slope No. 12, the cemetery appears as a small clearing just above the piles of unrecoverable and uneconomic material waste that stretches across the lower right to the upper left of the image. The buildings to the right (now demolished) once held train workshops while the overgrown area at the bottom left was occupied by beehive coke ovens. This is a landscape that continues to change as the traces of coal's infrastructures degrade, but it is also a landscape that marks the crucial "transition from slave-based agriculture to industrial economies," in Kim Gilmore's words, that "thrust ex-slaves and 'unskilled' laborers into new labor arrangements" that remade the exploitations of slavery into new forms of exploiting geological strata.[58] Writing the history of sites like these—fundamental if seldom visible components of the

---

57 For a description of the conditions at Pratt's Slope No. 12 see Blackmon, *Slavery by Another Name.* I have also drawn here from Brian Kelly, *Race, Class, and Power in the Alabama Coalfields, 1908–1921* (Urbana: University of Illinois Press, 2001).

architecture of an industrializing South—might ask us to begin from those graves, tracing backwards through the expansive, coercive mechanisms of dispossession (carried out through lawmaking, resource extraction, or building) that brought convict labor into the mines that fueled the decades after Reconstruction.

Brushy Mountain

On the night of July 14, 1891, striking coal miners and sympathizers from Coal Creek, Tennessee, and surrounding towns took up arms against the Tennessee Coal, Iron, and Railroad Company—though not, notably, against the forty convict laborers who had replaced them. They marched from Coal Creek along the railroad to neighboring Briceville, where they stormed the stockades of the coal-mining outfit that housed some of the state's leased prisoners.[59] The mine's security forces were overwhelmed, and the prisoners were liberated and sent via train to Knoxville with a telegram of demands for the recently-installed Governor John P. Buchanan, previously known for his support of labor.[60] Buchanan, fearing unrest, sent the prisoners and a state militia back to the mine, and the legislature eventually took measures to protect the convict-lease system. This was the opening salvo in an escalating series of conflicts between miners and the state, now known as the Coal Creek Wars, that resulted in three

58   Kim Gilmore, "Slavery and Prison—Understanding the Connections," *Social Justice* 27, no. 3 (Fall 2000): 198, History Is a Weapon, http://www.historyisaweapon.com/defcon1/gilmoreprisonslavery.html.

59   Coal Creek was renamed Lake City with the completion of the nearby Norris Dam in 1936, marking the region's remaking under the infrastructural auspices of the Tennessee Valley Authority. In 2014 the city was again renamed, styling itself Rocky Top, Tennessee, in the hopes of drawing tourism from the popular song by the same name.

60   This rendition of an often-told story relies largely on Karin A. Shapiro, *A New South Rebellion: The Battle against Convict Labor in the Tennessee Coalfields, 1871–1896* (Chapel Hill: University of North Carolina Press, 1998).

The remnants of Pratt's Slope No. 12, as photographed by
Jet Lowe in 1993. Library of Congress, Historic American
Engineering Record, AL-80-C-1.

further actions. In October and November of that year, over 300 convicts were freed from the same mine at Briceville alongside over 150 from nearby Oliver Springs. State documents record that 148 of these convicts were "released and not recaptured."[61]

This provisional solidarity between (largely white) miners and (largely black) prisoners over the course of a year may have been motivated by economic self-preservation—such solidarity was rarely displayed in the racial politics of union organizing in the Jim Crow South—but it points to a crucial juncture in the entangled history of Thirteenth Amendment labor and the extractive economy, in which workers, free and unfree, were allied in conflict with corporate interests. While Tennessee began leasing convicts shortly after the end of the Civil War, convict mining labor did not account for a substantial portion of Tennessee's industrial development. And yet, as Karin Shapiro has noted, between the coalfields and the construction of the railroads that opened them up, "the labor of Tennessee's convicts primed the economic pump of a pivotal extractive industry—coal mining—upon which many other industries depended."[62] In Tennessee, as in other Southern states, the fifteen years following the end of the Civil War saw the initial phase of carbon exploitation accompanied by the legislative expansion of convict mining labor to support it. By the 1880s, union coal miners' antagonism toward this cheapening of labor grew—revealing the extent to which the state did indeed rely on exploitation at the heart of its economic reconstruction.

The insurrections of the Coal Creek Wars may have been particularly dramatic, but they were of a piece with other Southern states. What followed, however, was something of a new development. Buchanan was reduced to run-

61 State of Tennessee, *Report of the Warden, Superintendent, and Other Officers of the Tennessee Penitentiary* (Nashville, 1893).
62 Shapiro, *A New South Rebellion*, 5.

ning a third-party campaign for reelection; the eventual victor, Governor Peter Turney, ran on a promise to purchase farmland and coalfields in order to build a new state penitentiary, which was successfully legislated in April 1893. This was accompanied by additional legislation, advocated by mining unions, that allowed cities to decline lowest-bid contracts when the costs were artificially depressed by convict labor. The result was that the Tennessee Coal, Iron, and Railroad Company found itself responsible for convicts who were no longer handily exploitable, effectively ending the practice of convict leasing (against the backdrop of the Panic of 1893 and the years-long depression that followed) when their existing contracts expired at the end of 1895.[63]

The solution to this twofold dilemma—surplus prisoners no longer absorbed by private interests, and thus the rising labor costs of the coal they had formerly produced as the work was done by laborers earning market wages—was Brushy Mountain State Penitentiary, which opened in 1896 in the town of Petros. Located some 25 miles down the road from Briceville atop the Cumberland Plateau, Brushy sat on 9,000 acres of geologically rich land bought by the state from the East Tennessee Land Company (a site that had deployed convict-lease labor in the years prior) and promptly set its prisoners to work extracting coal.[64] The first 210 convicts were former lessees who had been returned to the state, and their first project was the construction of the initial prison, framed and clad in wood, and a rail spur leading to the mine's works.[65] By the end of the year Brushy would hold up to 466 people with a continued influx of former lessees, 84 percent of whom

63   Shapiro, *A New South Rebellion*, 214–215.
64   This acreage is drawn from Schept and Mazurek, "Layers of Violence,"
      175. For a representative window into how the history of Brushy Mountain
      State Penitentiary is told to visitors, see "Brushy's History," Historic Brushy
      Mountain State Penitentiary, https://tourbrushy.com/history.
65   The uncited details that follow are drawn from the film shown to visitors to
      Brushy Mountain, as of the summer of 2019.

were black.[66] As the decades wound on, Brushy's crowding and unhygienic conditions eventually spurred the state to construct the building that still stands on the site today. Built in the early 1930s, again by prisoners, this structure was made of stone mined from a quarry on the property. The outer stone walls abut a bluff, blending the prison's limits into the geological substrate they were built from. The prison itself was outlined by a crenellated roofline in the shape of a Greek cross—a commonly reiterated sign of redemption through penitent labor, one that situates extraction as a means to personal reform and the prison as righteous shepherd.

During the 1930s, well after the end of the convict-leasing era, some 70 percent of Brushy's inmates were engaged in mining, but this was also a moment of transition in the organization of penal labor in the United States. In 1934 the Hawes-Cooper Act went into effect, which established that any goods produced by convict labor, when "transported into any State or Territory of the United States... shall be subject to the operation and effect of the laws of such State or Territory"—a law that allowed states to protect their own industries against prison-made goods from elsewhere.[67] In Tennessee, as in many other states, the prison system responded by shifting to a "state use" model that largely continues today, removing its mined coal and other convict produce from open markets. At the national level, in the same year, President Franklin Delano Roosevelt established Federal Prison Industries, Inc. (FPI), now known as UNICOR, which "matured into a national asset," as its promotional literature puts it, by supplying goods made by convict labor to the US military in World War II and which continues to produce goods for federal agencies.[68] A report on the "prison labor

66   This number is drawn from a report sent by Warden Baugh on November 30, 1896.

67   Hawes-Cooper Convict Labor Act, H.R. 7729, 70th Cong. (1929).

problem" sent to the White House by the US Prison Industries Reorganization Administration in 1937 notes that between 1923 and 1936, Tennessee's two penitentiaries grew in population from 1,630 to 3,090 (with the racial balance shifting back to become predominantly white, in part due to African American migration out of the state). During this same period the state's expenses increased by over \$300,000 while the revenues from the prisoners' labor declined by over a million dollars.[69] This report proposed diversifying the types of work being done by convicts and reducing the prisoner population at Brushy by closing the less productive No. 3 mine. "If it were not for the fact that the State had recently invested about \$46,000 in the new prison building," they added, "we would recommend unhesitatingly that Brushy Mountain be abandoned as a prison," as its Appalachian siting was understood as an impediment for future productive industries.[70] This marked a changing idea of "private interest" in the United States. The focus was no longer the competition between

68   UNICOR, *Factories with Fences: 85 Years Building Brighter Futures* (Petersburg, VA: UNICOR Print Plant, Federal Correctional Institute, 2018), 20, https://www.unicor.gov/publications/corporate/Factories WithFences_FY19.pdf. Today some 18,000 federal inmates work within the UNICOR program.

69   US Prison Industries Reorganization Administration, *The Prison Labor Problem in Tennessee: A Survey* (Washington, DC, 1937), 1–2. This same report notes that the convict-lease system that preceded Brushy Mountain "afforded unscrupulous lessees an opportunity to buy what amounted to slave labor, which could be exploited almost at will by means of poor housing, miserable clothing, scant rations, and long hours of work; discipline and punishment were usually in the hands of the employer's foremen, who used their power to extort as much work as possible. Brutal treatment was frequent and there were many fatalities." Little notice is paid to the fact that a similar description could be made of the state mining system, with the sole exception being that the state exerted its monopoly over these kinds of labor practices. US Prison Industries Reorganization Administration, *The Prison Labor Problem in Tennessee*, 3–4.

70   US Prison Industries Reorganization Administration, *The Prison Labor Problem in Tennessee*, 37. For example, this report noted that only 60 of Brushy Mountain's 11,000 acres were suitable for agricultural use.

The newly constructed stone version of Brushy Mountain
State Penitentiary in front of its wooden predecessor,
early 1930s.

free (perhaps unionized) labor versus unfree carceral labor, as it had been during the Coal Creek Wars that led to Brushy's creation. Rather, the terms of the debate had shifted to the competition between "private industry," and thus corporate profit, and state industries subsidized by penal labor. This new frame of reference, displaced from the politics of the workers themselves, provided the underpinnings for the political economies of carceral labor under late capitalism.

And yet mining continued at Brushy Mountain, decade by decade. By the penitentiary's annual report in 1943, the percentage of prisoners working in the mines was down to 23 percent. This was a tense moment in US coal production, with a half-million United Mine Workers (UMW) members going on strike and the federal government taking control of mining operations, but even with these headwinds for union labor, the inefficiency and costly nature of Brushy's mines rendered it an uncompetitive source of coal—to the point that more of its laborers were used on road crews than underground. The tide turned after a sit-down strike in the mines on the night of June 21, 1965, during which the foremen were taken hostage by the miners (equipped, as ever, with formidable tools). This episode was followed by exposés on convict mining and whippings at Brushy Mountain by the *Tennessean*'s Bill Kovach that brought renewed scrutiny to the practice, with one article noting the irony that the state's appropriations for coal mining at Brushy, $215,000, would buy more coal on the open market.[71] Later that summer the recently installed warden, Lake Russell, announced new vocational and educational initiatives at Brushy Mountain, and coal mining ended the following year. Beyond the evident

---

71   Bill Kovach, "Convict Coal Mining Is Holdover From Nineteenth Century,"
     Tennessean, June 27, 1965; Bill Kovach, "Spreadeagled Men Feel Bite
     Of a Heavy Leather Strap: Bars Shut Public Out, Convicts In," *Tennessean*,
     July 4, 1965.

economic motivations, other changes were afoot in the design of both state and national carceral environments. Not only had a maximum security "D-block" been added to the Brushy Mountain complex in 1957 but, in 1969, the entire facility was classified as a primarily maximum-security prison following the relocation of a number of low-risk prisoners to facilities outside its perimeters—one example among many of an increasing ethic of containment in the American prison, one with specifically prescriptive architectural stakes.

In the summer of 1972, Brushy's prison guards went on strike, and the state abruptly evacuated the prisoners to Nashville (along with a domesticated deer named Jeronimo, who would become a frequently invoked mascot of today's rebranded prison and its "colorful" past). The state attempted to auction off the prison in 1973, though failed when buyers were only interested in the site's "red dog," a slate-like byproduct from the production of coke that was at the time seen to be useful for paving dirt roads.[72] After further renovations, prisoners returned in 1976. In Brushy Mountain's second act, it evinced a new set of economic assumptions. Where the Tennessee prison system was hailed for its revenue production at the dawn of the twentieth century, headlines announcing that Brushy's reopening "perked up" the economic outlook of Petros and neighboring towns did so not because of the potential productivity of its prison industries but because of state-funded employment for guards.[73] No industries of substance were planned (though the possibility of a shoe factory employing fifty prisoners was briefly floated and never came to pass) beyond the maintenance of the

72   "Petros Prison to Be Sold by State: Bids to Be Taken Soon on Brushy
       Mountain Property," *Knoxville News-Sentinel*, December 19, 1973.
73   Willard Yarbrough, "Reopening of 'New' Brushy Mountain Prison Perks
       Up Economic Outlook in Petros Area," *Knoxville News-Sentinel*,
       August 29, 1976.

A Tennessee highway patrolman watching convict miners return to Brushy Mountain State Penitentiary after a sit-down strike, June 1965.

prison and the provision of clean laundry. Just as Brushy Mountain had monumentalized the end of Tennessee's convict-lease system in 1896 (by continuing it under the state's auspices), it stood at the American bicentennial as an anticipation of the contemporary tendency to see the Appalachian prison—now a site of governmental expense rather than coercive-extractive enterprise—as an avenue for post-coal revitalization.

Renewed Sites of Carceral Extraction

Decommissioned in 2009, Brushy has been turned into a tourist attraction in recent years. Unlike Newgate, or any number of exhibition mines in Appalachia, the experience of the mines themselves is not a part of the visitor's itinerary.[74] In some ways, Brushy is a characteristic object of penal tourism, one which differentiates itself from more famous sites of imprisonment through the trappings of Tennessee culture—complete with a "Warden's Table" restaurant serving barbeque, a working distillery producing "End of the Line" moonshine, and an outdoor country concert series in the prison yard.[75] A self-guided tour at Brushy commences with a video shown in the old chapel, added to the complex in the 1980s. While sitting in the pews, visitors get taken through the prison's historical arc in eighteen minutes, with particular attention paid to the most notorious prisoners (James Earl Ray's brief escape taking center stage), the grisliest of details concerning punishment and hard labor (whippings, hostage-taking,

---

74 For my own research on exhibition mines and mining museums in the region, see James Graham, "Making Coal Historical (a Road Trip)," *The Avery Review*, no. 35 (December 2018), http://averyreview.com/issues/35/making-coal-historical.

75 For an excellent analysis of the ideological dimensions of Brushy Mountain's redevelopment before its opening—particularly the Brushy Mountain Development Group's emphasis on craft production as a kind of carceral greenwashing—see Schept and Mazurek, "Layers of Violence."

and "the Hole"), and the "multigenerational family business" of prison employees. This last aspect is central to Brushy's historical reproduction—prisons, not unlike coal mines, claim the existence of emotional ties that extend beyond the simple provision of a paycheck, a rhetorical tendency that personifies and values the institution over and above the exploited individuals toiling within.

The exhibits in the museum include a wide array of contraband, shivs, tattoo guns—familiar displays of penal tourism that construct an all-too-easily digested image of prisoners justly punished, objects that aid in "circulating hegemonic logics about the violence of prisoners," as Judah Schept and Jordan E. Mazurek have put it.[76] Wandering the premises, one is meant to encounter former guards who work on site to share their stories. While the latest built and most secure cell block remains off limits, the visitor is allowed to explore the maximum security "D-block" as well as the central building, the cells still evincing the drawings and scrawls of their final occupants (a practice of auto-memorialization that is often remarked on in the literature around prison tourism).

But Brushy can also be read in other modes than prison-cell voyeurism, and in fact this carceral-extractive site had its own relationship to the cell, typically understood as the locus of the prisoner's custody. By working the prisoners in twelve-hour shifts, Brushy could house four prisoners per cell on only two beds—doubling its capacity by alternating shifts above- and belowground, depersonalizing the rooms themselves, and inscribing, as did *Ruffin v. Commonwealth*, an expanded vicinage of imprisonment. Prisoners were required to meet a fixed coal tonnage, receiving whippings if they fell short, a practice that continued until 1965. As at Pratt Mines, the architecture of extractive incarceration can also be read through

---

76   Schept and Mazurek, "Layers of Violence," 172.

the prison's outbuildings—the redemptive chapel, the mechanical sheds, and the portals into the mines up in the hills, which one can reach by trails elsewhere. The laundry takes a particular pride of place within the complex, since coal mining means, among other things, a great deal of washing. A 1928 report made by the federal government noted that towels were not provided to Brushy's incarcerated miners after taking showers, leading to improvements in the laundry facilities; in the 1950s and 1960s, the privilege of free laundry service was extended to the residents of Petros.

What kind of "carceral atmosphere" is this, to borrow a term from Jennifer Turner and Kimberly Peters, and what kind of frisson is brought forth by visiting Brushy Mountain?[77] Whatever empathy that is brought forth by the displays and the experience of the prison's spaces is, to borrow again from Saidiya Hartman, a fraught and ambivalent one, whatever the visitor's intentions or attitude toward the institutions this site marks the history of.[78] To its credit, this telling of Brushy's history does not shy away from the brutality of prison mining, the lines of race drawn within Tennessee's history of carceral extraction, or the illness and death that met unskilled laborers in unsafe and unsanitary conditions. And yet the story of Brushy is also told as an episode of Southern history from a colorful and dangerous past, one that distances the visitor from contemporary incarceration and the ongoing exploitation of Appalachian environments and convict labor as well as the full breadth of the prison's historical culpability.[79] In rendering it as a spectacle of remote misery—one that rarely questions the individual or collective stakes of imprisonment there, or the exploitative extractions that underpin the carbon economy—Brushy Mountain's museology sidesteps the possibility of connecting this site to the

77   Turner and Peters, "Unlocking Carceral Atmospheres."
78   Hartman, *Scenes of Subjection*, particularly chapter one.

conversations around environmental and social justice that urgently take place in the region.

Extractive Hinterlands

That the extraction of geological resources is reliably accompanied by the extraction of labor from the workers who do it—and, where possible, the extraction of additional margins of capital through financial machinations (such as tactical bankruptcies that minimize corporate responsibilities to out-of-work or retired miners or to communities affected by environmental devastation)—comes as no surprise to readers of history or the daily news. And while that exploitation takes many guises, the carceral state has been a persistent player in the development of geological resources, from the imprisoned Tories at Newgate to the coal-mining inmates of mid-1960s Tennessee. Attending to these seemingly idiosyncratic sites—which are not nearly so exceptional as they are sometimes made to seem—allows us glimpses into the political economies that motivate the changing guises of carceral labor.

Today, the coal country of the southern Appalachians continues to play something of an uncomplicated cameo in the national political imaginary of the United States. It is portrayed largely as a region hard hit by the opioid crisis, a polluted and diminished terrain sacrificed for its resources, a population susceptible to red-hat rallies promising coal's coming resurrection—narratives that do little to recognize formidable on-the-ground resistance to carbon and carceral economies.[80] A pervasive cultural shorthand

79   The question of potentially "flipping the prison" to other educative ends, a term that Schept and Mazurek borrow from the journalist Anna Clark, is discussed in Schept and Mazurek, "Layers of Violence," 184–186.
80   On this, see especially Elizabeth Catte, *What You Are Getting Wrong About Appalachia* (Cleveland: Belt Publishing, 2018). The online journal *Southerly: Ecology + Justice + Culture in the American South* is an excellent source of ongoing events and insightful essays; see https://southerlymag.org.

of equating "urban" with blackness and "rural" with white poverty further simplifies a complex cultural geography that is not nearly as schematic as it is often figured.[81] It is not *only* that the territory of Appalachian coal has been reappropriated for the ends of imprisonment, as a trade that allows prisons to be tidily removed from the blue-county capitals whose cities supply both the funds and the prisoners—though this is indeed the case. The entwinement of carbon and incarceration is longstanding and far-reaching, and together they have produced a joint extractive hinterland that has been a continuous presence within American capitalism as elsewhere.

81   David Todd Lawrence, "The Rural Black Nowhere: Invisibility, Urban-normativity, and the Geography of Indifference," *The Journal of the Midwest Modern Language Association* 48, no. 1 (Spring 2015): 221–244.

Sable Elyse Smith, *Coloring Book 9*, 2018. Screen printing ink, oil pastel, and oil stick on paper, 60 x 56 inches. Courtesy of the artist; JTT, New York; and Carlos/Ishikawa, London.

Together, Pat and Judge Friendly ride the elevator upstairs to a big room with benches. Lots and lots of people are waiting.

"It is hard to wait," says Judge Friendly.

"There are many families here, so we hope that everyone brings something to read or quiet puzzles to work on."

What 10 things don't belong in this picture?

FIRE CAMP, HIGHWAY, COAL MINE:
GEOGRAPHIES OF THE CARCERAL QUOTIDIAN

BRETT STORY

In 1972, seven months after prisoners at Attica Correctional Facility in upstate New York rebelled in what remains the largest prison uprising in US history, the French philosopher Michel Foucault described his visit there: "At first sight you have the impression that you are visiting more than just a factory, that you are visiting a machine, the inside of a machine."[1] Analogizing the prison as first a factory and then a machine was more than just literary flourish. It expressed Foucault's reading of the penitentiary apparatus as first and foremost a space—one made legible through its resemblance (or not) to adjacent architectures of modern life. Such architectures, Foucault argued, are themselves produced out of, and productive of, complex relations of power, some of which organize and disorganize the landscape in ways so quotidian that they seem completely benign.

Foucault is still today's most popular theorist of the prison as a space of power, despite having died in 1984 and having failed to predict, let alone explain, the systemic rise of mass incarceration in the United States and elsewhere from the 1970s onward. But if his spatial analysis charted new territory in the critical study of penal governance, it has since been eclipsed within the carceral literature by human geographers and sociologists, especially those working in the Marxist tradition who have sought to contextualize the prison system squarely within the development of neoliberal racial capitalism and its vicissitudes.

Geographers have made much of the way space is

1   Michel Foucault, "Michel Foucault on Attica: An Interview," by John K. Simon, in "Attica: 1971–1991, A Commemorative Issue," ed. Robert P. Weiss, special issue, *Social Justice* 18, no. 3 (1991): 26.

socially produced, arguing that space is a social practice through which, in turn, subjectivity is formed. We make space, and space makes us. We exist dialectically in our habits and habitations. As David Harvey puts it, "Space and the political organization of space express social relationships but also react back upon them."[2] Indeed, because the spatial organization of everyday life is a social product, arising from and co-constituent of purposeful social practice, space is both political and ideological.[3]

Space can also, therefore, be read; its contours and topographies can be mined for clues into the social relations and power struggles that configure and constrain our ways of being in the world. The prison is one such space—a building, most immediately, but one whose systemic import and political largess reaches far into the ordinary and so-called "free" spaces that constitute our communities and our habitats. If exceptional space is imagined as somehow outside of politics, then ordinary space is where politics organizes everyday life.

"Ordinary life, the life-world, the everyday, the quotidian, the low, the common, the private, the personal," as Tom Dumm puts it, is often sidelined in our culture's privileging of incarceration's most spectacular and seemingly exceptional manifestations.[4] It is ordinary space, however—where people live out their daily routines—that offers the most meaningful register of the deepening crises of downward mobility, the retrenchment of the social safety net, and the generalized precarity that the prison system

2   David Harvey, *Social Justice and the City* (Baltimore: Johns Hopkins University Press, 1973), 306.

3   See Harvey, *Social Justice and the City*; Edward W. Soja, "The Socio-Spatial Dialectic," *Annals of the Association of American Geographers* 70, no. 2: (1980): 207–225; Henri Lefebvre, *The Production of Space*, trans. D. Nicholson-Smith (Oxford: Blackwell, 1991); and Doreen Massey, *Space, Place, and Gender* (Minneapolis: University of Minnesota Press, 1994).

4   Thomas L. Dumm, *A Politics of the Ordinary* (New York: New York University Press, 1999), 1.

is tasked with managing. One witnesses in such spaces the reproduction of the status quo and *also* the kinds of crises that harbor the possibilities of change. As Lauren Berlant reminds us, "the ordinary is, after all, a porous zone that absorbs lots of incoherence and contradiction."[5] To consider "ordinary space" is therefore to contend with how the prison system etches its violence into the social fabric in ways as diverse and complex as they are quiet and mundane.

It is thus worth considering three quotidian land-scapes that each in their own way represents, expresses, and folds back onto the contemporary situation of mass incarceration in the United States. These sites can be viewed as external geographies of a sprawling prison regime whose operation is increasingly central to the functioning of the neoliberal capitalist state. We see in these spaces not only how the prison as a public institution is imprinted on the broader social landscape but also how such spaces are experienced, contested, and appropriated by the carceral subjects who inhabit them. We see the concept of resource extraction take on new meaning as coal mines are swapped for cell blocks; we see intimate relations of care intersect with public infrastructure to produce connection as well as isolation; and we see the very category of the criminal lose its ideological veil as "criminals" become "heroes" in landscapes that are at once worksites and carceral outposts.

The point of finding the prison in the fire camp, along the highway, and at the coal mine is, indeed, to make visible those relations of power reified in such built edifices as the penitentiary proper; relations of power that have been naturalized, vacated of historicity and social formation, such that it seems the prison has always been with us and will always continue to be. The purpose is to

5   Lauren Berlant, *Cruel Optimism* (Durham, NC: Duke University Press, 2011), 53.

The images that accompany this piece are stills from *The Prison in Twelve Landscapes*, directed and produced by Brett Story (New York: Grasshopper Film, 2016).

Marin County, California.

denaturalize the prison and see what is deliberately kept hidden: the organization of power and its contestations. The prison system is banal as well as brutal. We must read the landscape not just to be better spectators of our world, but rather so we might know its contingencies, and its fault lines.

Fire Camp

There is a fire raging over the mountains of Marin County, California. A group of women in boots, overalls, and gloves climb toward it in the night, carrying chainsaws and hose lines. For some of them, the vast vista of the mountain is a novelty, and many have not seen the night sky in years. All of these firefighters are wards of the state of California who, until their deployment to a prison fire camp, were incarcerated in one of the prisons in the state's massive constellation of penitentiaries.

In California's approximately thirty prison fire camps, minimum-security state prisoners are housed in small, open barracks, trained as firefighters, and deployed in crews of about fourteen to the front lines of some of the state's largest wildfires. The state boasts around 3,700 prison firefighters who they send out to do the hard and dangerous work of beating back flames and dousing hot spots.[6]

This work has never been more important. In October of 2017 alone a series of 250 wildfires burned across the state of California, part of the climate change–related trend toward ever more frequent and destructive wildfires across the west coast of North America. Indeed, six of California's most devastating wildfires occurred between 2015 and 2018. In 2018, the fires were even worse, registering 30

6   Peter Brook, "Unpacking the Media's Obsession with Prisoner Firefighters," *Medium*, April 9, 2019, https://medium.com/s/story/whats-with-all-the-photos-of-prisoner-firefighters-b7385489243f.

GEOGRAPHIES OF THE CARCERAL QUOTIDIAN

percent larger than the average fire over the previous
decade.[7] The California Department of Corrections and
Rehabilitation (CDCR) reports that the camp program
saves the state an estimated hundred million dollars annually—money we can assume would otherwise pay the sala-
ries of professional firefighters.[8] What might at other times
have been considered a site of extraordinary crisis, the
wildfire—and thus the fire camp—has become a kind of
generalized condition, as fires now rage every year across
the western coast with increasing frequency and voracity.

A prison firefighter might be deployed for months at a
time, moving up and down the state from San Diego all the
way to the Oregon border. They might spend twenty-four
hours at a time on a fire, earning, on average, $1 an hour
for each spent on the line. Other kinds of manual labor on
the fire crew are awarded closer to 32 cents per hour. While
there is no question this labor is exploitative, the presump-
tion that it is unwelcome among prisoners is unfounded.
Such are the contradictions of life and work in the unfree
conditions of incarceration, not to mention market capitalism more broadly. For many prison firefighters, the
work is actually a respite from the unrelenting boredom of
their sentence and also offers an opportunity to temporarily transcend the dehumanized subjectivity imposed upon
them on the basis of their criminal status.

As one prison firefighter puts it: "Here people out
there when we go out on a fire, regular citizens, are re-
spectful to you. You just saved their house, their crop, their
livestock, whatever. And they don't look at you like you've
got the blue on or the orange on. It's a whole different
world." As another describes it, "The public sees us as hero

7   Umair Irfan, "California's Wildfires are Hardly 'Natural'—Humans Made
    Them Worse at Every Step," *Vox*, November 19, 2018, https://www.vox.
    com/2018/8/7/17661096/california-wildfires-2018-camp-woolsey-
    climate-change.
8   Brook, "Unpacking the Media's Obsession with Prisoner-Firefighters."

firefighters. And I do too."[9] Prisoners are some of society's most demeaned and dehumanized subjects, and firefighters are among the most revered. The prison firefighter feels the effects of occupying both subjectivities at once.

The fire camp, as a carceral space, is full of these seeming contradictions. Sociologist Phil Goodman has written extensively about the multiple and mutable characterizations of this labor itself: exploitive *and* liberating, coerced *and* welcomed. Prisoners are trained. They develop essential and specialized skills. Once out, however, they are rarely able to translate those skills into secure employment in related sectors.[10]

The exploitation of prison labor is a favorite bogeyman of critics. Prisons, the thinking goes, serve capitalism by putting captives to work in a kind of neo-slavery marked by meager wages so profit-driven companies might produce goods more cheaply than possible in the "free world." In actuality, the Prison Industry Enhancement Certification Program (PIECP)—the federal agency with which companies wanting to hire incarcerated workers must register—reported that in 2018 only 5,000 people in prisons were under contract with private companies. That number amounts to less than 3 percent of the nation's prison population.[11] A larger number of incarcerated people do labor, like the prison firefighters, for government departments and institutions. But many more spend their days incapacitated as well as incarcerated. They are forced to do nothing, and their relationship to the job market and thus to

9   Interview transcripts from primary research provided to the author by Dr. Phil Goodman between 2008–2009.

10 Phil Goodman, "Hero *and* Inmate: Work, Prisons, and Punishment in California's Fire Camps," *WorkingUSA: The Journal of Labor and Society* 15, no. 3 (September 2012): 353–376.

11 Ruth Wilson Gilmore and James Kilgore, "Some Reflections on Prison Labor," *The Brooklyn Rail*, June 2019, https://brooklynrail.org/2019/06/field-notes/Some-Reflections-on-Prison-Labor.

the capitalist economy is better understood through the concept of surplus labor than through exploited labor.

The contradictions that mark the prison fire camp pose hard questions about ideology and subject formation: how the same person might occupy the place of both "hero" (the more-than-human) and "criminal" (the less-than-human) in the public imagination, and how wage-labor can operate as both an exploitative practice and a liberating alternative to the coerced idleness that marks most life in the contemporary carceral machine. Such critical questions do not have to stop at the fire line. Rather, they invite us to ask about the logics that underpin the prison system writ large, like why justice is understood as abandonment rather than investment, or how violence by the state can possibly be a remedy for other kinds of violence.

Highway

If you travel regularly to anywhere upstate from New York City or vice versa, you probably know at least one of the state's major highways fairly intimately. There's Interstate 87 (I-87), which reaches due north toward the Quebec border; I-90, which leans west toward Niagara Falls; and I-81, which services Syracuse and the towns to its north. Traveling these highways, the scenery changes little: exit ramps and on ramps, gas stations and dollar stores, cars jostling for lane space among cargo trucks and passenger buses.

What might not be visible is the way these highway routes divide also into prison routes. I-87 runs eventually to Upstate Correctional Facility in Malone, NY, and nearby facilities. I-81 will take you to the vicinity of Five Points and Auburn Correctional Facilities. I-90, meanwhile, leads towards Attica Correctional Facility, a fixture of the New York landscape since 1931. A bus traveling overnight from Manhattan along the Attica route will in fact stop at six

Bus to Attica, New York.

different facilities over the span of eight to ten hours: Groveland and Livingston at about 6 am, Wyoming and Attica an hour after that, and finally to Wende and Albion near the Canadian border.

As the country's incarceration rates have ballooned over the past half century, so too has the bus traffic along these highways. There are now, in New York State alone, more than a dozen different privately run buses and vans serving the population of visitors traveling from New York City to the state's primarily rural penal facilities and back again. A handful of them have been taking passengers to New York's prisons for almost forty years.

The majority of the state's penitentiaries are built in remote areas where land is cheap and where communities are hurting from various forms of economic decline and abandonment. They are often situated far from the urban neighborhoods where most incarcerated people come from and where their loved ones still reside. The highway is thus a space of circulation between the two poles of the contemporary prison regime: expensive state penitentiaries in poor rural towns and disinvested and criminalized neighborhoods in urban centers.

The bus is a vehicle for connection, but it is also its own kind of holding space where one endures the multiple insecurities—precarious housing, poor healthcare, and low wages—that neoliberal racial capitalism produces for those at the lowest echelons of the social order. On these buses, public infrastructure intersects with private service provision, as intimate relationships crosshatch the political geographies and coercive technologies of market capitalism and social control.

The bus riders themselves tend mostly to be low-income women of color. Their penance is also a labor: the socially reproductive work of caretaking across the fissures of the prison regime. Indeed, for those with intimates locked up in one of New York State's fifty-four prison facilities, these buses are likely both a lifeline and a "secondary imprisonment": the slow drudgery of traveling the highway its own form of "doing time" alongside one's incarcerated loved one.

Riders span all ages. They bring notes and care packages. They offer news from the family or the neighborhood. Their very presence is a reminder to prisoners and guards alike that to be incarcerated is not, in fact, to be unloved. Indeed, the stakes of these visits run high. Many visitors believe, with good reason, that the abuse prisoners face from guards increases in proportion to the degree that they are perceived as not having anyone on the outside who cares about them. In this sense, the act of riding the bus constitutes the work of social reproduction in a very literal sense—it is the work of keeping people alive.

Care work tends to be gendered female across all realms and income brackets. The prison system poses a particular violence in its very attempt to isolate, to break community, and to destroy relationships. Care work is deeply demanding and made more so by the increasing taxations of neoliberal austerity for those who already occupy the lowest rungs of a social order organized by class, race, and gender. The women who take the visitors' bus tend to work a lot, on all fronts, for very little. For this and many other reasons, the long, cramped, and often overnight bus trip only further exhausts the bodies, wallets, and psyches of those already worn out by capitalist life.

The complaints are small and ordinary, but they speak to the generalized condition of injury and deterioration felt by so many of the riders. For life caught in the crosshairs of the prison regime, systemic violence is felt as tedium, exhaustion, resource depletion, and the slow death attendant to inadequate healthcare. Riders complain of the physical and psychic agonies experienced on the bus: cramped quarters, snorers and crying children, needing to urinate, vans that refuse to stop, temperatures that are too hot or too cold, and the various holdups that prolong waiting times both outside and on the bus, like break-downs, drivers getting lost, and companies not departing until their seats are filled. Riders complain of drivers going too fast, tires skidding off asphalt, and the terror of being on the road during snowstorms. And they complain of not sleeping. Of staring out windows at long stretches of high-way, dimly lit in the hollows of deep night, for hours and for years.

Yet on the bus and in the visiting rooms, visitors also forge small solidarities. The prison isolates, but it also collectivizes. People spend a lot of time together in a shared space. Thus, the visitors riding the bus form bonds and share strategies for survival and endurance. One woman I met on the ride to Attica told me she brings two sets of extra clothes when she makes the journey: one for herself, and another for anyone else who might be found, upon arrival, in violation of one of the rules regarding attire.[12]

Ruth Wilson Gilmore notes how "prisons wear out places by wearing out people, irrespective of whether they have done time."[13] The prison bus, journeying across the great hallmark of American civic infrastructure, the inter-state highway, is one carceral site where this wearing out takes place. It is simultaneously where its primarily female riders demonstrate, and sometimes collectivize, the power of their caregiving—making common cause across the fractures of the prison regime to reproduce life and maintain its fragile, and necessary, social adhesions.

12   For more firsthand accounts of these trips, see the chapter "The Prison In-Between: Caretaking and Crisis on the Visitors' Bus" in my book *Prison Land: Mapping Carceral Power across Neoliberal America* (Minneapolis: University of Minnesota Press, 2019), 105–137.

13   Ruth Wilson Gilmore, *Golden Gulag: Prisons, Surplus, Crisis, and Opposition in Globalizing California* (Berkeley: University of California Press, 2007), 17.

Coal Mine

Even before construction on United States Penitentiary (USP) Big Sandy was completed in 2003, it began to sink. Literally sink. Below its foundation was an empty crater, or, more exactly, an abandoned coal mine, rendering the surface area fragile and insecure. Because of the costs of remediating and securing the facility on such precarious ground, the institution is the most expensive federal prison on record ever built. Twenty years later, some of the guard towers still tilt and some of the buildings are still partially sunken. Locals refer to the prison as "Sink-Sink," a clever play on the infamous "Sing Sing" penitentiary in New York.

The view from the site is magnificent. Rolling hills as far as the eye can see play host to over a hundred different species of trees. The complex ecology of the "Appalachian forest" forms one of the greatest floral provinces on Earth. Indeed, Appalachian Kentucky, where USP Big Sandy is perched, is often described as a place with "rich land and poor people."[14] Timber and coal have formed the backbone of the economy here for more than a century, but the ruthless extraction of the region's rich resources has declined alongside the incomes of its residents over the past four decades especially.

Martin County, where USP Big Sandy currently holds prisoners from as far as Hawaii and Alaska, is also home to the town of Inez, made famous as the site where US President Lyndon B. Johnson declared a national "war on poverty" in 1964. More than fifty years later, Martin County is still ranked the eleventh poorest county in the nation by median household income.

The problem across this county and Central Appalachia more broadly is unemployment. Or, more correctly,

14   R.D. Eller, *Uneven Ground: Appalachia since 1945* (Lexington: University Press of Kentucky, 2008).

Letcher County, Eastern Kentucky.

poverty, for of course wage-labor isn't the only possible way to ameliorate economic deprivation and its harms. The region has been hemorrhaging jobs for decades. Between 1979 and 2006, the number of people working in the mining industry in Kentucky decreased by over 60 percent.[15] The Gallup-Healthways Well-Being Index, which includes physical health and basic access, ranked Kentucky's fifth congressional district—covering all of Appalachian Kentucky—last out of 434 districts.[16] After more than a century of being barnacled to an increasingly mechanized and de-unionized coal economy, the counties of eastern Kentucky have in recent decades taken to courting state and federal prison construction as a putative remedy to their economic woes—hence the high-security facility for male prisoners built atop a mountaintop-removal site with a hollow core and a fragile floor.

Prisons are being actively promoted here, as in similarly depressed and disinvested regions, as an economic development strategy: the only hope locals have for new employment. The region has witnessed a prison-building boom since the turn of the century. In just one decade, between 2000 and 2010, Kentucky's prison population grew by a whopping 45 percent. And total state spending on penal institutions in the fiscal year 2009 reached $513 million—an almost fourfold increase since 1989.[17] Eastern Kentucky is now home to nine prisons in total—several of

15   Office of Energy Policy, *Kentucky Quarterly Coal Report: January to March 2019* (Frankfort: Kentucky Energy and Environment Cabinet, 2019), https://eec.ky.gov/Energy/News-Publications/Quarterly Coal Reports/2019-Q1.pdf.

16   Gallup-Healthways Well-Being Index, *State of American Well-Being: 2013 State, Community, and Congressional District Analysis* (Washington, DC: Gallup, 2014), http://cdn2.hubspot.net/hub/162029/file-610480715-pdf/WBI 2013/Gallup-Healthways_State_of_American_Well-Being_Full_Report_2013.pdf.

17   Judah Schept, "'(Un)seeing Like a Prison: Counter-Visual Ethnography of the Carceral State,'" *Theoretical Criminology* 18, no. 2 (May 2014): 304.

them, like USP Big Sandy, built directly on top of decommissioned coal mines.

The landscape can tell us many things, including how the contemporary carceral state animates a particular future. The post-coal towns of eastern Kentucky suggest that it does so, at least partly, by preying on gutted, economically devastated communities and dangling the promise of purposeful work in prison development. As per the wont of a capitalist economy, land is swapped from one extractive industry to another, repurposed in actual terrain and in local imaginaries. Coal mines become prison sites and former miners, prison guards. The capitalist state reproduces itself for a new generation.

Except that most unemployed miners can't actually find gainful employment in the prison business. Deemed too old, too sick, or simply just too numerous for the narrow belt of prison jobs that accompany each new opening, former miners rarely experience the employment boom promised by the prison boosters. As Sylvia Ryerson notes in a study of another new prison proposal in the region, USP McCreary, the qualifications for employment were outlined only after construction of the facility had begun, and, it turned out, actually disqualified most of the county's unemployed and underemployed men and women.[18]

We remedy nothing by building prisons. We certainly do not palliate the injuries etched into the landscape by extractive industries and their exploitation and then abandonment of workers. But if it is the surfeit of laborers, whether those in cities where prisoners come from or those in rural hinterlands where prisons are built, that are the true remit of the carceral state, then alternatives to the prison become easier to imagine. The resources of the region and the capacity of its people might be repurposed

18   Sylvia Ryerson, "Speak Your Piece: Prison Progress?" *The Daily Yonder*, February 20, 2013, https://www.dailyyonder.com/speak-your-piece-prison-progress/2013/02/20.

in such a way that its locals might work and live well again in circumstances that don't rely on a re-hazing of the landscape or the forced migration and mass incarceration of thousands of other poor people.

When we think of the prison, we tend to imagine a building. That makes sense: The earliest penitentiaries, first conceived and constructed some two centuries ago, were built primarily to move state punishment out of the public square and into a space hidden behind high walls and locked cell doors. These discrete sites of punishment have exemplified the contemporary prison system in our imagination as well as in our understanding of its architecture ever since. But "architecture" necessarily exists within something we call "infrastructures": what Brian Larkin describes as "matter that enable the movement of other matter."[19] The peculiarity of infrastructures stem, he says, from the fact that "they are things and also the relation between things."[20]

It is useful, politically as well as analytically, to consider the prison not just as an architecture but as an infrastructure in the sense that Larkin describes. Prisons are buildings, yes. But they are also manifestations of a society's organization of social relations. And they are *themselves* relations between things—between urban centers and rural hinterlands, between the state and industry, between capitalists and labor markets, between technologies of exploitation and means of social reproduction.

It is when they are considered just "things" or just "buildings" that prisons are most easily dismissed as natural and inevitable. They become reified. Their "thingness" obscures the underlying historical conditions and social contingencies that produced the prison in the first

19   Brian Larkin, "The Politics and Poetics of Infrastructure," *Annual Review of Anthropology* 42 (October 2013): 329.

20   Larkin, "The Politics and Poetics of Infrastructure," 329.

place and which the system continues to serve. The reified world must be challenged, argued the Marxist critic Georg Lukács, precisely because it appears to us as "the only possible world, the only conceptually accessible, comprehensible world vouchsafed to us humans."[21] Discerning these relations and processes requires at times a shifting of perspective and a reconsideration of spaces frequently dismissed within conventional penal study as outside the carceral apparatus and thus outside the field of inquiry.

The fire camp, the highway, and the coal mine all gesture toward the much larger infrastructural network that constitutes the sprawling and systemically entrenched US prison regime. These spaces manifest a set of contradictions, failed promises, and intimate dramas played out through the efforts of ordinary people to survive and live better. As such, these landscapes also stage the conditions for contestation and social struggle. Attica Penitentiary is one famous site where solidarities were forged in the name of freedom, but the prison bus, perhaps less spectacularly, is another. The ordinary, after all, is not only where everyday life is lived, but also where futures are built.

21   György Lukács, "Reification and the Consciousness of the Proletariat," in *History and Class Consciousness: Studies in Marxist Dialectics*, trans. R. Livingstone (Cambridge, MA: MIT Press, 1971), 119.

Sable Elyse Smith, *Coloring Book 10*, 2018. Screen printing
ink, oil pastel, and oil stick on paper, 60 x 56 inches. Courtesy
of the artist; JTT, New York; and Carlos/Ishikawa, London.

PROCESSING POWER:
ARCHIVES, PRISONS, AND THE ETHNOGRAPHY OF EXCHANGE

JARRETT M. DRAKE

Yale University and the United States Federal Bureau of Investigation (FBI) chose a conspicuous time to collaborate. The two institutions ostensibly share little in common. One is an Ivy League university located in the middle of a disproportionately Black, working-class city, while the other is the chief domestic law enforcement agency of the world's largest jailer. Divergent as these two entities might appear, their interests coalesced in 2016 when the nascent Movement for Black Lives reached a fever pitch. The previous year, demonstrators across the country took to the streets demanding justice for Black people whose lives had been stolen by the state: Sandra Bland in Waller County, Texas, Walter Scott in North Charleston, South Carolina, and Freddie Gray in Baltimore, Maryland. These three killings all took place in motion. Bland was driving and allegedly changed lanes without using a signal. Scott was running away from a traffic stop. Gray was being transported in the back of a police vehicle. Their mobility, in a sense, provided the immediate context for their demise at the hands of the state. The capture of Scott's murder on a mobile device placed the system of policing and prisons in the US under a renewed lens and level of scrutiny.

At stake in the wake of these killings was not just the credibility of a specific police department or county jail but the legitimacy of law enforcement writ large. The debate hit close to home for Yale too, given that in January 2015 a patrol officer from the university's police department pulled a gun on a Black student leaving the library and ordered him to the ground. Suspected of robbery, the student was asked to show his Yale ID and confirm his recent whereabouts. The damage of this brief yet almost deadly detention and interrogation cannot be undone, neither to the student nor to the public perception of policing.[1] These incidents contextualize the 2016 announcement from the FBI about its new partnership with Yale to launch the Future Law Enforcement Youth Academy (FLEYA). FLEYA, a training program for high school students in Connecticut, promises applicants an "inside look" at law enforcement:

> The students will receive specific classroom training and practical exercises in investigative forensics, use of cyber technology techniques for combating violent crime, counterintelligence, gang awareness, civil rights (hate crimes), and many more violations of state and federal law. This unique training will include classes with Assistant US Attorneys and State's Attorneys, local police, judges, and federal agents.[2]

Yale police chief Ronnell Higgins boasted that the academy typifies the university's provision of community programming.[3] But Higgins's celebration of enhanced relations with New Haven residents proved premature. Less than three years into the program, a Yale police officer drove his cruiser well beyond the limits of campus and into the nearby neighborhood of Newhallville to assist a

1   Charles M. Blow, "Library Visit, Then Held at Gunpoint," *New York Times*, January 26, 2015, https://www.nytimes.com/2015/01/26/opinion/charles-blow-at-yale-the-police-detained-my-son.html.

2   United States Federal Bureau of Investigation, "Now Accepting Applications for FBI/Yale Future Law Enforcement Youth Academy Program," press release, May 6, 2016, https://www.fbi.gov/contact-us/field-offices/newhaven/news/press-releases/now-accepting-applications-for-fbi-yale-future-law-enforcement-youth-academy-program.

3   Karen N. Peart, "Yale and FBI Launch Future Law Enforcement Youth Academy," *YaleNews*, May 10, 2016, https://news.yale.edu/2016/05/10/yale-and-fbi-launch-future-law-enforcement-youth-academy.

fellow officer from the bordering town of Hamden. The two cops, who both crossed jurisdictional boundaries, summarily opened fire on two young Black people seated in a car that police suspected had been used in a robbery. The Yale officer mercifully missed his intended targets. However, the Hamden officer did not, injuring the female passenger. After detaining the driver at the Hamden precinct, police later released him with no charges.[4] The incident inflamed tensions in the city yet brought no bearing on the FLEYA program. In fact, the FBI replicated the academy and later that year announced its partnership with Marquette University in the largely Black city of Milwaukee, Wisconsin.[5]

The mobility that threads all of these incidents together produces the fabric of contemporary carcerality. Prisons and jails no longer (if they ever did) exist exclusively as bounded sites, out of sight or out of mind. Rather, the prison has become as diffuse as those responsible for its propagation, including the armed agents of multibillion-dollar non-profit corporations such as Yale University. If, as Angela Y. Davis and Gina Dent suggest, the prison is a type of border, then it is also true that, similar to other borders, the prison is marked much more by its exchange than by its exclusion.[6] That is, fluidity—of processes, of people, of products—and not fixity best characterizes the

4   Nicholas Rondinone, "Woman Shot in New Haven after Hamden, Yale
     Police Open Fire on Man Suspected in Armed Robbery," *Hartford Courant*,
     April 16, 2019, https://www.courant.com/breaking-news/hc-br-new-
     haven-officer-involved-shooting-20190416-h7q7ldqenzg67pr7dtj72hdwfq-
     story.html.
5   United States Federal Bureau of Investigation, "FBI and Marquette Uni-
     versity Police Department to Host 2019 Future Law Enforcement Youth
     Academy," press release, February 20, 2019, https://www.fbi.gov/contact-us/
     field-offices/milwaukee/news/press-releases/fbi-and-marquette-university-
     police-department-host-2019-future-law-enforcement-youth-academy.
6   Angela Y. Davis and Gina Dent, "Prison as a Border: A Conversation on
     Gender, Globalization, and Punishment," *Signs* 26, no. 4 (2001): 1235–1241.

carceral landscape in the US, a reality no doubt replicated in the empire's ever-expanding borders.[7] This does not suggest a borderless society, but quite the contrary: borders are as abundant as ever, much like movements across them.

The prison's mobility presents an epistemological as well as ethnographic challenge. Where, after all, does one *look* to study a shifting site? The anthropologist Igor Kopytoff gives a glimpse of one approach to this question. In his study of commoditization as a process in which objects change conditions throughout their (inanimate) lives rather than retain a fixed status, Kopytoff argues for cultural biographies of objects—a way of seeing a thing "as a culturally constructed entity, endowed with culturally specific meanings, and classified and reclassified into culturally constituted categories."[8] I propose a parallel approach for the study of the prison, one that pursues not a cultural *biography of things* but rather an *ethnography of exchange.* Following the flow of goods and services across the prison border reveals its proximity to processes presumed to be remote and removed from carcerality altogether. In other words, this essay explores how the prison shows up in seemingly distinct spaces—not only producing the commodities of said spaces but also comprising their core constitution. In this way the prison presents itself as both a metaphorical and material necessity. The challenge then is to unpack, dismantle, and discard not just the prison itself but also its pervasive imprint, which can be found even in the most cloistered of corners.

7   Todd Miller, *Empire of Borders: The Expansion of the US Border around the World* (London and New York: Verso, 2019).

8   Igor Kopytoff, "The Cultural Biography of Things: Commoditization as Process," in *The Social Life of Things: Commodities in Cultural Perspective*, ed. Arjun Appadurai (Cambridge, UK: Cambridge University Press, 1986), 68.

ARCHIVES, PRISONS, AND THE ETHNOGRAPHY OF EXCHANGE

Ignoble Archives

By design, few corners are as cloistered as archives. The term itself contributes to its cloak. "Archive" simultaneously refers to historical documents preserved for future usage as well as to the edifices that house them and the organizations that manage them. Archivists, social scientists, and humanists have written extensively about archives as documents and archives as organizations, not to mention *the* archive.[9] Less commonly contested is the archive as edifice. Archives are typically situated at fringes, which functions to limit the number of people who make use of the documents in them. When housed in a library or museum, one must ordinarily go to the basement or the top floor, followed by a few tight turns around a couple of corners. Posted signs are rare occurrences. When housed independently, most archives border on invisibility—their opacity communicating to passersby that they ought to, indeed, pass by. This assumes, of course, that the archive is located somewhere that someone might pass by. Yet the opposite tends to be true. Traffic flows, or lack thereof, structure archives—few people stumble into them merely by curiosity, chance, or happenstance. This is the case from the national archives in Havana, Cuba, to the university archives of Harvard University. Archives, in a sense, are for seekers, not finders. Serendipity is so slight as to be a chimera.

The truly determined who make it to the front door of an archive may, after all, simply reach the front door and no further. Failure to obtain advanced approval from

9   For a discussion on the history of scholarship on archives, see Michelle Caswell, "'The Archive' Is Not an Archives: On Acknowledging the Intellectual Contributions of Archival Studies," *Reconstruction: Studies in Contemporary Culture* 16, no. 1 (2016), https://escholarship.org/uc/item/7bn4v1fk.

the archive or a lack of government-issued identification can end a visit before it even starts. If those hurdles are cleared, one earns the status of researcher with the right to request archival documents; not by name, of course, but by a unique inventory number.[10] The archivist at the reference desk will inform the researcher what items are prohibited in the reading room: no bags, no jackets, and no pens. They will assign the researcher a table in the reading room and mention that the wait time for documents depends on a number of factors. There may be a shift change or it may just be a bizarrely busy afternoon. The archive holds the most stringent of hours, so this should come as no surprise. But it always does. A dozen, or three, minutes might elapse before the researcher can finally see what they came to see. There are rules though. First, no documents can leave with the researcher. A search coming and going assures as much. Second, you must sit, however discomforting, so that the reading room attendant who is slightly perched above everyone can see both the researcher and the documents at all times. The black masking tape serves as a good guide. Third, and most importantly, you cannot (nor should you attempt to) use documents that another researcher is currently consulting. The archive must keep accurate statistics and maintain records of which researchers saw which (family) documents, in the event that a document leaves the premises. What, anyway, would an archive be without documents within its walls?

Archives, thus, also constitute a border. This border exists equally in its fixity and fluidity. The rarity of archival records, so the logics goes, requires the organizations that manage them to police their perimeters—at the very least to inform researchers that they have indeed entered a separate space. Yet, an archive also must maintain porous boundaries to engender processes of knowledge creation

10 See Elsie Freeman, "In the Eye of the Beholder: Archives Administration from the User's Point of View," *American Archivist* 47, no. 2 (1984): 111–123.

and dissemination. An archive thus attracts potential researchers in part through its support of past researchers who share their findings from previous visits. In this way, archives teeter on a tension: they must keep certain items *in* and keep certain people *out*, all the while ensuring a secured but steady cycle of those who enter and those who exit. The archive border consequently mirrors the prison border. Prisons, too, deploy procedures and practices to communicate to the incarcerated and those who visit them that they have also crossed into a wholly other world. Replacing "archive" with "prison," "archivist" with "guard," "researcher" with "visitor," and "document" with "incarcerated person" in the paragraph you just read does not impact its intelligibility:

> The truly determined who make it to the front door of a prison may, after all, simply reach the front door and no further. Failure to obtain advanced approval from the prison or a lack of government-issued identification can end a visit before it even starts. If those hurdles are cleared, one earns the status of visitor with the right to request an imprisoned loved one; not by name, of course, but by a unique inventory number.[11] The guard at the front desk will inform the visitor what items are prohibited in the visiting room: no bags, no jackets, and no pens. They will assign the visitor a seat in the visiting room and mention that the wait time for the imprisoned individual depends on a number of factors. There may be a shift change or it may just be a bizarrely busy afternoon. The prison holds the most stringent of hours, so this should come as no surprise. But it always does. A dozen, or three, minutes might elapse before the visitor can finally

11   See Megan Comfort, *Doing Time Together: Love and Family in the Shadow of the Prison* (Chicago: University of Chicago Press, 2008).

see who they came to see. There are rules though. First, no person can leave with the visitor. A search coming and going assures as much. Second, you must sit, however discomforting, so that the commanding correctional officer who is slightly perched above everyone can see both the visitor and the prisoner at all times. The black masking tape serves as a good guide. Third, and most importantly, you cannot (nor should you attempt to) see somebody that another visitor is already seeing. The prison must keep accurate statistics and maintain records of which visitors saw which confined persons, in the event that someone leaves the premises. What, anyway, would a prison be without prisoners within its walls?

But which came first: the modern archive or the modern prison? Michel Foucault in his landmark treatise *Discipline and Punish* offers a compelling connection between the two institutions. While he aims in this text to demonstrate the way prisons concentrate a form of disciplinary power previously distributed among other entities across European society, Foucault also emphasizes that discipline does not reside exclusively within a single institution, defining it instead as: "a type of power, a modality for its exercise, comprising a whole set of instruments, techniques, procedures, levels of application, targets; it is a 'physics' or an 'anatomy' of power, a technology."[12] These "modalities" and "techniques" necessitated a normalizing function capable of comparing and contrasting outputs from different people. For Foucault, the examination fulfilled this need. Exams—in asylums, in military barracks, in hospitals, in schools—positioned individuals in a panoptic web of writing, which fixed particular conditions of fitness, illness, or aptitude onto persons. These records

12   Michel Foucault, *Discipline and Punish: The Birth of the Prison,* trans. Alan Sheridan, 2nd ed. (New York: Vintage, 1995), 215.

retain accounts of people and as such are indispensable to discipline because they offer an ongoing observatory of behavior, with the intent, of course, to manipulate and manage the subject of the surveillance.

On the question of which, the archive or the prison, came first, Foucault is unequivocal: "It is probably to be found in these 'ignoble' archives, where the modern play of coercion over bodies, gestures, and behaviour has its beginnings."[13] Almost all subsequent meditations on the relationship between archives and prisons refer back to Foucault to frame their analyses.[14] In many ways Foucault floats as a specter that haunts as much as he helps. But what happens if one flips the frame away from seeing how the archive sustains the prison and instead puts into focus the ways that the prison sustains the archive? What if the link between these two sites is not merely metaphorical but material? What can be seen when the lens is adjusted to explore exchange and to look for labor? What epistemological possibilities emerge when the talk about time shifts to account for the "time of slavery?"[15]

13   Foucault, *Discipline and Punish*, 191. For a thorough rereading of Foucault's *Discipline and Punish* as well as the entire field of surveillance studies, see Simone Browne, *Dark Matters: On the Surveillance of Blackness* (Durham, NC: Duke University Press, 2015). Browne diligently highlights how Foucault's and the field's disregard of race and racism belies the fact that the "conditions of Blackness" form the basis of all contemporary surveillance dating back to the Middle Passage, which itself is, as Browne argues, one of the earliest mobile prisons that Foucault notably neglects.

14   For examples of three articles in this mold, see Eric Ketelaar, "Archival Temples, Archival Prisons: Modes of Power and Protection," *Archival Science* 2, no. 3 (2002): 221–238; Jarrett M. Drake, "Liberatory Archives: Towards Belonging and Believing" (keynote address, Community Archives Forum, Los Angeles, CA, October 21, 2016), https://medium.com/on-archivy/liberatory-archives-towards-belonging-and-believing-part-1-d26a aeb0edd1; Tonia Sutherland, "The Carceral Archive: Documentary Records, Narrative Construction, and Predictive Risk Assessment," *Journal of Cultural Analytics*, June 4, 2019, https://culturalanalytics.org/article/11047.

15   Saidiya V Hartman, "The Time of Slavery," *South Atlantic Quarterly* 101, no. 4 (2002): 757–777.

PROCESSING POWER

Factories with Fences

The Louisiana State Penitentiary tells a tale about time that must be seen to be believed. The largest maximum-security prison in the US maintains not just 18,000 acres of rich farmland nestled near the Mississippi River but also manages a museum. The Angola Museum at the Louisiana State Penitentiary differs from other prison museums—most notably those at Eastern State Penitentiary in Philadelphia, Robben Island outside Cape Town, and Alcatraz Island near San Francisco—in that it operates adjacent to a prison that is active, alive, and very much open for business. T-shirts emblazoned with the phrase "Angola—A Gated Community" go for twenty dollars. Tote bags and travel mugs that say the same cost eight and ten dollars.[16] The naked commercialism of the museum shop contrasts the narrative that the museum otherwise constructs about Angola. Its timeline charts a story of progress in which the prison's origin as a slave plantation and subsequent transition into a convict-leasing camp are remnants of a distant past. The museum intimates that the Angola of today is markedly different from the Angola whose exploitative, extractive, and excessive practices led a group of prisoners in the 1950s to object to the prison's harsh working and living conditions by slicing their Achilles tendons.[17] The penitentiary, in other words, has faced its forgettable past. What symbolizes this Sankofa better than the incarcerated people who deliver documents to the reading room?[18]

16   "Shop Angola," The Angola Museum at the Louisiana State Penitentiary, accessed November 15, 2019, https://www.angolamuseum.org/shop.

17   "History of Angola," The Angola Museum at the Louisiana State Penitentiary, accessed November 18, 2019, https://www.angolamuseum.org/history-of-angola.

18   Dennis Childs, *Slaves of the State: Black Incarceration from the Chain Gang to the Penitentiary* (Minneapolis: University of Minnesota Press, 2015), 103–104.

Ronald Brooks has a different history of the Louisiana State Penitentiary: his version is not history at all. Brooks and others imprisoned at Angola created the organization Decarcerate Louisiana to account for a persistent, even possibly unending historical present in which slavery and incarceration cannot be decoupled from one another.[19] Brooks expounds on this point in a video posted to Facebook: "We believe that federal and state constitutions that uphold slavery if a person is convicted of a crime is a dirty scheme; an evil plan put forward by modern day slave traffickers disguised as public official[s] and big businesses to re-enslave the 2.4 million Americans currently being warehoused and forced to work on prison farms across the United States of America."[20] His comments came after he and others organized a work strike in the spring of 2018 to draw attention to a brutal work regime at Angola centered on the harvesting of crops grown on the prison grounds.[21] Decarcerate Louisiana's action was part of a coordinated resistance inside prisons that year, culminating in a four-week strike led by incarcerated people across the country. First among the strikers' ten demands was a call to improve the overall "condition" of prisons, which might as well be understood in the context of a warming planet, given that 2018 registered as the fourth hottest year in

---

19 Ronald Brooks, "Decarcerate Louisiana for Sustainable Economies," *San Francisco Bay View*, January 3, 2017, https://sfbayview.com/2017/01/decarcerate-louisiana-for-sustainable-economies.

20 Decarcerate Louisiana (Ronald Brooks), Facebook Live video, filmed June 21, 2018, in Louisiana State Penitentiary, Angola, LA, https://www.facebook.com/story.php?story_fbid=310282476174390&id=100015779203681.

21 Bryce Covert, "Louisiana Prisoners Demand an End to 'Modern-Day Slavery,'" *The Appeal*, June 8, 2018, https://theappeal.org/louisiana-prisoners-demand-an-end-to-modern-day-slavery. See also Whitney Benns, "American Slavery, Reinvented," *The Atlantic*, September 21, 2015, https://www.theatlantic.com/business/archive/2015/09/prison-labor-in-america/406177.

recorded history.[22] The strike's second demand generated the most press coverage: an end to prison slavery.[23]

This demand makes reference, of course, to the Thirteenth Amendment of the US Constitution and its allowance of slavery or involuntary servitude for people convicted of crimes. Historically, organizers across (and within) prison borders have disagreed about the relationship between incarceration and enslavement.[24] Yet two trends prove true. First, nearly every prison uprising that publishes a set of demands mentions the paltry or nonexistent wages and the absence of basic workplace protections that mark prison labor, hence the frequent recurrence of the strike as an organizing tactic among people in prison.[25] Second, incarcerated people, like those enslaved under chattel slavery, were instrumental to most public works projects of the nineteenth and early twentieth centuries. Black women in Georgia toiled to construct roads all over the state following the decimation wrought by the US Civil

22   National Oceanic and Atmospheric Administration, United States Department of Commerce, "2018 Was 4th Hottest Year on Record for the Globe," press release, February 6, 2019, https://www.noaa.gov/news/2018-was-4th-hottest-year-on-record-for-globe. In addition to the increasingly unbearable heat waves that prisoners endure, climate change also means that during the winter months, prisoners face new cold extremes, made worse by insufficient or inoperable heating systems. See Tanya A. Christian, "Attorneys for Inmates at Brooklyn Jail without Heat, Electricity during Polar Vortex File Lawsuit," *Essence*, February 5, 2019, https://www.essence.com/news/attorneys-for-inmates-at-brooklyn-jail-without-heat-electricity-during-polar-vortex-file-lawsuit.

23   "Prison Strike 2018," Incarcerated Workers Organizing Committee, June 19, 2018, https://incarceratedworkers.org/campaigns/prison-strike-2018.

24   Dan Berger, *Captive Nation: Black Prison Organizing in the Civil Rights Era* (Chapel Hill: University of North Carolina Press, 2014), 186–188.

25   See for instance, California Prisoners Union, *The Folsom Prisoners Manifesto of Demands and Anti-Oppression Platform* (San Francisco: CONNECTIONS, 1970), https://www.freedomarchives.org/Documents/Finder/DOC510_scans/Folsom_Manifesto/510.folsom.manifesto.11.3.1970.pdf. The Folsom Manifesto also served as the blueprint for the demands issued in the 1971 Attica Uprising in New York, as detailed by Berger, *Captive Nation*, 3.

War.[26] Convict laborers in Louisiana built levees.[27] New York's notorious Sing Sing prison was built by people incarcerated at Auburn prison.[28] Thus, while surplus value may not be as central to incarceration as it was to chattel slavery, these historical continuities reveal that the issue of labor expropriation matters deeply for people imprisoned under an economic regime that simultaneously sees them as disposable on an individual basis yet indispensable on a collective one. In other words, to see the prison exclusively as an economic engine is to occlude its centrality in racial subjugation. Likewise, a failure to account for the prison's profitability vis-à-vis wage theft of incarcerated people is to mute the many voices coming from within the cage who, literally and figuratively, face the machinations of racial capitalism daily and cannot see it otherwise.[29]

As it is, too many in power already discount the experiences and hardships that plague prisoners. Warren Burger, Chief Justice of the US Supreme Court appointed by President Richard Nixon, wrote in 1982:

> Most prison inmates, by definition, are maladjusted people. From whatever cause—whether too little discipline or too much, too little security or too much, broken homes, or whatever—they lack self-esteem, they are insecure, they are at war with themselves as well as with society. They do not share the work ethic

26 See Talitha L. LeFlouria, *Chained in Silence: Black Women and Convict Labor in the New South* (Chapel Hill: The University of North Carolina Press, 2015); Sarah Haley, *No Mercy Here: Gender, Punishment, and the Making of Jim Crow Modernity* (Chapel Hill: University of North Carolina Press, 2016).

27 Childs, *Slaves of the State*, 121.

28 Jennifer Graber, *The Furnace of Affliction: Prisons and Religion in Antebellum America* (Chapel Hill: University of North Carolina Press, 2011), 106.

29 For records of some of these voices, see "#PrisonStrike," It's Going Down, accessed November 20, 2019, https://itsgoingdown.org/prisonstrike.

> concepts that made this country great... Place that
> person in a factory, whether it makes ballpoint pens,
> hosiery, cases for watches, parts of automobiles, lawn
> mowers, computers or parts of other machinery.[30]

Justice Burger publicly shared his hope that the impending boom in prison construction of the 1980s would "convert our 'warehouses' into factories with fences around them."[31] Burger was not alone in his thinking. William Norris, head of the computing firm Control Data Corporation, joined Burger for the "Factories with Fences" forum at George Washington University in 1984 and announced that his company operated partly under the auspices of the Minnesota State Prison where prisoners assembled computer equipment. In case there was any doubt as to why a prison might be an ideal supplier of discount labor, Norris made it clear: "When you think about it, there really isn't much difference between an inner-city poverty-stricken neighborhood and a prison."[32] The biggest difference, of course, is that work under the aegis of a state prison system allows for the suppression of wages both inside and outside the factory fence. Moreover, the so-called digital divide that came to characterize the late 2000s and early 2010s falls on its face with the reality that incarcerated people helped spur the dawn of the digital age, digitizing sensitive records for state governments and private businesses at least as far back as the late 1960s.[33] Defenders of this arrangement often cite the mundaneness of prison life as a reason that incarcerated

30   Warren Burger, "More Warehouses, or Factories with Fences?," *New England Journal of Prison Law* 8, no. 1 (1982): 116. For more on the idea of prison as a warehouse, see Ruth Wilson Gilmore, *Golden Gulag: Prisons, Surplus, Crisis, and Opposition in Globalizing California* (Berkeley: University of California Press, 2007).

31   Burger, "More Warehouses, or Factories with Fences?," 120.

32   William Raspberry, "Control Data Chief: Prison Productivity Matters," *Port Arthur News*, June 24, 1984.

people value any opportunity to leave their cells and keep busy. That is likely the case. Yet, their eagerness pales in comparison to someone like Bob Tessler, an executive of a data processing firm in Silicon Valley, who stated in no uncertain terms: "We have a captive labor force, a group of men who are dedicated, who want to work. That makes the whole business profitable."[34] While technology companies may have been the most aggressive and transparent in their pursuit of a coerced labor pool, they were far from the sole beneficiaries. It was just a matter of time until archives also began to reap the rewards of men and women working their fingers to the bone in service of a truly *digital* revolution. Nothing would be the same.

Archives underwent something like a fever during the 1990s. The Culture Wars set the context for the decade, but Annette Gordon-Reed's seismic study of the lineage linking former US president Thomas Jefferson to the descendants of Sally Hemmings, a woman whom he enslaved on his plantation, put genealogy—especially that of Black people in the country—into a public spotlight not seen since the 1977 miniseries *Roots*.[35] Almost overnight, identity became heritage and vice versa. In those intervening years, another movement was afoot too. The Church of Jesus Christ of Latter-Day Saints embarked on a massive archival endeavor to publish its vast holdings of genealogical records—stored within a vault carved beneath a mountain range in Utah—online. The church successfully launched its first iteration of FamilySearch in 1999, and within days

33   "Men Behind Bars Operate Booming Computer Service," *Red Bank Daily Register*, December 11, 1975; "Inmate Typing Pool in Use: To Transcribe Confidential Data," *The Victoria Advocate*, April 21, 1985; Matt O'Connor, "Firms, Prisons Join to Unlock Labor Pool: Use of Inmates Becomes Big Business," *Chicago Tribune*, December 13, 1987.

34   Christian Parenti, "Making Prison Pay," *The Nation*, January 29, 1996, 12.

35   Annette Gordon-Reed, *Thomas Jefferson and Sally Hemings: An American Controversy* (Charlottesville: University Press of Virginia, 1997).

the site attracted millions of visitors, instantly making it not just the most visited website for archival records but one of the most popular sites on the web.[36] The digital database now provided in electronic form what the Church's hundreds of family history centers across the country and world had been offering for decades: a peek into the past. However, the scanned copies of birth records, marriage certificates, and Freedmen's Bank files were static images whose text could not be searched, prompting FamilySearch to turn towards a familiar source to enable the documents' searchability: the labor of incarcerated people. Beginning in the early 1990s, FamilySearch opened one of its family history centers at the Utah State Prison. By 2014, it operated four family centers in just that facility.[37] At Utah State Prison alone more than a million names are indexed every year. Due to the program's success in Utah, FamilySearch has found willing partners in nearby states, conscripting workers from Idaho and Arizona, and has expanded into Utah's county jail system.[38] The Mormon interest in the project stems from the church's performance of "saving ordinances" for deceased people who never subscribed to the Mormon religion. These posthumous rituals, the church claims, release the dead from their "spirit prison."[39] Save a record, save a soul. But participation by people in-

36   Erik Davis, "Databases of the Dead," *Wired*, July 1, 1999, https://www.wired.com/1999/07/mormons.

37   Brooke Adams and Jim Dalrymple, "Inside Job: Inmates Help Further Mormon Genealogy Work," *The Salt Lake Tribune*, April 2, 2014, https://archive.sltrib.com/article.php?id=57682631&itype=cmsid.

38   Jordan Moroz, "Inmates Find Purpose Indexing Vital Records," *The Daily Universe*, February 6, 2015, https://universe.byu.edu/2015/02/06/being-set-free-through-indexing-the-positive-change-its-had-on-prison-systems1; and Glen N. Greener, "Pioneers Are Now Found in Local Jails," *FamilySearch Blog*, August 26, 2015, https://www.familysearch.org/blog/en/pioneers-local-jails.

39   Heather Whittle Wrigley, "Prisoners Rescuing Prisoners: Indexing at Utah State Prison," The Church of Jesus Christ of Latter-Day Saints, October 28, 2011, https://www.churchofjesuschrist.org/church/news/prisoners-rescuing-prisoners-indexing-at-utah-state-prison.

side prison walls is more ambiguous. They receive no wages whatsoever for the work, as the church considers its indexing program to be voluntary in nature and open to any person, incarcerated or not, who wants to help download files from its site and "donate" time as an indexer.[40] The men and women who come to the prisons' family history centers do so on their own free will, so the church contends, and thereby redeem their own salvation; to process a file is to perform a penitence of sorts. Moreover, advocates of the program take care to highlight the church's non-profit status as evidence that FamilySearch draws no direct financial benefit from the labor it extracts. Be that as it may, the hundreds of national and state governments that partner with FamilySearch by sharing their records for indexing and digitization certainly save untold millions of dollars.[41] Latent in the justification for the program is the acceptance of exploitation so long as its fruits can be enjoyed for private as well as public consumption. Despite the prevalence of neoliberal economic and social policies, public works in this regard persist not in the laying of brick and mortar but in the indexing and transcription of public documents. In fact, millions of archival records have been made available by incarcerated labor—reproducing a system of labor that has not reached such extents since the New Deal.

It was the New Deal, in part, that paved the way for

40   Shane Bauer, "Your Family's Genealogical Records May Have Been Digitized by a Prisoner," *Mother Jones*, August 13, 2015, https://www.mother jones.com/politics/2015/08/mormon-church-prison-geneology-family-search.

41   The Church of Jesus Christ of Latter-Day Saints "NARA and FamilySearch to Place Major Segments of National Archives Documents Online," press release, October 23, 2007, http://newsroom.churchofjesuschrist.org/article/ nara-and-familysearch-to-place-major-segments-of-national-archives-documents-online; and "Archives - About - Testimonials," FamilySearch, accessed November 20, 2019, https://www.familysearch.org/records/archives/ web/about-testimonials.

the state's (near) monopoly on prison labor. As contempt for private profiteers—in banks and prisons alike—mounted during the early 1930s, US President Franklin Roosevelt's administration established the Prison Industries Reorganization Administration (PIRA) to study the landscape of labor across the country's jails and prisons. The administration concluded with a recommendation that each state, under its respective Department of Corrections, establish its own "prison industries" program to charter and oversee semi-private corporations capable of producing a profit for the state by selling goods to state agencies and non-profit organizations.[42] These programs persist to this day. In fact, during the late 1990s, Congress convened a hearing to consider the impact of prison industries on private sector competitors. John M. Palatiello, Executive Director of the Management Association for Private Photogrammetric Surveyors (MAPPS), testified that the programs were on the verge of virtually bankrupting the business of digital cartography. In particular, the federal government's prison industry, UNICOR, and prison industries from Texas, Florida, and Oregon made it nearly impossible for private firms to compete. He explained how Oregon's operation "has become so pervasive that two MAPPS member firms have shut down their efforts to market these services to State and county government, as they are unable to compete with the below market prices and labor rates charged by the prisons," leading Palatiello to plead with the Congressional chairperson: "Mr. Chairman, rehabilitation and retraining are commendable goals for prison programs, but at what price? 'Penal' institution and 'penitentiary' get their name from the Latin 'poenalis,' meaning pertaining to punishment. Who is being punished

42   Kim Gilmore, "Slavery and Prison—Understanding the Connections," in "Critical Resistance to the Prison-Industrial Complex," ed. Critical Resistance Publications Collective, special issue, *Social Justice* 27, no. 3 (Fall 2000): 199.

here, the inmates who have committed a crime against
society, or the employees of private GIS firms who play by
the rules?"[43]

Palatiello's pleas fell on deaf ears. In the twenty
years since his testimony, state prison industry programs
have only expanded. A core component of that expansion
has been the provision of services marketed specifically
towards archives. Indeed, nearly a quarter of state prison
industries and the federal government offer an array of
services for special collections, historical societies, public
libraries, museums, or any entity where an archive might
be found.[44] The Oklahoma Correctional Industries (OCI),
for instance, operates a project that digitizes school yearbooks at no cost to the participating schools.[45] The OCI
"Yearbook Project" stretches far beyond the borders of Oklahoma—providing high-quality digital copies to schools in
places as remote as Washington (Everett), South Dakota
(Redfield), and Maine (Madawaska) to name a few.[46] Incarcerated people working on the "Yearbook Project" earn

43   *Prison Industry Programs: Effects on Inmates, Law Abiding Workers, and
      Business: Hearing before the House of Representatives Subcommittee on
      Oversight and Investigations of the Committee on Education and the Work-
      force*, 105th Cong., 2nd session (1998), testimony of John Palatiello, Exec-
      utive Director of Management Association for Private Photogrammetric
      Surveyors, 185, http://hdl.handle.net/2027/pst.000043016037. Palatiello is
      incorrect on the etymology of "penitentiary." The word derives from the
      Latin word *paenitentia*, meaning "repentance." For a closer look at the first
      penitentiary in the United States, see Caleb Smith, "Harry Hawser's Fate:
      Eastern State Penitentiary and the Birth of Prison Literature," in *Buried
      Lives: Incarcerated in Early America*, ed. Michele Lise Tarter and Richard
      Bell (Athens: University of Georgia Press, 2012), 231–258.

44   Alexis Logsdon, "Ethical Digital Libraries and Prison Labor?"
      (Presentation delivered at the Digital Library Forum, Tampa, FL, October
      15, 2019), https://osf.io/w7xe3.

45   "Non-Destructive Scanning: Yearbook Project," Oklahoma Correctional
      Industries Sales, accessed November 21, 2019, http://www.ocisales.com/
      non-destructive-scanning.

46   Julie Muhlstein, "Oklahoma Prisoners' Project Digitizes Everett High Year-
      books," *The Daily Herald*, June 7, 2016, https://www.heraldnet.com/news/

anywhere between fourteen and forty-three cents per hour for their efforts.[47] Utah Correctional Industries sells a full suite of archival tools: file naming (three cents), optical character recognition (three cents), microfiche and microfilm (eight cents), 600dpi scans (ten cents), and the nebulously named "archiving" (seven dollars).[48] Worker wages in Utah slightly edge out those in Oklahoma, ranging from sixty cents to $1.75 an hour, which is more than the nothing Texas pays prisoners for the work they do digitizing, georeferencing, and converting file formats.[49] It is important to note that the prison industry companies must produce a profit. Massachusetts, for example, which has an incarcerated population a fraction the size of Texas's and a (relatively) small number of 489 people working in its prison industry, generated over $18 million dollars in revenue in 2017 through Massachusetts Correctional Industries.[50] While the state does not presently provide archival services in its catalogue, it, along with many other states, uses its prison industry program

oklahoma-prisoners-project-digitizes-everett-high-yearbooks; Shiloh Appel, "Redfield High School Yearbooks from 1946–1989 Now Digitalized," *Redfield Press*, October 17, 2018, https://redfieldpress.com/article/redfield-high-school-yearbooks-from-1946–1989-now-digitalized; Morgan Mitchell, "Madawaska School History Goes Digital," *Fiddlehead Focus*, April 13, 2019, https://fiddleheadfocus.com/2019/04/13/news/community/top-stories/madawaska-school-history-goes-digital.

47   "Prison Wages: Appendix," Prison Policy Initiative, last modified April 10, 2017, https://www.prisonpolicy.org/reports/wage_policies.html.

48   Utah Department of Administrative Services, Division of Purchasing, and General Services, "Contract no. UCI1869: Data Entry, Scanning, and Micrographic Services," contract with Utah Correctional Industries, September 19, 2016, accessed December 12, 2016, http://purchasing.utah.gov/uci/UCI1869.pdf.

49   "Prison Wages: Appendix," Prison Policy Initiative; "Geographic Information System (GIS) Data Conversion Services," Texas Correctional Industries, accessed November 20, 2019, http://www.tci.tdcj.state.tx.us/services/gis.aspx.

50   Massachusetts Department of Correction, *Department of Correction Annual Report 2017* (Boston, 2018), https://www.mass.gov/doc/doc-annual-report-2017.

to manufacture much of the furniture sold to public agencies and non-profit organizations in the Commonwealth, especially the massive school system.[51] States such as Virginia even require state-funded universities—an institution in which archives are embedded—to buy goods from that state's Correctional Enterprises.[52] Archivists detest the hackneyed 'dust' metaphor that mainstream news outlets and even academics repeat ad nauseum about dusty documents in a dusty basement. But this metaphor has a much more material and physical significance. A prisoner in Texas serving a life sentence and working without pay for Texas Correctional Industries vomited and nearly fainted after inhaling sawdust from the furniture shop, which likely manufactures the desks, chairs, and tables that reside in reading rooms in archives across the state.[53]

Supporters of prison industry programs partially justify them on the basis that incarcerated people develop skills they can market upon their release from prison. Yet no amount of skill can overcome the fact that most archives lack basic policies to prevent discrimination against formerly incarcerated people during the hiring process.[54] The prison, in this sense, constitutes the condition of possibility for archives. Incarcerated workers labor with little

---

51 "Reupholstering behind Bars: Massachusetts Prisoners Repair Auditorium Chairs at ARHS, ARMS," *The Graphic*, June 3, 2019, http://thegraphic.arps.org/2019/06/reupholstering-behind-bars-massachusetts-prisoners-repair-auditorium-chairs-at-arhs-and-arms.

52 Erik Truong, "Products of Prison Labor on Campus," *Fourth Estate*, February 25, 2018, http://gmufourthestate.com/2018/02/25/products-of-prison-labor-on-campus.

53 Jayson Hawkins, "Sentenced to Life in Prison—And a Job Making Furniture," *The Marshall Project*, September 7, 2017, https://www.themarshallproject.org/2017/09/07/sentenced-to-life-in-prison-and-a-job-making-furniture.

54 Jarrett M. Drake, "Diversity's Discontents: In Search of an Archive of the Oppressed," *Archives and Manuscripts* 47, no. 2 (2019): 275, https://doi.org/10.1080/01576895.2019.1570470.

to no pay to produce indices, transcriptions, and copies of the most common types of archival records. Access to the past is thus mediated through a class of persons trapped in it. What is more, this class also constructs the reference desks and research tables that reflect the power dynamics central to the subjugation of imprisoned people and those who visit them. Far from peripheral, archives, like many other sites that seem distant, in fact depend on the capture and coercion that occur in prisons throughout the country. As such, the archive-border and the prison-border might be best described not by their imperviousness but by their interdependency. The two institutions coexist as coefficients, ultimately umbilical in their sustenance.

Ending the Exchange

If, as I have argued, archives sustain their operations in part from the persistence of the prison, then it follows that archives must also be transfigured in the larger political project to dismantle the systems and sites rooted in racial subjugation and economic exploitation. Two current archives—neither of which names itself as such—exemplify what this work looks like. The first is A Living Chance, a project launched by the California Coalition for Women Prisoners that records, preserves, and publishes the narratives of women sentenced to death by incarceration, known euphemistically as life without parole (LWOP).[55] The project models a way to mobilize archival efforts in support of larger organizing campaigns aimed at reducing the size of the carceral state. In a space that reminds these women of their un-belonging, A Living Chance exemplifies ways to build what the historian Kelly Lytle Hernández calls the "rebel archive."[56] It does the work of writing insurgent

55   California Coalition for Women Prisoners, A Living Change: Storytelling to End Life without Parole, multimedia archive, accessed November 25, 2019, http://alivingchance.com.

historical (counter)narratives that propose alternative epistemologies. That this archive does not have "a place on a map," as it were, can be read as intentionally and strategically location-less; or, actually, location-full, a mode of mobility that itself crowds out the space of the prison in both analog and digital realms.

The second is the project Testif-i | Storytelling for Change. Also focusing on the impacts of incarceration on women and the families they lead, this archive elevates stories often absent from the litany of programs, projects, and funding provided for boys and men caught in the clutch of cages.[57] Like A Living Chance, Testif-i is grounded within an existing abolitionist organizing effort, A New Way of Life Reentry Project, that focuses on, among other issues, family reunification. By identifying a targeted topic such as family reunification, the archive thus uplifts women's experiences from a range of backgrounds, avoiding the perilous "prison reformer" refrain that ranks who most deserves care and relief. Whereas archives actively obsess over the preservation of genealogical and (some) bloodline connections, prisons function as a structural severance of those ties. What is particularly rebellious about Testif-i is that it goes beyond providing stories of these women, a radical act on its own, and also offers information about voting rights and a recent legislative change in California that can aid women returning to the outside in accessing employment, housing, and education.Testif-i is a testament to how archives can be deployed to resist and rupture the processes of un-belonging that prisons

---

56   Kelly Lytle Hernández, *City of Inmates: Conquest, Rebellion, and the Rise of Human Caging in Los Angeles, 1771–1965* (Chapel Hill: University of North Carolina Press, 2017), 4.

57   A New Way of Life Reentry Project, Testif-i | Storytelling for Change, accessed November 25, 2019, http://testif-i.com. See also Testif-i's "Restore Your Rights," http://testif-i.com/restore-your-rights.

perpetuate, producing what the sociologist Mimi Sheller might classify as "citizenship from below."[58]

Archives, of course, are far from unique in their material connection to cages. Incarcerated people in California fight on the frontlines against the recurrent and raging wildfires for two dollars a day.[59] Harvard, like Yale, also has a curious connection to cages. Its multi-billion-dollar endowment is bolstered by the university's investments into the prison-industrial complex.[60] Prisons also provide political currency for elections. The US Census counts incarcerated people as part of the municipalities in which they are incarcerated while forty-eight states prevent prisoners from voting, meaning that the largely white, rural towns in which prisons are often located receive outsized numerical influence in state and federal elections. The disenfranchisement from the political process prompted the 2018 strike organizers to include the restoration of voting rights as their tenth and final demand, given that wage theft persists in part due to the state's rendering of imprisoned people as civically dead, leading Derrick Washington, an incarcerated organizer, to characterize his status as a "slave of the state of Massachusetts."[61]

By stripping incarcerated people of democratic rights, prisons strive to make non-humans out of humans and non-citizens out of citizens, marking prisons as formative sites of un-belonging. On the other hand, archives keep

58   Mimi Sheller, *Citizenship from Below: Erotic Agency and Caribbean Freedom* (Durham, NC: Duke University Press, 2012).

59   Kamala Kelkar, "Incarcerated Women Risk Their Lives Fighting California Fires—Part of a Long History of Prison Labor," *San Francisco Bay View*, October 25, 2017, https://sfbayview.com/2017/10/incarcerated-women-risk-their-lives-fighting-california-fires-part-of-a-long-history-of-prison-labor.

60   The Harvard Prison Divestment Campaign, *The Harvard-To-Prison Pipeline Report* (Cambridge, MA, October 2019), https://harvardprison divest.org/the-harvard-to-prison-pipeline-report.

61   Dana Liebelson, "In Prison, and Fighting to Vote," *The Atlantic*, September 6, 2019, https://www.theatlantic.com/politics/archive/2019/09/when-prisoners-demand-voting-rights/597190.

custody of the constitutions, laws, and judicial records that govern a democratic society. The accessibility of the archive, so the argument goes, reflects the fact that citizens have the ability to contest their grievances on the bases of documents stored at archives. Without them, it is argued, citizens are reduced to subjects incapable of holding those in power accountable for their actions and misdeeds.[62] In this sense, archives and prisons inhabit an inverse relationship through the establishment of who does and, more importantly, who does not constitute legitimate subjects before the specter of the state. Thus, the change of the Library of Congress subject heading from "illegal aliens" to "noncitizens" reflects a more accurate summation of the penal logic: much like citizens must be made, so too must non-citizens.[63] The archive shapes the former; the prison proscribes the latter.

The tentacles of carcerality ensnare even the most remote of institutions. Because of the prison's pervasiveness, it is incumbent to imagine interventions that intentionally dislodge, disrupt, and offer insurgencies against the technologies of un-belonging that prisons in particular engender. Nobody belongs in prison, and it is past time that academics, archivists, and architects push boundaries to build the conditions to make a world without them possible. To do so commands an insurgent intentionality and an orientation to the work that, if practiced, brings us all a little closer to a more approximate version of freedom. That is the labor, and if done correctly, that is also the liberation.

---

62   See Randall C. Jimerson, *Archives Power: Memory, Accountability, and Social Justice* (Chicago: Society of American Archivists, 2009).

63   Jasmine Aguilera, "Another Word for 'Illegal Alien' at the Library of Congress: Contentious," *New York Times*, July 22, 2016, https://www.nytimes.com/2016/07/23/us/another-word-for-illegal-alien-at-the-library-of-congress-contentious.html.

Sable Elyse Smith, *Coloring Book 13*, 2018. Screen printing ink, oil pastel, and oil stick on paper, 60.25 x 56 inches. Courtesy of the artist; JTT, New York; and Carlos/Ishikawa, London.

Together, Pat and Judge Friendly ride the elevator upstairs to a big room with benches. Lots and lots of people are waiting.

"It is hard to wait," says Judge Friendly.

"There are many families here, so we hope that everyone brings something to read or quiet puzzles to work on."

What 10 things don't belong in this picture?

"NOTHING STIRRED IN THE AIR":
AFFECT, SEXUALITY, AND THE ARCHITECTURAL TERROR OF THE RACIAL STATE

STEPHEN DILLON

In the essay "Reflections on Being Buried Alive," Susan Rosenberg describes her first time entering the Lexington High Security Unit for Women. Rosenberg, a white lesbian and member of a number of feminist and anti-racist revolutionary groups, writes:

> We stood at the electronically controlled metal gate under the eye of one of eleven security cameras, surrounded by unidentified men in business suits. We were wearing newly issued beige short sleeved shirts, culottes, and plastic slippers. We were in handcuffs. An unidentified man had ordered us placed in restraints while walking from one end of the basement to the other. The lights were neon fluorescent burning and bright, and everything was snow white—walls, floors, ceilings. There was no sound except the humming of the lights, and nothing stirred in the air. Being there at that gate looking down the cell block made my ears ring, and my breath quicken.[1]

What is remarkable about Rosenberg's writing from Lexington is the way it elucidates the material banality of carceral violence. A snow-white room. The humming of lights. Eleven cameras. Dead air. Her ears rang and her breath quickened, not at the spectacle of what was before her, but at its normality, its routineness, its technological perfection. The unimaginable violence of the Lexington

1   Susan Rosenberg, "Reflections on Being Buried Alive," in *Cages of Steel: The Politics of Imprisonment in the United States*, ed. Ward Churchill and J.J. Vander Wall (Washington, DC: Maisonneuve Press, 1992), 128.

High Security Unit was cloaked in a new visual episteme. It was clean, quiet, modern, rational, and orderly—men in suits, burning lights, plastic slippers. Lexington helped inaugurate a variety of psychological and physical contortions of the mind and body that are now so routine they remain invisible. Confronting the logics behind the unit would necessitate an epistemology able to see the rationality and mundaneness of contemporary carceral terror and its reproduction in walls, floors, and ceilings.

The Lexington High Security Unit embodied a new type of penal rationality that, even once Lexington was shut down in 1988 after Amnesty International declared it "deliberately and gratuitously oppressive," has spread to over sixty prisons across the country and the world.[2] These "control units"—prisons within prisons—instituted a more permanent and more enduring form of solitary confinement and sensory deprivation, which would come to be called "super-maximum security" or "supermax" prisons in the mid-1980s.[3] In these units people are confined to 6' by 8' cells for twenty-three hours a day, often indefinitely. There are no congregate exercise, dining, or work opportunities; no religious services; no relief. Most prisoners in control units will never see the horizon or night sky; they will never smell fresh air, hear trees rustling in the evening wind; they will never touch another human being. Many prisoners have lived in these "breathing coffins" for decades.[4] Prison administrators argue that control units assist with the management, control, and security of peo-

2   Mary O'Melveny, "Portrait of a US Political Prison—The Lexington High Security Unit for Women," in Churchill and Vander Wall, *Cages of Steel*, 119.

3   See Jean Casella, James Ridgeway, Sarah Shourd, eds., *Hell Is a Very Small Place: Voices from Solitary Confinement* (New York: New Press, 2016); Alan Eladio Gómez, "Resisting Living Death at Marion Federal Penitentiary, 1972," *Radical History Review*, no. 96 (Fall 2006): 59; and Colin Dayan, "Due Process and Lethal Confinement," *South Atlantic Quarterly* 107, no. 3 (Summer 2008): 496.

4   Gómez, "Resisting Living Death at Marion Federal Penitentiary," 61.

ple who have been designated "violent" or "disruptive"—
people who pose a threat to the safety and security of traditional high-security facilities and whose "behavior can be
controlled only by separation, restricted movement, and
limited access to staff and other inmates."[5]

Anti-racist, feminist, and queer activists were subjected to this new form of carceral state violence before it
rose to dominance in the 1990s. We can turn to their writings from prison as a critique of how carceral space was
animated anew in the aftermath of the radical and revolutionary movements of the 1960s and 70s, as well as how, in
particular, it began to directly target the feelings, senses,
and affects of imprisoned people, which were understood
to be potentially insurgent by the racial state. New forms
of penal design thus targeted these feelings, senses, and
affects in the name of counter-insurgency. When Rosenberg
looked down the cellblock, she saw something she couldn't
yet describe—something prisoners continue to say is inde-
scribable. She knew something was coming. And what she
saw made her senses fail.

The Architecture of Counter-Insurgency

The first control unit in the United States emerged as a
direct response to the radical and revolutionary movements of the 1960s and 70s, which intensified anti-prison
activism both within and outside prison walls. This moment, which Alan Eladio Gómez calls "the prison rebellion
years," connected the organizing efforts of prisoners to the
underground and aboveground leftist movements sweep-
ing the country and world from Oakland, Cuba, China,
and Chile to Puerto Rico, Paris, Germany, and Angola.[6]

5   Jerry R. DeMaio, "If You Build It, They Will Come: The Threat of Over-
     classification in Wisconsin's Supermax Prison," *Wisconsin Law Review*
     (2001): 208.

In 1972, just one year after the uprising and massacre at Attica prison in New York, there were over 40 prison rebellions in the United States.[7] The prison became a key site of struggle in larger national and international struggles against racism, colonialism, and war. Activists involved in Civil Rights, Black Power, Indigenous, Chicano, feminist, Asian-American, anti-capitalist, and anti-imperialist organizing were frequently arrested and incarcerated for their work. This meant that radicals and revolutionaries were inside prisons in large numbers. In addition, imprisoned people began their own organizing aligned with the radical and revolutionary politics gaining local, national, and international power. Their work was also bolstered by a variety of organizations involved in Black, Chicano, Native American, and Puerto Rican liberation movements, which understood the prison as *the* space that would ignite a new struggle for revolutionary transformation in the era immediately after the Civil Rights reforms of the mid-1960s. While the goal of the prison in this period was to suffocate anti-racist revolution, its architecture was understood by imprisoned people as a key site of insurgent, and sometimes utopic, possibilities. Radical and revolutionary activists increasingly saw the prison as the core of the racial state and ending incarceration as a means to end US empire and, perhaps, the United States itself. The control unit was designed to render these revolutionary possibilities impossible, unthinkable, and insensate.

6   For an overview of this era, see Dan Berger, *Captive Nation: Black Prison Organizing in the Civil Rights Era* (Chapel Hill: University of North Carolina Press, 2014); Stephen Dillon, *Fugitive Life: The Queer Politics of the Prison State* (Durham, NC: Duke University Press, 2018); Heather Ann Thompson, *Blood in the Water: The Attica Prison Uprising of 1971 and Its Legacy* (New York: Pantheon Books, 2016); and Emily Thuma, *All Our Trials: Prisons, Policing, and the Feminist Fight to End Violence* (Urbana: University of Illinois Press, 2019).

7   Gómez, "Resisting Living Death at Marion Federal Penitentiary," 65. See also Tom Wicker, *A Time to Die: The Attica Prison Revolt* (Chicago: Haymarket Books, 2011).

AFFECT, SEXUALITY, AND THE ARCHITECTURAL
TERROR OF THE RACIAL STATE

In April of 1972, the Federal Bureau of Prisons (FBP) transferred over 100 prisoners involved in organizing and activist work around the country to Marion Federal Penitentiary in Southern Illinois.[8] By isolating "problem" inmates within one institution, the FBP sought to control prison activism by subjecting prisoners at Marion to a new regime of behavior modification: brainwashing, sensory deprivation, medication, and prolonged isolation.[9] James Bennett, the director of the FBP for most of the mid-twentieth century, believed that criminality was a biological, permanent, yet treatable disease. Under his direction, Marion became a research lab for psychiatrists at the Center for Crime, Delinquency, and Corrections at Southern Illinois University in Carbondale.[10] Designed to cure criminal deviants, programs at Marion attempted to change prisoners' behavior, beliefs, and thoughts. In response to this regime of punishment, prisoners wrote and submitted a report to the United Nations and began working with the American Civil Liberties Union, National Association for the Advancement of Colored People, and the People's Law Office in Chicago. Prisoner organizing at Marion peaked after a Chicano inmate was beaten by guards and the resultant formation of the Political Prisoners Liberation Front—a racially diverse organization that led a series of labor strikes and work stoppages that shut down entire sections of the prison. Marion's administration responded by beating and gassing organizers and confiscating their legal materials. What followed next would change incarceration models for the next four decades. Authorities isolated members of the

8   Gómez, "Resisting Living Death at Marion Federal Penitentiary," 59.
9   Bill Dunne, "The US Prison at Marion, Illinois: A Strategy of Oppression,"
     in Churchill and Vander Wall, *Cages of Steel*, 38–82.
10   Dunne, "The US Prison at Marion, Illinois," 63.

Political Prisoners Liberation Front in special cells called "steel boxcars."[11]

Despite discourses about security and safety that attempt to legitimate and naturalize solitary confinement, Ralph Arons, a former warden at Marion, articulated the goal of the control unit more honestly: "The purpose of the Marion Control Unit is to control revolutionary attitudes in the prison system and in the society at large."[12] Critically, the goal of the unit was to manage *not* revolutionary action but rather radical and revolutionary orientations and dispositions. The unit aimed to annihilate *feeling* revolutionary. Marion targeted the body but also the knowledge, senses, feelings, and affects that were seen as threats to the prison and the security of the racial state more broadly. The control unit was designed to inhibit and abolish the epistemological and affective formations of the Third World left that undermined the naturalness of the prison and the racial state. In addition, the effects of the unit were not only aimed at prisoners but also "society at large." Arons observed what imprisoned people and scholars of incarceration have argued for decades: the prison's power is not insulated from the free world. The prison's violence disparately and asymmetrically shapes the experience of freedom for all people. He argued that the control unit's abolition of feelings inside would also alter and eradicate feelings on the outside. It was designed to send a message to prisoners and free world activists alike: anti-racist and anti-imperialist forms of organizing would be met with new forms of punishment, a "prison within a prison," a space beyond human contact and concern. Rosenberg would come to call the control unit "existential death," like being "buried alive." Other captives described it as a "white tomb," like being "in the grave."

11   Dunne, "The US Prison at Marion, Illinois," 75.
12   Fay Dowker and Glenn Good, "The Proliferation of Control Unit Prisons in the United States," *Journal of Prisoners on Prisons* 4, no. 2 (1993): 5.

AFFECT, SEXUALITY, AND THE ARCHITECTURAL TERROR OF THE RACIAL STATE

Disappearing insurgent and rebellious people was a way to efface and erase the new ways of knowing, feeling, and sensing created by the many social movements of the period. In this way, we can understand the control unit as a new manifestation of carceral space—a regime of "living death"—that sought to manage what could be known, felt, and sensed. The unit attempted to repress, contain, and preempt the forms of disobedience and insurgency inherent in the structural position of the prisoner.[13] Under the logic of the prison, the prisoner is already rebellious—already trying escape whether through contraband, writing, reading, touching, speaking. Seeing the stars, smelling the first thaw, feeling the sun on one's face are radical acts of freedom as the prison seeks to render them impossible. In other words, the prison is a form of war against bodily, affective, and collective freedom in all its racialized, gendered, and sexual lines of flight.

Disappearing the Senses

The US Bureau of Prisons announced the completion of the Lexington High Security Unit, a 16-bed high security unit at the existing federal penitentiary in Lexington, Kentucky, in the fall of 1986. The unit, which was entirely self-contained and underground, was the first maximum-security prison designed specifically for women in the federal system. Although it could accommodate sixteen female prisoners, it never held more than seven at any one time.[14] Susan Rosenberg, Alejandrina Torres, and Silvia Baraldini were the unit's first and longest held prisoners. Rosenberg and Baraldini had been involved with new left, Black

13   Dylan Rodríguez, *Forced Passages: Imprisoned Radical Intellectuals and the US Prison Regime* (Minneapolis: University of Minnesota Press, 2006), 188.
14   Jan Susler, "The Women's High Security Unit in Lexington, KY," *Yale Journal of Law and Liberation* 1, no. 1 (1989): 35.

liberation, and Puerto Rican liberation movements, and both had been charged with helping Assata Shakur escape from prison. Torres was part of the Puerto Rican liberation movement and in 1983 was charged with conspiring to overthrow the US government along with Edwin Cortes, Jose Alberto Rodriguez, and Jose Luis Rodriguez. All three women understood themselves to be political prisoners, or in the case of Torres, a "prisoner of war."[15] All three women reported being told they were placed in the unit due to their political affiliations—though nowhere were the goals, rules, and regulations governing their captivity in the unit officially recorded. Rosenberg was told, "You know, you're going to die here."[16] And yet, a few weeks into their incarceration, the warden also told her and Torres, "You can be transferred out of here if you renounce your associations, affiliations, and your... uh, err, uh... views. You can have the privilege of living out your life in general population."[17] The countless intuitional and legal contradictions and inconsistencies shaping the inner operations of the unit worked in tandem with its spatial dimensions, which destroyed the ability of the women to think and feel.

The control unit at Lexington had no natural light, no fresh air, no color, no sound. It was an environment of total isolation designed to "demoralize the prisoners" and also their friends, families, communities, and movements in the free world.[18] Contact between control unit prisoners and general population prisoners was an affective threat with material consequences—a glance, a wave, a nod, a soft smile, the sharing of information were all terrifying

15   Gilda Zwerman, "Special Incapacitation: The Emergence of a New Correctional Facility for Women Political Prisoners," *Social Justice* 15, no. 1 (Spring 1988): 31–47.

16   Susan Rosenberg, *American Radical: A Political Prisoner in My Own Country* (New York: Citadel Press, 2011), 78.

17   Rosenberg, *American Radical*, 79.

18   O'Melveny, "Portrait of a US Political Prison," 113; and Susler, "The Women's High Security Unit in Lexington, KY," 35.

AFFECT, SEXUALITY, AND THE ARCHITECTURAL
TERROR OF THE RACIAL STATE

to the prison, all potentially destabilizing. In her memoir,
Rosenberg describes an event that apprehends the power
and danger of affective connections between imprisoned
people, which helps contextualize the sensory deprivation
and isolation central to the unit at Lexington.

After her sentencing, Rosenberg was taken to a transport plane. It was winter and the plane was surrounded
by prison guards, police, and US marshals armed with
shotguns and automatic rifles. According to Rosenberg,
there was:

> a line of sixty men standing perpendicular to the tail
> of the plane. All of them were dressed in short-sleeved
> khaki shirts and pants and blue prison-issue slip on
> sneakers. They were handcuffed and chained. It was
> below freezing. Many were stamping their feet, jump-
> ing up and down and blowing air that formed frost.
> Almost all of them were young African Americans.
> They had been removed from the plane so I could be
> put on.[19]

As Rosenberg looked at the Black men standing in the cold
surrounded by white men with weapons, "time stopped,"
images of slave ships, shackles, and the "middle passage"
flashed before her eyes. Her "sadness turned to fury"
and she thought of John Brown for strength. Rosenberg
recounts that despite the "divide between us" she felt
"unity with the men."[20] As she was dragged from a car to
the plane, she "found her voice" and yelled to them, "I'm
sorry these police made you stand in the cold, brothers! I'm
sorry! They didn't need to do that!" For a moment the guns,
the fear, the chains, the cold, the agony, the isolation halted
in a silence.

19   Rosenberg, *An American Radical*, 42–43.
20   Rosenberg, *An American Radical*, 43.

> A man on the line called back: "Aren't you Susan? I was with Ray at MCC!"
>
> "Yes!" I shouted. "I am!"
>
> He turned to the others and said, "She is ours! She's Black Liberation Army!"
>
> Another man called out: "Thank God for the BLA! Don't worry, baby! The more they fear you, the more they respect you!"
>
> "We will win one day!" I yelled. "Maybe not now, but one day!"
>
> A third man said, "I know about Assata! Don't worry!"[21]

After these gestures of humanity and solidarity, the guards and police pointed their weapons at Rosenberg and the men. They dragged her to the plane. Once on board, Rosenberg was surrounded by marshals "whose duty it was to ensure that no one communicated with me."[22]

The affective isolation that was enforced on the transport plane extended to the unit itself. Whenever the women were taken from the control unit to a part of the larger prison they were shackled at the ankles and handcuffed at the wrists with a black box over them. During these transfers, the entire prison was locked down so that contact between control unit prisoners and the general population was impossible. Only a single prisoner could have one outside visitor at any one time. Guards often scheduled these visits for the same time and then canceled visitations once family and loved ones had arrived after traveling long distances. Phone calls were only allowed twice a week in short intervals.[23] Human rights groups were often denied access to the control unit because another visitation was already under way.[24] The women were barred from the

21   Rosenberg, *An American Radical*, 44.

22   Rosenberg, *An American Radical*, 45.

23   Susler, "The Women's High Security Unit in Lexington, KY," 36.

work, education, and rehabilitation programs offered to most prisoners in the general population.[25] The only work available to them was folding army shorts for six-and-a-half hours a day in a small, poorly ventilated room that used to be a utility closet. These policies constituted a form of social death.[26]

Central to the control unit's extreme isolation was an expansive system of monitoring. Fluorescent lights were kept on at all times. Every inch of space, including the showers, was surveilled by cameras. To block the cameras, the women hung sheets over the shower entrance, or refused to shower, or showered fully clothed.[27] All activities and conversations were recorded in written logs. Reading material and written correspondence were limited and always screened. Amnesty International wrote that if a prisoner wanted to see anything outside, "one has to put one's eye close to the mesh to get a fuzzy view of the limited view [due to a perimeter fence] beyond."[28] This meant that one was watched but could not see. They were assigned prison-issued clothing designed to ensure they looked "feminine."[29] Anytime they left their cells or the outdoor "recreation" cage, the women were strip searched by male guards.[30] The tactical deployment of sexual violence and

24   National Prison Project of the ACLU Foundation, "Report on the High
        Security Unit for Women, Federal Correctional Institution, Lexington,
        Kentucky," *Social Justice* 15, no. 1 (Spring 1988): 3.
25   National Prison Project, "Report on the High Security Unit for Women," 1–2.
26   See O'Melveny, "Portrait of a US Political Prison."
27   Rod Morgan, "Report for Amnesty International, International Secretariat
        RE: High Security Unit (HSU) for Women at Lexington Federal Prison,
        Kentucky, USA," appendix to Amnesty International, International
        Secretariat, *United States of America: The High Security Unit, Lexington
        Federal Prison, Kentucky* (London: Amnesty International, 1988), 7.
28   Morgan, "Report for Amnesty International," 6.
29   Richard Korn, "The Effects of Confinement in the High Security Unit at
        Lexington," *Social Justice* 15, no. 1 (Spring 1988): 10.
30   Morgan, "Report for Amnesty International," 7–8.

the production of statist conceptions of gender colluded with isolation and sensory deprivation to turn insurgent women into shadows of their former selves. In other words, gender violence was a weapon in the racial state's war on anti-racist liberation movements—it worked to disappear the women as activists and political prisoners at the same time it enforced statist visions of gender that rendered them hyper-visible as women.

Gender Violence and the Politics of Truth

One of the challenges of mounting legal battles against the unit, and indeed of writing about it now, is that very little is actually known about its origins or the details of its daily operation. In 1988, Rosenberg and Baraldini filed a lawsuit *Baraldini v. Meese*, which alleged that the FBP violated their First, Eighth, and Fifth Amendment rights. Lawyers for the defendants and plaintiffs in the case failed to discover any documentation outlining the planning objectives or commissioning procedures for the unit. The judge in the case found it astounding that a prison that cost over one million dollars to build produced no documents on long-term planning objectives or goals. In its report on the unit, Amnesty International confirmed, "Nothing… is known about the origins or planning of HSU."[31] Most of what *is* known was either recorded by the women themselves or discovered in a handful of letters between Amnesty International and the Federal Bureau of Prisons (FBP).

A central question throughout the case was *why* Rosenberg, Baraldini, et al. were imprisoned in the control unit. Was the FBP holding them because they were dangerous flight risks or because they were revolutionaries? Based on statements from different directors of the FBP, the official position was that the Lexington Control unit

31   Morgan, "Report for Amnesty International," 5.

was intended to hold high-security prisoners subject to "rescue attempts by outside groups" and to confine "females who have serious histories of assaultive, escape-prone, or disruptive activity." The women and their lawyers contested the FBP, insisting instead that the unit was designed as a "behavioral experiment in the control and [possible] breaking of women who may have constituted a security risk, but more importantly, held firm political views to justify their criminal actions and response to imprisonment." They believed the unit was intended to hold women political prisoners, even though the federal government recognized no such category. In letters back to Amnesty International, all of the women's allegations are denied. Lexington, according to the FBP, simply operated according to "normal FBP policy."[32] This question was finally answered when, after two years of operation and three months before it was shut down, a federal judge ruled that the government had unlawfully placed the women in Lexington because it found their political beliefs "unacceptable."[33]

The lack of documentation about the control unit structured what could be known about the conditions endured by women held there. Even simple details, like the size of cells, could not be confirmed. No one disputed that each cell contained a bed, a metal toilet, a metal shelf, a chair, a small metal cabinet, a notice board, and a color television. But according to Rosenberg every cell was a different size, and the one she was detained in measured 8' by 10.' Lawyers for the FBP claimed that every single cell was 100 square feet. Other discrepancies concerning what was real and what was imaginary also existed and were a central part of the unit's goals. Part of the difficulty of knowing the reality of the unit was architectural—the

32   Morgan, "Report for Amnesty International," 5.
33   O'Melveny, "Portrait of a US Political Prison," 118.

physical attributes of the unit produced hallucinations, memory loss, blindness, and other forms of mental and physical debility and incapacity. The women held at Lexington experienced chronic rage; claustrophobia; heart palpitations; depression; dizziness; visual disturbances; weight loss; insomnia; panic attacks; obsessive thoughts about dying or being killed; the forced reliving of past forms of sexual violence caused by "humiliating and physically injurious body search procedures"; non-stop hallucinations; and fear of mental breakdown.[34] They became unhinged from reality—objects moved, walls melted, and space contracted.[35]

Working for Amnesty International, Dr. Richard Korn stated that the unit was deliberately designed "to undermine their physical and mental wellbeing, that is, to destroy them physically and psychologically."[36] In a report on the health effects of the control unit by the ACLU, one woman said, "I feel violated every minute of the day."[37] Amnesty International described the unit as "deliberately and gratuitously oppressive."[38] In the 1989 documentary *Through the Wire*, Rosenberg maintains, "I believe this is an experiment being conducted by the Justice Department to try and destroy political prisoners and to justify the most vile abuse to us as women and as human beings, and [to] justify it because we are political."[39] For Rosenberg,

---

34 Korn, "The Effects of Confinement in the High Security Unit at Lexington," 14–16; and Richard Korn, "Follow Up Report on the Effects of Confinement in the High Security Unit at Lexington," *Social Justice* 15, no. 1 (Spring 1988): 25–26.

35 Lisa Guenther, "Subjects Without a World? An Husserlian Analysis of Solitary Confinement," *Human Studies* 34 (2011): 259.

36 Korn, "The Effects of Confinement in the High Security Unit at Lexington," 16.

37 O'Melveny, "Portrait of a US Political Prison," 116.

38 O'Melveny, "Portrait of a US Political Prison," 119.

39 Nina Rosenblum, dir., *Through the Wire* (New York: Daedalus Productions and London: Amnesty International, 1989), quoted in Rodríguez, *Forced Passages*, 243.

the control unit at Lexington was a specifically gendered
penal technology, one that destroyed gendered subjectivities by deploying material yet incomprehensible regimes
of violence. The philosopher Lisa Guenther describes this
instrumentalization:

> In nonincarcerated space, walls tend to function
> as supports for embodied personhood: constitutive
> limits that carve places out of pure depth, both stabi-
> lizing and continuing the dynamics of stable embod-
> ied consciousness. Walls offer protection and privacy;
> they mediate between inner and outer space. But
> what is the experience of walls like in a supermax
> unit, where the walls have no windows and the door
> does not open from the inside—where the white or
> gray ganzfeld gives the eyes almost nothing to "gear"
> into, just a smooth homogeneous surface or, in older
> prisons, a pockmarked surface carved with traces of
> other inmates, now absent.[40]

At Lexington, the white walls stood to support not
"embodied personhood" but an intellectual and affective
nothingness aimed at undoing and erasing non-normative
ways of being, thinking, and identifying. Walls were weapons in the war between the racial state and the flow and
flight of rebellious affects. While one of the unit's stated
goals was to contain "escape-prone" inmates (even though
all three women discussed here had perfect disciplinary
prison records), one of its other goals was to discipline,
manage, and control non-normative epistemologies, feelings, and affects. Korn testifies to the deprivation of knowledge and affect that is central to the unit's function:

40   Lisa Guenther, *Solitary Confinement: Social Death and Its Afterlives*
      (Minneapolis: University of Minnesota Press, 2013), 182.

For three of these women, whose ideology is an intrinsic part of their identity, the denial of a personal library is an unmistakable assault on their identity and their right to decide who they are. It is, additionally, an attack which is in itself ideological and violative of their rights as intellectually free and mature human beings. For people such as these, their books are a statement of who they are—a statement made by minds which instruct and respect them. These books are, in effect, their only other society, their only unfailing friends, and to deny them this companionship is as perverse as it is vicious... The point cannot be stressed too much. The officials who imposed this limitation are not unsophisticated, illiterate, provincials in some penological backwater. They are nothing if not carefully deliberate, in every detail. They know what they are doing, and why they are doing it. The prisoners know it too—and their inability to convey their understanding of this intellectually murderous limitation is part of the pain of it.[41]

By segregating the women from the general population, from their families and loved ones, from the sociality of books, and even from their own minds, the unit created a type of social and civil death that not only delegitimized subjugated forms of knowledge and feeling but also sought to eradicate them. Through its design, the unit worked to discipline and erase forms of knowledge that epistemologically undermined the racial state, the naturalness of incarceration, and the dominance of new ways of ordering economic and social life under neoliberalism. Indeed, memory loss was intrinsic to living in the unit, which meant the women's histories, convictions, politics, and feelings dissolved into the concrete around them.

41   Korn, "The Effects of Confinement in the High Security Unit at Lexington," 11.

AFFECT, SEXUALITY, AND THE ARCHITECTURAL
TERROR OF THE RACIAL STATE

This deprivation is not only evident in how knowledge was regulated within the unit but also in how the FBP shaped what could be known about it. It is worth quoting the Deputy Director of the FBP in order to understand the epistemological dilemma represented by Lexington for the women and their lawyers as well as scholars studying the history and design of prisons:

> The unit is not a control unit nor a disciplinary unit and sensory deprivation is not practiced nor condoned there... We have ensured that inmates in the unit have access to educational, religious, medical and mental health programs and we have established a small industries program there... All walls in the unit have been painted in soft, earth-tone graphics... The industries work area is well ventilated and has an outside window... It is not true that the women in the unit are subject to systematic strip searches whenever they leave or enter their cells. In fact, they are not subject to any search, including pat search, when they enter or leave their cells. Likewise, it is untrue that male guards accompanying Ms. Torres to a medical examination were allowed to watch her undress through an open door. There is no formal nor informal policy wherein security searches of inmates at Lexington are designed to humiliate prisoners... I assure you that the prisoners at Lexington are being confined in a humane and proper manner.[42]

According to the FBP and the forms of knowledge produced by the racial state, the prisoner's world and truth was a fiction. The control unit was not a control unit; walls were

42   J. Michael Quinlan to Ian Martin, letter, June 12, 1987, appendix to Amnesty International, International Secretariat, *United States of America: The High Security Unit.*

not white but earth-toned; a closet was not a closet but an "industries work area"; pat-downs and strip searches were figments of the imagination. Reconstituting our understanding of the function and design of the prison means embracing prisoners' fictive facts, hallucinations, obsessions, fears, and theories produced in states of absolute panic.

Rosenberg countered state violence and terror with writing, "I found a new way to survive by reading and writing and thinking with purpose."[43] Her lawyer told her to write down the forms of violation, pain, and horror that were too numerous to catalog during their visits, were so unimaginable they could not be conveyed by speech, or were simply unspeakable. Rosenberg's lawyer framed this process as building an archive that would contradict the state's account of Lexington and thus would produce a different conception of the truth: "Write it down, *for the record*. I half believed that keeping a record was a futile effort, and she half believed it would be of use in fighting for justice, but that sentence became a signal between us, a way to reference acts of violence too difficult to discuss."[44] The "record" in this formulation was a legal account that could potentially contest the state in court, but it was also an alternative record of events that could live on in places and times beyond the state's determination of what is real and true. Writing became a way to document the violence of the law and the terror of the unit—violence that the law itself could not register and a bodily and affective terror that would exponentially expand in the coming decades.

When Rosenberg first entered the unit, she noted its architecture—the walls, the lights, the floor, the ceiling. Her first reaction was affective—her ears rang and her breath quickened. Later in the passage that opened this essay, she describes a haunting that takes hold of her, a haunting that challenges the control unit's exceptionality:

43   Rosenberg, *An American Radical*, 86.
44   Rosenberg, *An American Radical*, 87.

> As I looked down the hallway, my mind filled up
> with images of other places that were centers of
> human suffering: death rows in Huntsville, Angola,
> and Comstock; white cells and dead wings in West
> Germany where captured enemies of the state expe-
> rience the severest effects of isolation; the torture
> center on Robben Island in South Africa and the La
> Libertad in Uruguay. All these images rose and fell,
> my ideas and goals—my whole life—passed before
> me, I began to disassociate from myself.[45]

The unit at Lexington was part of a carceral assemblage
of containment and immobilization spanning time and
space—from the apartheid cages of South Africa, to the
execution chambers of the southern United States, to the
control unit prison that held members of the Red Army
Faction in West Germany.

We can add to Rosenberg's list—the sweat box of the
plantation, the train cars of the convict-lease system, the
prison at Guantanamo, the camp, the gulag, the basement
prisons in Chile and Argentina, the administrative segregation cells that "protect" transgender prisoners, the caged
children at the US–Mexico border and on and on and on
and on and on and on and on. Rosenberg alerts us to an
international continuum of carceral counter-insurgency
that sought to eliminate leftist radical and revolutionary
futures. Solitary confinement was used against the Black
freedom movement in South Africa and Alabama. It also
targeted anti-imperialist and anti-capitalist insurgencies
in Uruguay and West Germany. Yet, as Rosenberg and
so many people held in a state of living death make clear
everyday through their writing, art, and organizing, other
possibilities live on inside this carceral continuum that

45   Rosenberg, *An American Radical*, 76.

bleeds across the fictions of liberal conceptions of time and space. The global rise of solitary confinement as a form of counter-insurgency was a response to the threat of international movements in defense of racialized life, and thus, all life. While walls and lights and bars sought to render human beings dead to themselves and the world, these same people modeled a new world inside the terror of the old. Even as it tried, the prison's steel and concrete could not kill the senses, dreams, desires, affects, and feelings of its captives.

We can turn to a poem written by political prisoner Katya Komisaruk, "They Are Searching," to see the struggle between the architecture of the prison and the affects of the prisoner.[46] The poem was published in the 1990 edited collection *Hauling Up the Morning: Writings and Art by Political Prisoners and Prisoners of War in the US*, which includes writings by Rosenberg and other women held at Lexington as well as dozens of other US-based political prisoners. In June 1987, Komisaruk hiked onto Vandenberg Air Force Base and destroyed a NAVSTAR computer designed to guide nuclear missiles. She was sentenced to five years in federal prison. Written during her incarceration, "They are Searching" highlights the relationship between captive feelings and the failure of architectures of capture:

46   Katya Komisaruk, "They Are Searching," in *Hauling Up the Morning: Writings and Art by Political Prisoners and Prisoners of War in the US*, ed. Tim Blunk and Raymond Luc Levasseur (Trenton, NJ: The Red Sea Press, 1990), 32–33.

AFFECT, SEXUALITY, AND THE ARCHITECTURAL TERROR OF THE RACIAL STATE

The officer puts out his hand as I leave building C.
I give him my jacket
And he checks the pockets.

The walk to my housing unit
is one hundred yards.
I keep my back straight, my head high.
Cameras, mounted on poles and walls
relay my progress to monitoring screens in Building A.
More guards watch through the mirrored windows of
Building B
as I approach.

At the door, another cop waits to explore my jacket again.
Finishing, she gestures with one hand,
indicating that I should turn my back to her.
Now I stand with feet apart,
arms stretched horizontally.
As she explores my thighs,
I stare into the distance,
demanding that my feet stay
disinterested and undisturbed.

Do they think it is so easy to find?
Do they imagine I will surrender it,
simply because they force me to spread my legs
while they investigate?

Fools.
I've never hidden it.
I carry it openly all the time.
And their kind attentions simply make it larger.

Cameras, guards, and doors work together to keep this un-namable something from getting inside the prison. For the guards, it appears to be something visible and tactile—a weapon, a note, a cigarette. They are looking for some-thing to confiscate—something threatening, something whose presence could upset the security and stability of one of the most powerful institutions in human history. The jacket and the pocket are so threatening they must be checked twice. The search involves an assault—"they force me to spread my legs," "as she explores my thighs." In this scene of institutionalized sexual assault, the body itself is conceptualized as a site of rebelliousness or insur-gency that must be investigated, watched, and surren-dered. These routine moments of assault and surveil-lance are pedagogical performances—moments when the prison attempts to teach the prisoner the order of things. This includes an attempt at total dominion over the captive body. Like the routine strip and cavity searches at Lexington, this assault, Komisaruk makes clear, is also aimed at her feelings and beliefs. Yet she refuses to surren-der—"I keep my back straight, my head high." The assault and regulation only "make it larger." Komisaruk has some-thing that can't be seen or felt or taken. And one purpose of the poem, and of *Hauling Up the Morning* more broadly, is to make "it" contagious so the reader is touched by how Komisaruk is touched and moved by how she is moved to survive and resist. The book and the poem show how the prison can't contain the affects of the prisoner. The unnam-able "it" that ends the poem escapes the prison through the poem itself.

Through their writing, Komisaruk, Rosenberg, and imprisoned people generally reach out for connection that challenges their social death. They posit a relational-ity where there is only supposed to be antagonism—pris-oner or free, criminal or innocent, dead or alive. Rosenberg made clear that Lexington was a sign of things to come. In fact, once it was shut down, a similar high security unit for leftist women opened in Marianna, Florida.[47] The warnings embedded in Rosenberg and Komisaruk's writing embody what Avery Gordon calls "the prisoner's curse." As Gordon writes, "the curse delivers to you a vision of your own deathly existence laid bare." This is because the "prisoner's fate is always bound up with those of us who are not yet captured, regardless of whether this relation is acknowledged."[48] The prisoner's curse, for Gordon, is a type of subjugated knowledge that can alter the course of events. The prisoner's curse can send reality reeling in a direction no one expected, sending the time of progress to unimaginable places because it highlights the constitutive relationship between the prison and the free world—between imprisoned space and space we imagine to be imbued with freedom. As Rosenberg writes, "Our lack of freedom does affect how free you are. If we can be violated, so can you."[49] It is not enough to change the spatial politics of the prison—larger cells, bigger windows, longer chains. The prison itself must become unimaginable and the prisoner with it.

47   Susler, "The Women's High Security Unit in Lexington, KY," 40.
48   Avery F. Gordon, "Methodologies of Imprisonment," *PMLA* 123, no. 3 (May 2008): 652 and 655.
49   Linda Evans, Susan Rosenberg, and Laura Whitehorn, "Dykes and Fags Want to Know: Interview with Lesbian Political Prisoners by the Members of QUISP," in *Imprisoned Intellectuals: America's Political Prisoners Write on Life, Liberation, and Rebellion*, ed. Joy James (Lanham: Rowan and Littlefield Publishing, 2003), 270.

SABLE ELYSE SMITH

Scale and infrastructure are sometimes weapons. And language is both. Scale and infrastructure are sometimes weapons. And language is both. Scale and infrastructure are sometimes weapons. And language is both. Scale and infrastructure are sometimes weapons. And language is both. Scale and infrastructure are sometimes weapons. And language is both. Scale and infrastructure are sometimes weapons. And language is both. Scale and infrastructure are sometimes weapons. And language is both. Scale and infrastructure are sometimes weapons. And language is both. Scale and infrastructure are sometimes weapons. And language is both. Scale and infrastructure are sometimes weapons. And language is both. Scale and infrastructure are sometimes weapons. And language is both. Scale and infrastructure are sometimes weapons. And language is both. Scale and infrastructure are sometimes weapons. And language is both. Scale and infrastructure are sometimes weapons. And language is both. Scale and infrastructure are sometimes weapons. And language is both. Scale and infrastructure are sometimes weapons. And language is both. Scale and infrastructure are sometimes weapons. And language is both. Scale and infrastructure are sometimes weapons. And language is both. Scale and infrastructure are sometimes weapons. And language is both. Scale and infrastructure are sometimes weapons. And language is both. Scale and infrastructure are sometimes weapons. And language is both. Scale and infrastructure are sometimes weapons. And language is both. Scale and infrastructure are sometimes weapons. And language is both. Scale and infrastructure are sometimes weapons. And language is both. Scale and infrastructure are sometimes weapons. And language is both.

Sable Elyse Smith, *7666 Days*, 2017. Digital c-print, suede, artist frame, acrylic, 48 x 40 inches. Courtesy of the artist; JTT, New York; and Carlos/Ishikawa, London.

Sable Elyse Smith, *8031 Nights*, 2018. Digital c-print, suede, artist frame, 48 x 40 inches. Photograph by Charles Benton. Courtesy of the artist; JTT, New York; and Carlos/Ishikawa, London.

Sable Elyse Smith, *8031 Days*, 2018. Digital c-print, suede, artist frame, 48 x 40 inches. Photograph by Charles Benton. Courtesy of the artist; JTT, New York; and Carlos/Ishikawa, London.

Sable Elyse Smith, *8032 Days*, 2018. Digital c-print, suede, artist frame, 48 x 40 inches. Photograph by Charles Benton. Courtesy of the artist; JTT, New York; and Carlos/Ishikawa, London.

Sable Elyse Smith, *8033 Days*, 2018. Digital c-print, suede, artist frame, 48 x 40 inches. Photograph by Charles Benton. Courtesy of the artist; JTT, New York; and Carlos/Ishikawa, London.

Sable Elyse Smith, *8093 Days*, 2019. Digital c-print, suede, artist frame, 49 x 41 inches. Courtesy of the artist; JTT, New York; and Carlos/Ishikawa, London.

I spent most of 2019 in a cabin in the pathway of a fracked gas pipeline at Unist'ot'en Camp on Wet'suwet'en territory, *yintah*. This is not the first infrastructure to invade Wet'suwet'en lands. In 1913, the town of Smithers was built as a stop along the Grand Trunk Pacific Railway in British Columbia. Local Wet'suwet'en people were moved to the reservations, displaced as space was made for settlers on newly occupied land. Now, the territory is bisected by Highway 16, the Highway of Tears, an infrastructure known primarily for the number of Indigenous women who have gone missing and been murdered along it.

On January 7, 2019, militarized police raided the Gidimt'en Access Point, the territory neighboring Unist'ot'en Camp. Wet'suwet'en people were torn from their own lands, and land defenders arrested at gunpoint. The raid was a violent enforcement of a court injunction that prohibited Wet'suwet'en people from blocking access to the Coastal Gaslink Pipeline after the company failed to obtain consent for its project from the hereditary chiefs of five Wet'suwet'en clans.

The late Secwepemc land defender and theorist Art Manuel called the injunction a "legal billy club."[1] Along with a flood of bureaucracy, permit extensions, reports, and requests for waiver of environmental conditions, the state has weaponized Canadian law in order to subvert Indigenous autonomy and the right of Indigenous peoples (under the UN Declaration on the Rights of Indigenous Peoples and Wet'suwet'en law) to control the access to and use of their traditional territories. Injunctions are a tool of the state. They facilitate invasion and punish expressions of Indigenous sovereignty and autonomy. They are also built for industry: a 2019 Yellowhead Institute report found that, in Canada, 76 percent of injunctions filed against First Nations by corporations are granted, while the courts deny 81 percent of injunctions filed against corporations by First Nations.[2]

The criminalization of Indigenous land defense means that police arrest Indigenous people for living on and exercising sovereignty over their own lands. It means that police are called on to force Indigenous people to solve their "disputes" with companies that refuse to ask for consent in colonial courts. And, once in those courts, it means the odds are in the favor of industry. The legal system is rigged to facilitate land theft.

The police function as private security for the pipeline company, and after the raid on January 7, they set up a mobile detachment along the logging road that leads to the camp: the "Community Indus-

1   Arthur Manuel and Grand Chief Ronald Derrickson, *The Reconciliation Manifesto: Recovering the Land, Rebuilding the Economy* (Toronto: James Lorimer, 2017), 215.
2   Shiri Pasternak and Hayden King, *Land Back: A Yellowhead Institute Red Paper* (Toronto: Yellowhead Institute, 2019), https://redpaper.yellowhead institute.org/wp-content/uploads/2019/10/red-paper-report-final.pdf.

try Safety Office." The Royal Canadian Mounted Police (RCMP) patrolled the territory several times a day over the course of the next year, surveilling and harassing land defenders and clients of the Unist'ot'en Healing Center, who had returned to the territory to reconnect with the land and attempt to heal from colonial trauma.

On January 4, 2020—in response to an interlocutory injunction from the court allowing the continued invasion and occupation of Wet'suwet'en territory—Wet'suwet'en hereditary chiefs evicted Coastal GasLink workers. They blockaded the Gidimt'en Access Point and closed access to Unist'ot'en village. In response to this action, BC Premier John Horgan said the "rule of law applies," which signaled that RCMP enforcement of the injunction was imminent, regardless of the demands of the hereditary chiefs. The "rule of law" carries with it an implicit, genocidal drive. If injunctions are a "legal billy club," then the "rule of law" means that Indigenous people are to be beaten into submission. The law, and the RCMP arriving to enforce it, are conceived and exercised to quell the threat of Indigenous insurrection.

I remained at Gidimt'en Access Point to support and enforce the hereditary chiefs' eviction and to assert the jurisdiction of Wet'suwet'en people over their unceded territories. For a month, both Gidimt'en Access Point and Unist'ot'en village were free from industrial traffic and police patrols (although industry and RCMP continued their surveillance using helicopters, planes, and drones). On February 7, approximately seventy tactical officers (alongside helicopters, police dogs, assault rifles, and snipers) raided the camp again. They surrounded the makeshift watchtower and repurposed school bus where I observed the invasion along with three other Indigenous people. To be clear: RCMP arrived with seventy armed officers to remove four unarmed Indigenous land defenders from the territory. They pointed snipers at us. They put tactical teams on snowshoes to surround us in the woods. They used large machinery to rip apart the gate protecting the territory. They arrested the four of us, and we spent three nights in holding cells while police tried to push release conditions that would disallow us from returning to the territory. Three days later, three Unist'ot'en matriarchs, along with Indigenous supporters, were torn from their ancestral territories and arrested during a ceremony for missing and murdered Indigenous women and girls. The red dresses that were hung to hold the spirits of the women and girls were torn down; the ceremonial fire was extinguished by police.

When we enforce Wet'suwet'en law, we face police violence. Wet'suwet'en law requires a fundamentally anti-capitalist, anti-colonial reorganization of relations. Trespass was, and is, strictly prohibited. The Wet'suwet'en hereditary governance system relies on the responsibility of hereditary chiefs to protect and manage their house group territories so that those territories are able to continue to feed future generations of Wet'suwet'en people. Prior to colonization, trespass and unauthorized harvesting by a neighboring house group territory had deadly consequences, as trespassers were literally taking food from the mouths of the children and grandchildren of chiefs. Trespass was punishable by death, and Wet'suwet'en protocols forbade the trespasser's family from exacting retribution or revenge for the sanctioned death of their relative. Wet'suwet'en law has always been, first and foremost, about the protection of the land and the survival of Wet'suwet'en people. Wet'suwet'en people are no longer allowed to enforce their laws in these ways, and the application of injunctions and the deployment of police have made new strategies to protect their territories illegal under Canadian law.

When contemporary infrastructures of invasion trespass on Wet'suwet'en territories, they threaten the ability of Indigenous people to feed themselves and to live on their lands. Dark House *yintah* is overrun with pipeline employees, private security, and police. There is a man camp in the middle of the main moose habitat. Hunting and trapping have been made impossible. The pipeline right-of-way is slated to run through a number of berry patches and medicine gardens. Protecting these sites has been criminalized. This is part of a long history of criminalizing Indigenous survival and cultural practice, from the outlawing of fishing weirs for Wet'suwet'en people in the early twentieth century, to the potlatch ban that effectively criminalized Indigenous law, to the current fight for Indigenous survival. Not only are pipeline infrastructures invasive, but the Canadian state's use of injunctions as a method of Indian removal makes these infrastructures carceral as well. Land defense is a pipeline to prison.

The response to the raids on Wet'suwet'en territory has been immense. Across the country, Indigenous nations and non-Indigenous communities blocked railways and highways, occupied ports and ferry terminals, paralyzed the Canadian economy under the slogans "Shut Down Canada," "Land Back," and "Reconciliation Is Dead." This collective response has condensed my research questions into a series of memes. (Are Indigenous youth doing better research than me?) But it has also provided the space to reflect on the nature of Indigenous resistance and solidarity.

Instead of focusing on the Coastal GasLink pipeline alone, or on oil and gas infrastructure more broadly, responses to the Wet'suwet'en invasion have targeted all major Canadian infrastructures. They have targeted Canada itself, and they have shut it down. The discourse has pivoted from a pipeline fight understood and waged on environmentalist terms to a nation-wide discussion about the jurisdiction of hereditary chiefs, the application of Indigenous rights and title, and the contested and fragile nature of state sovereignty given the long history of violent colonization, illegal settlement, and occupation. Statements of solidarity emerged to support rail blockades that recognized the role of the Canadian Pacific Railway (CPR) in earlier colonial invasions of Indigenous territory. The Chinese Canadian National Council chapter in Toronto linked CPR's role in the colonization of Indigenous peoples to the violence suffered by Chinese workers while building the railway and offered support and solidarity founded on a shared history of colonial harm. These responses to the invasion of Wet'suwet'en territory recognize the role of transportation infrastructures as tools of settler colonial invasion.

The communities of solidarity that formed in the wake of recent incursions encourage healthier relations with each other, with the land, and with our other-than-human relations. In Victoria, for example, Indigenous youth and non-Indigenous supporters occupied the legislature steps for fifteen days, and organizers across Turtle Island worked together to reclaim Indigenous spaces and push back against industrial invasions on Wet'suwet'en lands. The fight is not over, and Coastal GasLink continues to push through construction without Wet'suwet'en consent. But the relations built and strengthened through this movement are built to outlast this colonial juggernaut, to see us through to a just and sustainable future on our lands.

Remember this feeling. On the day of the eviction, the chiefs met and decided it was time. They put on their blankets, drummed, told stories by the fire. The last worker left the territory. We could all breathe relief and sleep soundly knowing there were no violent men creeping behind us or occupying the land.

The moose came back.

After Freda served the eviction notice, she saw three moose on her way back home beside the Wedzin Kwah. There are tracks everywhere. The animals are celebrating. This is their *yintah*. Several weeks later, we harvest a young bull moose on Gidimt'en territory. I help process it and haul a hindquarter 5 kilometers up the road, over the fallen trees protecting Gidimt'en Access Point. We send some meat to the head chief of the territory; the rest is shared between the camps—for the first time in a year it is possible to feed ourselves from the land.

The moose offer themselves, again.

There is balance.

We set up a canvas tent in the middle of their empty man camp. In the morning, the sunrise is brilliant, and we stand between the mountain and the sun in a place where Wet'suwet'en and Gitxsan warriors once readied themselves for battle, once hastily made weapons and tools, once rested before crossing the mountain pass—in a place where herds of caribou flowed on migration routes now lost.

This route, the Kweese trail, tells a war story that is not mine to tell. But I can say that it goes back to a time before the invaders, before the occupiers. When the Wet'suwet'en went to war on the coast, they brought back stories and crests. It is a part of who they are as people, part of their *kungax* (stories/history).

This trail has been used every year since, as the moose migrate down from the mountains toward the river. And so their return also marks a victory; there has been a war against our animal relatives too. They walk the ancient trails on pathways of older wars. They are with us, as they always have been.

"We're doing this for you, moose," Freda says on the way back from serving the eviction. And they reciprocate in turn—meat for the winter, meat for the feast, a relationship restored.

—Anne Spice, "Pipelines to Prison," April 2020

Lily, a Gidimt'en youth, waits for moose stew cooked on a wood stove. Credit: Michael Toledano.

Wedzin Kwah River, headwaters of Wet'suwet'en territory
and the boundary between Unist'ot'en and Gidimt'en
territories. Credit: Michael Toledano.

Red dresses suspended on the bridge leading to Unist'ot'en territory in honor of Missing and Murdered Indigenous Women. Credit: Michael Toledano.

Salmon hangs in a smokehouse at the Gidimt'en Access Point. Credit: Michael Toledano.

Freda Huson, Chief Howilhkat and spokesperson for the Unist'ot'en. Credit: Michael Toledano.

FIGHTING INVASIVE INFRASTRUCTURES: INDIGENOUS RELATIONS AGAINST PIPELINES

ANNE SPICE

Critical infrastructure refers to processes, systems, facilities, technologies, networks, assets, and services essential to the health, safety, security, or economic well-being of Canadians and the effective functioning of government... Disruptions of critical infrastructure could result in catastrophic loss of life, adverse economic effects, and significant harm to public confidence.[1]

In Unist'ot'en territory in northern British Columbia, Canada, clan members of the Wet'suwet'en people have built a permanent encampment in the pathway of numerous potential and proposed pipelines. In response to the characterization of these pipeline projects as "critical infrastructure," the camp's spokesperson, Freda Huson, notes that the pipelines were proposed through the clan's best berry patches. By resisting pipeline construction, she explains, "What we're doing here is protecting *our* critical infrastructure."[2] The language game of the response inverts the promise and inevitability of settler infrastructures but does not replace them with a network that works within the same epistemological and ontological relations

This piece originally appeared in "Indigenous Resurgence, Decolonization, and Movements for Environmental Justice," ed. Jaskiran Dhillon, special issue, *Environment and Society: Advances in Research* 9, no. 1 (September 2018): 40–56.

1   Public Safety Canada, *National Strategy for Critical Infrastructure* (Ottawa: Government of Canada, 2009), 2.

2   See Freda Huson in Al Jazeera's documentary video: AJ+, "Unist'ot'en Camp: Holding Their Ground Against Oil and Gas Pipelines," YouTube, November 18, 2015, https://www.youtube.com/watch?v=5qUw3bqIHks.

to land and kin. When I asked Freda to describe the difference between industry conceptions of critical infrastructure and the infrastructures that sustain Indigenous life on Unist'ot'en *yintah* (territory), she told me this:

> So industry and government always talk about critical infrastructure, and *their critical infrastructure is making money, and using destructive projects to make that money*, and they go by any means necessary to make that happen... So for us, our critical infrastructure is the clean drinking water, and the very water that the salmon spawn in, and they go back downstream and four years, come back. That salmon is our food source, it's our main staple food. That's one of our critical infrastructures. And there's berries that are our critical infrastructure, because the berries not only feed us, they also feed the bears, and the salmon also don't just feed us, they feed the bears. And each and every one of those are all connected, and without each other, we wouldn't survive on this planet... For example, the bears will eat the berries and they'll drop it, and the waste that comes out of the bear, it's got seeds in it, so that germinates and we get more berries. We need the bears in order to keep producing our berries, and same with the salmon. The bears eat the salmon as well, because once the salmon spawn, they end up dying anyways, and that becomes food for the bears, so it's not being wasted. All of that is part of the system that our people depend on, and *that whole cycle and system is our critical infrastructure*, and that's what we're trying to protect, an infrastructure that we depend on. And industry and government are pushing these projects that would destroy that critical infrastructure, most important to our people.[3]

Here, Freda Huson appropriates the term "critical infrastructure" to index the interconnected networks of human and other-than-human beings that sustain Indigenous life in mutual relation. This network stands in stark contrast to the critical infrastructures of government and industry—infrastructures that are meant to destroy Indigenous life to make way for capitalist expansion. By contrasting these two meanings under one term, she brings attention to the underlying driving force of industrial infrastructure, exposing the lie that these projects are creative/productive and instead insisting that they are regressive/destructive and embedded in a capitalist system that is fundamentally at odds with the cycles and systems that make Indigenous survival possible.

Infrastructure vis-à-vis Settler Colonialism

How, then, can an anthropology of infrastructure address the radical vision of Indigenous resistance to settler infrastructures? Brian Larkin defines infrastructures as:

> Built networks that facilitate the flow of goods, people, or ideas and allow for their exchange over space. As physical forms they shape the nature of a network, the speed and direction of its movement, its temporalities, and its vulnerability to breakdown. They comprise the architecture for circulation, literally providing the undergirding of modern societies, and they generate the ambient environment of everyday life.[4]

3   Emphasis added. See Anne Spice, "Heal the People, Heal the Land: An Interview with Freda Huson," in *Standing with Standing Rock: Voices from the #NoDAPL Movement*, ed. Jaskiran Dhillon and Nick Estes (Minneapolis: University of Minnesota Press, 2019).
4   Brian Larkin, "The Politics and Poetics of Infrastructure," *Annual Review of Anthropology* 42 (October 2013): 328.

Larkin advocates for a systems analysis of infrastructures and stresses that infrastructures are networks that cannot always be reduced to the technologies or materials that make them up: "infrastructures are matter that enable the movement of other matter... They are things and also the relation between things."[5] As such, infrastructures "create the grounds" of operation for other objects. Looking at infrastructures as systems, Larkin argues, allows us to attend to how the definition of an *assemblage as infrastructure* works to categorize the world. This act of definition "comprises a cultural analytic that highlights the epistemological and political commitments involved in selecting what one sees as infrastructural (and thus causal) and what one leaves out."[6] As the Canadian government's definition of "critical infrastructure" above makes clear, these political commitments may come into conflict, as infrastructures are proposed across territories that Indigenous peoples have never surrendered to the Canadian state. By linking an anthropology of infrastructure, settler colonial studies, and critical Indigenous studies, it is possible to understand the emergence of "critical infrastructure" as a settler colonial technology of governance and expropriation in lands now claimed by Canada.

An anthropology attentive to settler colonial power relations must consider not only "our" analytic categories (as anthropologists), but also the categories that wield and carry the authority (and violence) of the settler state. The government mobilizes the language of "critical infrastructure" to transform oil and gas infrastructures from industry projects into crucial matters of national interest. That authority is buoyed further by the genealogy of the concept of infrastructure itself, which Larkin shows is the genealogical descendant of Enlightenment ideas about modernity and progress. While the categorization of

5   Larkin, "The Politics and Poetics of Infrastructure," 329.
6   Larkin, "The Politics and Poetics of Infrastructure," 330.

oil and gas technologies as "critical infrastructure" is a relatively recent move, the discursive positioning of infrastructure as a gateway to a modern future has been used in state-building projects around the world for some time now. The conflict over oil and gas infrastructures, however, is more than a disagreement about what "counts" as infrastructure and what does not. Embedded in Larkin's definition of infrastructure is a tacit assumption that infrastructures, as "things and also the relation between things," are inanimate, are not alive. Freda Huson calls attention to the salmon, the berries, and the bears that form "our critical infrastructure." This living network is not an assemblage of "things and relations between things" *but a set of relations and things between relations*. These are relations that require caretaking, that Indigenous peoples are accountable to. And they are relations that are built through the agency of not only humans but also other-than-human kin. The bears and the salmon create and maintain the assemblage as much as (or more than) humans do. Infrastructure, then, attempts but fails to capture the agentive and social network through which Indigenous life is produced.[7] These assemblages exist whether or not they are framed or captured by anthropological theory.

The comparison between oil and gas infrastructures and Indigenous assemblages, however, helps to illuminate how the binaries of civilized/savage and culture/nature continue to operate within anthropological theory to code the built environment of "modern societies" as a mark of progress and a space of political reckoning while obscuring the Indigenous relations these infrastructures attempt

7   These productive networks are better described by Ruth Wilson Gilmore's concept "infrastructures of feeling." Asking how structures of feeling are produced and relations rearranged, she suggests that the Black Radical Tradition and other revolutionary knowledges are formed and maintained through connections that arc toward freedom and challenge the structures of racial capitalism.

to replace. If the infrastructural is what is seen as causal, and the definition of the infrastructural does not capture Indigenous assemblages that sustain life, then what do we make of the causal force of other-than-human relations (the water, the bears, the berries, the salmon)? Put another way, how do Indigenous peoples mobilize relational systems—or how are Indigenous peoples mobilized by commitments to these systems—against oil and gas infrastructures when these are naturalized as the "ambient environment of everyday life?" To answer these questions, I make two central assertions. First: the characterization of oil and gas pipelines as "critical infrastructures" constitutes a form of settler colonial invasion, and second: Indigenous resistance to oil and gas infrastructures, through suspension, disruption, and blockages, protect our relations against the violence of settler colonial invasion and open alternatives for living in good relation to our territories.

Field Insights: Critical Infrastructure

I visited Unist'ot'en Camp for the first time in the summer of 2015. I responded to their call for support on the ground after increased industry pressure and police presence threatened to breach the borders of their territory to begin construction of pipelines on their land. The atmosphere at the camp was tense, in part because the stakes of participation in Indigenous resistance to pipelines were both raised and unclear. For the first few days, I sat by the fire alone, feeling the distrust and fear in the gaze of the Indigenous peoples gathered. In a matter of weeks, these people would grow to be my dearest friends, but in those first tense and heated days they could not afford to trust a stranger. In May of that year, the Canadian legislature had passed Bill C-51, which redefined "activity that undermines the security of Canada" as "any activity... if it undermines the sovereignty, security, or territorial integrity of Canada or the lives or the security of the people of Canada."[8] Activities explicitly listed include "interference with the capacity of the Government of Canada in relation to intelligence, defense, border operations, public safety, the administration of justice, diplomatic or consular relations, or the economic or financial stability of Canada," "terrorism," and "interference with *critical infrastructure*." An emergent category for the governance of crisis, the Canadian government defines critical infrastructure as "the processes, systems, facilities, technologies, networks, assets, and services essential to the health, safety, security or economic well-being of Canadians and the effective functioning of the government."[9] The United States operates under a similar definition of critical infrastructure as "systems and assets, whether physical or virtual, so vital to the United States that the incapacity or destruction of such systems and assets would have a debilitating impact on security, national economic security, national public health or safety, or any combination of those matters."[10] Canada and the United States also coordinate to protect and maintain cross-border critical infrastructures that facilitate the flow of goods, capital, and people between the two countries. Because the discourse of critical infrastructure is tightly linked to one of "national security" as well as one of "economic well-being," there is discursive and legal space open for an understanding of oil and gas pipelines as critical infrastructure because of the economic reliance of both the United States and Canada on revenue from

8   Bill C-51, *Anti-Terrorism Act*, 2nd sess., 41st Parl., 2015 (Can.), http://www.parl.gc.ca/HousePublications/Publication.aspx?Language=E&Mode=1&DocId=7965854.

9   Public Safety Canada, *National Strategy for Critical Infrastructure*, 2.

10   Barack Obama, "Directive on Critical Infrastructure Security and Resilience, February 12, 2013," Presidential Policy Directive No. 21, in *Public Papers of the Presidents: Barack Obama, 2009–2017*, 16 vols. (Washington, DC: Government Printing Office, 2018) 9:106–9:115.

fossil fuels. Threats to pipeline projects, then, can be cast as threats to national (economic) security, and these definitions of critical infrastructure make it possible to place resistance to fossil fuels in the same category as domestic terrorism. Despite the fact that the reoccupation of traditional territory at Unist'ot'en Camp has always been peaceful, supporters in 2015 worried that they could be cast as terrorists simply by helping Unist'ot'en people to re-establish a home on the territory they have cared for for thousands of years.

This concern was amplified by the apparent coordination between oil and gas industry personnel and police. Supporters on their way to Unist'ot'en Camp were surveilled; police checkpoints stopped cars on the logging road and issued tickets for broken taillights and cracks in windshields. In between police visits meant to intimidate supporters, industry executives attempted to "negotiate" entry onto Unist'ot'en territory. These tactics mirrored the industry-police collaboration made clear in a leaked report from the Royal Canadian Mounted Police (RCMP) Critical Infrastructure Intelligence Assessment Team titled *Criminal Threats to the Canadian Petroleum Industry*.[11] The report's key findings draw attention to "a growing, highly organized and well-financed, anti-Canadian petroleum movement, that consists of peaceful activists, militants, and violent extremists, who are opposed to society's reliance on fossil fuels," and the capacity of "violent anti-petroleum extremists" to "engage in criminal activity to promote their anti-petroleum ideology."[12] The report's dismissal of environmental concerns with climate change and environmental destruction as "anti-petroleum ideology" is matched with an uncritical ventriloquism of indus-

11   Royal Canadian Mounted Police (RCMP), *Criminal Threats to the Canadian Petroleum Industry* (Ottawa: Critical Infrastructure Intelligence Assessments, 2014).

12   RCMP, *Criminal Threats to the Canadian Petroleum Industry*, 1.

try statements and concerns. The report is particularly concerned with "violent aboriginal [sic] extremists," and their ability to garner wide national and international support for actions against oil and gas incursions into Indigenous territories. An unmarked binary operates throughout the report: privatized oil and gas technologies and pipelines are "critical infrastructures" in need of increased securitization and protection, while protection of Indigenous lands and ecologies is extremist ideology.

In the lands now occupied by Canada, the state's approach to Indigenous protest has shifted under Prime Minister Justin Trudeau's government, which has fully embraced the politics of recognition with its accompanying reconciliation pageantry. On National Aboriginal Day in 2016, the Trudeau government released a statement on the government's approach to Indigenous peoples, saying: "No relationship is more important to our government and to Canada than the one with Indigenous peoples. Today, we reaffirm our government's commitment to a renewed nation-to-nation relationship between Canada and Indigenous peoples, one based on the recognition of rights, respect, trust, cooperation, and partnership."[13] Despite these statements of "recognition," Indigenous peoples remain in a deeply subordinated relationship to Canada, and political claims to land and self-governance are repeatedly squashed in favor of cultural exchange.[14] The Prime Minister's statement of recognition itself embodies this by reciting the language of a nation-to-nation relationship as the route to reconciliation but ending with the facile suggestion that reconciliation can be practiced by

13   Justin Trudeau, "Statement by the Prime Minister of Canada on National Aboriginal Day," press release, June 21, 2016, https://pm.gc.ca/eng/news/2016/06/21/statement-prime-minister-canada-national-aboriginal-day.

14   Glen Sean Coulthard, *Red Skin, White Masks: Rejecting the Colonial Politics of Recognition* (Minneapolis: University of Minnesota Press, 2014); and Audra Simpson, *Mohawk Interruptus: Political Life across the Borders of Settler States* (Durham, NC: Duke University Press, 2014).

Canadians reading more books by Indigenous authors: "I invite you to join the #IndigenousReads campaign to help raise awareness and understanding through shared culture and stories and encourage steps toward reconciliation with Indigenous peoples."[15]

While the government shifts the focus to "shared culture and stories" and away from Indigenous claims to land and sovereignty, oil and gas infrastructures have continued to operate as emblems of national progress and resource wealth. Resource extraction is coded as "critical" to national well-being and is normalized as unavoidable common sense. While the veneer of cooperation and negotiation has thickened under Trudeau, the underlying approach to the oil and gas industry has remained consistent with past governments. In the Speech from the Throne presented by Stephen Harper's government in 2013, the Government of Canada highlighted the role of resource extraction in Canada's future: "Canada's energy reserves are vast—sufficient to fuel our growing economy and supply international customers for generations to come... A lack of key infrastructure threatens to strand these resources at a time when global demand for Canadian energy is soaring... Canada's natural wealth is our national inheritance."[16]

In a continuation of this approach to oil and gas, Justin Trudeau gave the keynote speech to a meeting of oil and gas executives in Houston, Texas, noting that "no country would find 173 billion barrels of oil in the ground and just leave them there."[17] His speech was met with a standing ovation. The naturalization of oil and gas extrac-

15   Trudeau, "Statement by the Prime Minister of Canada on National Aboriginal Day."

16   Government of Canada, "Speech from the Throne to open the Second Session Forty First Parliament of Canada," October 16, 2013, Parlinfo, Parliament of Canada, transcript, https://lop.parl.ca/sites/ParlInfo/default/en_CA/Parliament/procedure/throneSpeech/speech412.

17   Jeremy Berke, "'No Country Would Find 173 Billion Barrels of Oil in the

tion and the securitization of pipelines as "critical infrastructures" serve to link industry profits to national security, criminalizing Indigenous dissent and recasting destructive infrastructure projects as natural outgrowths of the settler state. Given the use of the term "critical infrastructure" to legitimize extractive projects that have not received the free, prior, and informed consent of Indigenous nations guaranteed under United Nations Declaration on the Rights of Indigenous Peoples, the intersections between official state definitions of "infrastructure" and the tactics and technologies of settler colonialism merit further explanation.[18]

Invasive Infrastructures

This essay takes up Patrick Wolfe's assertion that settler colonial "invasion is a structure not an event" and turns to one of invasion's contemporary material forms—oil and gas infrastructure.[19] In North America the expansion of oil and gas networks is tightly linked to the continued displacement, pacification, and expropriation of unceded and Treaty-guaranteed lands historically inhabited and cared for by Indigenous peoples. Pipelines, like other modern infrastructures, are not events, but they are event-ful: rooted in a settler future, they enable a material transit of empire, and this movement is hailed as an inevitable and necessary pathway to progress.[20] Pipelines become a key link between the expropriation of Indigenous

Ground and Just Leave Them': Justin Trudeau Gets a Standing Ovation at an Energy Conference in Texas," *Business Insider*, March 10, 2017, http://www.businessinsider.com/trudeau-gets-a-standing-ovation-at-energy-industry-conference-oil-gas-2017-3.

18   UN General Assembly, Resolution 61/295, United Nations Declaration on the Rights of Indigenous Peoples, A/RES/61/295 (September 13, 2007), http://www.un.org/esa/socdev/unpfii/documents/DRIPS_en.pdf.

19   Patrick Wolfe, "Settler Colonialism and the Elimination of the Native," *Journal of Genocide Research* 8, no. 4 (2006): 388.

homelands and industrial expansion, environmental crisis, and imperialist war. Oil and gas flow out of occupied Indigenous territories and fuel the maintenance of environmentally and socially devastating ways of life. Despite this imperial "transit," settler state discourse imagines "critical infrastructures" as assemblages that serve the Canadian public, need protection, and reimagine the social good in terms of the aggregate economy.[21] Yet as Unist'ot'en spokesperson Freda Huson makes clear, Indigenous resistance to "critical infrastructures" contests the very category of infrastructure itself, asserting alternative ontological and epistemological modes of relating to assemblages that move matter and sustain life.

As the "undergirding of modern societies," critical infrastructures are infrastructures of invasion.[22] By facilitating capitalist exchange, reproducing and encouraging new forms of white land ownership, and cementing settler ontologies that naturalize the existence and domination of the nation-state, infrastructures carry the colonial dispossession that travels through them, as they are used to extend settlements' reach into Indigenous territories that remain unceded, unsurrendered to the Canadian state, or protected under Treaty agreements with Indigenous nations. The settler state is built through a network of infrastructures, which must be normalized and maintained to assert settler jurisdiction toward nation-building projects.[23]

Infrastructures that transport people have been identified as formations of settler colonization. The railroads that facilitated westward expansion onto Indigenous ter-

20   Jodi Byrd, *The Transit of Empire: Indigenous Critiques of Colonialism* (Minneapolis: University of Minnesota Press, 2011).

21   Timothy Mitchell, *Carbon Democracy: Political Power in the Age of Oil* (London and New York: Verso, 2011); and Michelle Murphy, *The Economization of Life* (Durham, NC: Duke University Press, 2017).

22   Larkin, "The Politics and Poetics of Infrastructure," 328.

23   Shiri Pasternak, "Jurisdiction and Settler Colonialism: Where Laws Meet,"

ritories in Canada and the United States were deeply colonial projects requiring the labor of Chinese immigrants as well as the displacement of Indigenous peoples in order to build capital and deliver settlers to the West.[24] Manu Vimalassery describes how the land grants underwriting the Central Pacific Railroad link the assertion of settler sovereignty to underlying Indigenous claims to land—the practice of "counter-sovereignty" in this case uses railroad infrastructure to both build on and replace pre-existing Indigenous sovereignties to shape and expand colonial geographies.[25] Other transportation infrastructures operate this way, as well. As Penny Harvey and Hannah Knox make clear in their book *Roads: An Anthropology of Infrastructure and Expertise*, roads and highways are fully entangled in politics at both the micro and macro levels.[26] Madhuri Karak uses the case of Odisha, India, to trace how roads are used to aid counter-insurgency efforts to remove guerrillas and facilitate land-grabbing. The association of roads with military presence led local people to take paths, avoiding the "shiny asphalt highway" even if this was an added inconvenience.[27] And as Roxanne Dunbar-Ortiz notes, the extensive roadways used by North American Native peoples as trade routes prior to colonization have been paved over, forming the major highways of the United States and obscuring the mobility and presence of Native

in "Law and Decolonization," ed. Stacy Douglas and Suzanne Lenon, special issue, *Canadian Journal of Law and Society* 29, no. 2 (August 2014): 145–161.

24   Iyko Day, *Alien Capital: Asian Racialization and the Logic of Settler Colonial Capitalism* (Durham, NC: Duke University Press, 2016).

25   Manu Vimalassery, "The Prose of Counter-Sovereignty," in *Formations of United States Colonialism*, ed. Alyosha Goldstein (Durham, NC: Duke University Press, 2014): 88.

26   Penny Harvey and Hannah Knox, *Roads: An Anthropology of Infrastructure and Expertise* (Ithaca, NY: Cornell University Press, 2015).

27   Madhuri Karak, "Choosing Paths, Not Roads," *Engagement* (blog), Anthropology and Environment Society, May 24, 2016, https://aesengagement.wordpress.com/2016/05/24/choosing-paths-not-roads.

peoples, both historically and in the present.[28] Thus, in crucial ways, the concept of modern infrastructure elides the supposedly "nonmodern" assemblages of Indigenous peoples that were transformed into settler property and infrastructure. Settlers acquired their "modernity" as infrastructures facilitated dispossession while disavowing their roots in Indigenous organizations of space. If settler colonialism is a structure that "destroys to replace," then transportation infrastructures are themselves settler colonial technologies of invasion.[29]

These transportation infrastructures intersect with oil and gas projects as both are increasingly grouped under the definition of critical infrastructures secured by the state in Canada and the United States. Furthermore, the danger of transporting oil by rail is often used to argue for the construction of "safer" pipelines, ironically acknowledging the possibility of the railroads creating contamination, death, and disaster (as if they didn't cause these things from their inception), while pushing oil pipelines as further incursions onto Indigenous territories in the name of "public safety."[30] Since the very beginning of the settler colonial project in North America, infrastructures have been sites of contact, violence, tension, and competing jurisdiction. Deborah Cowen emphasizes not only the temporality of infrastructures that reach toward aspirations of their completion but also their entanglement with the past:

Infrastructures reach across time, building uneven relations of the past into the future, cementing their persistence. In colonial and settler colonial contexts,

28 Roxanne Dunbar-Ortiz, *An Indigenous Peoples' History of the United States* (Boston: Beacon Press, 2014), 28–30.

29 Wolfe, "Settler Colonialism and the Elimination of the Native."

30 James Wilt, "How the Spectre of Oil Trains is Deceptively Used to Push Pipelines," *The Narwhal* (formerly *Desmog Canada*), January 6, 2017, https://thenarwhal.ca/how-spectre-oil-trains-deceptively-used-push-pipelines.

infrastructure is often the means of dispossession, and the material force that implants colonial economies and socialities. Infrastructures thus highlight the issue of competing and overlapping jurisdiction—matters of both time and space.[31]

The infrastructures that support oil and gas development form a network of completed and proposed projects that are embedded in the national imaginaries of settler colonies while also reaching beyond international borders. They enable the material transit of energy as well as the ideological claims of settler sovereignty over Indigenous territory.[32] In the case of Unist'ot'en Camp, pipelines currently proposed through the unceded territories of the Wet'suwet'en nation in northern British Columbia, Canada, rely on fracking fields to the northeast and the construction of liquefied natural gas (LNG) export facilities on the coast. The controversial proposed Keystone XL pipeline would transport oil from the Alberta tar sands across the United States border to meet up with existing pipelines in Nebraska. Michael Watts has referred to this network as an "oil assemblage," and anthropologists have attended to the material and political consequences of oil as it travels through these networks.[33] In the case of Indigenous resistance to oil and gas assemblages, these

---

31 Deborah Cowen, "Infrastructures of Empire and Resistance," *Verso* (blog), January 25, 2017, https://www.versobooks.com/blogs/3067-infrastructures-of-empire-and-resistance.

32 For an excellent report on the political context of pipeline infrastructures and their claims to Indigenous territories, see Katie Mazer and Martin Danyluk, *Mapping a Many Headed Hydra: The Struggle Over the Dakota Access Pipeline* (Toronto: Infrastructure Otherwise, 2017), http://infrastructureotherwise.org/DAPL_Report_20170921_FINAL.pdf.

33 Michael Watts, "Securing Oil: Frontiers, Risk, and Spaces of Accumulated Insecurity," in *Subterranean Estates: Life Worlds of Oil and Gas*, ed. Hannah Appel, Arthur Mason, and Michael Watts (Ithaca, NY: Cornell University Press, 2015), 211–236; and Douglas Rogers, "Oil and Anthropology," *Annual Review of Anthropology* 44 (2015): 365–380.

pipeline infrastructures also carry the work of jurisdiction and the assertion of political claims to territory and resources. Proposed pipelines assume and assert settler jurisdiction over the unceded Wet'suwet'en territories in British Columbia in order to usher in prosperity for the Canadian public, and they do so in concert with transportation infrastructures. When police approached the border of Unist'ot'en territory in 2015, they told us that our actions were not allowed because we were blocking a "public highway" (a logging road). Hence, the language of infrastructure is used to delegitimize Indigenous claims to territory by replacing them with allusions to the legality of "public" access. The extraction of oil and gas is normalized, and the petro-economy invades Native lands in the name of the settler public, extending the net of economic relations reliant on oil and gas and making it harder and harder to imagine and also live into relations outside of capitalism.

As Aileen Moreton-Robinson has pointed out, settler nation-states are steeped in "possessive logics" that dispossess Indigenous nations both historically and in the present through the enduring reproduction of white possession.[34] Material infrastructures such as the buildings, roads, pipes, wires, and cables that make up cities are built alongside and on top of Indigenous sovereignties. These sovereignties, Moreton-Robinson insists, still exist, but are "disavowed through the materiality of these significations, which are perceived as evidence of ownership by those who have taken possession."[35] Indigenous peoples resisting the infrastructures of oil and gas recognize the power of a pipeline to reinscribe white possession on their territories. These are also infrastructures of white supremacy. For the Unist'ot'en clan of the Wet'suwet'en nation, resistance to the construction of pipelines in their territory is

---

34   Aileen Moreton-Robinson, *The White Possessive: Property, Power and Indigenous Sovereignty* (Minneapolis: University of Minnesota Press, 2015).

35   Moreton-Robinson, *The White Possessive*, xiii.

resistance to the invasion of the Canadian state onto territories they have never ceded or surrendered to the province or the crown. Unist'ot'en people regularly remind visitors to their land that it is not Canada, it is not British Columbia, it is unceded Wet'suwet'en territory. Oil and gas companies, on the other hand, publicize their projects by hailing settler publics through possessive investment in Indigenous territories as a pathway to prosperous settler futures. Oil and gas extraction and infrastructure reproduce the settler state, not only through the dispossession of Indigenous peoples but also through the generation, maintenance, reproduction, and naturalization of settler ontologies. In the case of pipelines, the land through which pipelines are built is not owned by oil and gas companies but is drawn into the oil and gas assemblage as a form of white dominion—Indigenous sovereignty stands in the way of oil and gas infrastructures by asserting a prior jurisdiction over territory. While oil and gas companies strive to present their projects as just another national infrastructure—TransCanada's Coastal Gaslink pipeline is even pitched as a boon to other infrastructures: "Annual property tax revenues generated from the project can also help build important infrastructure that we rely on every day like roads, schools and hospitals"—white possession continues to naturalize projects that cut through Indigenous territories in service of the national interest.[36]

As Indigenous feminist scholars continue to remind us, the work of white possession in settler states traffics in patriarchal notions of ownership and property that have implications for ways of relating beyond heteropatriarchal settler normativity.[37] Reclaiming relations beyond invasive infrastructures means acknowledging the violence

36   Coastal GasLink, "The Benefits," in *Coastal GasLink Pipeline Project* (Calgary: TransCanada, 2017), https://www.tcenergy.com/siteassets/pdfs/natural-gas/coastal-gaslink/transcanada-2017-coastal-gaslink-project-overview.pdf.

FIGHTING INVASIVE INFRASTRUCTURES

done by prioritizing technical and technological infrastructure as the work of national progress. The settler state shapes narratives around infrastructure projects that make them out to be a part of the natural advancement of the nation-state while masking the violence they cause to Indigenous land and bodies, especially the bodies of women and girls.[38] Oil and gas extraction, in particular, creates spaces of unchecked white masculinity in which incidents of violent abduction, abuse, and rape of Indigenous women and girls have skyrocketed.[39] Attention to alternatives would recognize the work done by generations of women and Two-Spirit people to protect and maintain the assemblages that sustain Indigenous life in the face of settler colonial invasion—work that Dakota scholar Kim TallBear

37   Maile Arvin, Eve Tuck, and Angie Morrill, "Decolonizing Feminism: Challenging Connections between Settler Colonialism and Heteropatriarchy," *Feminist Formations* 25, no. 1 (Spring 2013): 8–34; Joanne Barker, introduction to *Critically Sovereign*, ed. Joanne Barker (Durham, NC: Duke University Press, 2017), 1–44; Mishuana Goeman, *Mark My Words: Native Women Mapping Our Nations* (Minneapolis: University of Minnesota Press, 2013); and Lisa Kahaleole Hall, "Navigating Our Own 'Sea of Islands': Remapping a Theoretical Space for Hawaiian Women and Indigenous Feminism," in "Native Feminism," ed. Mishuana R. Goeman and Jennifer Nez Denetdale, special issue, *Wicazo Sa Review* 24, no. 2 (Fall 2009): 15–38.
38   Jaskiran Dhillon, "Indigenous Girls and the Violence of Settler Colonial Policing," *Decolonization: Indigeneity, Education & Society* 4, no. 2 (2015): 1–31; Toni Jensen, "Women in the Fracklands: On Water, Land, Bodies, and Standing Rock," *Catapult*, January 3, 2017, https://catapult.co/stories/women-in-the-fracklands-on-water-land-bodies-and-standing-rock; and Audra Simpson, "The State is a Man: Theresa Spence, Loretta Saunders, and the Gender of Settler Sovereignty," in "On Colonial Unknowing," ed. Alyosha Goldstein, Juliana Hu Pegues, and Manu Vimalassery, special issue, *Theory & Event* 19, no. 4 (2016).
39   G. Gibson, K. Yung, L. Chisholm, and H. Quinn with Lake Babine Nation and Nak'azdli Whut'en, *Indigenous Communities and Industrial Camps: Promoting Healthy Communities in Settings of Industrial Change* (Victoria, BC: Firelight Group, 2017); Toni Jensen, "Women in the Fracklands"; and Women's Earth Alliance and Native Youth Sexual Health Network, *Violence on the Land, Violence on Our Bodies: Building an Indigenous Response to Environmental Violence* (Berkeley, CA: Women's Earth Alliance; Toronto: Native Youth Sexual Health Network, 2016).

calls "caretaking relations."[40] In spaces of land defense and Indigenous resistance across Canada and the United States, women have led movements to protect the land and water and to reinvigorate alternatives to infrastructures threatening destruction of land and Indigenous ways of life.[41]

Anthropology of Infrastructure

Infrastructure is by definition future oriented; it is assembled in the service of worlds to come. Infrastructure demands a focus on what underpins and enables formations of power and the material organization of everyday life in time and space. Cowen offers an expansive definition of infrastructures as "the collectively constructed systems that also build and sustain human life," and terms the alternatives to state systems "fugitive infrastructures."[42] While fugitive infrastructure may not be an obvious place to start, anthropology must break from the reification of infrastructure's stated purpose and imposed coherence. Fugitivity calls our attention to the ways the organization of time, space, and the material world are organized by power, yet constantly disrupted and remade. An analysis that dwells in "fugitivity" attends to that which can be gleaned from spaces of power.[43] With Cowen's frame of "fugitive infrastructures" we can draw attention to the

40   Kim TallBear, "Badass (Indigenous) Women Caretake Relations: #NoDAPL, #IdleNoMore, #BlackLivesMatter," Hot Spots, *Fieldsights*, December 22, 2016, https://culanth.org/fieldsights/badass-indigenous-women-caretake-relations-no-dapl-idle-no-more-black-lives-matter; see also the emerging *Voices: Indigenous Women on the Frontlines Speak* project, which compiles Indigenous women and Two-Spirit people's stories in a book and zine series, http://voicesbook.tumblr.com.

41   The Kino-nda-niimi Collective, *The Winter We Danced: Voices from the Past, the Future, and the Idle No More Movement* (Winnipeg: ARP Books, 2014).

42   Cowen, "Infrastructures of Empire and Resistance."

43   Fred Moten and Stefano Harney, *The Undercommons: Fugitive Planning and Black Study* (New York: Minor Compositions, 2013).

material, social, and economic networks that flourish in the space opened by industry pressure and the threat of environmental devastation. The concept of "fugitivity," however, has temporal and theoretical limitations in relation to Indigenous movements. While Indigenous movements may disrupt settler infrastructures and the capitalist relations they sustain, these movements are not transitory, fleeting, or temporary.[44] Furthermore, Indigenous peoples are not fugitives "on the run" from settler governance. Instead, resistance to invasive infrastructures requires standing in place, in our territories, and insisting on our prior and continuing relationships to the lands, kin, and other-than-human relations that those infrastructures threaten. Indigenous blockades, checkpoints, and encampments slow and disrupt flows of extractive capital and the ideological project of settler sovereignty while also strengthening alternative relations that tend to the matter beyond what is usually considered the "built environment." As such, these are not simply spaces of negation (as the oft-repeated phrase "no pipelines" might suggest) but also spaces of radical possibility under Indigenous leadership and jurisdiction—possibility that is deeply threatening to the continued operation of the capitalist settler state.

As Larkin notes, the Enlightenment underpinnings of "infrastructure" root the term in the building of modern futures.[45] Indigenous blockades of "critical infrastructures" disrupt the reproduction of settler futures through assertion of Indigenous jurisdiction, placing the settler future in suspension. Shiri Pasternak and Tia Dafnos describe how blockades trigger state securitization: "Simply put, Indigenous peoples interrupt commodity flows by asserting

---

44 Anne Spice, "Interrupting Industrial and Academic Extraction on Native Land," Hot Spots, *Fieldsights*, December 22, 2016, https://culanth.org/fieldsights/interrupting-industrial-and-academic-extraction-on-native-land.

45 Larkin, "The Politics and Poetics of Infrastructure."

jurisdiction and sovereignty over their lands and resources in places that form choke points to the circulation of capital. Thus, the securitization of 'critical infrastructure'—essentially supply chains of capital, such as private pipelines and public transport routes—has become a priority in mitigating the potential threat of Indigenous jurisdiction."[46] Pasternak and Dafnos draw attention to the particular circuitry of oil and gas infrastructures in the global system of capitalist "just-in-time" production. The attention to systems, here, considers the materiality of oil and pipelines, but insists that the pipeline infrastructure be understood within the particular networks of circulation it enables. When the Canadian state steps in to protect "critical infrastructures" by securitizing risk, we might ask, "Critical to what and to whom?" What subjects and publics are hailed into infrastructure projects, and how are they reproduced? Managing "critical infrastructures," then, is primarily about colonial governance. Pasternak and Dafnos argue that this shift in governing strategies has positioned industry and corporations as partners in national security, marking Indigenous jurisdiction as a "risk" to be mitigated. This shift in governance reinscribes settler colonial dispossession through the legal and material network built to support pipeline infrastructure. Movements to block critical infrastructures, such as those enacted across the country during the Idle No More movement (the "Native winter" of 2012–2013), highlight the ability of dispersed Native nations to significantly alter the circulation of capital by shutting down highways, bridges, and railroads. By participating in the politics of blockades, Indigenous activists are correctly identifying the reliance of the petro-state on energy infrastructure and forcing

---

46   Shiri Pasternak and Tia Dafnos, "How Does the Settler State Secure the Circuitry of Capital?" *Environment and Planning D: Society and Space* 36, no. 4 (2018): 741.

open the contradiction between proposed and presumed energy infrastructure on stolen land.

The naturalization of resource extraction projects and the suspension of Indigenous life through settler infrastructure projects combine to mask the ways in which the language of infrastructure itself can work to legitimize "modern" assemblages like pipelines while rendering invisible the living assemblages that would strengthen Indigenous sovereignty and lifeways. If, following Larkin, we turn to "what one sees as infrastructural (and thus causal) and what one leaves out" as a window into state aspirations and intentions,[47] the Canadian context of oil and gas extraction returns the following conclusion: in the eyes of the Canadian state, oil and gas pipelines count as infrastructural, while the relations of rivers, glaciers, lakes, mountains, plants and animals, and Indigenous nations are the natural resources to be modernized as commodities or subjects. Here, Larkin's note that infrastructures "literally provid[e] the undergirding of modern societies" raises a crucial question.[48] If those modern societies have settled, colonized, and attempted to eliminate existing Indigenous nations and political orders, does the word "infrastructure" itself denote an apparatus of domination?[49] Here, the very act of defining infrastructures as tools of the state takes for granted the state's ontological claims. "What one leaves out" of the definition of infrastructure is a world of relations, flows, and circulations that the settler state has attempted to destroy and supplant.

47   Larkin, "The Politics and Poetics of Infrastructure," 330.
48   Larkin, "The Politics and Poetics of Infrastructure," 328.
49   *Gunalchéesh* (thank you) to a reviewer for pointing out that this is also true of the word "sovereignty." See Lenape scholar Joanne Barker's edited collection *Sovereignty Matters: Locations of Contestation and Possibility in Indigenous Struggles for Self-Determination* (Lincoln: University of Nebraska Press, 2005) as well as her introduction to *Critically Sovereign* for a discussion of Indigenous appropriations of sovereignty.

INDIGENOUS RELATIONS AGAINST PIPELINES

A number of scholars have connected infrastructures to state promises of modernity, progress, and nationhood.[50] The promise of oil, Fernando Coronil explains, allows the state to perform all kinds of "magic"; Andrew Apter explores this magic through the dramaturgy and spectacle underlying oil and the mirage of progress in Nigeria.[51] Oil infrastructures in particular also produce spectacular forms of breakdown. As Susan Leigh Star notes, infrastructures often "become visible upon breakdown."[52] The BP oil spill or the Exxon Valdez bring the particular materiality of infrastructures (a "leak" in an oil rig; the crash of a tanker) into high relief. But the focus on breakdown reinforces a slippage between actually existing and future infrastructures—a slippage that is both enforced by oil and gas companies who operate as if pipelines are already built and therefore inevitable and by environmental activists who operate on the assumption that the pipeline WILL break (they always break). But what of infrastructures that do not yet exist? How might spaces of anticipation, spaces slated as "energy corridors," work as transit to capitalist petro-futures? And how might these futures be disrupted?

50 Laura Bear, *Lines of the Nation: Indian Railway Workers, Bureaucracy, and the Intimate Historical Self* (New York: Columbia University Press, 2007); Fernando Coronil, *The Magical State: Nature, Money, and Modernity in Venezuela* (Chicago: University of Chicago Press, 1997); Elizabeth Emma Ferry and Mandana E. Limbert, introduction to *Timely Assets: The Politics of Resources and Their Temporalities*, ed. Elizabeth Ferry and Mandana Limbert (Santa Fe, NM: School for Advanced Research Press, 2008), 3–24; John Gledhill, "'The People's Oil': Nationalism, Globalization, and the Possibility of Another Country in Brazil, Mexico, and Venezuela," *Focaal* 52 (2008): 57–74; and Rudolf Mrazek, *Engineers of Happy Land: Technology and Nationalism in a Colony* (Princeton, NJ: Princeton University Press, 2002).

51 Coronil, *The Magical State*; Andrew Apter, *The Pan-African Nation: Oil and the Spectacle of Culture in Nigeria* (Chicago: University of Chicago Press, 2005).

52 Susan Leigh Star, "The Ethnography of Infrastructure," *American Behavioral Scientist* 43, no. 3 (November/December 1999): 382.

While anthropological definitions of infrastructure carry the political weight of state and industry projects, they have also made space to investigate the affective, social, and temporal aspects of infrastructure. Akhil Gupta compels anthropologists to look to the temporality, not only the spatiality, of infrastructure.[53] Gupta explains that infrastructure can illuminate social futures, since state infrastructure projects are often long-term investments. Infrastructures "tell us a great deal about aspirations, anticipations, and imaginations of the future... what people think their society should be like, what they might wish it to be, and what kind of statement the government wants to make about that vision."[54] Gupta's attention to temporality can help to articulate also how visions of the future within a nation are fractured and competing. If we refuse the idea that there is one unified "society" (and the attendant epistemological and ontological claims of what "society" is vis-à-vis the state, nature, morality, and technology) for whom infrastructures are meant to function, we may start to see how infrastructures materialize temporal logics. Pipelines, then, become an inevitable harbinger of social progress, and they are proposed across territories as if they are already bringing the benefits of their completion. The temporality of infrastructure construction further brings with it reorganizations of experience. The new socialities and relations formed through infrastructures are themselves worthy of study. AbdouMaliq Simone's concept of "people as infrastructure" explains that attempts to govern through the built environment or to separate distinct populations through networks of services often fail—Simone pays attention to the actually existing material and social networks on the ground

---

53   Akhil Gupta, "The Infrastructure Toolbox: Suspension," Theorizing the Contemporary, *Fieldsights*, September 24, 2015, https://culanth.org/fieldsights/suspension.

54   Gupta, "The Infrastructure Toolbox: Suspension."

in inner-city Johannesburg, South Africa, noting that "the growing distance between how urban Africans actually live and normative trajectories of urbanization and public life can constitute new fields of economic action."[55] In the suspension, failure, or rupture of government intentions to govern through infrastructure, other social and temporal worlds develop.

Governments intending to extend settler colonial control over Indigenous lands through pipeline construction face the continued resistance of Indigenous peoples, forcing oil and gas projects to linger for years between proposal and completion. Gupta characterizes this state of suspension: "Suspension, then, instead of being a temporary phase between the start of a project and its (successful) conclusion, needs to be theorized as its own condition of being. The temporality of suspension is not between past and future, between beginning and end, but constitutes its own ontic condition just as surely as does completion."[56] For many Indigenous peoples, the completion of pipelines includes the inevitable spill, the environmental catastrophe, the destruction of ways of life. Holding projects in suspension, then, is a key tactic of Indigenous resistance.

Indigenous feminist perspectives, however, point to how suspension also characterizes Indigenous life under settler occupation. Southern Paiute anthropologist Kristen Simmons explains, "Suspension is a condition of settler colonialism—it suffuses all places, and keeps in play the contradictions and ambiguities built into the colonial project."[57] Simmons explains how settler colonialism creates an atmosphere of violence, both through the suspension of toxic chemicals in the air and the ways that these

55   AbdouMaliq Simone, "People as Infrastructure: Intersecting Fragments in Johannesburg," *Public Culture* 16, no. 3 (Fall 2004): 428.
56   Gupta, "The Infrastructure Toolbox: Suspension."
57   Kristen Simmons, "Settler Atmospherics," Member Voices, *Fieldsights*, November 20, 2017, https://culanth.org/fieldsights/settler-atmospherics.

suspensions create the "normal" conditions of Indigenous life. Settler colonialism preys on our porosity and vulnerability to toxicity, wearing on our health and bodies while chemically altering our atmospheres. Simmons theorizes this combination of chemical suspension and the suspension of Indigenous life as "settler atmospherics."[58] The normalization of settler colonial violence is accomplished through shifts in our atmosphere as well as discursive regimes. Here we can also look to Traci Voyles's Indigenous feminist–informed *Wastelanding*; Voyles shows how the discourses about land in the US Southwest shape settler colonial violence—the land is cast as already wasted, allowing the continued settler appropriation of resources and reckless contamination of land and water.[59] The settler accumulation of energy, capital, and territory is reliant on the parallel distribution of toxicity and violence to Indigenous nations, and forms of immediate state violence (like the militarized response to Standing Rock water protectors) are tied to the slow environmental destruction of Indigenous homelands.[60]

The uneven distribution of infrastructures also draws attention to who is seen to be part of a society worth reproducing and who is not. Recall Harper and Trudeau advertising the future of Canada through pipelines and energy infrastructures while minimizing the threats to Indigenous sovereignty and the environment required to complete these state-building projects. The effects are dramatic abandonments and exclusions from the social benefits promised by modernity's infrastructures in order to secure resource extraction. As Tess Lea and Paul

58   Simmons, "Settler Atmospherics."
59   Traci Brynn Voyles, *Wastelanding: Legacies of Uranium Mining in Navajo Country* (Minneapolis: University of Minnesota Press, 2015).
60   Teresa Montoya, "Violence on the Ground, Violence below the Ground," Hot Spots, *Fieldsights*, December 22, 2016, https://culanth.org/fieldsights/violence-on-the-ground-violence-below-the-ground.

Pholeros point out in the settler state of Australia, outward appearance of infrastructure can be deceiving.[61] In their discussion of state provision of housing for Aboriginal peoples in Australia, they document the systematic disrepair, incompleteness, and poor design of Aboriginal housing. Houses provided for Aboriginal families may look like houses, but they are not. Their pipes lead to nowhere; they are constructed with cheap and crumbling materials. These "not-houses" draw attention to the way in which infrastructure can, through its pull to the literal, mask the material conditions lurking just underneath the surface.[62] Infrastructures in settler states like Australia, the United States, and Canada keep Indigenous nations in suspension as a condition of settler colonial expansion and extraction—while infrastructures of resource extraction roll in with government approval and corporate money.

Larkin, Gupta, and Lea and Pholeros emphasize the temporality of infrastructure and the contingent link between proposed infrastructure projects and their materialization. Like many infrastructures that are subject to state investment, oil and gas infrastructures are aspirational. They anticipate the circulation of certain materials, the proliferation of certain worlds, the reproduction of certain subjects. But, sometimes, their bluster hides their tenuous nature, and their future-focus creates an opening in which other possibilities can assert themselves. While Prime Minister Justin Trudeau has heralded his government's approval of two major pipeline projects, another was cancelled after many years of Indigenous resistance and a lack of proper consultation with Indigenous peoples.[63] If

61   Tess Lea and Paul Pholeros, "This Is Not a Pipe: The Treacheries of Indigenous Housing," *Public Culture* 22, no. 1 (Winter 2010): 187–209.

62   Lea and Pholeros, "This is Not a Pipe."

63   John Paul Tasker, "Trudeau Cabinet Approves Trans Mountain, Line 3 Pipelines, Rejects Northern Gateway," *CBC News*, November 29, 2016, http://www.cbc.ca/news/politics/federal-cabinet-trudeau-pipeline-decisions-1.3872828.

FIGHTING INVASIVE INFRASTRUCTURES

Indigenous resistance forces pipeline projects into suspension, futures might grow in the space between proposal and completion (a space that, if Indigenous land defenders have their way, leads to the reversal of settler colonialism).

Field Insights: Relations against Pipelines

Before heading out to Unist'ot'en Camp for the second time in 2016, I drove a rusting Toyota truck up to the Yukon territory, following my parents along the Alaska Highway and stopping to camp along the way. My mother grew up in Whitehorse, Yukon, and left home to go to school in Alberta when she was eighteen. We were going up to attend a memorial service for her cousin, a man who she says was like her brother growing up. We were going, also, to meet and re-meet my family.

I was nervous. Having grown up on Treaty 7 territories in southern Alberta, I felt like an interloper and outsider. The day after we arrived in Whitehorse, my auntie had a barbeque for family. She put the word out, expecting a handful of people. Suddenly, the house was full. Dozens of people, all related to me. All my relations. I sat outside with a moose burger in one hand, talking to a maybe-cousin of mine. "So," he says, "how are we related?" Um, I don't know. "Someone told me you're an anthropologist?" Yeah, you could say that. "Uh… shouldn't you know?" He convinces me to make a kinship chart. I find a piece of chart paper and sit down on the deck. People gather around, and I map out our relations. A giant, sprawling tree. Over the next week I go over the chart, adding in forgotten relatives, piecing it together. When I see my relatives in the streets of Whitehorse, they come and ask me how my anthropology project is going. They introduce me to others: "This is Anne, she's an anthropologist, you're cousins." I am unquestionably part of this family. Here it is, on paper in front of me. Here it is, in the way I am addressed—Lee's daughter. Lori's niece. All of us are descendants of my great-grandmother, Jenny LeBarge, though we can now trace the tree back further, back a few more generations to ancestors whose names are all Tlingit or Southern Tutchone, not the names of the places the colonizers found them. Our family name—LeBarge—is a misspelled tribute to Lake LeBerge, which was named for a French-Canadian explorer. So we're named for a place that was named for a white man. Not that there weren't names for us, or the lake for that matter, before all that. The lake: Tàa'an Män, Southern Tutchone; Kluk-tas-si, Tagish; Tahini-wud, Tlingit. And my people weren't even really from there; we migrated in from the coast of Alaska. White explorers were lazy historians.

After a week in Whitehorse, in the area that my people called Kwanlin (Southern Tutchone for "water running through a narrow place"—the Yukon river running through Miles Canyon), I drive down through the neighboring territories of Tagish, Kaska Dena, Tahltan, Gitxsan, Wet'suwet'en. Arriving on Unist'ot'en *yintah*, I am exhausted and reeling. I arrive in the midst of preparations for a northern Indigenous youth art camp and busy myself with preparing food, helping to lead activities, and making the youth feel welcome and supported in that space. During the final week of the camp, after a trip out berry picking with all of the youth, we get a moose. After it is shot, we run up to where it fell. I see its breath stop. All the youth gather around to help skin and gut it, and I work to do this myself for the first time.

After we get the moose and get back to camp, after the moose is tucked into the smokehouse, after all the youth are in bed and everyone else is sleeping or out watching the northern lights, I reflect on what this means for me as a neighbor of the Wet'suwet'en people. Skinning the moose, I've never felt so sure that I was in the right place. Here, on the territories of others, my ancestors are teaching me. That moose is my relation; this land is my responsibility. Much of my time left at camp is taken up with the work of butchering the moose with an Indigenous (but not Wet'suwet'en) friend. I feel entirely bound up in my responsibilities to the moose, and when a bowl of moose meat spoils after we give it to some supporters to pressure can, I am sick with sadness and anger. Next time, we tell each other, we won't let this happen. This is when I realize I have wholly committed myself to a "next time," and the pull back to the land is so strong that when I arrive in New York City I am ill for weeks, heartsick as my connection to both territory and people wears under the strain of distance, the fast-paced crunch of capitalist time, the pressing need for me to make my "summer research" legible and theoretical and fundable.

It has become clear to me that spaces like Unist'ot'en Camp are doing more than blocking pipelines. The work of undoing settler colonial invasion requires blocking, resisting, and suspending the infrastructures of oil and gas and the systemic dominance of capitalism. It also requires attending to and caring for the networks of relations that make Indigenous survival possible. These are the relations that linked my nation to the Wet'suwet'en people before our territories felt the first footsteps of white settlers. These are the relations that bring Indigenous youth back onto the land and into material relation with the other-than-human beings that share their territories. These are the relations that connect me to other Indigenous peoples as we struggle to regain ancestral skills that we have lost. These are the Indigenous assemblages that recognize our dependence on other-than-humans for our survival as peoples. These are the relations threatened by invasive infrastructures and their toxic consequences. If the moose, the berry patches, the salmon, the bears are destroyed, so are we.

Stephen Collier and Andrew Lakoff detail how "critical infrastructures" in the United States became objects of national security as events threatening infrastructures over the course of the twentieth century were increasingly understood as threats to "vital systems" supporting the collective life of the United States.[64] In both Canada and the United States, these systems are sometimes threatened by the jurisdiction of Indigenous peoples, whose land forms the conditions of possibility for collective life on this continent. When Indigenous land defenders point to "our critical infrastructures," they are pointing to another set of relations that sustains the collective life of Indigenous peoples—the human and non-human networks that have supported Indigenous polities on this continent for tens of thousands of years. Indigenous peoples reject the idea that the way of life supported by pipeline infrastructure should be accelerated or intensified and instead step into the vulnerable and volatile space between the proposal and potential completion of pipelines to protect the land, water, air, plant, and animal relations. By doing so, they attend to the "vital systems" that form alternatives to capitalist exploitation, alternatives to oil-soaked futures, alternatives to the unquestioned occupation of the settler state. By performatively "seeing like an oil company," land defenders appropriate the language of infrastructure to question the terms of industrial invasion onto their territories.[65] And by building alternatives based on Indigenous relations of ethics and care in the aspirational space of proposed pipeline routes, encampments like Unist'ot'en Camp challenge the destructive teleology of settler petrofutures. At Unist'ot'en Camp, the hosts remind visitors, "This is not Canada, this is not British Columbia, this is

64 Stephen J. Collier and Andrew Lakoff, "The Vulnerability of Vital Systems: How 'Critical Infrastructure' Became a Security Problem," in *Securing the Homeland: Critical Infrastructure, Risk and (In)security*, ed. Myriam Dunn and Kristian Søby Kristensen (New York: Routledge, 2008), 17–39.

65 James Ferguson, "Seeing Like an Oil Company: Space, Security, and Global Capital in Neoliberal Africa," *American Anthropologist* 107, no. 3 (2005): 377–382.

unceded Wet'suwet'en territory." If the space of the camp is not Canada today, then perhaps it is an opening into a more reciprocal Indigenous tomorrow, beyond the perpetual incursions of settler colonial domination. Yet an analysis of how these futures are anticipated and brought into existence is only possible if we center Indigenous feminist methodologies that work against the inevitability of settler modernity and make room for the resurgent infrastructures that sustain human and other-than-human relations. We must critically analyze the tactics and strategies of colonial domination while strengthening our relations. We can do this by supporting spaces of resistance like Unist'ot'en Camp, by holding each other accountable for the relationship-building work that underlies everything we do. We can challenge the inevitability of settler colonial invasion by returning to the networks that have sustained us for tens of thousands of years on our territories and by living into better relations with each other and our other-than-human kin. We pick the berries, skin the moose, protect the water. We feed *our* critical infrastructures, in hopes that they will flourish again.

Sable Elyse Smith, *Coloring Book 16*, 2018. Screen printing ink, oil pastel, and oil stick on paper, 60 x 50 inches. Courtesy of the artist; JTT, New York; and Carlos/Ishikawa, London.

ZEROES AND ONES:
CARCERAL LIFE IN THE DATA WORLD

WENDY L. WRIGHT

As we begin to encounter the true shape of the twenty-first century, surveillance, power, and control are taking on radically new structures, transforming the nature of incarceration, criminal justice practice, and a broad range of social forms. Technologies of surveillance and data extraction are developing at a near-unimaginable pace. While the day-to-day life of the average person living in the United States has already been transformed in barely more than a decade by the advent of the smartphone—which has changed how we conduct business, how we raise children, how we experience time, and how we love—the promised future of the "Internet of Things" foretells a dimensional shift in the role of data and its capture across human experience. Re-engaging the dialectical nature of surveilling technologies in Bentham's panopticon and Foucault's carceral system with these technological frameworks offers new ways to understand how power functions in this era. This essay takes up a novel conceptualization of carceral surveillance to assess new forms of criminal justice supervision as the leading edge of a broader shift toward a "total" carceral schema realized through the data revolution. That is, the expansion of state surveillance, most typically identified through technologies such as biometric monitoring and facial recognition, must be considered part of the same schema as the private data revolution, which is based on ostensible consent but expands the potentiality of coercion.

A total carceral schema must be understood to encompass both explicitly carceral space (such as prisons and jails) and the expansive, near unlimited space of invasive, perpetual surveillance of private telecommunication networks. It is "total" to the extent that it encloses the breadth of experience. Michel Foucault, like Jeremy Bentham, centered the prison in *Discipline and Punish* but drew lines to other institutions, like hospitals and schools, which retain the promise of development and liberation more plausibly than correctional facilities *and* still demand conformity. It might be said that the worst school is worse than the best prison, but, in general, the prison is both a subjectively and objectively more dominating structure. So we have a both/and, in which the physical instantiation of the carceral is at once everywhere and a very specific somewhere.[1]

In describing the movement of the carceral across society, Foucault offered the analogy of circles emanating out from a stone thrown in a pond, with the prison at the center of this concentric resonance. Foucault's "carceral archipelago" has become the carceral ocean.[2] The intensity of total carcerality might be more accurately imagined as waves peaking in some places—yet rather than dissipating in others, the gravitational force of the carceral perpetually reforms, such that the origin and the directionality of it remains obscured.[3] The experience of this new carcerality may be banal, as being monitored becomes a daily, expected element of everyday life, but missed in that banality is the aggressive expansion of state potentiality. The manipulation of data by corporate actors conditions daily life and simultaneously creates avenues for state control.

1   Foucault tends to neglect the fact that the state is still ready and willing to use unmediated violence to achieve its ends—even if, in general, it prefers the soft touch of discipline—and even resists the idea that the state's primary characteristic is its wielding of violence.

2   Michel Foucault, *Discipline and Punish: The Birth of the Prison*, trans. Alan Sheridan (New York: Vintage, 1977), 297.

3   It may be argued that Foucault himself moved beyond this spatial analogy as he developed his theory of biopolitics. However, retaining carcerality as the frame centers the materiality and structural elements wherein power and politics might be meaningfully engaged.

By attending to those who already exist at the kinetic juncture of state surveillance capacities—those under GPS surveillance, for example—the nature of this total carcerality and the threat to political life it presents can be mapped. Carcerality is now held in potential across the lived landscape. We are entering an era in which the traditional and obvious forms of carceral control are fused with the boundless technological framework of data capture—creating a new carceral schema that seeks (largely successfully) to penetrate the entirety of sociopolitical life.

The expansion of technological surveillance in the broader economy and in the specific area of criminal justice constitutes one carceral schema. Prefiguring the data revolution, "mass incarceration" radically replaced carcerality. The sheer scale of incarceration and the focus on criminalizing poor communities of color has produced a political order recreated through carcerality.[4] Ruth Wilson Gilmore and Judah Schept, amongst others, have incisively analyzed how prisons have extended the carceral into new economic, social, and political arenas—how, in the words of Brett Story, prisons now comprise a carceral geography that extends into "places where everyday life happens and is reproduced... where people encounter the political and economic structures that produce and uphold the social order."[5] Each of these places and arenas yields to carceral logics of conformity, docility, and objectification.[6] State

4   See Marie Gottschalk, *Caught: The Prison State and the Lockdown of American Politics* (Princeton, NJ: Princeton University Press, 2016); Amy E. Lerman and Vesla M. Weaver, *Arresting Citizenship: The Democratic Consequences of American Crime Control* (Chicago: University of Chicago Press, 2014); and Katherine Beckett and Naomi Murakawa, "Mapping the Shadow Carceral State: Toward an Institutionally Capacious Approach to Punishment," *Theoretical Criminology* 16, no. 2 (2012): 221–244.

5   See Brett Story, *Prison Land: Mapping Carceral Power Across Neoliberal America* (Minneapolis: University of Minnesota Press, 2019), 140; Ruth Wilson Gilmore, *Golden Gulag: Prisons, Surplus, Crisis, and Opposition in Globalizing California* (Berkeley: University of California Press, 2007); and Judah Schept, *Progressive Punishment: Job Loss, Jail Growth, and the*

surveillance capacitates this process through the dialectical practice of constantly re-defining the non-criminal as a norm against which communities will be measured: through police judgment, punitive workfare guidelines, zero-tolerance schools, so on.

Carceral Narrowing, Carceral Expansion?

The carceral, broadly, is characterized by a shift from the active hand of a coercive state power to an authority dispersed across the public and private realms. Replacing an immediate fear of state violence is a prisoner self-disciplining and self-disciplined. Behaviors, actions, and even thoughts are conditioned by constant reiterations of norming forces. The shape of this discipline—physical and ideological—in turn comes to shape behavior and undermine self-determination. The extent to which carcerality exists across political life—and across the lives of all subjects of modern state institutions—is the extent to which carcerality has been instantiated beyond the prison.

Carcerality, as it appears across its history, uses internal and external incentives that function dialectically to order and produce certain kinds of behaviors and certain kinds of people. Carcerality produces pliant subjects, less able or less willing to resist arbitrary power—not always or even typically out of a conscious fear or desire to obey, but rather because conformity is internalized as natural, useful, and sensible. Commonplace notions of cleanliness, of order, even of modernity are prioritized as the norming power of the carceral conditions public space for ease of inspection.

Neoliberal Logic of Carceral Expansion (New York: New York University Press, 2015).

6   It is crucial, however, to note that carceral expansion is not uncontested. As carceral institutions undermine the possibilities for self-determination, human will and initiative respond imperfectly, always creating cracks in the carceral continuity.

The carceral is also always already value-laden—discipline shapes the subject according to the goals of dominant power while presenting a neutral, deracinated visage. Efficiency seems like a reasonable institutional virtue, but it may easily undermine other potential values, of sociality or of creativity, and, more importantly, undermine self-determination at the individual and collective levels. The carceral shapes toward dominant power—and it increases its pathologizing and coercive tendencies the further a person moves outside the constructed norm. When it is impossible to conform to the default, by reasons of core identity, for example, the subject may be pushed beyond survival or recognition, made to fit the carceral norm by procrustean measures: cultural markers, social preferences, and even biological features might be prohibited or condemned. As Enora Brown notes, being subjected to "carceral virtues" is a "systemic and symbolic violence"—carceral virtues dehumanize as they construct unruly figures outside of, and without, civic virtues.[7] Brown writes specifically of the creation of racial categories to justify carceral control, of the "poor-Black-violent girls" who are "pathologized as parasitic, undeserving, dangerous."[8] The US model of carceral materialities has always been a racial framework, defining Blackness as unruly and thus criminal, simultaneously in need of and resistant to the disciplining structure of carceral institutions. As was understood (and intended) in its earliest articulations, carceral surveillance functions to produce docile subjects—subjects who are simultaneously less and less able to form and enact willing acts that stray from the molded path and

7   Enora Brown, "Systemic and Symbolic Violence as Virtue: The Carceral Punishment of African American Girls," in *The Routledge Handbook of Poverty in the United States*, ed. Stephen Nathan Haymes, María Vidal de Haymes, and Reuben Jonathan Miller (Abingdon, UK: Routledge, 2015), 398–405.

8   Brown, "Systemic and Symbolic Violence as Virtue," 399, 400.

also more and more able to facilitate the controlling gaze. The carceral produces a ruly consciousness that develops in relation to both external confines and self-discipline (conscious and unconscious). *Unruly* bodies experience increasing pressure until they bend or break, castigated for their unruliness even as some of those "broken" bodies are defined *per se* as always already outside the bounds of the rule.

As an inherently surveilling form of power, the carceral norm is built through the collection and reflection of mass data. In Bentham's vision, data about the behavior of the incarcerated would generate an aspirational standard of conforming behavior. Collected data is used to both assess in relation to the norm and refine the norm itself.[9] As expanded modes of surveillance become possible within and beyond the prison, the stringency of assessing the norm intensifies, while the norm narrows. With near total surveillance made possible with the data revolution, the forces of the norm and control are maximal. Human complexity itself is pathologized. Further, these norms have also been mobilized by the state via its criminal apparatus; criminalization is the process of marking

9   Foucault assumed that this process of assessment was a function of power. Yet even beyond a theoretical or genealogical account, this collection and assessment of mass data can also be traced in the material record of labor. As Matthew Desmond argues, modern productivity models re-enact the controlling violence of the plantation. Enslavers originated and developed practices of record-keeping that identified possible levels of productivity that, once they were identified as possible, became the standard required of the rest—enforced with the full violence of the racial state. Desmond writes that, in antebellum North Carolina, this meant "having hands line-pick in rows sometimes longer than five football fields allow[ing] overseers to spot anyone lagging behind. The uniform layout of the land had a logic; a logic designed to dominate. Faster workers were placed at the head of the line, which encouraged those who followed to match the captain's pace." See Matthew Desmond, "In Order to Understand the Brutality of American Capitalism, You Have to Start on the Plantation," in "The 1619 Project," special issue, *New York Times Magazine*, August 14, 2019, https://www.nytimes.com/interactive/2019/08/14/magazine/slavery-capitalism.html.

an observable behavior as worthy of state violence. The collection of data enables the deployment of state power; it also, in iterative waves, creates the terrain from which future norms will be narrowed. Every action—movement, purchase, click, glance—is something to be quantified, measured, and capitalized for the state's purposes; lagging behind or surging ahead are errors to be rectified through discipline toward power's goals.

From the emergence of the prison as an architectural and ideological form, the carceral has tended toward bourgeois, white supremacist, and Puritanical values, wielding its power through surveillance, humiliation, and the constant threat of violence. While disciplining power is, like the watchman at the center of the panopticon, difficult to perceive directly, its long genealogy is consistent. Jen Manion argues that the emergent prison in early independent America was a key factor in shaping the country's social and governing structure, as "a diverse class of white men, from ruling elites to middling artisans, cast their lot with the penitentiary system, hoping it would make them better men, bring back the gender roles of old, cultivate industrious habits, contain the threat of free blacks and immigrants, and regulate illicit sex."[10] The carceral, in its most originary and dispersed form, inherits and replicates the hegemonic virtues of the old guard.

Market Power? State Power?

The recent rise in the use of surveillance technologies for corrections practice has eroded the boundary of the prison wall, refiguring brick-and-mortar boundaries through an electronic web. This is not a shift or re-location, but a radical re-placing of carceral power—as in, the carceral extends its reach into previously uncontrolled places. Daniel Kato

10   Jen Manion, *Liberty's Prisoners: Carceral Culture in Early America* (Philadelphia: University of Pennsylvania Press, 2015), 1.

identifies the rise of non-prison-based supervision as "more of a realignment than an end of the carceral state."[11] Jackie Wang emphasizes this re-establishment as occurring through a process of accumulation, writing that "once 'digital carceral infrastructure' is built up, it will be nearly impossible to undo, and the automated carceral surveillance state will spread out across the terrain."[12] The digital capacity of the state exists and will exist as solidly as roads and bridges and dams. This policing and corrections infrastructure has been built and centered around the monitoring of those who have come under the purview of law enforcement agencies. Approximately 4.5 million people in the United States are subject to community-based supervision (primarily probation, parole, and pre-trial release), with a small but growing number of those supervised by the use of developing technological mechanisms.[13] Originally conceptualized as an alternative to incarceration, tech-based surveillance increasingly intensifies and extends coercive state force; it subsumes those who previously might have been unsupervised, or supervised through less invasive, relatively manual means, under an algorithmic and all-encompassing monitorial regime.

Currently, the most prevalent form of individual technological supervision is GPS or location-based tracking. Commonly referred to as ankle bracelets, these shackles are typically affixed to the wearer and are only intended to be removed by a supervising authority. Depending on the sophistication of these tracking devices, they might

11   Daniel Kato, "Carceral State 2.0?: From Enclosure to Control and Punishment to Surveillance," *New Political Science* 39, no. 2 (2017): 198.

12   Jackie Wang, *Carceral Capitalism* (South Pasadena: Semiotext(e), 2018), 251.

13   Beckett and Murakawa, "Mapping the Shadow Carceral State"; and Adam Gelb, Juliene James, and Amy Solomon, *Probation and Parole Systems Marked by High Stakes, Missed Opportunities* (Philadelphia: Pew Charitable Trusts, 2018), https://www.pewtrusts.org/-/media/assets/2018/09/probation_and_parole_systems_marked_by_high_stakes_missed_opportunities_pew.pdf.

provide 24/7 location data, warn if a person is out past their curfew or is simply out of place, and require random check-ins from a specific land-based phone line. If the device is removed by the wearer, a non-compliance advisory is typically triggered, notifying the supervisor who is supposed to respond via a warrant or arrest. The newest technologies, such as those created by Scram Systems or Telmate, deploy smartphone-based technology, which verifies identity via facial or other biometric-recognition data combined with the GPS included in the phone.[14] As the 5G revolution and the "Internet of Things" continue to roll out, monitoring is increasingly embedded across physical and personal landscapes. While e-carceration techniques are typically framed by proponents as a more humane, cost-effective, and less invasive alternative to the prison, those who have experienced it testify to a radically different experience— arguing that it must be properly understood as a form of incarceration *per se*. Further, as lawmakers have accepted the benefits of electronic monitoring as truisms, there has heretofore been minimal accountability in either the practices or goals of electronic monitoring.[15] Instead of a benign, progressive softening of state coercion, the intensity and reach of criminal supervision in the community has, per legal scholars R.J. Miller and Amanda Alexander, created a new status of diminished civil and social rights, that of "carceral citizenship." Under this designation, the carceral citizen is continuously/permanently excised from a range of experiences including voting, freedom of movement, and rights to employment and to housing. That is to say, they

14   For a brief tutorial video on these technologies, see the Telmate Guardian app video here: http://guardianmonitor.com/faq/getting-started-with-guardian.

15   For more information on e-carceration visit James Kilgore's "Challenging E-Carceration" project, https://www.challengingecarceration.org. Kilgore has written extensively on how state legislatures have almost never reviewed the practices of state and local agencies in charge of electronic monitoring programs.

are deprived from the meaning-making centers of sociopolitical life.[16]

Under today's data regime, previously unsurveilled bodies become automatic subjects of carceral attention. State monitoring of place (the specific, identified, already meaningful) has been re-placed by the monitoring of space (the general, geographic, not yet meaningful). The blanketing of both sites of specific interest and sites considered not-yet-of-interest with active and passive regimes of technological surveillance and control has created a new context of possible and anticipatory enforcement (perhaps even of "continuous flow" or "just-in-time" enforcement), which criminologists Fergus McNeill and Kristen Beyens have described as "mass supervision."[17] The civil rights organization Electronic Frontier Foundation lists nine different "street-level surveillance" technologies deployed by policing organizations: automatic license plate readers; body cameras; cell-site simulators (which divert cell phones in a given area and record descriptive information about each device); drones and unmanned aerial vehicles; stationary and mobile security cameras; and face, tattoo, and iris recognition.[18] These invasive technologies transform the default state of human experience from one of

16   Reuben Jonathan Miller and Amanda Alexander, "The Price of Carceral Citizenship: Punishment, Surveillance, and Social Welfare Policy in an Age of Carceral Expansion," *Michigan Journal of Race and Law* 21, no. 2 (2016): 291.

17   Geographers distinguish between "places," which are defined by the social process of meaning-making, and "spaces," which are in contrast considered "blank." See Tim Cresswell, *Place: A Short Introduction* (New York: John Wiley & Sons, 2013). Here, place is specifically identifiable, while space— also monitored—is reconstructed as a place worthy of suspicion and control via the surveilling technology. For more on mass supervision, see Fergus McNeill and Kristel Beyens, "Introduction: Studying Mass Supervision," in *Offender Supervision in Europe*, ed. McNeill and Beyens (New York: Palgrave Macmillan, 2013), 1–18.

18   "Street-Level Surveillance: A Guide to Law Enforcement Spying Technology," Electronic Frontier Foundation, https://www.eff.org/issues/street-level-surveillance.

presumed privacy to one of hyper-conspicuousness, which in turn produces the carceral—observed, managed, disciplined—subject. A recent piece in the *Atlantic* describes the latest technology of Persistent Surveillance Systems:

> A fixed-wing plane outfitted with high-resolution video cameras circles for hours on end, recording everything in large swaths of a city. One can later "rewind" the footage, zoom in anywhere, and see exactly where a person came from before or went after perpetrating a robbery or drive-by shooting… or visiting an AA meeting, a psychiatrist's office, a gun store, an abortion provider, a battered-women's shelter, or an HIV clinic. On the day of a protest, participants could be tracked back to their homes.[19]

Whereas the past 200 years of professional police investigations have emphasized the gathering of data, this moment in technological history reconditions the gathering of data as *prior* to the investigation. Data collection, AI, and machine learning become the context, rather than the practice, of investigation.[20]

This radical shift in how the state coercive apparatus conceptualizes daily life as evidence or as a legible site of investigation renders the entire population into legitimate and constant subjects of intense state scrutiny. While

---

19 Conor Friedersdorf, "Mass Surveillence Is Coming to a City Near You," the *Atlantic,* June 21, 2019, https://www.theatlantic.com/ideas/archive/2019/06/mass-surveillance-tech/592117.

20 Supreme Court jurisprudence lags behind technological development, often taking years to assess new technologies. It has remained almost entirely silent on the development of policing technologies—which have revolutionized the nature of investigation. See Andrew Guthrie Ferguson, *The Rise of Big Data Policing: Surveillance, Race, and the Future of Law Enforcement* (New York: New York University Press, 2017); Sarah Brayne, "Big Data Surveillance: The Case of Policing," *American Sociological Review* 82, no. 5 (October 2017): 977–1008; and Andrew D. Selbst, "Disparate Impact in Big Data Policing," *Georgia Law Review* 52, no. 1 (2017): 109–185.

the massification of this process is new, its significance and consequences extend already-existing, highly invasive, and racialized policing and surveillance practices, which, for communities of color, have been a part of "normal" political life. Stop and frisk, for example, might be considered a similar, though more "manual," incursion of state power into the daily lifespace of young Black and brown men in New York City.[21] Stop and frisk, experienced as a political violence, disrupts subjective processes of self-realization and self-determination. This analogy both warns of and invokes a recognition of the viciousness of state invasion into daily life.

Data Beyond the State?

Technological surveillance is of course not limited to the criminalized—as the density of this carceral infrastructure expands, the more the mass public becomes subject to consistent potential and actual disciplinary state control. These technologies intensify state presence in the space of the everyday via the commercial. While the nature of the modern bureaucratic state has been to create the legal and regulatory frameworks of lived personal experience—through zoning, land-ownership incentives and structures, the presence or lack of police officers and materiel—the rise of technological management is changing the quality of state-individual relations. Under today's new surveillance modus, all space is potentially carceralized. While this claim might seem extreme, when new state capacities are considered in concert with the capacious and under-regulated practices of private data organizations, the reach of *potentially* carceral supervision is near limitless, and that potential, as is the nature of the carceral, will necessarily affect human subjectivity. As

21   Wendy L. Wright, "Finding a Home in the Stop-and-Frisk Regime," *Social Justice* 43, no. 3 (2016): 25–45.

Julie Cohen reminds, "Commercial information collection has become a nearly continuous condition."[22] When you are walking (while carrying your phone) or driving your OnStar-equipped vehicle (whether you've paid for it or not), even when you drop out of the always-monitored service area, the boundaries of your movement are trackable. The nature of new commercial technologies functions such that even when you are not directly in contact with surveilling technology, it records when you enter and exit direct surveillance and collates this information as interpretable data. Therefore, even when you are out of the current reach of technological surveillance, your status is knowable, observed, and recorded—and may be retained indefinitely. In addition to the production and retention of data on one's movements, whereabouts, preferences, associations, and economic activities, the rise of virtual assistants, smart "things," and wearable technology makes the depth and breadth of this knowledge about the individual unfathomable—the ocean looms. Even our thoughts might soon be aggregated, as start-ups explore ways to monetize brain waves and hormones.[23]

What, here, is the nature of re-/de-tention? If data, collected over the expanse of a lifetime, can be mobilized to narrow a choice architecture such that will is nearly foreclosed and that a *total* management of the subject becomes possible, does data retention then become an always potential detention? Simultaneously, as the peccadillos of life are captured and catalogued, to what degree can the state pretextually enforce itself to achieve political ends?[24] As private industry revolutionizes the ways that data might

22   Julie E. Cohen, "The Biopolitical Public Domain: The Legal Construction of the Surveillance Economy," *Philosophy & Technology* 31, no. 2 (2018): 219.

23   Tekla S. Perry, "New Wearable Sensor Detects Stress Hormone in Sweat," IEEE Spectrum, July 20, 2018, https://spectrum.ieee.org/view-from-the-valley/biomedical/diagnostics/new-wearable-sensor-detects-stress-hormone-in-sweat.

be produced, collected, analyzed, and commoditized, the state is, by virtue of extant legal and political structures, ready to reap the harvest.

Google's Sensorvault, which holds detailed location data on hundreds of millions of devices from over the past decade or so, is accessible by police agencies with a warrant request. This is the case with almost all data produced, from Amazon orders to blood tests. In early 2019, the *New York Times* reported on Google's "geofence" technology that creates a dragnet focusing on a time and a place, rather than on a specific person, creating pools of "suspects" for police to review.[25] Even those places without cellular coverage—increasingly limited to rural and sparsely populated, often poor regions—produce capturable data, as people move in and out of coverage zones.[26] State power has largely remained unchallenged here because of the dominant ideology around criminality. Mass incarceration,

24   Case law in Whren v. United States, 517 US 806 (1996) and elsewhere establishes that police who have justified reasonable suspicion or probable cause for stop or detention may do so, even if the event establishing reasonable suspicion or probable cause is only a *pretext* for the goal that the officer hopes to achieve. In *Whren*, officers suspected that a vehicle's occupants might have been involved in the drug trade. Officers stopped the vehicle for failing to use a turn signal. During the course of the stop, they observed crack cocaine in the vehicle. But for the traffic violation, officers would not have had the power to stop Whren's vehicle, but the pretext permitted them to lawfully do so. Given the pervasiveness of potential legal sanction, from jaywalking to traffic offenses to drug use—all extremely common but typically unprosecuted transgressions—pretextual power may be near infinite.

25   Jennifer Valentino-DeVries, "Tracking Phones, Google Is a Dragnet for the Police," *New York Times*, April 13, 2019, https://www.nytimes.com/interactive/2019/04/13/us/google-location-tracking-police.html.

26   While rural regions are often subject to minimal cellular coverage, prison studies scholars like Ruth Wilson Gilmore, Judah Schept, and Brett Story have noted that sites of rural post-industrial economic collapse have increasingly become attractive sites for building new prisons. Prisons promise to be economic boons for struggling communities. Ironically, this means that at sites where the new carceral surveillance recedes, the old carceral concrete is reasserted.

modern criminalization, and the near-unchecked expansion of state potential has been legitimatized on the basis of its targets, which are so often seen as *rightly* the targets of state control. The range of surveilling strategies used against those who are criminalized are justified by pre-/ co-existing racial and class biases. Angela Y. Davis has argued that expansions of state violence are seen as acceptable when used first against those considered at the far margins of society. Only once this violence is normalized can it then be deployed without critique closer and closer to the supposed center—thus creating a new baseline of state power.[27] Criminal justice practice thus must be considered a kind of "technology" in the Foucauldian sense, wherein technology is more fully considered the domain of *techne*, the Greek category of practical knowledge, and is inextricably connected to the function of power. Police *know* how to police based on previous practices that are applied to new situations. Coercive practice is developed, deployed, and seen as legitimate against particularly maligned, vulnerable targets—targets that are typically racialized, class-located, and otherwise considered unruly. Were the objects of this violence seen as less *deserving* of violence, the dominant (purportedly democratic) center might object to novel expansions of coercive power. However, once a technology is deployed against the maligned mark, it easily slips and shifts from the cutting edge to the collected arsenal. The practice becomes a technology to be deployed as a matter of tactical expertise. Thus, the mobilization of surveillance is met without resistance; it is legitimate before judgment is even passed.

Locating carcerality within new technico-legal forms reveals that the continuum is pervasive even as it is also

27   Angela Y. Davis, "Class and the Prison Industrial Complex," (paper presented at Rethinking Marxism's 4th International Conference, "Marxism 2000: The Party's Not Over," University of Massachusetts at Amherst, September 21–24, 2000), YouTube, https://youtu.be/xTmiH1G_v5Q.

experienced differently by differently situated individuals. The modern state of surveillance crosses public and private, consented and coerced, intrusive and unknowable. Surveillance and digital discipline are ubiquitous: in most urban and suburban contexts, almost no one exists outside of a complicated push and pull of virtual supervision. The constant "sharing" of personal data—location, purchasing habits, browsing habits, communication partners and topics—creates, too, a baseline acquiescence to the leash of a corporate supervisor who is always a request away from state collaboration. While this data is initially collected by the private sphere, it is also almost all subject to state capture, due to a legal framework that renders both software and hardware easily accessible with minimal due process.

Here, the traditional juridical tools of Supreme Court review are out of balance with the expansive knowledge (and concurrent potential for control) offered by technological surveillance. The Fourth Amendment declares that "the right of the people to be secure in their persons, houses, papers, and effects, against unreasonable searches and seizures, shall not be violated." It has been interpreted almost entirely through the next half of the sentence, "and no warrants shall issue, but upon probable cause." In recent years, the Supreme Court has extended Fourth Amendment protections to digital data, following a fairly consistent, if not entirely robust, expectation that executive branch investigations will require warrants. Examples of the limitations that the Court has placed include a prohibition on warrantless use of thermal imaging to detect "grow operations" from outside of a building and a prohibition on the warrantless covert placement of a GPS tag on a car.[28] In 2018, acknowledging that current data records "give the Government *near perfect surveillance* and

28   See Kyllo v. United States, 533 US 27 (2001) and United States v. Jones, 565 US 400 (2012).

allow it to travel back in time to retrace a person's whereabouts," the Court confirmed that warrants were required when seeking records from private holders of data (i.e. telecommunications corporations).[29] However, these limitations extend only to whether warrants are required. Crucially, the Court declines to pursue *any* limitation on what is permissible under a reasonable search once the indefinite standard of probable cause is achieved.[30] Police are permitted that "near perfect surveillance," so long as there is a warrant or the officer determines themselves to have firsthand probable cause (that determination can be judicially reviewed retroactively and can result in evidence suppression if a court finds that the officer did not have cause).

The Court has articulated probable cause as "a flexible, common-sense standard, merely requiring that the facts available to the officer would warrant a man of reasonable caution to believe that certain items may be contraband or stolen property or useful as evidence of a crime; it does not demand any showing that such a belief be correct or more likely true than false."[31] Further, reliance on the "reasonable person standard," or what an imagined person might find reasonable—imagined and found reasonable by a judiciary long dominated by propertied white masculinity—has long been discussed as problematic. It is a standard that replicates the biases of dominant culture. It grants legal sanctuary to those who act with clear racial animus while it reconstructs the actions

29   Emphasis added. Carpenter v. United States, 585 US_(2018).
30   Legal scholars have debated the chaining of lawful search to warrants. Most visibly, Akhil Reed Amar has argued that warrants are not required, as searches may be "reasonable" without warrants. However, this has been largely an argument to expand policing powers, arguing that police need not seek warrants if other measures of reasonability are met. See Akhil Reed Amar, *The Law of the Land: A Grand Tour of Our Constitutional Republic* (New York: Basic Books, 2015).
31   Texas v. Brown, 460 US 730 (1983).

of racial and religious minorities as genitivally transgressive. The construction of some subject locations as inherently more suspect than others has been explored with regards to multiple subject identities: Khalil Muhammad has examined the historical process by which Blackness became criminalized; Jasbir Puar has explored the reduction of post–9/11 Muslim identity to the figure of the terrorist.[32] Probable cause is a barrier against absolute arbitrariness, and typically not much more. But most criticism has focused on the limits of the process prior to granting of the warrant. There has been minimal consideration of the transformation of what is available post-warrant. That a warrant is required is a valuable recognition that digital surveillance is an exertion of state coercion, but the crux is what becomes possible on the counterbalance. A traditional search is a snapshot of a moment in time, what is granted under a warrant granting access to data under the new model is a comprehensive view of a life. The extent of what the state can capture, with a remarkably low bar to reach, represents a radical shift in the relationship between the state and its subjects.

Data World Order

Even beyond the potential and actual use of surveillance (and its data) for criminal justice purposes, the data revolution as a whole is a carceral apparatus. The nature of carcerality is to enclose, foreclose, extract, and mold according to principles and logics of governmentality, which, as a range of interdisciplinary scholars have argued, is the

---

32   See Khalil Gibran Muhammad, *The Condemnation of Blackness: Race, Crime, and the Making of Modern Urban America* (Cambridge, MA: Harvard University Press, 2011); and Jasbir K. Puar, *Terrorist Assemblages: Homonationalism in Queer Times* (Durham, NC: Duke University Press, 2007).

process by which data becomes useful: quantified, intelligible, commoditized, valorized.

Scholars have disagreed on how to characterize the domination of data. Some, like Shoshana Zuboff, take a maximalist approach, arguing (persuasively) that this turn ought to be understood as "surveillance capitalism," an "economic order that claims human experience as free raw material for hidden commercial practices of extraction, prediction, and sales" and "a parasitic economic logic in which the production of goods and services is subordinated to a new global architecture of behavioral modification."[33] Nick Couldry and Ulises Mejias agree on the issue of scale but argue that "data colonialism" is a more accurate and historically useful framework to articulate the era: "While the modes, intensities, scales, and contexts of dispossession have changed, the underlying function remains the same [as colonialism]: to acquire resources from which economic value can be extracted."[34] Julie Cohen offers a perhaps more meso-level analysis: data, contra the force of commercial extraction and exploitation, is constructed as a biopolitical public domain—a legal construct framing the process of extraction and ownership as a natural, inevitable consequence of the existence of data, rather than as a politico-economic structure designed to legitimize the expropriation of data from the masses to the bourgeois elite. The biopolitical public domain, in her words, "naturalizes practices of appropriation by data processors and data brokers, positions the new data refineries and their outputs as sites of legal privilege, and elides the connections between information and power. That process subtly and durably reconfigures the legal and economic playing

---

33   Shoshana Zuboff, *The Age of Surveillance Capitalism: The Fight for a Human Future at the New Frontier of Power* (London: Profile Books, 2019), 8.

34   Nick Couldry and Ulises A. Mejias, *The Costs of Connection: How Data Is Colonizing Human Life and Appropriating It for Capitalism* (Stanford, CA: Stanford University Press, 2019), iv.

field, making effective regulation of its constituent activities more difficult to imagine."[35]

Common across these critical data arguments is the construction of data as that which is extracted from a subjected public, often with performative consent, but without meaningful consent, choice, or even knowledge. Beyond the mere collection of extant data is the understanding that as data extraction becomes a primary mode of capitalist accumulation, human relations become increasingly determined to conform to the demands of data production. This is an intensification of the mechanisms of capitalist extraction into non-labor activities. While twentieth-century capitalist industrialization maximized the extractive possibilities of market consumption, twenty-first-century data capitalism transforms all human activity into "raw material" to be extracted, processed, and rendered for profit.[36]

However, these large-scale indictments largely ignore the work of the state, except for its neoliberal role in creating and maintaining the market conditions for smoother capitalist expansion. That the state is a leading actor in extracting data for state interests, producing data for its own and market use, and mobilizing data as a form of punishment and as its legitimating framework for other uses of *bodily* coercion is a matter largely ignored. As scholars of criminal justice surveillance have shown, the state engages in all of the actions decried in private actors, *but with the force of legitimate violence behind it*. This era of data is an intensification of capitalist exploitation, but it is simultaneously and through identical means an intensification of the state's capacity for bodily domination. In *The Age of Surveillance Capitalism*, Zuboff gives a dire final warning: "Surveillance capital derives from the dispossession of human experience, operationalized in its unilateral and

35   Cohen, "The Biopolitical Public Domain," 231.
36   Cohen, "The Biopolitical Public Domain," 214.

pervasive programs of rendition: *our lives are scraped and sold to fund their freedom and our subjugation, their knowledge and our ignorance about what they know.*"[37] Yet this critique of capital is only partial without acknowledging the interplay between state coercion and market extraction.

Surveillance capitalism continues the general capitalist process of converting sites of self-determination into sites for profit. Yet as a carceral schema, the politics of data become more clear. While the effect on those under house arrest is a different sort of limitation of freedom (and a more extreme violence) than on those whose data is scraped from regular engagement with Alexa, the wielding of data about the self for state and market purposes that are definitively not one's own self-determined goals or interests reveals that both are functioning under a carceral logic. The body has become an object site, its humanity, with attendant demands like dignity, privacy, and, self-determination, seconded to state and market purposes.

The Total Carceral Schema as a Politics

The ultimate stakes of living under a total carceral schema are, in fact, unknowable. As the central feature of carceral surveillance is the internalization, legitimation, and naturalization of the reproachful gaze, the subverted will is unable to entirely escape the superstructure of carceral capital. The extent to which human life is instrumentalized—rendered useful for the expansion of corporate-state power and profit—is the manifestation of the undermining of human self-determination. The access to and transformation of the entirety of life, up to and including the texture of interiority—through expansive biometric data but also through preference management—represents a fundamental shift in the status of the individual. Under

37   Emphasis in the original. Zuboff, *The Age of Surveillance Capitalism*, 466.

totalitarian rule, one could not express, even among intimates, one's subversive feelings for fear of betrayal to the state. A future in which the state has access to the data revolution might create a world in which to even have subversive feelings is to betray oneself—and that it might be increasingly impossible to imagine subversion portends a framework wherein basic concepts of freedom, personhood, and the political itself are difficult to imagine.

Returning to the center of the carceral may give insight to its broader expanse. James Baimbridge, GPS-tracked parolee, articulates the challenge of existing under the surveillance state: "Even in prison, I didn't feel so overwhelmed with worry about doing something wrong when I'm doing everything right."[38] Baimbridge's experience has confirmed that his status is determined not by his own behavior but rather by the threat of arbitrary state force. Across the carceral schema our existence is determined by the potential threat and its concealed technological mandate. What might we wish for, if we moved through the world with neither a supervisory eye nor an engineered choice architecture?

[38]   James Baimbridge as told to Beatrix Lockwood, "My GPS-Tracked Life in Parole," *The Marshall Project*, October 28, 2019, https://www.themarshall project.org/2019/10/28/my-gps-tracked-life-on-parole.

Sable Elyse Smith, *Coloring Book 25*, 2018. Screen printing
ink, soft pastel, and oil stick on paper, 60 x 50 inches.
Courtesy of the artist; JTT, New York; and Carlos/Ishikawa,
London.

DESIGN OF THE SELF AND THE RACIAL OTHER

MABEL O. WILSON

> This "space of Otherness" line of nonhomogeneity had then functioned to validate the socio-ontological line now drawn between rational, political Man (Prospero, the settler of European descent) and its irrational Human Others (the categories of Caliban [i.e. subordinated Indians and the enslaved Negroes]).
> —Sylvia Wynter, "Unsettling the Coloniality of Being/Power/Truth/Freedom"

In 2014 the San Francisco–based Architects/Designers/Planners for Social Responsibility (ADPSR) requested the American Institute of Architects (AIA) adopt a rule prohibiting architects from designing buildings for the purpose of execution, torture, or solitary confinement. An estimated 80,000 prisoners currently live in some form of solitary confinement, including those housed in "supermax" prisons designed specifically to segregate. Not only are black and Hispanic men and women disproportionally represented in the prison population, but they are also disproportionally represented among those sentenced to solitary confinement.[1] ADPSR was unequivocal in its stance that

Epigraph from Sylvia Wynter, "Unsettling the Coloniality of Being/Power/Truth/Freedom: Towards the Human, After Man, Its Overrepresentation—An Argument," *The New Centennial Review* 3, no. 3 (Fall 2003): 313–314. This piece originally appeared in Nick Axel, Beatriz Colomina, Nikolaus Hirsh, Anton Vidokle, Mark Wigley, eds., *Superhumanity: Design of the Self* (New York: e-flux Architecture, 2018).

1   New York Advisory Committee to the US Commission on Civil Rights, *The Solitary Confinement of Youth in New York: A Civil Rights Violation* (Washington, DC: US Commission on Civil Rights, 2014), 19. See, https://www1.nyc.gov/assets/boc/downloads/pdf/NYSAC%20to%20U.S.%20Commission%20on%20Civil%20Rights.pdf.

Prison Map, developed by Josh Begley, is "not a map—
it's a snapshot of the earth's surface, taken at various points
through the United States." See http://prisonmap.com.
Courtesy of Josh Begley.

spaces purposefully designed to facilitate cruel, inhumane, and degrading acts should not be sanctioned by the profession and are "fundamentally incompatible with professional practice that respects standards of decency and human rights."[2] The AIA declined their request to amend its Code of Ethics (the organization reconsidered its initial response but has still not made the addition). Given that architecture is one of the least racially diverse professions in the United States (according to the Department of Labor, over 80 percent of architects are white), it comes as little surprise that an effort to ban the design of spaces for the unethical treatment of a largely black and brown incarcerated population would fail.[3]

That gap in understanding incarceration's impact on black and Hispanic Americans may have to do in part with who designs prisons, but it is also influenced by architecture's own genealogy in racialized modern discourses of history and science. It's an outcome of how theories of architecture and theories of the racial paradigm of human difference—modern discourses that engage the human needs and modern subjectivity—emerged from Enlightenment and post-Enlightenment thought.

Eighteenth-century debates among European architects on the aesthetic character and historical origins of architecture spurred the abandonment of classical architectural theory. These formative treatises on modern architecture also drew upon epistemic and ontological queries

2   Architects/Designers/Planners for Social Responsibility, "AIA Code of Ethics Reform," updated September 4, 2018, https://www.adpsr.org/aiaethics.

3   US Bureau of Labor Statistics tabulates demographic data on professions. See "Labor Force Statistics from the Current Population Survey," US Bureau of Labor Statistics, http://www.bls.gov/cps/cpsaat11.htm. Recent statistics on prison construction note that supermax prisons cost two to three times more than other facility types. See Sal Rodriguez, *Fact Sheet: The High Cost of Solitary Confinement* (Washington, DC: Solitary Watch, 2011), https://solitarywatch.org/wp-content/uploads/2011/06/FACT-SHEET-The-High-Cost-of-Solitary-Confinement2.pdf.

in both natural history and philosophy about the nature of humans, the world, and the cosmos. During this same period, secular forms of knowing the world continued to upend ecclesiastical doctrines. The European—the philosophe, the revolutionary, the citizen, and the architect—believed himself to be self-determined and self-conscious. It was an act of self-fashioning that Boris Groys—writing about design modernism at the beginning of the twentieth century—asserts was "the ultimate form of design"; that is, "the design of the subject."[4] As the power and influence of Christianity waned, design became a vehicle for self-realization whereby "the problems of design are only adequately addressed if the subject is asked how it wants to manifest itself, what form it wants to give itself, and how it wants to present itself to the gaze of the Other." What Groys identifies as "self-design" I would argue emerged much earlier in the Enlightenment, when an understanding of personhood was formed by distinguishing the essence of the self not only from others, but also from other things.

Also by design, Europe distinguished itself from its Others, a critical socio-political context that Groys's analysis also does not take into account. As different kingdoms throughout the fifteenth and sixteenth centuries launched explorations and colonizing missions to the New World, Africa, and Asia, Europeans began to see themselves and their continent as unique and superior. Religious and lay scholars not only began to differentiate the human species from other animal and plant species, but also began to observe and rationalize the differences in appearance and behaviors seen in those people encountered on their colonial voyages. For Denise Ferreira da Silva, "the productive narratives of science and history have consistently contained the others of Europe outside of the subject that emerged in post-Enlightenment Europe."[5] The racial

4   Boris Groys, "The Obligation to Self-Design," *e-flux Journal*, no. 00 (November 2008): 2.

became discursively productive of concepts and representations of human difference, ones that established hierarchies of mental and physical fitness affirming why
Europeans were the most capable of advancing world civilization; in other words, why they were most capable of
being modern.

Racial difference also became productive of the material conditions of modern life, fueling the unequal distribution of the resources—food and shelter—that sustain
it. To expand and entrench their imperial power over
Europe's Others, Europeans constructed colonial settlements composed of an architectural ensemble of docks,
storehouses, government buildings, plantations, and slave
quarters. In the colonies, the transatlantic slave trade
and the enslavement of Africans—rationalized through
the pretext that they were inferior and lacking faculties of
reason—provided a key labor force to cultivate rice, sugar,
and tobacco, particularly during the eighteenth and nineteenth centuries. The wealth gleaned from the movement
of slaves, raw materials, and finished goods to market
not only filled Europe's treasuries, bank accounts, church
coffers, and private fortunes, but also financed a building
boom in the metropoles of governmental offices, universities, cathedrals, banks, stock exchanges, factories, and
country estates.[6]

With the exception of the Haitian Revolution, the
French and Americans failed to put an end to chattel slavery after their respective revolutions, despite the fact
that its logic ran against the grain of modern democracy's
values of self-determination and natural rights. As self-
governing, democratic nations formed—no longer under

5   Denise Ferreira da Silva, *Toward a Global Idea of Race* (Minneapolis:
     University of Minnesota Press, 2007), xviii.

6   See Eric Williams, *Capitalism and Slavery* (Chapel Hill: University of North
     Carolina Press, 1994); and Simon Gikandi, *Slavery and the Culture of Taste*
     (Princeton, NJ: Princeton University Press, 2011).

divine rule of monarchies—new civic architecture needed to be designed and built, including prisons, an integral part of the judicial functions of the new governments. But the presence of Europe's Others in the United States—Native Americans, as well as, and more specifically, freed and enslaved blacks—complicated how prisons were designed and utilized, and how the newly constituted democratic values of America clashed with its slave-based economy.

Architectures of Punishment or Penitence

In the first decades of the nineteenth century, the statesmen, natural philosopher, planter, and architect Thomas Jefferson designed a prison for nearby Cumberland County in the Piedmont region of Virginia where his plantation Monticello was located. In 1823 the prison plans were adapted and built in Nelson County at the request of his friend Joseph Carrington Cabell, whose family owned several plantations in the region. Jefferson's efficient, compact design contained seven cells, including one for solitary confinement, which was to be used for "ill behaved prisoners."[7] Jefferson provided an extensive list of materials—brick for walls, iron for grating, tin for floors, and wood for rafters—along with their quantity and price specifications and the cost of free labor (the labor of slaves owned by contractors was left unaccounted). Construction details were calculated for security, cleanliness, and durability. Prefiguring Michel Foucault's observation that the body served "as object and target of power," Jefferson placed a privy in the corner of each cell that was to be limed daily,

7   Thomas Jefferson, architectural plan for prison, n.d., N488 (verso), Thomas Jefferson Papers: An Electronic Archive, Architectural Drawings, Miscellaneous Buildings, Massachusetts Historical Society, Boston, published as electronic resource in 2003, http://www.masshist.org/thomasjeffersonpapers/doc?id=arch_N488verso.

Thomas Jefferson's plan of a prison in Piedmont, Virginia;
1 sheet, 2 pages, undated. Identification number: N488.
Courtesy of the Coolidge Collection of Thomas Jefferson
Manuscripts, Massachusetts Historical Society.

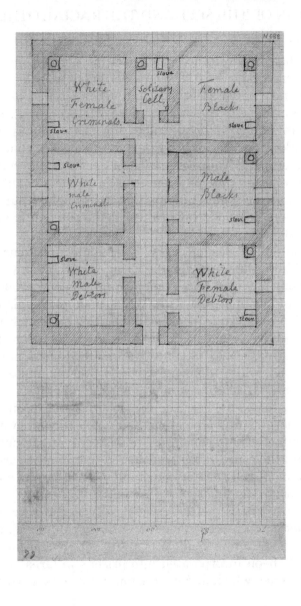

White
Female
Criminals.

stove

Solitary
Cell.

stove

Female
Blacks

stove

stove

White
male
Criminals

Male
Blacks

stove

White
Male
Debtors

stove

White
Female
Debtors

stove

99

along with a stove.[8] With taxonomic precision, the architect labeled the cells according to crime, gender, and race.

The first two cells were designed to hold "White Male and Female Debtors." Located on either side of the front entrance to the prison, these cells were most accessible to public visitors—indicating that debtors would most likely go free once creditors were satisfied that debts had been paid. The segregation of debtors and criminals likely reflected class differences in the prison's population, as well as the understanding that debt might result from imprudent decisions, but crime was the outcome of deeper moral deficiencies.

Jefferson designed the left-middle and rear cells for "White Male and Female Criminals." Under Virginia common law, men and women could be sentenced for a range of criminal activities. White male criminals could be imprisoned while awaiting trial, punishment, or death, while white women were less likely to be incarcerated for lengthy periods of time. The institution of marriage ensconced white women—wives, mothers, and daughters—in the private realm of domestic regulation, meaning that husbands bore the responsibility for disciplining their morality and protecting their virtue. If white women, particularly thieves and prostitutes, were caught violating the law, the courts often transferred them to the care and guidance of religious or charitable reform organizations, rather than sending them to prison.[9]

In between the two corner cells at the rear of the jail, Jefferson placed a narrow solitary confinement cell. This type of confinement was an invention that had only recently been incorporated into prisons in Great Britain and France, which Jefferson came into contact with and

---

8   Michel Foucault, *Discipline and Punish: The Birth of the Prison*, trans. Alan Sheridan, 2nd ed. (New York: Vintage Books, 1995), 136.

9   Mark E. Kann, *Punishment, Prisons, and Patriarchy: Liberty and Power in the Early American Republic* (New York: New York University Press, 2005), 81.

learned from while serving as a diplomat to France shortly after the end of the Revolutionary War. In Paris, Jefferson, working with French architect Charles-Louis Clèrisseau, designed civic buildings for the state of Virginia, which included the Virginia State Capitol building, a residence for the governor, and a state prison. Jefferson took interest in the designs for a French solitary confinement prison by architect Pierre Gabriel Bugniet, on which Jefferson loosely based his Virginia state prison design. Bugniet's scheme advocated the idea that introspection and reflection could reform immoral behavior.[10] His plan also organized courtyards and windows between cells to facilitate circulation of air to stem sickness.[11] These prospects of moral and physical regeneration fascinated Jefferson, noting in his autobiography:

> I had heard of a benevolent society, in England, which had been indulged by the government, in an experiment of the effect of labor, in *solitary confinement*, on some of their criminals... This I sent to the Directors [in charge of constructing Virginia's capital], instead of a plan of a common prison, in hope that it would suggest the idea of labor in solitary confinement, instead of that on the public works.[12]

Jefferson was also aware that northern Quakers advocated solitary confinement as a form of penitence for criminal

10 The concept of penitentiaries spread quickly in the United States beginning with the construction of Walnut Street Prison in 1774, established by a group of Quakers led by Benjamin Franklin. Michel Foucault described Walnut Street as an experiment where "life was partitioned according to an absolutely strict time-table, under constant supervision." Foucault, *Discipline and Punish*, 124.

11 Howard C. Rice, Jr., "A French Source of Jefferson's Plan for the Prison at Richmond," *Journal of Society of Architectural Historians* 12, no. 4 (December 1953): 28–30.

12 Thomas Jefferson, *Autobiography of Thomas Jefferson* (Mineola, NY: Dover Publications, 1959), 42.

behavior and activities, which they considered to be more humane and just than the cruel corporeal punishments administered by temperamental sovereigns.[13]

Jefferson's nation-building project, which included the building of new civic architecture to house the institutions while representing the values of the nation, aimed to elevate and maintain the moral character of naturalized Americans. His ideal citizen was the white yeoman farmer whose free labor would build the foundations of American democracy. To produce such a population, the new nation needed institutions like penitentiaries to exercise control across the disparate thirteen colonies. Those men and women who strayed toward vice and criminal activities would have the opportunity for moral improvement and rehabilitation at society's expense. Based upon Jefferson's earlier recommendations, Virginia erected architect Benjamin Henry Latrobe's designs in 1797 for a penitentiary in Richmond. These spaces of criminal reform, whose functions aimed toward what Foucault called "the deprivation of liberty," were reserved, however, for white citizens. Yet by 1820, enslaved and freed blacks comprised more than a third of the population of the United States.[14]

The Negro: Human or Subhuman?

Enlightenment and post-Enlightenment naturalists argued vociferously over the monogenetic or polygenetic origin of humans, speculating on whether Africans, Asians, and Native Americans had developed from the same species as Europeans. Geography and geology proved central to these questions of character and physiognomy. For Immanuel Kant, "Negroes and Whites are not

---

13 Foucault, *Discipline and Punish*, 124.
14 Foucault, *Discipline and Punish*, 232. The total slave population in Virginia in 1820 was 425,153. The number of freed men and women totaled 39,889, making them 9 percent of the total black population in the state.

different species of humans (for they belong presumably to one stock), but they are different *races*, for each perpetuates itself in every area, and they generate between them children that are necessarily hybrid, or blendlings (mulattoes)."[15] Whether humans of African descent had the ability to reason, and therefore the moral and intellectual capacity to create anything more than a "primitive" culture, was studied by natural philosophers and historians who largely relied on reports and diaries from colonial voyagers for their research and analysis.[16] Pondering the nature of national character, Kant, for example, observed:

> Mr. [David] Hume challenges anyone to cite a single example in which a Negro has shown talents, and asserts among the hundreds of thousands of blacks who are transported elsewhere from their countries, although many of them have even been set free, still not a single one was ever found who presented anything great in art or science or any other praiseworthy quality.[17]

Through their comparative analysis of physical and mental traits, as well as climate and geography, most naturalists concluded Africans and Negroes to be an inferior race with little or no capacity to evolve beyond a primitive state no matter where they lived.

The need to set a firm national economic foundation after the War for Independence rendered enslaved labor indispensable to rebuilding the nation's wealth. It was also

15   Immanuel Kant, "On the Different Races of Men" (1777), in *Race and the Enlightenment: A Reader*, ed. Emmanuel Chukwudi Eze (Cambridge, MA: Blackwell Publishers, 1997), 40.

16   See David Bindman, *Ape to Apollo: Aesthetics and the Idea of Race in the Eighteenth Century* (Ithaca, NY: Cornell University Press, 2002).

17   Immanuel Kant, "On National Characteristics, So far as They Depend upon the Distinct Feeling of the Beautiful and Sublime," in Eze, *Race and the Enlightenment*, 55.

necessary for sustaining the life and livelihoods of its white population. The end of the US Civil War brought constitutional amendments that granted emancipation, citizenship, and legal protection to all, but before this, blacks had toiled under common laws and brutal slave codes that rendered them without rights. Most lived among white Americans whose socio-cultural beliefs and practices dehumanized them without reprieve. Any injustice or criminal act upon enslaved blacks was typically resolved outside the judicial system. If they were charged with a crime, trial would take place in front of white judges and be decided upon by all-white juries. As Saidiya Hartman writes about why the rape of enslaved women, for instance, was rarely adjudicated, "the invocation of person and property made issues of consent, will, and agency complicated and ungainly."[18]

In his *Notes on the State of Virginia*, Jefferson expressed his "physical and moral objections" to the Negro based on observations of comportment and character of his more than one hundred slaves at Monticello. What he saw as the Negro's inability to appreciate beauty except in the most sensual manner or to create works of true aesthetic value except out of mimicry provided Jefferson with evidence of their natural mental inferiority. In their faculties of recollection, they are equal to whites, observed Jefferson, but the Negroes' ability to reason, to comprehend mathematics and sciences is certainly inferior. "In their imagination," Jefferson condemned, "they are dull, tasteless, and anomalous."[19]

A proponent of natural rights—that all men are born free—Jefferson had advocated for the incremental emancipation of slaves and for the elimination of the international slave trade early in his political career. But emancipation

18   Saidiya V Hartman, *Scenes of Subjection: Terror, Slavery, and Self-Making in Nineteenth-Century America* (New York: Oxford University Press, 1997), 80.

could only be successful as a national enterprise if blacks, he claimed, once freed, left the United States and immigrated to colonies in the West Indies or Africa. "Why not retain and incorporate blacks into the state?" asked Jefferson in *Notes on the State of Virginia*. Because of "deep rooted prejudices entertained by the whites; ten thousand recollections, by the blacks, of the injuries they have sustained; new provocations; the real distinctions which nature has made."[20] Jefferson's proposition, which paralleled similar movements in England that established Sierra Leone in 1787, would become the foundation for the colonization movement in the United States. The American Colonization Society was founded in 1816, whose members included William Thornton, the architect of the US Capitol, and the son of British architect Benjamin Henry Latrobe. With the foundation of Liberia in 1821 by the United States, integration of blacks into the fabric of the nation was not a desired course of action. The colonization movement, which formed from an alliance between white Northern abolitionists and mid-Atlantic slaveholders who held similar views to Jefferson's, tacitly agreed that there was no place for the freed Negro in America's democratic society or within its national boundaries.

We can now return to Jefferson's 1823 design for the county prison and unpack the significance of the cells reserved on the right-middle and rear for "Black Men and Women." It is notable that Jefferson did not include the labels "debtor" or "criminal" on these cells; rather, they were most likely designed to hold captured slaves who had escaped either from their masters or while in transit

19   See Thomas Jefferson, "Query XIV: The Administration of Justice and Description of the Laws?," in *Notes on the State of Virginia* (Paris, 1785), Avalon Project: Documents in Law, History, and Diplomacy, Yale Law School, accessed July 22, 2016, https://avalon.law.yale.edu/18th_century/jeffvir.asp.

20   Jefferson, "Query XIV: The Administration of Justice and Description of the Laws?"

westward for sale to till in the frontier territories created from Jefferson's purchase of the Louisiana Territory. In other words, these prison cells served as holding cells for private property.

Authorities rarely incarcerated enslaved men and women for criminal activity, but instead implemented harsh measures—beatings or death—for improper and unlawful behavior.[21] Unless the public prosecution of a slave's criminal deed, such as plotting insurrection, murder, or violence against a white person, could function as a deterrent to slave disobedience, disciplining the enslaved body fell under the jurisdiction of their owners who meted out various forms of punishment for minor infractions. The fabrication and use of iron shackles, collars, bridles, and regular displays of punitive justice at the whipping post within the slave quarters were regimes of violence deployed by slavers, owners, overseers, and slave patrols to subdue a person and maintain lawful and submissive behavior. The black slave body became the site of what Hartman calls the "routinized violence of slavery."[22] Through these means, Southerners made the disciplining of slave populations a private rather than public matter, which was also an attempt to keep the dispute over slavery's inhumanity out of the public space of political debate.

The two "Black" cells would have also held free black men and women who had committed crimes. Fearing freed slaves would become a financial burden, undermine the wages of white workers, pose a criminal threat, or incite slave rebellions, Virginia in 1793 restricted the migration of freed blacks to the state and required that manumitted men and women either register with local authorities or leave the state within a year of their liberation.[23] Failure to

---

21   Paul Finkelman, "Slavery in the United States: Persons or Property?," in *The Legal Understanding of Slavery: From the Historical to the Contemporary*, ed. Jean Allain (Oxford: Oxford University Press, 2012), 105–134.

22   Hartman, *Scenes of Subjection*, 4.

migrate would entail forfeiture of their freedom. Any freed black person caught committing a crime would be arrested and, depending on the severity of the crime, possibly sold back into slavery. Freed blacks were given higher penalties and longer sentences for criminal acts. Despite a lack of civil liberties—freedom of movement, higher taxes, and threats of violence and enslavement—many freed blacks chose to remain near enslaved family members.[24] By 1820 some 30,000 free-people resided in Virginia.

Virginia, like other Southern states, refused to recognize the humanity and equality of black people. To be of African descent in antebellum Virginia meant one could only live as property in the system of chattel slavery. Certainly, to be free and black was an anomaly. Lacking rights and citizenship and reduced to the status of a possession, blacks were dehumanized under Virginia's law, the very laws which constituted the spaces of everyday life. Jefferson, like many of the ruling planter class, had depended his entire life on enslaved blacks to take care of his family's personal needs wherever he traveled and to work his various plantations in Virginia. Through his prison plan for nearby Cumberland and Nelson counties, Jefferson had designed a racialized apparatus of modern incarceration, a typology of captivity and violence that has continued to evolve through the twenty-first century.

From Plantation to Prison

Debates on racial character and physiognomy remained active until the "Sciences of Man," disciplines such as biology, anthropology, and sociology that were invented during the nineteenth century, naturalized earlier concepts of

23   Ellen D. Katz, "African-American Freedom in Antebellum Cumberland County, Virginia—Freedom: Personal Liberty and Private Law," *Chicago Kent Law Review* 70, no. 3 (April 1995): 952.
24   Katz, "African-American Freedom," 952–953.

Chandra McCormick, *Line Boss, Angola State Penitentiary*, 2004. Courtesy of the artist.

racial difference. Ferreira da Silva writes that with objective fact the "scientists of man attempted to prove... what eighteenth-century naturalists could only describe and the philosophers who framed man could only postulate."[25] By the twentieth century, race and raciality—the productive signifiers of race—had rationalized and naturalized the physical (bodily) and mental (moral) inferiority of Europe's Others as fact. The logics of modern planning, development policy, and neoliberal economics justified their continued dehumanization and marginalization in the slum, the ghetto, the favela, the projects, the banlieue, and, of course, the prison.

Plantation enclosures link directly to the carceral spaces of prisons. During post–Civil War Reconstruction, Louisiana erected, for example, its new prison on parcels of land from several plantations known as Angola, named for the region of Africa where the plantation's slaves had originated. The plantation's old slave quarters remained in active use at Angola prison, as did the farming operations and the regimes of violence exacted on black convicts—who, like their enslaved ancestors, were also leased out for the profit of the prison's management and the state. The adaptation of Angola plantation to a prison tethers the abuses of slavery to modern incarceration. Today, the 18,000-acre Louisiana State Penitentiary at Angola, known as "The Farm," operates as the largest maximum-security prison in the United States. Sentences to solitary confinement can last for decades in its supermax cellblocks.[26]

The billion-dollar prison-industrial complex, an increasingly privatized, corporate-managed system, continues slavery's vicious dehumanization of black men and

---

25   Ferreira da Silva, *Toward a Global Idea of Race*, 120.
26   See Thomas Beller, "Angola Prison in the Shadow of Slavery," *New Yorker*, August 19, 2015, http://www.newyorker.com/culture/cultural-comment/angola-prison-louisiana-photos; also see "The Angola Three," Amnesty International, http://www.amnestyusa.org/our-work/cases/usa-the-angola-3.

women. ADPSR's request to the AIA marks one noble effort to disentangle the architect's expertise from their centuries-long productive engagement with America's inhumane and exploitive carceral system. ADPSR's goal is to limit architects from profiting off of the design of the most violent spaces of the prison-industrial complex. Perhaps then, the profession will recognize that black lives actually do matter.

Sable Elyse Smith, *Coloring Book 26*, 2018. Screen printing ink, white out, and oil stick on paper, 60 x 50 inches. Courtesy of the artist; JTT, New York; and Carlos/Ishikawa, London.

BACKWARD TO WAYWARD: LISTENING TO ARCHIVES OF DISCIPLINARY EDUCATION IN PHILADELPHIA

LESLIE LODWICK

This essay traces the long history of a particular site of domination and resistance, forced subjecthood and collective refusal. The disciplinary school brought to task in this essay captures the way in which spaces of education are both produced by and productive of social, racial, and political anxieties, as well as, more specifically, highly-constructed ideas about certain kinds of students. Thus, the material, pedagogical, and institutional evolution of the Daniel Boone School in Philadelphia must be situated within—or between—accounts of the undisciplined: the pathologized and the racialized, the knowable and the unknowable, the heard and the unheard, the acquiescent and the unyielding, the backward and the wayward. Doing so reveals how student subjectivities and racial boundaries are normalized but also how they are undone.

Constructing a Backward Pathology

In 1911, Dr. Lightner Witmer, a professor at the University of Pennsylvania and an early founder of clinical psychology, outlined an epistemology of normal adolescence:

> The first step toward the understanding and adequate training of normal and gifted children in the public schools is to understand the problem of individual training with backward and mentally defective children. This arises from the fact that the minds of these children are less complicated and move more slowly than the minds of normal or gifted children. We are therefore able to learn more about a defective

child than about the mind of a normal child, and we shall acquire the necessary knowledge concerning normal children first through a better understanding of defective children.[1]

Witmer's theory of knowledge linked, as it constructed, ideas of normality and abnormality, giftedness and defectiveness, public duty and private duty. Even more, it attempted to formalize a rehabilitative connection between school and laboratory. The production of a "normal" child depended on the existence of an oppositional "backward" child, one whose mind could be studied, analyzed, known, and put to use. Witmer's epistemology formed the basis for a model of education that in turn naturalized, reproduced, and spatialized the artificial separation and real segregation of children. His writings were fundamental to the rapidly developing idea of special education—that some students were unable to learn in the same environments and spaces as others—and, more specifically, to how this idea was taken up across Philadelphia Public Schools in the early twentieth century.

Witmer's understanding of "backwardness" was productive of individuals and of society. To be "backward" was, according to Witmer, to be "more or less defective mentally and physically" and in possession of "moral symptoms which aroused grave apprehension in the minds of those concerned for their future welfare and standing in society."[2] "Backward" was a catchall, encompassing those with hearing or vision impairment, unspecified learning disabilities, developmental delays, or the pathologized effects of trauma and poverty. According to Witmer, attending to

1   Lightner Witmer, *The Special Class for Backward Children; An Educational Experiment Conducted for the Instruction of Teachers and Other Students of Child Welfare by the Psychological Laboratory and Clinic of the University of Pennsylvania* (Philadelphia: The Psychological Clinic Press, 1911), 5.

2   Witmer, *The Special Class for Backward Children*, 1.

backward youth became a social and pedagogical issue best *handled* through the institution of the public school—in cooperation with Pennsylvania's juvenile delinquency statutes around waywardness in the nineteenth and twentieth centuries.[3] Though perhaps less draconian than the New York Wayward Minor Acts, the laws structuring waywardness in Philadelphia were equally presumptive and unquestioningly enforced and sought to hand those children with a supposed predisposition to crime—as primarily decided through neighborhood, and thus class and race—over to the state.[4] During Witmer's time, backwardness begat waywardness, and thus it served as an ideal apparatus for turning class and race into pathological and scientifically explained phenomena.

Writing twenty-five years before Witmer opened his clinic, Bradford K. Pierce, affiliated with New York's House of Refuge and the Wayward Minor Acts, warned of the same corruptible force of racialized poverty and its generational impact that Witmer hypothesized in his later experiments, writing, "The immense importation of the poorer and lower classes of Europe, the most destitute portion of which lingers in our Eastern cities, greatly increases the statistics of exposed and criminal children. Poor blood, low moral culture, the pinch of poverty, the habit of indulgence, predispose this class to early crime."[5] To be sure, the child in Pierce's paranoid projection, one predisposed toward criminality, was implicitly aligned with an "other" set in opposition to whiteness. As the non-white population grew in Philadelphia throughout the Progressive Era due to

3   Witmer, *The Special Class for Backward Children*, 5.
4   Peter D. Garlock, "'Wayward' Children and the Law, 1820–1900: The Genesis of the Status Offense Jurisdiction of the Juvenile Court," *Georgia Law Review* 13, no. 2 (1979): 341.
5   Bradford K. Pierce, *A Half Century with Juvenile Delinquents; Or, the New York House of Refuge and Its Times* (New York: D. Appleton & Co., 1869), 249–250.

"At the Parting of the Ways: Ought We Allow Human Material Like This to be Wasted and Destroyed to Develop Physical Degeneracy, Mental Retardation, and Moral Delinquency?" From Lightner Witmer, "The Restoration of Children of the Slums," *Psychology Clinic* 3, no. 9 (1910).

AT THE PARTING OF THE WAYS

OUGHT WE TO ALLOW HUMAN MATERIAL LIKE THIS TO BE WASTED AND DESTROYED,
TO DEVELOP PHYSICAL DEGENERACY, MENTAL RETARDATION AND MORAL DELINQUENCY?

waves of immigration from Europe and the Southern United States, whiteness was constructed in a certain image, non-whiteness in another. With the first wave of the Great Migration, in which 140,000 black people moved to Germantown, white Philadelphians relocated to the outskirts of the city, making way for an additional influx of immigrants from Italy, Ireland, and Poland. That the problem children in Witmer's writings are frequently described as *looking* typically Irish, Italian, Yiddish, or some other "coarse parental lineage" is notable—for immigrants had not yet been accepted or opted into whiteness.[6] To appear to be other than white was a direct correlate to backwardness, and thus a threat to whiteness, especially as it was produced and reproduced in the institution of the school.[7] Of this yoking of racialized physical attributes to supposed inherent mental and moral capacities, David Bindman writes, "The science of aesthetics was conceived of as a way of ordering and codifying the 'lower' mental processes in man that were not and could not be governed by reason."[8] For Witmer, aestheticized race continued to be a factor in his scientific construction of a student other, one predetermined to function at the periphery of normativity. By the 1920s, the growing Germantown posed an ideological and racial threat that needed to be managed at the developmental level. Witmer's methods of managing and segregating difference offered a way to do that.

6   US Bureau of the Census, "Population—Pennsylvania, Table 13: Composition and Characteristics of the Population for Wards of Cities of 50,000 or More, Philadelphia," in *Fourteenth Census of the United States, 1920*, vol. 3, *Population, 1920: Composition and Characteristics of the Population by States* (Washington, DC: Government Printing Office, 1922), 896. For additional reading on becoming white, see James Baldwin, "On Being White... And Other Lies," *Essence*, April 1984, Anti-Racism Digital Library, https://sacred.omeka.net/items/show/238.

7   Witmer, *The Special Class for Backward Children*, 42–114.

8   David Bindman, *Ape to Apollo: Aesthetics and the Idea of Race in the Eighteenth Century* (Ithaca, NY: Cornell University Press, 2002), 19.

In the early days of special education, Witmer and school district administrators used the term "orthogenic" to signify a student unable to function in the normative classroom environment and in need of remedial instruction. Reportedly coined by Witmer and then superintendent Dr. Oliver Cornman, "orthogenic" dealt with the science of "making people right."[9] Witmer believed that with special classes a "subnormal" student with disciplinary problems could be rehabilitated or perhaps made "normal" with proper care and restored to their neighborhood school. He also believed that the only way for special education to properly function was through a formal institutional channel between school district and university-affiliated psychology clinic.[10] According to the 1920–1921 Philadelphia School Survey, between 1909 and 1921 the number of classrooms for orthogenic students increased from 48 to 136. By 1921, students were classified even more specifically as either "orthogenic disciplinary" or "orthogenic backward," and by 1922 there were 104 orthogenic backward classes and 32 orthogenic disciplinary classes across Philadelphia public schools.[11] The lines between these two categories were blurry—the factor determining how children were sorted into disciplinary classrooms was often whether or not they were perceived likely to commit future crimes by administrators, and thus in greater need of being made "right." In Philadelphia's School District 6—home to Germantown and home to more immigrants from Italy, Ireland, and the black South than any other neighborhood in the city—the number of

9   W. Herbert Grigson, "Physical and Health Education in Special Classes: The
     Physical Education Program in Orthogenic, Backward, and Disciplinary
     Classes," *The Journal of Health and Physical Education* 2, no. 4 (1931): 15.

10   Witmer, *The Special Class for Backward Children*, 7.

11   Pennsylvania State Department of Public Instruction, *Report of the Survey
     of the Public Schools of Philadelphia*, vol. 3 (Philadelphia: The Public
     Education and Child Labor Association of Pennsylvania, 1922), 11–20.

"Expressive Work in Detail: Giving Back the Talk at the Opening Exercises," from Lightner Witmer, *The Special Class for Backward Children; An Educational Experiment Conducted for the Instruction of Teachers and Other Students of Child Welfare by the Psychological Laboratory and Clinic of the University of Pennsylvania* (Philadelphia: The Psychological Clinic Press, 1911).

III. EXPRESSIVE WORK IN DETAIL.
GIVING BACK THE TALK AT THE OPENING EXERCISES.

orthogenic disciplinary classrooms was nearly triple that of other school district areas.[12]

Typologically, the orthogenic school was linked to the home in a more concrete sense too. Writing on the need for the restorative public school, Cornman cited the private failures of "dissolute parents" in "semi-slum districts."[13] Witmer, too, frequently attributed "backwardness" to the impoverished home. He went as far as to argue that the home environment of a child is more influential on their ability to perform in a "normal" classroom than is their "fixed" mental capacity—the worst environment being that of "very poor homes… usually found in the foreign quarters of the city where the parents are densely ignorant and incapable of giving adequate oversight to the children."[14] That Witmer's theories of normalization linked the family and the home to the production of mental and physical abnormality is crucial for understanding their wide adoption. If families could not be helped, either because of entrenched poverty or perceived cultural obstinacy, then schools were the necessary disciplinary corrective, not only to the backward student but also to the backward home:

> When a boy comes into the school and manifests obstinacy there, we must remember that his behavior is in large part a product of his home treatment… Many children show lack of discipline in the schools when eight, fifteen, or perhaps twenty years old, because the initial lack of discipline was in the first, second, or third year of the child's life. These problems are

12   David W. Young, "'You Feel So Out of Place': Germantown's J. Gordon Baugh and the 1913 Commemoration of the Emancipation Proclamation," *The Pennsylvania Magazine of History and Biography* 137, no. 1 (2013): 79–93.

13   Lightner Witmer, "A Psychological Clinic," in "Race Improvement in the United States," special issue, *The Annals of the American Academy of Political and Social Science* 34, no. 1 (July 1909): 151.

14   Witmer, *The Special Class for Backward Children*, 38.

> being turned over to the schools. The home is practi-
> cally asking the school to remedy its defects. We must
> assist the home in the better training and disciplining
> of these children before and after they enter school.[15]

Witmer thus positioned his own research as a social necessity—something that could correct the failures of the
family, which he and others came to evaluate through
the lens of poverty and race.[16] That his epistemology was
absorbed into the public school system provided proof of
the school's role in naturalizing, normalizing, and thus
legitimizing values produced outside of it; it confirmed the
school's force as a mechanism of ideological management
in concert with other social institutions.

As the official psychological advisor for the Philadelphia public school system, Witmer consulted with
the city's schools for years, organizing and maintaining its orthogenic classrooms and an entire orthogenic
disciplinary school—setting the trajectory of the city's
approach to special education, which maintained its core
structuring even as the discursive framing and naming
of reform schools changed over the course of the twentieth century. The misguided and racially motivated *belief*,
which appeared throughout his writing, that poor children were actually happier when separated from "normal"
classrooms rationalized the continued existence and ongoing proliferation of orthogenic schooling.[17] This, together
with the fear that the commingling of "backward" students

---

15   Witmer, "A Psychological Clinic," 143.
16   In 1910, Witmer writes, "To conserve the children of the next generation,
      however, we must begin by restoring their future parents, the children
      of this generation. We should offer the slum parent something better than
      a choice between race suicide and child murder." See Lightner Witmer, "The
      Restoration of Children of the Slums," *Psychological Clinic* 3, no. 9
      (1910): 280.
17   Witmer, "A Psychological Clinic," 149–152.

"Marching Drill: To Line Up as Shown in the Illustration Required Four Or Five Weeks' Work," from Lightner Witmer, *The Special Class for Backward Children; An Educational Experiment Conducted for the Instruction of Teachers and Other Students of Child Welfare by the Psychological Laboratory and Clinic of the University of Pennsylvania* (Philadelphia: The Psychological Clinic Press, 1911).

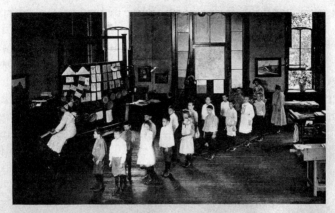

IV. MARCHING DRILL.
TO LINE UP AS SHOWN IN THE ILLUSTRATION REQUIRED FOUR OR FIVE WEEKS' WORK.

(again, mentally, morally or disciplinarily) with "normal" students would negatively influence or proximally corrupt the latter, led to an unofficial system of spatial segregation in the city's schools. Against the backdrop of Philadelphia's wayward minor laws, waywardness as a pathology—vis-à-vis backwardness, which needed to be contained and corrected in the service of preserving the ongoing production of whiteness—was embedded pedagogically and spatially in the long-term planning endeavors of the city's public school administrators.[18]

Schooling the Wayward:
The Evolution of Boone, Kane, and Camelot

In 1931, W. Herbert Grigson—the then Supervisor of Physical and Health Education for Philadelphia Public Schools—wrote a four-part series of essays on orthogenic disciplinary education in the *Journal of Health and Physical Education*. The series made explicit the racist and classist beliefs of his contemporaries, which had become imbricated and normalized in the formation of disciplinary school spaces and programming in Philadelphia. To be not only non-white but now specifically black became synonymous with waywardness, and these racial categories were concretized in the formation of disciplinary boundaries. Grigson writes,

When in the throes of an angry outburst there is no telling what they may do. Colored pupils are more unstable emotionally than native white. Boys' disciplinary schools in other cities with few colored pupils bear out the truth of this statement.[19]

18   Garlock, "'Wayward' Children and the Law, 1820–1900," 341.
19   W. Herbert Grigson, "Physical and Health Education in Special Classes: History, Problems, and Special Methods," *The Journal of Health and Physical Education* 2, no. 3 (1931): 54. The following three essays were

For Witmer, the corrupting force of poverty and of other racial, cultural, and national formations threatened the progress of whiteness and proximally produced the backward child. Grigson's text marked a shift toward a system that understood backwardness and waywardness to be constituted by race—and toward a racialized hierarchy of disciplinary students. It established blackness as something to be managed through the institution of the school and described a new expression of disciplinary student formation. The throes, the anger, the outbursts, the instability, and the unpredictability assigned to non–"native white" students were more forwardly punishable. Grigson's text constructed outlawed emotions according to race, and it anticipated both the set of harsh punitive measures that would be developed to suppress this vitality or emotionality and the corollary collective impulse to resist the categorization and coercion of the racialized disciplinary student.

The origins of pathologized and racialized waywardness can only be fully understood by considering the spatial evolutions and sonic means of its continued production, as well as by considering the resistance and social agency of students. Despite Grigson's attempt to produce a fixed and undeniable disciplinary subject, an alternative reading of his statement leads to Rinaldo Walcott's description of blackness "as a sign, one that carries with it particular histories of resistance and domination."[20] Therefore, this essay seeks to interrogate the nuanced spatial histories of a disciplinary reform that reifies racial boundaries in the context of student resistance. It traces the first

published in issues 4, 9, and 10 of the same volume, respectively. See also Grigson, "Physical and Health Education in Special Classes: The Physical Education Program in Orthogenic, Backward, and Disciplinary Classes."

20   Rinaldo Walcott, *Writing Black Canada*, 2nd rev. ed. (Toronto: Insomniac Press, 2003), 27, quoted in Simone Browne, *Dark Matters: On the Surveillance of Blackness* (Durham, NC: Duke University Press, 2015), 8.

disciplinary school in Philadelphia—and one of only a handful of disciplinary schools throughout the twentieth century—across time. That is, it tells an account of subject formation both bound to the desire for control within the disciplinary institution and inextricably linked to a collective, indexical student refusal that nullified the enactment of that control. What follows is an attempt to describe the contours of a "particular" history and site "of resistance and domination."

The Daniel Boone School opened in 1929 in the working-class immigrant neighborhood of Fishtown, Philadelphia—strategically located outside of the wealthy city center among a growing Catholic and Jewish population and developing black neighborhood. Intended specifically for students classified as having "disciplinary" problems, the school was built by district architect Irwin T. Catharine as part of a larger school-building campaign undertaken by the district.

Boone, like Catharine's other school buildings, was constructed in the same collegiate Gothic style as nearby University of Pennsylvania. This was not accidental; Catharine and school board members sought to express the elevated status of public education as a socially ameliorative force. Boone had elaborate stained glass windows, decorative tile mosaics, brick cornices, and arched limestone—indicative of the influence of Witmer's ideas (particularly the link between special education and university-affiliated clinic or lab) on public school administrators but also of the changing aesthetics and practices of spatial reform more broadly. The Lancasterian model of schools in Philadelphia had come under increasing scrutiny. Reformers like Witmer and Catharine sought a less militant and more apparently gentle form of rehabilitation.[21] Catharine's school designs were a campaign—aimed to make students feel connected to their education, rather than disconnected from it, and to restore faith in public schools. Faith in the institution came with its interior marble, indoor plumbing, collegiate stylings, double-loaded corridors, high ceilings, auditoria, and gymnasia. Though smaller in scale than Catharine's other schools, Boone was no different. It was to be a manageable architectural microcosm of the larger neighborhood school, except its pupils would be students with behavioral issues; it was not intended to be singularly punitive or more readily surveilled than other schools at the time of its design and construction. According to Witmer, even this permanent district-run disciplinary school was to be a temporary solution—second fiddle to the pedagogical experiments he was conducting in his clinic to determine the best strategies for "rehabilitation" and forced normalization.

By the 1960s, however, the popular use of the medical term "orthogenic" had entirely fallen out of use, and with Witmer's death in 1956, the relationship between his psychology clinic and the public school system had dissolved. Boone, which had over the years aligned itself with harsher disciplinary practice, came under increasing scrutiny in the 1960s (a scrutiny that would last through the 1980s), in large part because of a series of exposés in the *Philadelphia Inquirer* that detailed excessive violence against students, physical restraint and abuse by staff, and allegations of little to no classroom instruction.[22] Students reported that Boone functioned not like a school but like a series of holding rooms for students the district did not know what to do with. Amidst increasing

21 Dell Upton, "Lancasterian Schools, Republican Citizenship, and the Spatial Imagination in Early Nineteenth-Century America," *Journal of the Society of Architectural Historians* 55, no. 3 (1996): 250.

22 Harry J. Karafin, "Penna. Probes Job Abuses, Wage Chiseling, Beatings At City Disciplinary School," *Philadelphia Inquirer*, February 24, 1960; John P. Corr, "'I'd Do Anything to Keep My Child Out of This School,'" *Philadelphia Inquirer*, February 13, 1970.

racial tension in Philadelphia and nationwide, and amidst a supposed "discipline problem" across public schools in the city, Mayor Frank Rizzo called for more disciplinary schools and higher enrollments in them.[23] Daniel Boone School thus relocated into the former building of the larger Elisha Kent Kane School in North Philadelphia in 1984.[24] The four-story masonry building, just 3 miles west of the original Boone School in a predominantly black neighborhood, could enroll up to 375 students—substantially more than the smaller Boone School in Fishtown.[25]

Originally intended to offer vocational training for students with disabilities, the Kane School building was built in 1963. It had seven large workshop classrooms for vocational-based activities, including shoe repair, barbering, and home economics. In Boone's early days at Kane, administrators maintained some of the original vocational training designed for the original school with the hope that disciplinary students, like students with disabilities, would benefit from the same work-based pedagogical programming. At this point, though no longer associated with clinical psychology, the message was still clear: students deemed to have disciplinary problems had the same pedagogical needs as students with disabilities and could be served by the same spatial arrangements. This message did not last long.

Fueled in large part by waves of gun violence in the city in the 1980s and a racialized fear of student violence, Boone's choice-based educational programming, sports, and vocational training were eliminated and replaced with

23   "'Principals keep telling me that there is a need for a special school where we'll turn these kids around,' says Rizzo." See "Rizzo Backs School for Problem Pupils" *Philadelphia Daily News*, November 24, 1971.
24   Juan Gonzalez, "School District Regains Balance, Pays Back $8.5M to City," *Philadelphia Daily News*, May 31, 1984.
25   "Closing of the Boone School Is Given Tentative Approval," *Philadelphia Inquirer*, January 24, 1984; "New Kane School Opened by City," *Philadelphia Inquirer*, December 4, 1963.

stricter classroom management. This closure echoed a larger nationwide anxiety, which stemmed from the infamous Reagan-era report *A Nation at Risk*. *A Nation at Risk* warned that, compared to the students of other nations, US students were missing essential school-based training in math, science, and reading and taking too many non-essential (vocational) courses: "Our society and its educational institutions seem to have lost sight of the basic purposes of schooling, and of the high expectations and disciplined effort needed to attain them."[26] Discipline was reframed as a necessary national good and the backbone of a newly reformed system of education that emphasized colorblind objectivity. The report continued,

> The people of the United States need to know that individuals in our society who do not possess the levels of skill, literacy, and training essential to this new era will be effectively disenfranchised, not simply from the material rewards that accompany competent performance, but also from the chance to participate fully in our national life.[27]

A Nation at Risk "effectively" promised to strip individuals—particularly those unable, incapable, and uninclined to participate in the reformed systems of education outlined in it or simply those who were averse, who resisted, who fell behind, who didn't fall in line, who didn't possess appropriate "competency"—of political purchase and of the right to engage in larger national politics and civic processes. Like the earliest disciplinary schools that

26   National Commission on Excellence in Education, *A Nation at Risk: The Imperative for Educational Reform, A Report to the Nation and the Secretary of Education* (Washington, DC: United States Department of Education, 1983), 5–6.

27   National Commission on Excellence in Education, *A Nation at Risk*, 7.

constructed and enforced racial boundaries through separation, *A Nation at Risk* outlined an educational model that
determined degrees of citizenship through exclusion. It
expressed a form of punitive disciplinary power, a pointed
rebuke and threat to specific communities and specific individuals: to be rendered incompetent or backward would be
to be deprived of participating in the public sphere and to
be untethered from the rest of society.

Within the shared context of US public schools, the
political anxieties that produced *A Nation at Risk*—the
fear of losing an upper-hand in science and technology
to foreign powers—can be understood as an extension of
nineteenth-century nativist concerns about the corrupting influence of non-"native" white and black immigrants
on a white moral society. They each express anxious, even
macabre optimism about the reformatory capacity of
public school to combat political and systemic anxieties.
Post–*A Nation at Risk*, the disciplinary school, in particular, operated in this space of fear. This national shift—
toward rigorous academic training (particularly in science
and math) alongside the elimination of arts and vocational
programs—found particular resonance in Philadelphia,
where it was taken up to justify misplaced fears about
"urban" students having too much choice and too much idle
time and institutions having too little control. Consistent
with other schools in the district, entire wings of Boone
were shuttered, workshops locked, and sports and vocational programs eliminated.

The turn toward zero-tolerance policies in the 1990s
was linked to the 1994 federal Gun Free Schools Act,
which made federal funding contingent on state expulsion
rules for students suspected of firearm possession. Many
districts across the US also included other offenses like
fighting and drug possession as part of these new zero-tolerance policies. In Pennsylvania, zero tolerance initially
intended to "assign explicit, predetermined punishments

to specific violations of school rules regardless of the situation or context of the behavior."[28] In Philadelphia, the policies evolved to include suspension or expulsion for school-uniform violations, for "ongoing open defiance," and for "habitually disruptive behavior." A report published by Philadelphia's youth-led organization Youth United for Change in 2011 found the city's zero-tolerance policies to be singular: "There may be no other large, urban school system that matches the District in its promotion of zero tolerance and in the heavy use of out of school suspensions, expulsions, disciplinary transfers to alternative schools, referrals to law enforcement and school-based arrests."[29] Under the zero-tolerance regime, "minor, or even trivial" student infractions—talking back, having a cell phone, being late or cutting class, smoking, graffitiing, and fighting—have outsized consequences distributed unevenly according to race: expulsion, school arrest, and forced transfer to disciplinary institutions.[30]

In 2004, the School District of Philadelphia entered into an operational contract with Camelot Education, a Texas-based charter school company that would come to operate dozens of transitional, restorative, and accelerated "alternative" charter schools nationwide. This union not only

28   Youth United for Change, Advancement Project, and the Education Law Center, *Zero Tolerance in Philadelphia: Denying Educational Opportunities and Creating a Pathway to Prison* (Philadelphia: Youth United for Change, 2011), 19, https://www.atlanticphilanthropies.org/wp-content/uploads/2015/09/Zero-Tolerance-in-Philadelphia-2.pdf.

29   Youth United for Change et al., *Zero Tolerance in Philadelphia*, 2.

30   "In fact, Black students were over two-and-a-half times more likely to be suspended than White students in 2008–2009 and Latino students were over one-and-a-half times more likely to be suspended than their White peers. Thus it is largely Black and Latino students who are excluded from school by these practices, which inevitably deepens the district-wide disparities in educational achievement along racial lines." See Youth United for Change et al., *Zero Tolerance in Philadelphia*, 17.

433   LESLIE LODWICK

turned Boone into a for-profit charter school but also
resulted in Camelot Education's first school: Camelot
Academy at Boone. That Camelot at Boone is a charter
school is not insignificant.[31] The school is unique among
charters for its operational contract with the district:
Camelot at Boone functions formally as the disciplinary
(or "transitional") wing of the school district, whereas most
charters operate at least semi-autonomously. It is also
certainly not unique: Camelot at Boone is part of a nationwide trend toward charter schools aligned with Obama-
era education policies and practices that include high-
stakes testing, tracking, and arguments for "school choice."
The charter school movement in the United States in the
early 2000s was largely fueled by the desire for market-
based educational options that could serve as alternatives
to public, private, or parochial schools. And they remain
incredibly controversial for reasons too numerous to re-
count in full here.[32]

31   The charter/district arrangement functions similarly to a public/private
     partnership in which public funding goes to a private company in the form
     of per-pupil spending, and a combination of publicly funded district re-
     sources and private money go toward curriculum, maintenance, and
     programming. In 2017, Camelot took in nearly $10 million from its Philadel-
     phia schools. See Sarah Carr, Francesca Berardi, Zoë Kirsch, and Stephen
     Smiley, "'That Place Was Like A Prison,'" *Slate*, March 8, 2017, http://www.
     slate.com/articles/news_and_politics/schooled/2017/03/camelot_schools_
     takes_its_discipline_too_far_say_current_and_former_students.html.
32   In short, critics have pointed to free-market, for-profit schools as insuf-
     ficient substitutes for state-run neighborhood or community-based schools
     for reasons such as financial mismanagement of state funding by executive
     boards and CEOS; a lack of educational expertise and training among
     school leadership; uneven disciplinary practices and high expulsion rates;
     inadequate commitment to special education and/or students with disabil-
     ities; and the failures of a lottery system and other exclusionary practices
     that determine both how students pick and choose their schools and
     where they attend. For more nuanced accounts of the historical and present
     context of charter schools see Eve L. Ewing, *Ghosts in the School Yard:
     Racism and School Closings in Chicago's South Side* (Chicago: University
     of Chicago Press, 2018); Pauline Lipman, *The New Political Economy of
     Urban Education: Neoliberalism, Race, and the Right to the City* (New York:

Camelot at Boone complicates a particular problem that underpins charter schools, more broadly. Charter schools are built on the alluring illusion and promise of "choice," which, for families disillusioned by inadequate public schools in their communities, is entirely and understandably compelling.[33] Discursively, they have been portrayed as a choice in communities where there have historically been fewer opportunities for choice making in the context of free, public education. This idea of choice rationalizes, perpetuates, and reproduces educational practices that are distinctly inequitable and unequal. Yet in the case of Camelot at Boone, as a for-profit disciplinary school, there is no choice: attendance is compulsory (or as the school says, "assigned"), the student body made of forced transfer students. This is not a charter school that allows families to choose among a number of "equal" choices, but rather the end of the line for students looking the justice system in the face. The logic behind the wide adoption of charter schools as choice based begins to crumble in the context of forced transfer or the "alternative charter."

The educational environment at Camelot at Boone enacts a space of racialized enclosure. Families and com-

Routledge, 2011); and Shawn Ginwright, *Black Youth Rising: Activism and Radical Healing in Urban America* (New York: Teachers College Press, 2010).

33   In *Market Movements: African American Involvement in School Voucher Reform*, Tom C. Pedroni argues that for many families, charter schools are simply a workaround to obstinate and unequal public schools. He very importantly cautions against seeing charter advocates as "dupes" who side with conservative agendas but rather as conscious social actors working under the constraints of systemic inequity. And to that end, there are a number of charter schools operating within social justice frameworks toward equality and radical pedagogy. I do not find fault with these charter schools or with charter school advocates but with the discursive process that makes charter schools seem like an actual choice between equal opportunities. See Tom C. Pedroni, *Market Movements: African American Involvement in School Voucher Reform* (New York: Routledge, 2007).

munities are not only virtually choiceless in whether to allow their students to attend as they would a non-disciplinary charter school, but the charter school company is also subsequently paid for a student's continued enrollment in the form of per-pupil state-allocated funding. Camelot at Boone profits from this fabricated need for rehabilitation, which attempts to render students sent there fungible. 2019 demographic data from the School District of Philadelphia reveal that 97 percent of Camelot's student body identify as black. Compared to 43 percent of students across the district self-identifying as black, this number demonstrates a clear racialized disparity in enrollment between disciplinary and non-disciplinary neighborhood schools.[34] Damien Sojoyner, in *First Strike: Educational Enclosures in Black Los Angeles*, insists that enclosure, as a mechanism by which black life and culture is coerced, suppressed, and circumscribed, offers a way to think against the deficient theory of school-to-prison pipelines. Camelot at Boone as an institution offers a *specific* mode or instance of black enclosure within public education that forecloses certain possibilities and ranks and determines the worth, welfare, and value of black life.[35]

Camelot at Boone is a profitable space of choicelessness for the wayward. Throughout the twentieth century, as the wayward, like the disciplinary student at Boone and then Camelot at Boone, was racialized, waywardness—managed via zero-tolerance policies, mandated attendance, and harsh disciplinary practice—became increasingly compulsory through forced enrollment. Like other alternative disciplinary schools, Camelot at Boone is a separate and unequal space of civic engagement, which

---

34   "District Enrollment Open Data," School District of Philadelphia, June 1, 2019, https://www.philasd.org/performance/programsservices/open-data/school-information/#district_enrollment.

35   Damien M. Sojoyner, *First Strike: Educational Enclosures in Black Los Angeles* (Minneapolis: University of Minnesota Press, 2016).

offers separate and unequal opportunities for expelled students to practice their right to public education. The burden of rehabilitation is placed on students as they work to be restored to their neighborhood school. The individual responsibility that permeated *A Nation at Risk* permeates Camelot at Boone as one's ability to return to their home school is contingent on choosing good behavior, on seeking normativity, on proving "competent performance." Even to families of expelled students, the disciplinary, alternative charter school is presented as a choice: families and students are told to choose rehabilitation rather than risk expulsion from the district altogether, thereby relinquishing their right to public education. The choice at Camelot at Boone is predetermined by the spectacle of possible disenfranchisement and deprivation that accompanies it.

Throughout the nearly one-hundred-year life of the school—whether as Daniel Boone or as Camelot at Boone—the institution has been marred by controversy. A 2017 *Slate* article detailed student allegations of abuse and exploitation at Camelot schools across the country that were strikingly similar to claims made by Boone students in the *Philadelphia Inquirer* nearly sixty years prior.[36] *Slate's* exposé of Camelot detailed the sanctioned and unsanctioned uses of force at the institution:

> There is nothing in the written policies of Camelot schools that mentions [a violent practice called] slamming, but there is something called "handle with care." This protocol calls for staff members to use a series of de-escalation strategies on disruptive students, starting with nonverbal cues, such as eye contact, and moving on to verbal redirection. If the

36   Harry J. Karafin, "Wetter Praises Boone Principal: Knowledge of Abuses Denied," *Philadelphia Inquirer*, February 25, 1960.

students fail to respond to the less intrusive efforts, the staff member is supposed to pin children's hands behind their backs, lead them over to a wall, and ease them into a seated posture. Camelot parents typically sign consent forms allowing school staff to physically restrain their children as a last resort.[37]

Former teachers employed by Camelot attested to the fact that, in practice, the official "handle with care" policy was not just in response to "disruptive" students, not just "a last resort," but rather part of a daily climate of violence at the school.[38] "Handle with care" manifests a longer history of force that extends the zero-tolerance policies of the 1990s and the production of early-twentieth-century waywardness. Within the context of a compulsory charter school, "handle with care" is just another form of custodial care and rehabilitation that exerts its power through forced subjecthood. The social relations contained within the disciplinary school create and define their own boundaries, communications, realities, and logics—which serve to link race and disciplining, waywardness and reform.

These logics of institutional violence are materialized spatially as well. It is important to remember that the Elisha Kent Kane School building that now houses Camelot at Boone was not designed to be a space of rehabilitation for students living under the conditions of trauma or poverty but was designed rather as a vocational training space for students with disabilities.[39] With the "non-

---

37   Carr et al., "'That Place Was Like A Prison.'"
38   A 2017 *PhillyVoice* article also details allegations of physical force by administrators, like "choke holds" and "body slamming," as well as the bullying and berating of students. Sarah Carr, Zoë Kirsch, Francesca Berardi, and Stephen Smiley, "Philly, 2 Other Cities Question For-Profit Manager of Alternative Schools," *PhillyVoice*, March 30, 2017, https://www.phillyvoice.com/philly-2-other-cities-rethink-profit-manager-alternative-schools.
39   Again, designed as an occupational school, Elisha Kent Kane School had seven metal and woodworking shops, a home economics suite, an

essential" programs shuttered, Camelot at Boone is a space, following Sojoyner, designed to be *liminal*. Liminality at Camelot at Boone manifests and functions in many ways. It is, of course, a space that claims to be transitory and temporary, one that operates in neither the public nor private sphere. But it also is a space marked by spatial disinvestment. The school's disrepair suggests that the disciplinary school student has no particular spatial need other than a barely adequate classroom.[40] The total lack of spatial consideration and upkeep is productive of a certain kind of student. It is a mechanism of devaluation— and those sentenced to Camelot at Boone are certainly aware of their de-prioritized existence as *students* of the school district. This "otherness" is captured in the transitional hold of Camelot at Boone, in the individual burden of restoration and rehabilitation, in the restrictive environment where only a certain normativity is designed and enforced by administrators, teachers, and school policies.

adjustment room, and a series of special activities rooms in addition to its twelve classrooms. The school did not specifically define the needs or disabilities of its students. It was a self-described "special educational school" for "retarded educable youngsters." The students at Elisha Kent Kane School mostly appear in the archive in news on "special" sports victories and participation in events associated with the Special Olympics in the 70s and early 80s. See "New Kane School Opened by City," *Philadelphia Inquirer*, December 4, 1963; Robert A. Thomas, "6 New City Schools: All Will Open Their Doors by Early Next Year to Meet Record 273,900 Enrollment," *Philadelphia Inquirer*, September 8, 1963; and Juan Gonzalez, "Board Votes to Close Kane School in N. Philadelphia," *Philadelphia Daily News*, June 21, 1983.

40   A 2017 Facilities Operation Survey found that Camelot Academy at Boone was in need of $14,026,762 worth of repairs. It listed the nonexistent security system, malfunctioning radiators and heating/cooling system, the lack of outdoor space, broken fire alarms, clocks, bells, doors, and windows, and asbestos removal as the most immediate concerns. As of 2017, the space was not ADA compliant and many of the bathroom fixtures were non-operational. See School District of Philadelphia, *Facility Condition Assessment Summary Report*, 2018, https://www.philasd.org/capitalprograms/wp-content/uploads/sites/18/2017/06/Camelot-Academy-Boone.pdf.

The disciplinary institution serves to establish a spatial distinction between the dispossessed and the free, the expendable and the nonexpendable, the abnormal and the normal, and to manifest the ongoing production of racial boundaries of this transitional space.

At Camelot at Boone, the doors are locked, hallways secured, and windows and lockers nailed shut—students are unable to walk freely, open a closed door, change the temperature by opening a window, or feel curious about the way brick or concrete walls feel against their hands. Students are told to walk silently, hands clasped behind their backs, and to touch nothing. This is an implicit pedagogy of space for the wayward that instructs how some students should engage with educational institutions. It is a space that actively attempts to circumscribe the student and to produce their deviancy. The documented culture of forced violence works together with the space, which is marked by foreclosed opportunities, to convey specific messages about who has access to what kinds of spaces and what kinds of education and who should instead be made proximal to everyday violence.

Disciplinary power at Camelot at Boone is conveyed through surveillance *and* spectacle. On the co-existence of these two regimes of power, Jonathan Crary argues, "Spectacular culture is not founded on the necessity of making a subject *see*, but rather on strategies in which individuals are isolated, separated, and *inhabit time* as disempowered."[41] In the case of Camelot at Boone, students are forced into (performing) spectacle by way of an imposed process of separation, categorization, and hierarchization—and, again in Crary's words, it "is not an optics of power but an architecture" that renders students subject to it knowable in ways beyond the visual.[42] In *Dark Matters:*

41   Jonathan Crary, *Suspensions of Perception: Attention, Spectacle, and Modern Culture* (Cambridge, MA: MIT Press, 1999), 3. Emphasis in the original.

42   Crary, *Suspensions of Perception*, 74–75.

LISTENING TO ARCHIVES OF DISCIPLINARY EDUCATION IN PHILADELPHIA

On the Surveillance of Blackness, Simone Browne offers another way of understanding these concomitant forms of subjection, writing that an "understanding of the ontological conditions of blackness is integral to developing a general theory of surveillance and in particular racializing surveillance—when enactments of surveillance reify boundaries along racial lines, thereby reifying race, and where the outcome of this is often discriminatory and violent treatment."[43] At Camelot at Boone, surveillance and the production of a knowable, racially-bound subject is not solely based on looking but on listening—for signs of disruption and to the sounds of resulting force used to suppress it.

Behavior management specialists sit at the ends of long halls and listen to students as they move through the day. Sound is used to exert authority through making, hearing, and silencing noise. The sound of "handle with care" and zero tolerance echoes through silent concrete hallways in spectacular performances of power. Camelot at Boone's locked lockers are not just residual reminders of the freedom students elsewhere in the district enjoy but physical platforms for noise as students are "slammed" against them—they are instruments that sound particular violences and particular warnings. Instead of removing the lockers when student access to them was taken away in the 1990s, administrators nailed some shut and continued to use the rest for storage.[44] Sharp, loud, and resonant, the noise of a student against one of these lockers reverberates through the halls and signals the bodily consequences of misbehavior and of punishment. Their continued presence in the classroom, though not functional as intended, are functional as signs of students' circumscribed experience,

---

43   Browne, *Dark Matters*, 8.

as resounding material tools of administrative control, and as tools of surveillance.

Spectacle is communicated sonically as a means to order students through the specter of violence. While misbehaved classrooms are punished with silent lunches, does the absence of sound produce or signal compliance? What power does the sonic have when it is taken? Tina Campt writes that "the *choice* to 'listen to' rather than simply 'look at' images is a conscious decision to challenge the equation of vision with knowledge by engaging photography through a sensory register that is critical to Black Atlantic cultural formations: sound."[45] How might listening differently—that is, listening as a non-surveilling gesture—allow us to hear not fixed subjects but rather open registers of sonic formation, civic participation, and collective refusal? How might spectacle and surveillance be unbound through listening to photographs? Images of disciplinary students mark a conversation with the state. What is this conversation and what can be heard from accounts of the wayward, disciplinary student through this act of listening?

44   I worked at Camelot at Boone from 2012–2013 as a secondary teacher, and the history of the building became known to me through conversations with administrators and long-serving teachers. Many of the locker doors were also removed in years prior. Students were not allowed to store any personal items or school supplies in them, which was a redundant rule since all their personal items were collected (and held throughout the day) before they even stepped through the metal detector at the entrance of the school. These policies were in place because of a fear that students were bringing weapons into the school, but, more than anything, they seemed to emphasize that students in this specific disciplinary school space had to relinquish certain freedom, autonomy, and rights. These practices worked to define a space apart from their former neighborhood schools, where they would have had more control over their bodies and their personal belongings.

45   Tina Campt, *Listening to Images* (Durham, NC: Duke University Press, 2017), 6. Emphasis added.

LISTENING TO ARCHIVES OF DISCIPLINARY EDUCATION IN PHILADELPHIA

Wayward Accounts

In *Wayward Lives, Beautiful Experiments*, Saidiya Hartman wipes away the Witmer-esque layers of facts, figures, biases, and "official" knowledges shaping, pathologizing, obstructing, confining the lives of wayward black women in the early to mid-twentieth century. She writes,

> In my search for her, I soon encountered all the others hovering about her—the sociologist, housing reformer, probation officer, club woman, social worker, vice investigator, journalist, psychiatrist—all of them insisting their view of her was the truth. One of them was always there, standing in my way, blocking my path, whenever I encountered her.[46]

Hartman instead recounts the ordinary lives, intimacies, struggles, freedoms, upheavals of the wayward—offering different ways of knowing, seeing, giving voice to the so-called unruly, the disruptive, the troublesome, the "backward," which resist the forced subjecthood of pathologized and racialized waywardness.

Crucial to an account of the extended life at Boone is a consideration of the lived-inness of the disciplinary school. It is not accurate to describe Camelot at Boone as a mastered or controlled space, as the students who occupy them are neither. Disciplinary school students are not passive subjects but active social agents, who draw on robust community networks, political power, histories of resistance, friendship, and intellect.[47] Students take up space of their own and actively resist the flattening and disembodying gestures naturalized there. This daily spatial and sonic resistance denies the pathologizing of

46   Saidiya V Hartman, *Wayward Lives, Beautiful Experiments* (New York: W.W. Norton and Co., 2019), 33–34.

Ted Silary, "A Boon for Boone: Woman Coach Earns Respect of Tough Guys," *Philadelphia Daily News*, January 8, 1988. Photograph by G. Lole Grossmann.

Philadelphia Daily News
Friday
January 8, 1988
Mike Rathet, Executive Sports Editor

SPORTS

Scoreboard: Pages 122-120
TV Weekend: Page 118
Briefly: Page 110
Horse Racing: Pages 110, 109

A Boon For Boone

Woman Coach Earns Respect Of Tough Guys

By TED SILARY
Daily News Sports Writer

Kevin Smith was aware by early November that Bill Manson had decided to quit coaching the varsity basketball team at Daniel Boone School.

What Smith wanted to know was, who had been selected as Manson's replacement?

"When I went to talk to Mr. Manson, he was acting like he didn't want to tell me," Smith said. "It was like he was giving me the runaround. I finally said, 'Come on, Mr. Manson. What's up? Who's going to coach us?' Then he said, 'All right . . . It's Miss Stewart.'"

With that, Kevin Smith, a 6-4 senior center with incredible leaping ability, responded, "Miss Stewart??!!"

Kevin Smith did not realize, but a woman coaching a boys varsity basketball team in this city is not unprecedented — Geri Zambrano steered Kensington in its Public League debut season (1981-82) and for half of the 1982-83 season before a battle against cancer forced her out. Another woman, Andrea Sullivan, completed the season. Zambrano died that July.

Kensington was a tough place to coach, but Muriel Stewart bit off a much, much larger chunk when she decided to coach hoops at Boone.

Boone, located at 26th and Jefferson streets in North Philadelphia, is one of the school district's two remedial disciplinary schools for boys (the other, Octavius Catto, is at 42nd and Ludlow streets in West Philly.) What that means is, Boone's student body — approximately 285 in grades five through 12 — is comprised completely of young men who caused problems in their former school.

See WOMAN Page 113

Boone School coach Muriel Stewart is surrounded by her players

Staff Photography by S. Lois Grossmann

Propp Makes Strong Return

By JAY GREENBERG
Daily News Sports Writer

Brian Propp is one of the best toys the Flyers ever bought themselves. For nine years, he has run and run and run, to 310 goals and 393 assists, only once having to go into the shop for major repairs.

That was last year, when his left knee sustained 27 games worth of damage. He also got an eight-game poke in the eye the season before that. Most recently, there was the six-game layoff for strained ligaments in his left knee from which he returned last night with two goals in the Flyers' 6-4 win over the St. Louis Blues at the Spectrum.

But he has not missed more than four contests in any other season. Clearly, if another Brian Propp would come along, designed exactly the same way the one the Flyers were fortunate enough to find with the 14th pick of the 1979 draft, Consumer Reports would wholeheartedly recommend they buy it.

Three Flyer coaches, including the present one, have been frustrated at times with Propp's unwillingness to take charge of situations that demanded it. But eventually they come to understand what Propp, in his passive resistance to being pressured by anything or anybody, was telling them all along:

To leave him alone. You just turn the key in his back and let him go. You don't need to yell at him, you don't need to bench him, and you don't often need to change his batteries to make him run, either.

All you have to do is accept that he is a very good player, but not quite a superstar. And, at the end of the season, wonder where the Flyers would have been without him.

The years have produced only outward changes in Propp. A marriage has come and gone and so has a wide variety of hairstyles and clothes, much to the bewilderment and amusement of his teammates. If there is any difference at all, it is that Propp, who will turn 29 next month, has ever so slightly begun to grasp his mortality.

Otherwise everything remains the same, including the Blues' inability to grasp Propp. Propp, who also had an assist in his comeback appearance, and linemates Rick Tocchet and Pelle Eklund totaled 12 points, ir

See PROPP Page 126.

Inside on the NFL

- Didinger on Watson: **Page 127**
- Oilers vs. Broncos: **Page 125**
- Eagles' Carter Injured: **Page 127**
- Vikings vs. 49ers: **Page 124**
- Colts vs. Browns: **Page 125**
- Redskins vs. Bears: **Page 124**

blackness and takes on innumerable forms. Campt again asks a number of questions that frame a relationship with (here architectural) sound and resistance:

> How do we build a radical visual archive of the African Diaspora that grapples with the recalcitrant and the disaffected, the unruly and the dispossessed? Through what modalities of perception, encounter, and engagement do we constitute it?... What is the place in this archive for images assumed only to register forms of institutional accounting or state management? How do we contend with images intended not to figure black subjects, but to delineate instead differential or degraded forms of personhood or subjection—images produced with the purpose of tracking, cataloguing, and constraining the movement of blacks in and out of the diaspora?[48]

So what does one find with Hartman and Campt as guides when navigating the archives that constitute Boone? What is captured in this archive of images? How might these reimagined, refigured documents reveal those who, as Campt writes, "face down the image that would negate the complicated truth of the lives they have lived, in order to

47   It is also vital to note the hundreds of formerly-employed teachers at Boone/Camelot who have actively resisted the disciplinary school student formation and worked to provide counter-narratives and rich instruction to students. Educators must also be considered social agents who are working within systemic constraints. During my time at Camelot at Boone, it was clear how passionately devoted many of the teachers were to working with the highest-need students in the city and to helping them navigate the biased economic, education, and judicial systems they found themselves in. This often meant forming alternative pedagogical interventions dedicated to care and to working with families. This is even reflected in the historical record of the school. See statements from educators in Valeria M. Russ, "A Tough Class of Kids," *Philadelphia Daily News*, February 10, 1986; and Ted Silary, "A Boon for Boone: Woman Coach Earns Respect of Tough Guys," *Philadelphia Daily News*, January 8, 1988.

48   Campt, *Listening to Images*, 3.

interrupt the narrative of their own demise that threatens to extinguish their capacity to claim a life lived in dignity and complexity"?[49]

To search the archive of Philadelphia daily newspapers for photographs of students at Daniel Boone School or Camelot at Boone is to be met with a certain "quietness." There are dozens of photoless entries in crime blotters, recording those Boone students alleged to be involved with violence, theft, and arson. These records aim to register some inevitable "type" of wayward student doomed to produce and reproduce violence and criminality. The frequency of this photographic absence speaks loudly—on one hand about laws protecting photographs of minors and on the other about the conscious refusal to be represented as criminal. What could a reading of this absent visuality as resistance offer disciplinary student formation? Perhaps, as with the young females in Hartman's *Wayward Lives, Beautiful Experiments*, we should read these quiet figures as revolutionaries rejecting misplaced attempts at control masked as reform. Writing of the then photographs and sociological surveys of Philadelphia's black Seventh Ward and attempts to offer visual evidence of its inevitable production of waywardness, Hartman writes,

> The outsiders and the uplifters fail to capture it, to get it right. All they see is a typical Negro alley, blind to the reality of looks and the pangs of desire that unsettle their captions and hint at the possibility of a life bigger than poverty, at the tumult and upheaval that can't be arrested by the camera. They fail to discern the beauty and they see only the disorder, missing all the ways black folks create life and make bare need into an arena of elaboration.[50]

49   Campt, *Listening to Images*, 109.
50   Hartman, *Wayward Lives, Beautiful Experiments*, 5–6.

Valeria M. Russ, "A Tough Class of Kids," *Philadelphia Daily News*, February 10, 1986. Photograph by Denis O'Keefe.

Staff Photography by Denis O'Keefe

Teacher Robert Bush aids Ralph Wills (left) and Tony Jardine, both 15, at Boone School

A TOUGH CLASS OF KIDS

DISCIPLINARY SCHOOLS MARK A FINAL CHANCE

By **VALERIA M. RUSS**
Daily News Staff Writer

I t is lunchtime at the Daniel Boone School in North Philadelphia and the hallways are mostly clear. A couple of teachers are clustered around the front security desk when a slender, smooth-faced boy of 15 walks by, wearing a green army jacket with its hood pulled up over his head.

"Hey, Walter, where you been, man? I haven't seen you for a while," music teacher Bob Bush calls out.

"Locked up," Walter mumbles, eyes downcast.

Walter says he has been away for a month and a half at the Glen Mills School in Delaware County, a reformatory school where students are sent by the courts after an arrest on criminal charges.

Walter says he had been wrongly accused of participating in the subway mugging of a man whose gold chain was stolen.

He says two other young men committed the robbery but told police that Walter had been with them.

"I was with them, but I didn't do it." Of Boone School, he said, "I like it, but I need more help."

■

Boone School is the last chance for Walter and others like him in the Philadelphia School District. It is one of the district's three disciplinary schools.

Most students get assigned to these schools because they have been chronic troublemakers at other schools. Fighting, truancy, vandalism, assaults on teachers or criminal activity outside of school are typical offenses.

But Boone is not a fortress with locks and bars. It is not much different from any other school. There is one security official posted at a desk in the first-floor hallway. Teachers usually monitor the hallways between classes.

The school's library is usually locked, but the classrooms are not and there is grillwork on the windows outside the principal's office, rather than iron bars.

Located for years at Hancock Street and Wildey in Fishtown, Boone moved to its current location at 26th Street and Jefferson — into the old Elisha Kane School — two years ago after the School District sold the old Boone school building.

■

The atmosphere in the classrooms at Boone is informal and teachers give students more leeway than would be acceptable in other schools.

On a recent morning in Walter Hawkins' social studies class, five students out of 12 on the roll have made it to class. The high absenteeism is typical. The

See **BOONE** Page 12

Joy McIntyre, "Graduates Special at Boone," *Philadelphia Daily News*, June 19, 1980. Photograph by Sam Psoras.

Graduates Special At Boone

By JOY McINTYRE

Around the corner from the Schmidt brewery, near where a wrecking ball is dismantling an abandoned bank building, there's a school for the boys nobody else wants.

Or can handle.

Kids who fight, kids who hit teachers, kids who "are known to the courts and agencies" attend the all-male Daniel Boone School at Hancock and Wildey Sts.

DAVID ROSOFF, the principal, looks at the problem differently. To him, these are special kids who need help.

"I felt that if there were some kind of divine mission on this earth (for me) this was it," said Rosoff, who's been at Boone 13 years.

Something must be working at Boone, because nearly 30 of its students received high school diplomas this month.

"To me it's just a piece of paper showing I did my 12 years," said Leonard Mason, 18, as he wiped down tables in the lunchroom one recent afternoon.

But, Mason said, "I hope maybe it will help me get a job."

NO ONE KNOWS why these students make a friend of trouble.

Rosoff said the youths who attend the combination junior and senior high school have low self-images.

Photographed by Sam Psoras

Boone graduates Mason (left) and Johnson with diplomas

Unsuccessful in school, in trouble with the law, the kids can misbehave out of frustration.

A chance to learn a trade can change that. And some even discover that they can get a sense of accomplishment just from doing well in school.

MASON VIEWS his graduation as a form of status within his family.

"It's the only reason I'm going to school," he said. "I'm the first one (in his family) to get a diploma ....As long as I've got it, it's all right with me."

Mason, who was thrown out of regular high school for fighting with a teacher, has a school-arranged job at the Philadelphia Navy Yard waiting for him after graduation.

Vice Principal Clifford Lipkin said students at Boone are taken out of their neighborhood schools and thus removed from gang pressure to mis-

behave. "Most boys have few friends here," he said.

"I GET ALONG with the students here," said Darrick Johnson, 18. "They don't cause trouble." Johnson dropped out of school for two years. Even so, he can still receive a diploma as long as he passes the required exams.

Johnson, too, will work at the Navy Yard in the maintenance department after graduation, probably making less money than he made as a drop-out working in construction.

But, said Johnson, "I came back to school to get my diploma. I'm really glad to get it. I waited so long."

Couple Honore...

Hartman's reading of waywardness recovers a space of possibility and social upheaval, which shuts down the provisions of the Wayward Minor Acts claiming that "the definition of a wayward minor includes only *non-criminal acts but which indicate the imminence of future criminality.*"[51] What possibilities are there in a reclamation of waywardness in students under zero tolerance? What could a photographic counter-archive offer in terms of resistance? Campt writes of photographic archives of black youth:

> Refusing to wait passively for a future posited as highly likely or inevitable for black urban youth, the sitters actively anticipate their premature deaths through these photos. In doing so, they enact anterior practices of fugitivity through their refusal to be silenced by the probability of a future violent death they confront on a daily basis. Through these images they fashion a futurity they project beyond their own demise... Their praxis of refusal consists of transforming mundane acts of image making into quotidian practices of fugitivity.[52]

While at Camelot at Boone, the elevated volume of the performance of control during the school day is set in relief to the silence that this control mandates, students' "lower frequencies" must not be understood as expressions of passivity. Student quietness resists knowability. It is a sonic and visual mode of refusal—a student can't be transformed into the "wayward" without accompanying data—which works to reject the supposed knowledge of the state that pathologizes blackness into something to be reformed or subdued. It's urgent to know that students at Camelot at Boone are adolescents, sentient social beings, capable

51 Hartman, *Wayward Lives, Beautiful Experiments*, 223. Emphasis in the original.
52 Campt, *Listening to Images*, 109.

of understanding and resisting the complexities of educational inequity, and also students with families, hopes, dreams, and futures. These are students who are gifted intellectually, who are artists, thinkers, musicians, mathematicians, scientists, and storytellers; sons and daughters; and holders of vast knowledges both inside and outside the institution of the school.

When there are images of students at Boone in the photographic archives, they are mostly images of kids looking and acting like kids. In 1986, the *Philadelphia Daily News* published an article titled "A Tough Class of Kids." The story was accompanied by a photograph of two Boone students at their desks as a teacher stands between them evaluating their work. It is a ubiquitous and informal classroom scene: a scene that could be from any school, anywhere in the US. These are not the unruly, the violent, the defiant, the unreasonable, the "chronic troublemakers" that the article describes. To some, the photograph might be evidence that whatever tough reform-based curriculum being employed at Boone is working. *Or*, more likely, it suggests instead that when students were asked to be photographed as students for a newspaper, they did. Through these images, the students reject the reduction of black life. They instead project, to echo Campt, a futurity of complexity, dignity, and life lived. Emitting their own frequency, these images refuse the peculiar listening of surveillance and deny the pathology of waywardness.

This theory of sonic surveillance still seeks to hold buildings accountable, as well as those who build them, use them, and institutionalize them. A surveillable subject needs an environment that lends itself to surveillance, and space continues to produce itself as needed, here through sound and architecture in addition to everyday spatial practices and pedagogies. Yet the subject produced by the disciplinary school is not reduced or flattened, and the potentiality of current and future resistance must be held in sonic tension with further attempts at disembodiment. Alexander Weheliye writes in *Phonographies: Grooves in Sonic Afro-Modernity*, "On the one hand this (dis)juncture between sound and source render[s] sound more ephemeral, since it fail[s] to provide the listener with a 'human' point of reference. On the other hand, sound gain[s] materiality in the technological apparatuses and the practices surrounding these devices, and in the process rematerialize[s] the human source."[53] That is, sound also inherently contains the kinetic potential for human resistance.

---

53   Alexander G. Weheliye, *Phonographies: Grooves in Sonic Afro-Modernity* (Durham, NC: Duke University Press, 2005), 7.

Sable Elyse Smith, *Coloring Book 28*, 2019. Screen printing ink and oil stick on paper, 60 x 50 inches. Courtesy of the artist; JTT, New York; and Carlos/Ishikawa, London.

NO PLACE LIKE HOME:
PRACTICING FREEDOM IN THE LOOPHOLES
OF CAPTIVITY

JASMINE SYEDULLAH

There is nowhere to just sit in the place where I live. The apartment we rent is small. It has two bedrooms and one and a half baths. We are four beings: me, my love, our teenage daughter (whom my love raised mostly as a single parent), and an aging, very protective, very loud Miniature Pinscher, all brimming with love and life, and all black. If you follow the Hudson River 80 miles north from New York City, you will eventually find our town. Historically black but increasingly gentrified, Beacon is nestled between river and mountains. Wealthy New Yorkers moving up from the city have displaced black homeowners, crowded and slowed street traffic, and, like so many places these days, their arrival is a sign that we might not be able to get a bigger place here any time soon. We will likely need to fight to hold on to what we have.

Space is limited these days. Space to live, to work, to travel. We live in a cultural moment that asks that we maximize the capacity of everything that supports us to hold more than it was ever designed to bear. While the land on which we live holds many more truths, possibilities, and teachings than we can touch from above, too many of us are disconnected from it, distracted by the roar of our own efforts to keep up with so-called progress. The spaces we inhabit seem to leave little room for imagining what alternatives exist to the hoarding, hunting, and fencing tendencies of settler colonial homemaking that mark the American Dream with so much violence. Rather than

Deep appreciations to Saredo Ali for their close readings and generous editing of this piece—it is a blessing to work with students with such brilliant minds, elegant skills, and creative spirits as yours! Thank you!

letting go of what is not working for us, we are taught to hold on for dear life to all we have, as if holding more things than there is time to manage, use, or enjoy will make us feel more at home.

Decolonizing our sense of being at home in settler colonial logics is a practice that takes time. Time working in community, learning from those most directly affected by the limits of their protections. In her collaboratively written self-published community textbook *Poverty Scholarship: Poor People-Led Theory, Art, Words, & Tears Across Mama Earth*, sisSTAR Lisa "Tiny" Gray-Garcia teaches that

> Us poor and homeless people in the US are in a state of emergency—between the demolitions of thousands of units of public housing, the extreme rise in gentrification and evictions of low-income and working class elders and families and the concurrent rise in the criminalization of unhoused encampments and our bodies... it is so urgent for people to listen to our own innovative solutions to poverty and homelessness—solutions like Poverty Scholarship and the Homefulness Project.[1]

For the last twenty-two years, Tiny, a formerly homeless single parent, has worked collaboratively to organize formerly and currently unhoused communities and to lift up the voices of those most directly impacted by displacement and urban development, making links between gentrification and the displacement of native peoples across this country. Folded into the incredibly rich text she produced with her community of Poverty Scholars is the

---

1   Lisa "Tiny" Gray-Garcia, Dee Garcia, and the POOR Magazine Family, *Poverty Scholarship: Poor People-Led Theory, Art, Words, & Tears Across Mama Earth* (Oakland, CA: POOR Press, 2019), 38. Gray-Garcia is also the author of *Criminal of Poverty: Growing Up Homeless in America* (San Francisco: City Lights, 2006).

idea that homemaking is a necessarily alchemic process of transformation. Transforming distraction into discipline, chaos into care, harm into healing, alienation into accountability, pathology into possibility is an ongoing practice of improvising on reality, as prison abolition activist Liz Samuels would say.[2] If we were all always waiting for the right place and space to practice letting go of what is not serving us, then we might never take the time to feel ourselves beyond the real press of the systems, isms, and conditions we struggle to breathe within. Our containment within them does not have to be the only thing that shapes us. When talking about her own experiences growing up houseless, being displaced, and having to drop out of school in the sixth grade, Tiny writes, "I did not have the time away from earning a loaf of bread... I did not even have the privilege of an organized life, the privilege of knowing what I would be doing from one moment to the next."[3] And yet, the idea of home that was born from her struggles to survive without one seeded something completely revolutionary.

Without access to the necessary resources, making time to imagine home otherwise, to create space for healing, is a challenge compounded by the stigma and discrimination of a society that conspires to keep those without resources, in Tiny's words, "silenced: incarcerated, criminalized, displaced, homeless, disabled, marginalized, sorted, separated, and extinguished."[4] Rather than waiting for the perfect conditions to repair the wounds of surviving intergenerational trauma and oppression, Tiny worked with her mom, whom we all knew as Mama Dee, to create

2   Liz Samuels, "Improvising on Reality," in *The Hidden 1970s: Histories of Radicalism*, ed. Dan Berger (New Brunswick, NJ: Rutgers University Press, 2010), 21–38.

3   Gray-Garcia et al., *Poverty Scholarship*, 31.

4   Gray-Garcia et al., *Poverty Scholarship*, 22.

space on the road, along the way, within shelters, within welfare offices, on the streets, and on buses to practice liberation—space well within reach of the carceral forces designed to survey, criminalize, and punish, yet far enough from view to make a way out of no way. Tiny and Mama Dee seeded space for homemaking in the midst of struggle, a sense of home that grew amid the suffocation of living in crisis.

I met Dee and Tiny and the Poverty Scholars a year after graduating from college and moving across the country from New York to California. In college I studied ideas of freedom from as many angles as I could. I took classes in theater, philosophy, creative writing, literature, and classics. It was in a religious studies course that I encountered a contemplative practice of freedom. The practice did not require much, just a place free enough from my own patterns and compulsive practices of perfectionism to step back from the press and weight of all that was touted as a sign of progress or success; a place to get to know myself beyond the performance of being a good student, a good daughter, beyond the anxiety, beyond the depression, beyond the imposter syndrome, beyond the tokenization. I practiced meeting myself on my meditation cushion, in the silence of my sitting practice three times a week, twenty minutes at a time, and, slowly, I began to take account of all I was holding.

While I was practicing sitting meditation in the enclosures of the Ivy League, Tiny and Mama Dee were practicing "homefulness" while struggling to survive what they call "houselessness." Homefulness began as a dream, a joint mother-daughter imagination of

> a flat or house with at least four bedrooms, art/community meals, shared child care, and revolutionary case management (poor people-led support by any means necessary...), sliding scale sweat-equity to

pay for rent (i.e. a non-ableist, concept of whatever
you are able to do based on your time, energy, physical challenges, etc., which sometimes means cooking
meals, helping with child care, or paper-work, admin,
rides, etc.).[5]

Tiny and Mama Dee practiced their imagination of home,
a home neither had experienced but knew was possible,
while weathering the repeated trauma of displacement
and disenfranchisement. They "slogged through a several
hundred page HUD [US Department of Housing and
Urban Development] application to make Homefulness a
HUD funded project," Tiny writes. All that was "approved
were more contracts for the devil-opers who already got
millions of dollars for politricked approved housing projects like 'Master leases for Single Room Occupancy' Hotels,
or shelter plus care transitional housing projects."[6] Ten
years later, while I was living in Santa Cruz studying political theory, slave narratives, and abolitionist social movements, Tiny was becoming a scholar of the streets again,
this time with her son.

At age twelve, Tiny's son Tiburcio Garcia wrote a
poem titled "Houseless":

On the sidewalk the pounding of feet passing by. We
holding up cardboard signs and all we usually get
a wary eye. Always moving. People think we loot-
ing. We are treated like criminals for sleeping on the
street even though America is the one who made sure
we had nothing to eat. This country left us jobless,
friendless, loveless, and most of all houseless.[7]

5   Gray-Garcia et al., *Poverty Scholarship*, 298.
6   Gray-Garcia et al., *Poverty Scholarship*, 298.
7   Gray-Garcia et al., *Poverty Scholarship*, 294.

Homefulness was more than a place for Tiny, more than a project. It was a practice of tirelessly and unapologetically working toward the realization of a vision of home that could hold more than just herself and her child, one strong enough to hold the whole community of unhoused mamas and children and elders and community members who they were working with as advocates, journalists, and activists. Their imagination of home grew out of their work as founders of a grassroots media network run for and by those most impacted by the aggressive gentrification of San Francisco, called POOR Magazine. For more than twenty years the reporting/supporting protocol of the Poverty Scholars has centered town hall–type gatherings in the POOR Magazine newsroom during which folks find home in telling each other their stories, their lived experiences of poverty, and in teaching others to do the same. The Poverty Scholars curated space to stand against the press of social isolation and political paralysis. Their media activism is unapologetically displacing the dismissal, invisibility, illegibility, and despair of living in poverty with the truth of their lives and their visions for the future.

Homefulness became a collective practice of poverty scholarship, of transformative healing and resistance to the displacement of gentrification. Poverty scholarship, writes Tiny, "enables us poverty scholars to re-envision ourselves as liberators of ourselves, our families, our communities, our elders, our cultures. It allows us to delink ourselves from the middle-class media makers, missionaries, social workers, and nonprofit industrial complexes (NPICs), and nongovernmental organizations (NGOs), and their controlled systems of housing, education, service provision, art making and care-giving."[8]

I was a Poverty, Race, and Media intern for the interdependent media project at POOR Magazine starting in

8   Gray-Garcia et al., *Poverty Scholarship*, 30.

PRACTICING FREEDOM IN THE LOOPHOLES
OF CAPTIVITY

2002. The project operated out of an abandoned office space in the quickly gentrifying urban landscape of displacement that was and still is San Francisco. Mama Dee's teachings turned me right side out, dee-programmed and re-programmed my sense of what a "good" student wrote like. Dee renamed me, said Spirit called me Fatima, and helped me put my newfound rage at having come out of the Ivy League more lost than when I'd entered to good use by holding me accountable to what I'd learned there. Rather than letting my education alienate me from my new teachers, I found myself living for the one day a week they trained interns. I was 3,000 miles away from home and falling in love with Mama Dee's five-minute-long voicemails chastising my elitism and schooling me on how to tell the truth when I write. She taught me how redistributing what I gathered at elite institutions could keep me connected to my own Poverty Scholar ancestors and that they could teach me more than the degrees I held would ever dare. Along with Krip-Hop Nation founder and disability justice and Poverty Scholar Leroy Moore and the POOR Magazine family, Tiny and her beloved Mama Dee taught me how to distinguish between what it feels like to perform solidarity while standing apart from those I am moved to stand for and what it is to revise and reprise the way I stand with chosen family until the I becomes we. Over time my sense of home has grown beyond biology, beyond the academy, beyond a personal responsibility to myself and my household to include the dreams for the future that made my own dreaming possible.

Too many of the homemaking practices we inherit from national narratives and even spiritual traditions fence in and imprison our imagination of freedom. Even the Buddhist tenets of mindfulness and of being with what is can risk becoming alibis for middle-class detachment from accountability for the "privileges" of economic inequality, discrimination, and what we in the academy might call the necropolitics of urban renewal. Being with what is is not a passive act but a radical practice of deconstruction and reimagination. It means bearing witness to reality to transform it, to improvise on it. Co-creating practices of radical homemaking, repair, and transformation while swimming against the currents of capitalism, settler colonialism, and liberal sentimentality is the kind of labor of love that requires rest, space for recuperation, and collective healing. While reproductive homemaking practices of personal liberation, popularly understood as "self-care," require resources of indulgence and distance from the day-to-day things as they are—on our own, on a mat, on a cushion, on our property, behind closed doors and security systems—they are, for the Poverty Scholars, necessarily practices of collective survival that require forming unlikely partnerships and taking up space in public places in as-of-yet-unimagined ways.

In one instance, as Tiny writes in a recent essay,

> We launched a formal collaboration with a Bay Area agency that ran locked placements and schools inside and outside the public school system for severely emotionally disturbed youth... Our belief was that all members of the community needed to learn, grow, resist, and heal together, overcoming our collective experiences of broken school systems and/or broken or disempowered families that had been impacted or destroyed by the crime of poverty and or racism.[9]

Teaching in the system this way led to opportunities to teach in universities and colleges, semester-long sessions led by those most effected by poverty for those with some of the greatest distance from it.

9   Lisa "Tiny" Gray-Garcia, "Poverty Scholarship," *Educating for Equity* 14, no. 2 (Fall 2007): 62, https://www.reimaginerpe.org/node/1188.

PRACTICING FREEDOM IN THE LOOPHOLES
OF CAPTIVITY

What I am learning from their scholarship is that the practices of homemaking we have been taught to carry can only carry us so far. That all of our fates are intimately interconnected and our own ability to provide food and shelter for ourselves and our family is insufficient in itself to improve the life chances and quality of life for those who have little or no access to housing. What I am learning is that lack of access to some is a crisis for us all. The collective denial of our interconnectedness as co-habitants of our society, our community, our country, our planet has material consequence. Nationalist ideals about what counts as home, about who can practice it and where and on what authority, keep our collective imaginations of what home-making could look like limited by notions of personal responsibility, and render ideas like universal income, universal health care, and housing as a human right distant impossibilities. The real challenge is not just one of space. It is not even just one of design. It is one of imagination. How do we practice a kind of homemaking that is freed from the nationalist idealism and exceptionalist perfectionism of individualism and personal responsibility? How do we uproot ourselves from ways of homemaking that are not serving so many of us and take refuge in a co-created *practice* of homemaking that centers the voices, vision, and leadership of those most vulnerable, those who know how to survive displacement, deferment, detention, and destruction, in the fray, on the way, in the meanwhile? What if the spaces where we have been taught to feel most at home are holding us captive? What if the people and places we fence ourselves off from contain the very imaginations of home we need to liberate us all?

Living in the Loopholes

467   JASMINE SYEDULLAH

NO PLACE LIKE HOME

We who believe another world is possible know another US is necessary, and we are learning, from each other, how to live with ourselves as biological and chosen family, hidden in plain sight, in the loopholes of settler logics of incarceration, where the hold of oppression can be compromised, cracked open, undermined, sabotaged, and subverted, without notice when possible. Though not all the ways folks are learning to live and love in the loopholes of the intersecting structures of settler colonial logics that conspire to keep us silenced can be ethically documented (that is, without compromising their efficacy), some of the ways I am learning to live and love in the loopholes look like redistributing college capital to community activist/teacher/scholars, bringing Tiny and Leroy Moore to campus as guest lecturers, centering the knowledge production of cultural workers and self-taught intellectuals who never went to college or never received formal degrees in my college courses, and building community across lines of race and class privilege with folks in my neighborhood, in the places I live, work, play, and create. These lines of sight and accountability are the do-it-ourselves networks we pull on in times of collective crisis. For displaced peoples, these mutual-aid cultures of redistribution, education, healing, and advocacy have a long history. The places and practices of homemaking that escaped and emancipated formerly enslaved communities relied on during and after the Civil War refused the conventions of personal responsibility; these communities pooled resources for everything from housing to education to burial. These practices were documented in grassroots media networks, in narratives, speeches, novels, and essays. About a decade ago my studies led me to the writings of antislavery abolitionist Harriet Jacobs, a domestic fugitive slave and mother from North Carolina who self-authored the only full-length slave narrative of record by a formerly enslaved woman.

PRACTICING FREEDOM IN THE LOOPHOLES
OF CAPTIVITY

In *Incidents in the Life of a Slave Girl, Written by Herself,* Harriet Jacobs recounts the story of her escape from slavery. Before she was legally freed, Jacobs, who writes under the pseudonym Linda Brent in her narrative, was taught to read and write by her mother's mistress. Until the age of twelve, Jacobs lived a life as the mistress's maid, relatively free from the horrors of slavery. With her mistress's death, however, she was left to the woman's young niece and came to live on a plantation under Dr. Flint, a man who would assume ownership of Jacobs until her child mistress came of age. He was wealthy and well-known among the enslaved community for his pursuits of his bondwomen. It was not long before Jacobs became the object of his obsession.

Unlike other slave narratives that chart a more direct journey up from slavery, the story of escape that Jacobs tells takes a more circuitous route. It is not one where she suffers the trails of escape alone, leaving behind her uncles and aunts and cousins and grandmother, nor is it one with a happy ending. It is instead one that brings her, as she says, "something akin to freedom." A central incident of Jacobs's life was her relationship with Mr. Sands, a white unmarried lawyer whose affections she entertained because, she hoped, they would be strong enough to save their future children from a life of slavery, as was the law. Jacobs knew what it meant to be an enslaved woman and knew that, given her status, she would not likely escape slavery's claim over black women's reproductive bodies and labor, so she used her sexuality as a shield against the totalizing reach of slavery. In the highly unsanctioned relationship with Mr. Sands, she found just enough defense against the entitlements of her master's power over her; she found a loophole in his hold on her imagination of both escape and home. Dr. Flint tried relentlessly to appeal to Jacobs's desire for freedom, tempting her with promises of

NO PLACE LIKE HOME

protection from servitude should she consent to live in a home built far enough from the main house to be hidden from his wife. Jacobs writes:

> When I found that my master had actually begun to build the lonely cottage, other feelings mixed with those I have described. Revenge, and calculations of interest, were added to flattered vanity and sincere gratitude for kindness. I knew nothing would enrage Dr. Flint so much as to know that I favored another; and it was something to triumph over my tyrant even in that small way... Pity me, and pardon me, O virtuous reader! You never knew what it was to be a slave, to be entirely unprotected by law or custom; to have the laws reduce you to the condition of chattel, entirely subject to the will of another.[10]

Finding escape within the constraints of the places she called home became a practice of survival. Living in the loopholes of a law that conscripted children born to enslaved women to the condition of their mothers, rather than being wholly subject to it, created space beyond the law, a loophole for Jacobs to be something more than property, more than a domestic vessel for the homemaking of another. It created space for her to practice a homemaking of the future on the run, in flight.

When neither Jacobs's affair with her neighbor nor the two children she bore with him compelled Dr. Flint to let her go, she conspired to have Mr. Sands buy the children's freedom. However, Dr. Flint learned of her plan and threatened to "break" her children by selling them South should she continue to evade and refuse him. Jacobs had her sights set on a vision of freedom that could not be gifted or bartered and so with her closest friends and family, she

10   Harriet A. Jacobs, *Incidents in the Life of a Slave Girl, Written by Herself,* ed. Jean Fagan Yellin (Cambridge, MA: Harvard University Press, 1987), 55.

hatched a plan to escape his hold altogether and move them all closer to freedom. Rather than leave her children at the mercy of a resentful and vengeful master, her friends and family conspired to make it seem as if Jacobs had run away to the North—tucking her away and out of sight in a makeshift garret in a toolshed that sat on her grandmother's property. Escaped and at home in a place no bigger than a coffin, Jacobs took refuge in a space where she could be neither free nor enslaved. This space was her "loophole of retreat." From this place she was able to remain out of her master's grasp but within reach of her children and community for nearly seven years. She could listen to the voices of her children as they played in the street below and watch over them through holes in the wall of her hiding place while remaining invisible to those who hunted her. From this place she began to free herself from the spaces of subjection that kept her captive within the hold of slavery.

Jacobs's practice of living in the loopholes, in close proximity to both those captive relations still in bondage and those who had found freedom, followed in a tradition of collective liberation she learned from her grandmother who had spent years while enslaved working to buy freedom for herself and her children by baking cookies in the middle of night. These "midnight bakings," as she called them, took place after her grandmother's responsibilities to her mistress were fulfilled. With the money she saved from their sale, Jacobs's grandmother was able to buy her own freedom, as well as that of her son. Though much of what she saved was stolen from her by Dr. Flint, whose promise to pay her back went unfulfilled, she used the rest of the money to buy a home not far from where her remaining family lived as slaves, and continued to work to save money to buy freedom for them all.

"I bored three rows of holes, one above another; then I bored out the interstices between." Harriet A. Jacobs, *Incidents in the Life of a Slave Girl, Written by Herself,* ed. Jean Fagan Yellin (Cambridge, MA: Harvard University Press, 1987), 175.

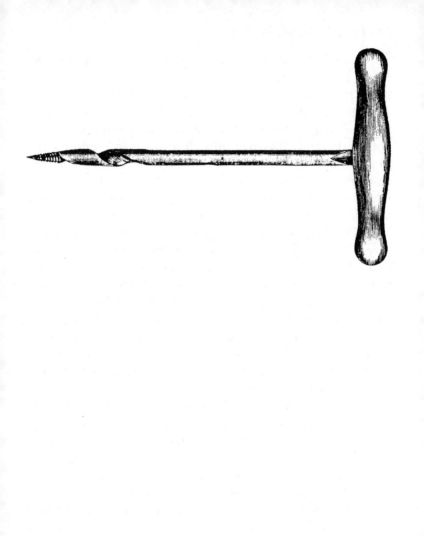

Grandmother's home became Jacobs's refuge. Jacobs's uncle, her grandmother's freed son, carved Jacobs's hiding space into the toolshed's roof and sealed it with a trapdoor. Though she inhabited this 9-by-7-by-3-foot crawl space as a place of refuge, life in this loophole was neither promising nor predictable. Its cover offered little opportunity for her to move or stand. It provided limited protection from the elements and from vermin. Nevertheless, Jacobs concedes, "there was no place where slavery existed, that could have afforded me so good a place of concealment."[11]

The loophole of retreat was more than a physical place: it was a generative space for creating much-needed mental distance from the quotidian violence of plantation life, distance from the ideological and architectural conscriptions of slavery's domestication of her imagination of freedom and her future. Jacobs's escape within the loophole suggests that it is always possible to create space for opposition within the hold of structural violence and domination, to move closer to freedom while still within the borders of hostile territory.

While fugitive solo journeys North structured the slave narratives of her male counterparts, Jacobs's loophole of retreat was more consistent with the "bondwomen who, for short periods of time, occasionally ran away from overwork, violence, planter control... Called 'runaways' by antebellum blacks and whites, and 'truants' and 'absentees' by historians, such women did not tend to make a break for freedom in the North, but sought temporary escapes from... oppressive regimes."[12] Hidden within the American ideals of home—held dear in nationalist rhetoric of homeownership today—is another history of home-making in which home was a prison for black communities

---

11   Jacobs, *Incidents in the Life of a Slave Girl*, 117.
12   Stephanie M. H. Camp, *Closer to Freedom: Enslaved Women and Everyday Resistance in the Plantation South* (Chapel Hill: University of North Carolina Press, 2004), 35–36.

under slavery. The image of home we have inherited may have a beautiful edifice, but, alongside the terrorist history of genocidal, deterritorialized indigenous nations that "settled" this country, it is saturated with the violent rape of black women and the theft of their children for the purposes of creating homes, wealth, and protection for others.

Moving closer toward freedom began as a series of sensory deprivations from the dispossessions and distractions of enslavement and developed into a practice of taking refuge in the undervalued spaces of her prison-home-plantation landscape. In addition to the garret space, Jacobs also took refuge beneath the floorboards of a neighbor's kitchen. Like a ghost among her captors, Jacobs haunted her hunters, as well, walking among them undetected disguised as a sailor. Living between containment and contract, she became something other than slave or fugitive. She was neither free nor captive. Her friends and family helped her take up the work of homemaking as a co-created space of revolutionary action, as a kind of freedom she could not have otherwise imagined. Living in the loopholes of slavery's hold on black life provided physical and figurative time and space away from the either/or entrapments of freedom and bondage, which slavery made all but inescapable.

As a poor black mother living in the time of slavery, there was no place to find the kind of freedom the free people of the North enjoyed. There was no being at home in freedom, even after the Constitutional end of slavery, for black women. No authority that could protect their lives from the will of entitled men. No shield to defend the idea that their lives mattered.

To borrow from Valerie Smith, Jacobs's loophole of retreat is a double signifier: a place of both withdrawal and confinement.[13] It provides the space for strategic retaliation and reorientation and offers a new perspective from which to surveil the effects of slavery. Inhabiting her own loophole in the landscape of both freedom and captivity, Jacobs's narrative asks: What if there is, has been, and would be no escape from slavery? What if freedom is not slavery's end but merely a suspended uncharted space of license, not only a way to keep black bodies captive, to use and dispose of them, to kill them with impunity or just leave them to die, but also a space where anything and everything is possible within, thinking with Christina Sharpe's work, the hold, the hull, the wake of antiblack trauma?[14] It is in this loophole space that she bore an end to her bondage and began seeding the conditions of possibility for slavery's abolition.

When I shared an early draft of this essay with Tiny, she proclaimed how very much Mama Dee had loved the narrative of Harriet Jacobs—that it had been a source of strength that inspired the dreams of homefulness she fought to realize her whole life. While homemaking has had many faces on this stolen land, the one that *Incidents* bears represents homemaking as an embodied practice of reclaiming that which was stolen. In this way the abolition of slavery is more than a political movement or ideology, it is the collective reclamation, reappropriation, and repair of black maternal reproduction, its function, and its futures. It is fugitive by its very nature, speculative by design. In an essay about the work of abolition, Alexis Pauline Gumbs writes,

> What if abolition isn't a shattering thing, not a crashing thing, not a wrecking ball event? What if abolition is something that sprouts out of the wet places

13   Valerie Smith, *Self-Discovery and Authority in Afro-American Narrative* (Cambridge, MA: Harvard University Press, 1987), 29.

14   Christina E. Sharpe, *In the Wake: On Blackness and Being* (Durham, NC: Duke University Press, 2016).

in our eyes, the broken places in our skin, the waiting
places in our palms, the tremble holding in my mouth
when I turn to you? What if abolition is something
that grows?[15]

So many of our national narratives and imagined
ideals of home are domesticated by settler logics rooted
in old oppositional understandings of freedom—mastery
or bondage, domination or containment. Keeping Jacobs
in mind, we might think with Gumbs's portrait of abolition as rupture rather than wrecking ball to ask: What
if the political project of abolition requires building trapdoors into the very architecture of our confinement? What
if it requires carving out hiding spaces within hostile home
spaces to stow dreams of futures we can only dare imagine
when no one is watching? A keepsake within the confines of
carceral landscapes, Jacobs's narrative carves new subversive openings into our collective understanding of caretaking and homemaking *and* even into the kinds of freedom slavery's end produced. Rather than dreaming of a
sometime someplace where the time and space of slavery
is somehow lifted from the blood-soaked soil—is somehow
redeemed and rendered obsolete—Jacobs's loopholes leave
blueprints for imagining how we might be made brave
enough by our bondage to take the distance we need to see
the world as it is, see how it could be, and act to revise
it! Captive fugitives from the time of slavery, those who
imagined a way out without leaving their people behind,
left traces of their imaginations of homemaking for us to
take up in our own radical acts of liberation. Captive fugitives model what it means to wake up from this horrific

15   Alexis Pauline Gumbs, "Freedom Seeds: Growing Abolition in Durham,
       North Carolina," in *Abolition Now! Ten Years of Strategy and Struggle
       against The Prison Industrial Complex*, ed. CR10 Publications Collective
       (Oakland: AK Press, 2008), 145.

history to seed alternative practices of liberation wherever we encounter slavery's domestication of freedom, the unfinished work of abolition—unsettling the way we imagine freedom and captivity, what they look like, how they feel, sowing different ways to collectively live within their hold while working to grow otherwise. Rather than become hostage to the ideals and protocols of homemaking we have been handed, Jacobs asks that we aggressively contemplate if this freedom we've inherited is really the "freedom" we need to feel at home after all.

Fugitive Abolitionist Architectures of Black Feminist Homemaking

It was through her encounters with her children's father and her retreat into her grandmother's garret that Jacobs cultivated a black feminist abolitionist consciousness of homemaking and developed an image of herself as a person in community with other captive fugitives and abolitionist co-conspirators. Jacobs's self-authorization is an expression, to borrow from the thought of black feminist political theorist Joy James, of the power of the "captive maternal."[16] Joy James's theory of the captive maternal interrogates how the creative force of black life is systematically subjected to serve as the literal and analytic fulcrum, as she imagines it, against which the womb of Western power grows. We see this dynamic at play in Jacobs's narrative. What drives Dr. Flint's desire to control his "slave girl" is a complex web of economic, sexual, and patriarchal desire to take her power to bolster or leverage his own—in as many ways as possible. James argues that the survival of black life under such conditions is evidence

---

16   Joy James, "The Womb of Western Theory: Trauma, Time Theft, and the Captive Maternal," in *Carceral Notebooks*, ed. Bernard E. Harcourt, vol. 12, *Challenging the Punitive Society*, ed. Perry Zurn and Andrew Dilts (New York: Carceral Notebooks, 2016), 253–296.

that the creative force of the captive maternal could not be wholly yoked by bondage.

Jacobs is one of many in a lineage of caretakers and homemakers criminalized for their defense of their families, refuges, and futures. James's theory of the captive maternal demonstrates how practices of homemaking in hostile territories are passed down through the writings, witnesses, and testimonies of those held in bondage but who refuse to be wholly domesticated by their subjection. Captive maternals ensure their co-created fugitive homemaking practices survive and move from the time of slavery to the time of so-called freedom. From fugitive formerly enslaved Jacobs to fugitive political prisoner Assata Shakur, from aggrieved mother Margaret Garner to murdered mother Korryn Gaines,[17] "the economies of pleasure and domination in democracy are tied to bondage of various forms facing the captive maternal," James explains. "With power understood in its pornographic rather than erotic forms... the captive maternal necessarily has to reinvent herself in the world through struggle and theorizing."[18] Though the world might have seen her and her practice of liberation as unbecoming for a lady, Jacobs wrote her testament of resistance into and against the world's moral compass—humanizing her experience for those "women of the North," as she writes in her preface, and, in doing so, making space for countless wayward others like her to also lay claim to the emancipatory power of the divine feminine.

17 See LaShonda Carter and Tiffany Willoughby-Herard, "What Kind of Mother Is She?: From Margaret Garner to Rosa Lee Ingram to Mamie Till to the Murder of Korryn Gaines," *Theory & Event* 21, no. 1 (January 2018): 88–105.

18 Joy James, "Political Trauma," in *The Bloomsbury Handbook of Twenty-First-Century Feminist Theory*, ed. Robin Truth Goodman (New York: Bloomsbury Academic, 2019), 352.

Joy James's theory of the captive maternal deconstructs the ways that people across the spectrum of gender identity leverage the creative power generated from the constraints of enslavement, incarceration, policing, and exile toward their own liberation. We need only turn to the context of displacement and gentrification in the contemporary moment to see how the loss of one person's freedom can quite literally be the condition of possibility for another to move closer to it. The captive maternal is, however, not only concerned with their own survival but also that of future generations. Throughout her work, James charts the protocols of captive-maternal homemaking as a radical unsettling of settler colonial divisions of labor, legitimacy, and authority. She argues that the captive maternal calls out and implicates the implicit and explicit perpetuation of Western philosophy's sanctioned and justifiable violence against and theft of captive stories, realities, bodies, imaginations, lives, and communities in the name of freedom— its hoarding, as Poverty Scholar Tiny would say, of what is not theirs in ways that buttress power without shame or fear of impunity. Through James we can see how the principles and protocols of homemaking as we have inherited them in the West seed a mindset of piracy within the American Dream—the self-appointed right to take whatever one wants, by force if necessary, to make oneself at home.

Rather than join the chorus of political theorists who declare that sovereignty is a necessary prerequisite for self-determination, James proposes a theory of freedom that cannot be conjured from expectation but only born out of practice: "Suffering produces the conditions under which sanctuaries are imagined, and constructed within minds, at times extended into the physical world."[19] To imagine a kind of freedom, a kind of home, and a kind of safety, that

19   James, "The Womb of Western Theory," 281.

those who consider themselves free, home, and safe cannot yet imagine: that is the mission of the captive maternal. To gather up the resources for homemaking on the run, in the streets, in hiding. On the rough road of praxis, fugitive homemaking is a practice of sitting with things as they are, so that their loopholes may be identified, located, and lived in until our illicit inhabitation transforms the landscape of our containment from the inside out. In this way, fugitive abolitionist homemaking becomes a co-created collective resistance to inequity as it arises, on the ground, in real time, against further enclosures or capture. There is anonymity in this audacious irreverence toward the master narrative, in seeing the loopholes in its hubris. Too sure of itself to concede to the credibility of a slave girl's critique, Jacobs's *Incidents* is not silenced by the yoke, but it slips it, to invoke Ralph Ellison here, to survive slavery's relentless surveillance.

Captive maternals are guaranteed no happy endings, but their stories become beacons in the spaces of containment we find ourselves in today. Though, in the end, there is no home for Jacobs and her children and no reward or glory bestowed on her for the triumph of her escape, we still have her story and its evidence of written protest against the moral integrity of the institution itself. Homeless but free, lawful but nearly lost to the archive of the abolitionist tradition, Jacobs's *Incidents in the Life of a Slave Girl, Written by Herself* represents a dream of glory that is full of a kind of homemaking that ends neither with the bill of sale nor with the national victory of Constitutional emancipation.[20]

20　For more than half a century after Jacobs's death, *Incidents* was believed to be a work of fiction. It was historically authenticated by literary historian Jean Fagan Yellin in the 1980s, who was inspired by black feminists working from/within marginalized positions of black liberation movements to establish a lineage of black women's contributions to abolition reaching back from Jim Crow and Reconstruction to the anti-slavery movement. Angela Y. Davis's and Hortense Spillers's studies of gender, race, and place

Rather, Jacobs chronicles her dream of glory as an ongoing practice of liberation brought to life and made possible by the fugitive abolitionist homemaking practices of clandestine political communities.[21]

Despite the ways "the state," as ethnic studies scholar Lisa Lowe reminds us, "subsumes colonial violence within narratives of modern reason and progress," the circulation of Jacobs's testament against slavery and others like it continue to create space for freedom beyond the protections of the law—and beyond the time of emancipation, the era of Reconstruction, and Jim Crow, and through the movements for black lives from Civil Rights to today.[22] The inscriptions of these dreams of freedom are nailed to the trapdoors of the peculiar institution and reside in the hidden corners of Jacobs's as-yet-unrealized imagination of freedom. They remain emergent, some hundred-plus years later, in the leveraging of, as Tiny writes,

> blood-stained Amerikkklan Dollarz to facilitate the "purchase" of stolen land on Turtle Island... In this East Oakland community, where many of POOR Magazine's family members have been gentrified out of, or currently dwell houselessly or in different forms of at-risk housing... the first HOMEFULNESS site

in the 1970s drew special attention to Jacobs's narrative, situating it within a praxis of black feminist activism and thought that retreated from both the paternalism of black liberation movements as well as from the white supremacy of women's liberation movements.

21　A note of clarification here: The narrative omission of names is a protocol of resistance in itself, one rooted in a political context in which the end of slavery is still uncertain and the ramifications for being associated with efforts to hasten its end—especially in the South—could prove fatal. Jacobs, in renaming herself, the figures of her story, and the location of her origin in fidelity to the fugitive community of underground railroad conductors, authors a reclamation of the virtues of anonymity, a refutation of the fungibility of the slave relation toward the destruction of plantation household.

22　Lisa Lowe, *The Intimacies of Four Continents* (Durham, NC: Duke University Press, 2015), 2.

> includes sweat-equity co-housing for 4–10 landless, houseless/landless families in poverty, as well as a site for PeopleSkool, a multigenerational, multilingual school based on an indigenous model of teaching and learning, POOR Magazine peoples media center, Uncle Al & Mama Dee's Social Justice and Arts Café and Tierra Madre Garden where we... grow food for the whole community.[23]

Asè!

While all the places I call home—this mind, this body, this two-bedroom apartment in a gentrifying hamlet on the Hudson—are all far more crowded than they are still or silent, there is space within the noise of my own rushing, panic, planning, and anxiety to watch myself, to become at home in these feelings, to see them and lovingly revise them rather than stand in opposition or be held hostage by them. Come what may, I can still myself to sit with what really matters.

Through poverty scholarship, the wayward, the houseless, the fugitive, and the exiled outlaws can breech the conditions of their captivity, however temporarily. Impossible to wholly assimilate or co-opt in nationalist narratives of progress, there is no place where fugitive affiliations are not being aggressively formed and passed on in hiding, in make-shift shelters, in swampy in-between spaces, in stolen moments—in the wet places, the broken places, the waiting places—all tethered together with the deconstructed reconstructed remnants of forced dispersal and criminalization and the dispossessions of a patrilineally domesticated landscape of fugitive life. The places where Jacobs, Mama Dee, Tiny, Tibu, and captive

---

23   Gray-Garcia et al., *Poverty Scholarship*, 307.

maternal others find refuge often unsettle the dreamscapes, landscapes, and timescapes of a colonizer's horizon, the cherished attribute of the privileged, the privatized, the lawful, the white and black, the women and men, the opportunists and their calculated casualties of consumptive and compulsive practices of domestic violence. With no self to defend and no place to call their own, Jacobs, Mama Dee, and others effectively author immanent critiques of slave ideology and respectability politics—they co-create a congregational confrontation with colonial logics from within capitalist constraints, one that springs from the dark briar of seemingly uninhabitable impossibility and spreads like wild fire.

By defending homemaking as a fugitive project rather than as a territorializing one, as the right of the fugitive, the formerly enslaved, the landless, the houseless, the spectacle, and the suspect, there is no place like home simply because home is more than a place. It is a space of practice, a space to practice liberation that retreats from the seductions of settler colonial logics, that seeds power beyond binary understandings of freedom and bondage. Being at home in the world, as it is, is all the space we need to locate the loopholes in the domestic landscapes we have inherited, to leverage their lack of oversight, and to envision alternative ways to see ourselves and the prisons we inhabit, taking refuge in the speculative shelter of our witness, our stories, and their wildest imaginations of home.

Sable Elyse Smith, *Coloring Book 29*, 2019. Screen printing ink and oil stick on paper, 60 x 50 inches. Courtesy of the artist; JTT, New York; and Carlos/Ishikawa, London.

Thanks for visiting!

ACKNOWLEDGMENTS

ISABELLE KIRKHAM-LEWITT

No one writes alone. I never write alone. As an editor, I mean this quite literally. Most writing I do every day happens in the margins of someone else's text. It is never done in isolation. It is always in dialogue. It is intimate, inconclusive, and reciprocal. Adrienne Brown, Stephen Dillon, Jarrett M. Drake, Sable Elyse Smith, James Graham, Leslie Lodwick, Dylan Rodríguez, Anne Spice, Brett Story, Jasmine Syedullah, Mabel O. Wilson, and Wendy L. Wright: Thank you for your trust and your openness. Thank you for not only sharing your writing and thinking with me but for creating the time and space to have such prolonged conversations across drafts, through email, in person, and over coffee. I am moved and guided by your work.

Writing carries all the ways one is formed in the world—which is why my thanks for this book are inseparable from the bibliography that follows. This project emerged out of frustration with the discipline of architecture for the limited ways it teaches architects to understand the built environment's relationship to and participation in the carceral state. It was frustration that led me through books and other disciplines; to archives; across sites of oppression and resistance; through Black geographies; to abolition feminism; that introduced me to the folx whose thinking has inspired this book, whose work has changed the way I see the world, and whose writing is in this volume—in actual essays, excerpts, footnotes, citations, and sentiments. As a register of what is in the book, though, the bibliography also includes many sources that evidence how the violence of the carceral state is produced and sustained and that document the quality of life under today's prison regime. I consider these materials equally important as indictments that invite more research, more work, more action, and more resistance within and beyond the discipline.

This project is directed towards abolition: it is assembled with the aim of organizing new ideas, of writing together, of inviting new research trajectories, and of co-producing a certain "counter-hegemonic discourse," as bell hooks names it, that will help abolitionist positions take root in architecture.[1] That is why no acknowledgment is greater than the acknowledgment of my indebtedness to those who have been fighting for the end of prisons, police, settler colonialism, racialized, gendered, and sexualized violence as a matter of life and death every day. I follow your lead and stand beside you.

I am also endlessly indebted to everyone who labored over this book with me, in big, small, and all ways. Wade Cotton, Emma Larson, Sabine Fayoux Cantillo, Carlo Bailey, Kaitlyn Kramer, Justine Holzman, Scott Hunter, Miranda Lievsay, and ":": each of you have taught me what it means to work in, and "collaboratively from," friendship.[2] Thank you for reading, talking, pushing, fighting, translating, and accompanying me on this project. To my brother Sam Lewitt: Thank you for so tirelessly and critically engaging with my work, for responding to my writing, for taking in all my anxiety and returning it to me as a something to read, and, for as long as I can remember, sharing and sowing seeds of communism. Milo Ward and Jordan H. Carver, my faux-peer-reviewers on the introduction: Thank

1   bell hooks, "Choosing the Margin as a Space of Radical Openness," *Framework: The Journal of Cinema and Media*, no. 36 (1989): 15–23.

2   Céline Condorelli and Avery F. Gordon, "The Company She Keeps: A Conversation with Céline Condorelli and Avery F. Gordon," part one and two (Chisenhale Gallery, September 26, 2013), How to Work Together, https://howtoworktogether.org/wp-content/uploads/htwt-think_tank-celine_condorelli_avery_gordon-the_company_we_keep.pdf; and https://howtoworktogether.org/wp-content/uploads/htwt-think_tank-celine_condorelli_avery_gordon-the_company_she_keeps_part_two.pdf.

you for pushing me to the limits of my own knowledge, for pointing out my blind spots, and for asking all the difficult questions that I continue to be happily stuck on. Laura Coombs: You are a sensitive and fierce book maker. You continually show me that editorial questions are design questions (and vice versa)—and your attentiveness to the particularities of print have moved this project in so many new directions. Thank you for insisting that even the smallest moment in a book is something to be designed with the biggest care. Grace Sparapani: Thank you for somehow managing to do the impossible as a copyeditor: for simultaneously reviewing each piece for Chicago Style, for knowing when to break the rules, and for whole-heartedly reading each essay. You were a remarkable second-set of eyes on this book. Emma Leigh Macdonald and Zoe Kauder Nalebuff: Thank you for doing the tedious task of turning all the footnotes in this book into a bibliography and for doing it with such careful consideration. To my brilliant colleague-editors at Columbia Books on Architecture and the City: thank you for meeting me day in and day out with endless curiosity and rigor. James Graham: Thank you for carving out the space for me to do this project in the first place. Jesse Connuck: Thank you for maintaining that my introduction could be an introduction. And Joanna Joseph: Thank you for holding me accountable every step of the way. This project would not have happened without the support of Columbia GSAPP, Dean Amale Andraos, and the Graham Foundation, and without Janette Kim and Rachel G. Barnard, who went out on a limb to sponsor the initial proposal for this book. Thank you all. And lastly to my partner Nick Morris: Thank you for modeling how to write honestly, for building a life practice with me, and for encouraging that I sit patiently with discomfort.

Here's to abolishing carceral society.

BIBLIOGRAPHY

"A Striking Scene: The Exchange of Prisoners at the Dade County Coal Mines." *The Atlanta Daily Constitution*, April 9, 1879.

"Closing of the Boone School is Given Tentative Approval." *Philadelphia Inquirer*, January 24, 1984.

"Convicts Who Are in Demand after Serving Terms." *New York Times*, June 4, 1911. https://timesmachine.nytimes.com/timesmachine/1911/06/04/106783727.pdf.

"Corrections Corporation of America's Founders Tom Beasley and Don Hutto." *The Nation*, February 27, 2013. Video, 2:47. https://www.youtube.com/watch?v=DAvdMe4KdGU.

"Dade County Coal Mines." *Atlanta Weekly Constitution*, July 20, 1886.

"Inmate Typing Pool in Use: To Transcribe Confidential Data." *Victoria Advocate*, April 21, 1985.

"Men Behind Bars Operate Booming Computer Service." *Red Bank Daily Register*, December 11, 1975.

"New Kane School Opened by City." *Philadelphia Inquirer*, December 4, 1963.

"Petros Prison to Be Sold by State: Bids to Be Taken Soon on Brushy Mountain Property." *Knoxville News-Sentinel*, December 19, 1973.

"Richmond Items." *New Orleans Times-Picayune*, January 15, 1871.

"Rizzo Backs School for Problem Pupils." *Philadelphia Daily News*, November 24, 1971.

"Senator Brown's Convicts: An Attempt Being Made to Starve Them into Submission." *New York Times*, July 14, 1886.

"The Leased Convicts of Georgia." *New York Times*, July 26, 1881.

A New Way of Life Re-Entry Project. "Restore Your Rights." Testif-i. http://testif-i.com/restore-your-rights.

Abdullah, Melina. "Why LA's DA Refuses to Prosecute Killer Cops." Interview by Sonali Kolhatkar. *Rising Up with Sonali,* September 29, 2017. Video, 13:28. https://www.risingupwithsonali.com/2017/09/29/why-las-da-refuses-to-prosecute-killer-cops.

Abolition Collective. *Abolishing Carceral Society.* Abolition: A Journal of Insurgent Politics. Brooklyn, NY: Common Notions, 2018.

Adams, Brooke, and Jim Dalrymple II. "Inside Job: Inmates Help Further Mormon Genealogy Work." *Salt Lake Tribune*, April 2, 2014. https://archive.sltrib.com/article.php?id=57682631&itype=cmsid.

Aguilera, Jasmine. "Another Word for 'Illegal Alien' at the Library of Congress: Contentious." *New York Times*, July 22, 2016. https://www.nytimes.com/2016/07/23/us/another-word-for-illegal-alien-at-the-library-of-congress-contentious.html.

BIBLIOGRAPHY

Ahmed, Sara. "A Phenomenology of Whiteness." *Feminist Theory* 8, no. 2 (2007): 149–168.

Ahmed, Sara. *On Being Included: Racism and Diversity in Institutional Life.* Durham, NC: Duke University Press, 2012.

Ahmed, Sara. *What's the Use?* Durham, NC: Duke University Press, 2019.

Alexander, Michelle. *The New Jim Crow: Mass Incarceration in the Age of Colorblindness.* New York: New Press, 2012.

Amar, Akhil Reed. *The Law of the Land: A Grand Tour of Our Constitutional Republic.* New York: Basic Books, 2015.

American Civil Liberties Union. "LA County Jails." https://www.aclu.org/issues/prisoners-rights/cruel-inhuman-and-degrading-conditions/la-county-jails.

Amnesty International. "The Angola Three." http://www.amnestyusa.org/cases/the-angola-3.

Anders, Marjorie. "Counties Turning to Privately Operated Jails." *Clovis News Journal,* August 4, 1985.

Angola Museum at the Louisiana State Penitentiary. "History of Angola." https://www.angolamuseum.org/history-of-angola.

Angola Museum at the Louisiana State Penitentiary. "Shop." https://www.angolamuseum.org/shop.

Appel, Shiloh. "Redfield High School Yearbooks from 1946–1989 Now Digitalized." *Redfield Press,* October 17, 2018. https://redfieldpress.com/article/redfield-high-school-yearbooks-from-1946-1989-now-digitalized.

Apter, Andrew. *The Pan-African Nation: Oil and the Spectacle of Culture in Nigeria.* Chicago: University of Chicago Press, 2005.

Architects/Designers/Planners for Social Responsibility. "AIA Code of Ethics Reform." https://www.adpsr.org/aiaethics.

Arvin, Maile, Eve Tuck, and Angie Morrill. "Decolonizing Feminism: Challenging Connections between Settler Colonialism and Heteropatriarchy." *Feminist Formations* 25, no. 1 (2013): 8–34.

Austin, James, and Garry Coventry. *Emerging Issues on Privatized Prisons.* Washington, DC: Bureau of Justice Assistance, 2001. https://www.ncjrs.gov/pdffiles1/bja/181249.pdf.

Austin, James, Wendy Naro-Ware, Roger Ocker, Robert Harris, and Robin Allen. *Evaluation of the Current and Future Los Angeles County Jail Population.* Denver, CO: JFA Institute, 2012. https://www.aclu.org/sites/default/files/field_document/austin_report_20120410.pdf.

The Avery Review. "Control Systems." http://averyreview.com/topics/control-systems.

Ayers, Edward L. *Vengeance and Justice: Crime and Punishment in the Nineteenth-Century American South.* New York: Oxford University Press, 1984.

Baimbridge, James. "My GPS-Tracked

Life in Parole." As told to Beatrix Lockwood. *The Marshall Project*, October 28, 2019. https://www.themarshall project.org/2019/10/28/my-gps-tracked-life-on-parole.

Baldwin, James. "On Being White… And Other Lies." *Essence*, April 1984. Anti-Racism Digital Library. https://sacred.omeka.net/items/show/238.

Barker, Joanne. Introduction to *Critically Sovereign*, edited by Joanne Barker, 1–44. Durham, NC: Duke University Press, 2017.

Barker, Joanne. *Sovereignty Matters: Locations of Contestation and Possibility in Indigenous Struggles for Self-Determination*. Lincoln: University of Nebraska Press, 2005.

Bauer, Shane. *American Prison: A Reporter's Undercover Journey into the Business of Punishment*. New York: Penguin Press, 2018.

Bauer, Shane. "Today It Locks Up Immigrants. But CoreCivic's Roots Lie in the Brutal Past of America's Prisons." *Mother Jones*, September/October 2018. https://www.motherjones.com/crime-justice/2018/09/corecivic-private-prison-shane-bauer-book.

Bauer, Shane. "Your Family's Genealogical Records May Have Been Digitized by a Prisoner." *Mother Jones*, April 13, 2015. https://www.motherjones.com/politics/2015/08/mormon-church-prison-geneology-family-search.

Bear, Laura. *Lines of the Nation: Indian Railway Workers, Bureaucracy, and the Intimate Historical Self*. New York: Columbia University Press, 2007.

Beaumont, Gustave de, and Alexis de Tocqueville. *On the Penitentiary System in the United States, and Its Application in France; With an Appendix on Penal Colonies, and Also, Statistical Notes*. Translated by Francis Lieber. Philadelphia: Carey, Lea & Blanchard, 1833.

Beckett, Katherine, and Naomi Murakawa. "Mapping the Shadow Carceral State: Toward an Institutionally Capacious Approach to Punishment." *Theoretical Criminology* 16, no. 2 (2012): 221–244.

Beller, Thomas. "Angola Prison in the Shadow of Slavery." *The New Yorker*, August 19, 2015. https://www.newyorker.com/culture/photo-booth/angola-prison-louisiana-photos.

Benns, Whitney. "American Slavery, Reinvented." *The Atlantic*, September 21, 2015. https://www.theatlantic.com/business/archive/2015/09/prison-labor-in-america/406177.

Benson, Sara M. "Democracy and Unfreedom: Revisiting Tocqueville and Beaumont in America." *Political Theory* 45, no. 4 (August 2017): 466–494.

Benson, Sara M. *The Prison of Democracy: Race, Leavenworth, and the Culture of Law*. Berkeley: University of California Press, 2019.

Berger, Dan. *Captive Nation: Black Prison Organizing in the Civil Rights Era*. Chapel Hill: University of North Carolina Press, 2014.

Berke, Jeremy. "'No Country Would Find 173 Billion Barrels of Oil in the Ground and Just Leave Them': Justin Trudeau Gets a Standing Ovation at an Energy Conference in Texas."

BIBLIOGRAPHY

Business Insider, March 10, 2013. http://www.businessinsider.com/trudeau-gets-a-standing-ovation-at-energy-industry-conference-oil-gas-2017-3.

Berlant, Lauren. *Cruel Optimism*. Durham, NC: Duke University Press, 2011.

Bill C-51, *Anti-Terrorism Act*. 2nd sess., 41st Parl., 2015 (Can.). http://www.parl.gc.ca/HousePublications/Publication.aspx?Language=E&Mode=1&DocId=7965854.

Bindman, David. *From Ape to Apollo: Aesthetics and the Idea of Race in the Eighteenth Century*. Ithaca, NY: Cornell University Press, 2002.

Biss, Eula. "Time and Distance Overcome." *The Iowa Review* 38, no. 1 (Spring 2008): 83–89.

Black Lives Matter Los Angeles. "Prosecute Police Who Kill Our People." OrganizeFor, September 11, 2017. https://campaigns.organizefor.org/petitions/los-angeles-county-da-prosecute-police-who-kill-our-people.

Black Lives Matter Los Angeles. "Sign BLMLA's Petition to Prosecute Police Who Kill Our People." Black Lives Matter, October 17, 2017. https://blacklivesmatter.com/sign-blmlas-petition-to-prosecute-police-who-kill-our-people.

Blackmon, Douglas A. *Slavery by Another Name: The Re-Enslavement of Black People in America from the Civil War to World War II*. New York: Doubleday, 2008.

Blow, Charles M. "Library Visit, Then Held at Gunpoint." *New York Times*, January 26, 2015. https://www.nytimes.com/2015/01/26/opinion/charles-blow-at-yale-the-police-detained-my-son.html.

Boos, Peter E. "Runaway REIT Train? Impact of Recent IRS Rulings." *Tax Notes*, September 15, 2014. http://www.taxhistory.org/www/features.nsf/Articles/FFF8F863CF33DB1E85257E1B004BAD8F?OpenDocument.

Bratton, William, and George Kelling. "There Are No Cracks in the Broken Windows." *National Review*, February 28, 2006. https://www.nationalreview.com/2006/02/there-are-no-cracks-broken-windows-william-bratton-george-kelling.

Brayne, Sarah. "Big Data Surveillance: The Case of Policing." *American Sociological Review* 82, no. 5 (October 2017): 977–1008.

Brook, Pete. "Unpacking the Media's Obsession with Prisoner-Firefighters." *Medium*, April 9, 2019. https://medium.com/s/story/whats-with-all-the-photos-of-prisoner-firefighters-b7385489243f.

Brooke-Eisen, Lauren. *Inside Private Prisons*. New York: Columbia University Press, 2017.

Brooks, Ronald. "Decarcerate Louisiana." Filmed June 21, 2018. Facebook Live video, 7:28. https://www.facebook.com/100015779203681/videos/310282476174390.

Brooks, Ronald. "Decarcerate Louisiana for Sustainable Economies." *San Francisco Bay View*, January 3, 2017. https://sfbayview.com/2017/01/decarcerate-louisiana-for-sustainable-economies.

Brown, Adrienne, and Valerie Smith. *Race and Real Estate*. New York: Oxford University Press, 2016.

Brown, Enora. "Systemic and Symbolic Violence as Virtue: The Carceral Punishment of African American Girls." In *The Routledge Handbook of Poverty in the United States*, edited by Stephen Nathan Haymes, María Vidal de Haymes, and Reuben Jonathan Miller, 398–405. Abingdon, UK: Routledge, 2015.

Browne, Simone. *Dark Matters: On the Surveillance of Blackness*. Durham, NC: Duke University Press, 2015.

Burger, Warren E. "More Warehouses, or Factories with Fences Commentaries." *New England Journal on Prison Law* 8, no. 1 (1982): 111–120.

Burroughs, Nannie Helen, and Charles Spurgeon Johnson. *Negro Housing; Report of the Committee on Negro Housing*. Edited by John M. Gries and James Ford. Washington, DC: President's Conference on Home Building and Home Ownership, 1932.

Butler, Octavia. "An Interview with Octavia Butler." By Randall Kenan. *Callaloo* 14, no. 2 (Spring 1991): 495–504.

Byrd, Jodi. *The Transit of Empire: Indigenous Critiques of Colonialism*. Minneapolis: University of Minnesota Press, 2011.

Caldwell, Alicia A., and Chris Kirkham. "Washington Attorney General Sues Motel 6 for Sharing Guest Info with Feds." *Wall Street Journal*, January 3, 2018. https://www.wsj.com/articles/washington-attorney-general-sues-motel-6-for-sharing-guest-info-with-feds-1515016334.

California Coalition for Women Prisoners. A Living Chance: Storytelling to End Life Without Parole. Multimedia archive. http://alivingchance.com.

California Prisoners Union. *The Folsom Prisoners Manifesto of Demands and Anti-Oppression Platform*. San Francisco: CONNECTIONS, 1970. https://www.freedomarchives.org/Documents/Finder/DOC510_scans/Folsom_Manifesto/510.folsom.manifesto.11.3.1970.pdf.

Camp, Jordan T. *Incarcerating the Crisis: Freedom Struggles and the Rise of the Neoliberal State*. Berkeley: University of California Press, 2016.

Camp, Jordan T., and Christina Heatherton. *Policing the Planet: Why the Policing Crisis Led to Black Lives Matter*. London and New York: Verso, 2016.

Camp, Stephanie M. H. *Closer to Freedom: Enslaved Women and Everyday Resistance in the Plantation South*. Chapel Hill: University of North Carolina Press, 2004.

Campt, Tina. *Listening to Images*. Durham, NC: Duke University Press, 2017.

Caron, Denis R. *A Century in Captivity: The Life and Trials of Prince Mortimer, a Connecticut Slave*. Durham: University of New Hampshire Press, 2006.

Carpenter v. United States, 585 US_ (2018).

Carr, Sarah, Francesca Berardi, Zoë

BIBLIOGRAPHY

Kirsch, and Stephen Smiley. "'That Place Was Like A Prison.'" *Slate*, March 8, 2017. http://www.slate.com/articles/news_and_politics/schooled/2017/03/camelot_schools_takes_its_discipline_too_far_say_current_and_former_students.html.

Carr, Sarah, Zoë Kirsch, Francesca Berardi, and Stephen Smiley. "Philly, 2 Other Cities Question For-Profit Manager of Alternative Schools." *PhillyVoice*, March 30, 2017. https://www.phillyvoice.com/philly-2-other-cities-rethink-profit-manager-alternative-schools.

Carter, LaShonda, and Tiffany Willoughby-Herard. "What Kind of Mother Is She?: From Margaret Garner to Rosa Lee Ingram to Mamie Till to the Murder of Korryn Gaines." *Theory & Event* 21, no. 1 (January 2018): 88–105.

Casella, Jean, James Ridgeway, and Sarah Shourd, eds. *Hell Is a Very Small Place: Voices from Solitary Confinement*. New York: The New Press, 2016.

Caswell, M. L. "'The Archive' Is Not an Archives: On Acknowledging the Intellectual Contributions of Archival Studies." *Reconstruction* 16, no. 1 (2016). https://escholarship.org/uc/item/7bn4v1fk.

Catte, Elizabeth. *What You Are Getting Wrong about Appalachia*. Cleveland: Belt Publishing, 2018.

Chakravartty, Paula, and Denise Ferreira da Silva. "Accumulation, Dispossession, and Debt: The Racial Logic of Global Capitalism—An Introduction." *American Quarterly* 64, no. 3 (September 2012): 361–385.

Chávez, Lydia. *The Color Bind: California's Battle to End Affirmative Action*. Berkeley: University of California Press, 1998.

Chicago Commission on Race Relations. *The Negro in Chicago: A Study of Race Relations and a Race Riot*. Chicago: University of Chicago Press, 1922.

Child, Deborah M. "Richard Brunton: An Artist of No Ordinary Character." *Journal of the American Revolution*, May 7, 2015. https://allthingsliberty.com/2015/05/richard-brunton-an-artist-of-no-ordinary-character.

Childs, Dennis. *Slaves of the State: Black Incarceration from the Chain Gang to the Penitentiary*. Minneapolis: University of Minnesota Press, 2015.

Christian, Tanya A. "Attorneys for Inmates at Brooklyn Jail without Heat, Electricity during Polar Vortex File Lawsuit." *Essence*, February 5, 2019. https://www.essence.com/news/attorneys-for-inmates-at-brooklyn-jail-without-heat-electricity-during-polar-vortex-file-lawsuit.

Church of Jesus Christ of Latter-day Saints. "NARA and FamilySearch to Place Major Segments of National Archives Documents Online." Press release, October 23, 2007. http://newsroom.churchofjesuschrist.org/article/nara-and-familysearch-to-place-major-segments-of-national-archives-documents-online.

City of Los Angeles v. Patel, 576 US__ (2015). https://www.supremecourt.gov/opinions/14pdf/13-1175_k537.pdf.

Clegg, John, and Adaner Usmani. "The Economic Origins of Mass Incarceration." *Catalyst Journal* 3, no. 3 (Fall

2019). https://catalyst-journal.com/vol3/no3/the-economic-origins-of-mass-incarceration.

Cliche, Spencer. "Reupholstering behind Bars: Massachusetts Prisoners Repair Auditorium Chairs at ARHS, ARMS." *The Graphic*, June 3, 2019. http://thegraphic.arps.org/2019/06/reupholstering-behind-bars-massachusetts-prisoners-repair-auditorium-chairs-at-arhs-and-arms.

Clover, Joshua. *Riot. Strike. Riot.: The New Era of Uprisings*. London and New York: Verso, 2016.

Cluckey, Amy, and Jeremy Wells. Introduction to "Plantation Modernity," edited by Amy Cluckey and Jeremy Wells. Special issue, *The Global South* 10, no. 2 (Fall 2016): 1–10.

Cohen, Julie E. "The Biopolitical Public Domain: The Legal Construction of the Surveillance Economy." *Philosophy & Technology* 31, no. 2 (2018): 213–233.

Cohen, Stanley. "The Punitive City: Notes on the Dispersal of Social Control." *Contemporary Crises* 3 (1979): 339–363.

Collier, Stephen, and Andrew Lakoff. "The Vulnerability of Vital Systems: How 'Critical Infrastructure' Became a Security Problem." In *The Politics of Securing the Homeland: Critical Infrastructure, Risk, and (In)Security*, edited by Myriam Dunn and Kristian Søby Kristensen, 17–39. New York: Routledge, 2008.

Comfort, Megan. *Doing Time Together: Love and Family in the Shadow of the Prison*. Chicago: University of Chicago Press, 2008.

Condorelli, Céline, and Avery F. Gordon, "The Company She Keeps: A Conversation with Céline Condorelli and Avery F. Gordon." Chisenhale Gallery, September 26, 2013, https://howtoworktogether.org/wp-content/uploads/htwt-think_tank-celine_condorelli_avery_gordon-the_company_we_keep.pdf.

Connecticut Department of Economic and Community Development. *Old New-Gate Prisoner List*. Hartford, 2015. https://portal.ct.gov/-/media/DECD/Historic-Preservation/04_State_Museums/Old-New-Gate-Prison-and-Copper-Mine/Old-New-Gate-Prisoner-List.pdf?la=en.

Connolly, N. D. B. *A World More Concrete: Real Estate and the Remaking of Jim Crow South Florida*. Chicago: University of Chicago Press, 2014.

CoreCivic. *2018 Annual Report*. http://ir.corecivic.com/static-files/3cc197ff-e1a0-495a-b1fc-1c347733d320.

CoreCivic. Company presentation. Recorded June 7, 2017, at REITWeek 2017: NAREIT's Investor Forum, New York. Webcast. https://reitstream.com/webcasts/reitweek2017.

CoreCivic. "CoreCivic Acquires 28 Property, 445,000 SF Portfolio of GSA Leased Assets." Press release, January 6, 2020. http://ir.corecivic.com/node/20826/pdf.

CoreCivic. "Corrections Corporation of America Rebrands as CoreCivic." News, October 28, 2016. https://www.corecivic.com/news/corrections-corporation-of-america-rebrands-as-corecivic.

CoreCivic. *ESG Report: Environmental,*

BIBLIOGRAPHY

Social and Governance, 2018. https://www.corecivic.com/hubfs/_files/2018-ESGReport.pdf.

CoreCivic. Form 10-K for the fiscal year ended December 31, 2018 (February 25, 2019). http://ir.corecivic.com/static-files/f289bea9-086c-4540-82b2-114dbfb95e4e.

CoreCivic. Form 10-K for the fiscal year ended December 31, 2019 (February 20, 2020). http://ir.corecivic.com/static-files/acc01462-f138-4e80-a699-10db834fec73.

CoreCivic. "Myth vs. Fact: CoreCivic's Valued but Limited Role in the Immigration System." https://www.corecivic.com/hubfs/_files/Myth%20Versus%20Fact%20CoreCivic%20Private%20Detention.pdf.

Coronil, Fernando. *The Magical State: Nature, Money, and Modernity in Venezuela*. Chicago: University of Chicago Press, 1997.

Corr, John P. "'I'd Do Anything to Keep My Child Out of This School.'" *Philadelphia Inquirer*, February 13, 1970.

Costa Vargas, João, and Moon-Kie Jung. Introduction to *Antiblackness*, edited by João Costa Vargas and Moon-Kie Jung. Durham, NC: Duke University Press, forthcoming.

Couldry, Nick, and Ulises A. Mejias. *The Costs of Connection: How Data Is Colonizing Human Life and Appropriating It for Capitalism*. Stanford, CA: Stanford University Press, 2019.

Coulthard, Glen Sean. *Red Skin, White Masks: Rejecting the Colonial Politics of Recognition*. Minneapolis: University of Minnesota Press, 2014.

Covert, Bryce. "Louisiana Prisoners Demand an End to 'Modern-Day Slavery.'" *The Appeal*, June 8, 2018. https://theappeal.org/louisiana-prisoners-demand-an-end-to-modern-day-slavery.

Cowen, Deborah. "Infrastructures of Empire and Resistance." *Verso* (blog), January 25, 2017. https://www.versobooks.com/blogs/3067-infrastructures-of-empire-and-resistance.

Crary, Jonathan. *Suspensions of Perception: Attention, Spectacle, and Modern Culture*. Cambridge, MA: MIT Press, 1999.

Cresswell, Tim. *Place: A Short Introduction*. New York: John Wiley & Sons, 2013.

Curtin, Mary Ellen. "Convict-Lease System." In *Encyclopedia of Alabama*. Alabama Humanities Foundation, May 13, 2019. http://www.encyclopediaofalabama.org/article/h-1346.

Cybersecurity and Infrastructure Security Agency. "Sector-Specific Agencies." Last modified August 22, 2018. https://www.cisa.gov/sector-specific-agencies.

Davis, Angela Y. *Abolition Democracy*. New York: Seven Stories Press, 2005.

Davis, Angela Y. *Are Prisons Obsolete?* New York: Seven Stories Press, 2003.

Davis, Angela Y. "Class and the Prison Industrial Complex." Paper presented at Rethinking Marxism's 4th International Conference, "Marxism 2000: The Party's Not Over," University of Massachusetts at Amherst, September 21–24, 2000. Video, 42:27.

https://youtu.be/xTmiH1G_v5Q.

Davis, Angela Y., and Frank Barat. *Freedom Is a Constant Struggle: Ferguson, Palestine, and the Foundations of a Movement*. Chicago: Haymarket Books, 2016.

Davis, Angela Y. "Globalism and the Prison Industrial Complex: An Interview with Angela Y. Davis." By Avery F. Gordon. In Avery F. Gordon, *Keeping Good Time: Reflections on Knowledge, Power, and People*, 46–57. Abingdon, UK: Routledge, 2016.

Davis, Angela Y. "Political Prisoners, Prisons, and Black Liberation." May 1971. History Is a Weapon. https://www.historyisaweapon.com/defcon1/davispoprprblli.html.

Davis, Angela Y., and Gina Dent. "Prison as a Border: A Conversation on Gender, Globalization, and Punishment." *Signs* 26, no. 4 (2001): 1235–1241.

Davis, Erik. "Databases of the Dead." *Wired*, July 1, 1999. https://www.wired.com/1999/07/mormons.

Davis, Mike. *City of Quartz: Excavating the Future in Los Angeles*. 6th ed. London and New York: Verso, 2006.

Dawson, Michael C., and Megan Ming Francis. "Black Politics and the Neoliberal Racial Order." *Public Culture* 28, no. 1 (January 2016): 23–62.

Day, Iyko. *Alien Capital: Asian Racialization and the Logic of Settler Colonial Capitalism*. Durham, NC: Duke University Press, 2016.

Dayan, Colin. "Due Process and Lethal Confinement." *South Atlantic Quarterly* 107, no. 3 (Summer 2008): 485–507.

DeMaio, Jerry R. "If You Build It, They Will Come: The Threat of Overclassification in Wisconsin's Supermax Prison." *Wisconsin Law Review* (2001): 207–248.

Dent, Gina. "Stranger Inside and Out: Black Subjectivity in the Women-in-Prison Film." In *Black Cultural Traffic: Crossroads in Black Performance and Black Popular Culture*, edited by Harry Elam and Kennel Jackson, 17–18. Ann Arbor: University of Michigan Press, 2003.

Desmond, Matthew. *Evicted: Poverty and Profit in the American City*. New York: Crown Publishers, 2016.

Desmond, Matthew. "In Order to Understand the Brutality of American Capitalism, You Have to Start on the Plantation." In "The 1619 Project." Special issue, *New York Times Magazine*, August 14, 2019. https://www.nytimes.com/interactive/2019/08/14/magazine/slavery-capitalism.html.

Dhillon, Jaskiran. "Indigenous Girls and the Violence of Settler Colonial Policing." *Decolonization: Indigeneity, Education & Society* 4, no. 2 (2015): 1–31.

Dhillon, Jaskiran, and Nick Estes, eds. *Standing with Standing Rock: Voices from the #NoDAPL Movement*. Minneapolis: University of Minnesota Press, 2019.

Dillon, Stephen. *Fugitive Life: The Queer Politics of the Prison State*. Durham, NC: Duke University Press, 2018.

Donziger, Steven. "The Hard Cell." *New York Magazine*, June 9, 1997, 26–28.

BIBLIOGRAPHY

Dowker, Fay, and Glenn Good. "The Proliferation of Control Unit Prisons in the United States." *Journal of Prisoners on Prisons* 4, no. 2 (1993): 1–10.

Drake, Jarrett M. "Diversity's Discontents: In Search of an Archive of the Oppressed." *Archives and Manuscripts* 47, no. 2 (2019): 270–279.

Drake, Jarrett M. "'Graveyards of Exclusion:' Archives, Prisons, and the Bounds of Belonging." Keynote address at the Scholar and Feminist Conference, Barnard Center for Research on Women, New York, February 9, 2019. https://medium.com/community-archives/graveyards-of-exclusion-archives-prisons-and-the-bounds-of-belonging-c40c85ff1663.

Drake, Jarrett M. "Liberatory Archives: Towards Belonging and Believing." Keynote address at the Community Archives Forum, University of California, Los Angeles, October 21, 2016. https://medium.com/on-archivy/liberatory-archives-towards-belonging-and-believing-part-1-d26aaeb0edd1.

Dumm, Thomas L. *A Politics of the Ordinary.* New York: New York University Press, 1999.

Dunbar-Ortiz, Roxanne. *An Indigenous Peoples' History of the United States.* Boston: Beacon Hill Press, 2014.

Dunne, Bill. "The US Prison at Marion, Illinois: A Strategy of Oppression." In *Cages of Steel: The Politics of Imprisonment in the United States,* edited by Ward Churchill and J.J. Vander Wall, 38–82. Washington, DC: Maisonneuve Press, 1992.

Egan, John. "How One Private Prison REIT Is Trying to Diversify." *National Real Estate Investor,* March 22, 2019. https://www.nreionline.com/reits/how-one-private-prison-reit-trying-diversify.

Electronic Frontier Foundation. "Street-Level Surveillance: A Guide to Law Enforcement Spying Technology." https://www.eff.org/issues/street-level-surveillance.

Eller, Ronald D. *Uneven Ground: Appalachia since 1945.* Lexington: University Press of Kentucky, 2008.

Ely, Richard T. "Private and Public Colonization." *National Real Estate Journal* 26, no. 6 (1923): 46–49.

Enns, Peter K. *Incarceration Nation: How the United States Became the Most Punitive Democracy in the World.* Cambridge, UK: Cambridge University Press, 2016.

Evans, Linda, Susan Rosenberg, and Laura Whitehorn. "Dykes and Fags Want to Know: Interview with Lesbian Political Prisoners by the Members of QUISP." In *Imprisoned Intellectuals: America's Political Prisoners Write on Life, Liberation, and Rebellion,* edited by Joy James, 261–278. Transformative Politics Series. Lanham: Rowman & Littlefield, 2003.

Ewing, Eve L. *Ghosts in the School Yard: Racism and School Closings in Chicago's South Side.* Chicago: University of Chicago Press, 2018.

FamilySearch. "Archives - About - Testimonials." https://www.familysearch.org/records/archives/web/about-testimonials.

Farzan, Antonia Noori, and Joseph Flaherty. "Attorneys Suspect Motel 6 Calling ICE on Undocumented Guests." *Phoenix New Times*, September 13, 2017, https://www.phoenixnewtimes.com/news/motel-6-calling-ice-undocumented-guests-phoenix-immigration-lawyers-9683244.

Felker-Kantor, Max. *Policing Los Angeles: Race, Resistance, and the Rise of the LAPD*. Chapel Hill: University of North Carolina Press, 2018.

Ferguson, Andrew Guthrie. *The Rise of Big Data Policing: Surveillance, Race, and the Future of Law Enforcement*. New York: New York University Press, 2017.

Ferguson, James. "Seeing Like an Oil Company: Space, Security, and Global Capital in Neoliberal Africa." *American Anthropologist* 107, no. 3 (2005): 377–382.

Ferguson, John D., and Damon T. Hininger. *A New View of Corrections: 2012 Annual Letter to Shareholders*. Nashville: CCA, 2012. http://ir.corecivic.com/static-files/56582057-2c3f-42df-9f63-b768e6d73872.

Ferreira da Silva, Denise. *Toward a Global Idea of Race*. Minneapolis: University of Minnesota Press, 2007.

Ferry, Elizabeth, and Mandana Limbert. Introduction to *Timely Assets: The Politics of Resources and Their Temporalities*, edited by Elizabeth Ferry and Mandana Limbert, 3–24. Santa Fe, NM: School for Advanced Research Press, 2008.

Finkelman, Paul. "Slavery in the United States: Persons or Property?" In *The Legal Understanding of Slavery: From the Historical to the Contemporary*, edited by Jean Allain, 105–134. Oxford: Oxford University Press, 2012.

Flaherty, Joseph. "Motel 6 to Settle Class-Action Discrimination Lawsuit Over Collusion with ICE." *Phoenix New Times*, July 9, 2018, https://www.phoenixnewtimes.com/news/phoenix-civilian-review-board-defund-the-police-11474245.

Foner, Eric. *Reconstruction: America's Unfinished Revolution, 1863–1877*. New York: Harper & Row, 1988.

Fort, William E. *Let's Get Rid of Alabama's Shame: The Convict Lease or Contract System: Facts, Figures, Possible Remedies*. Birmingham, AL: Statewide Campaign Committee for the Abolishment of the Convict Contract System, 1923. https://cdm16044.contentdm.oclc.org/digital/collection/p4017coll8/id/13001.

Foucault, Michel. *Discipline and Punish: The Birth of the Prison*. Translated by Alan Sheridan. New York: Vintage Books, 1977.

Foucault, Michel. "Michel Foucault on Attica: An Interview." By John K. Simon. In "Attica: 1971–1991, A Commemorative Issue," edited by Robert P. Weiss. Special issue, *Social Justice* 18, no. 3 (Fall 1991): 26–34.

Franke, Katherine. *Repair: Redeeming the Promise of Abolition*. Chicago: Haymarket Books, 2019.

Freedom for Immigrants. "Our Founding." https://www.freedomforimmigrants.org/our-founding.

BIBLIOGRAPHY

Freeman, Elsie T. "In the Eye of the Beholder: Archives Administration from the User's Point of View." *The American Archivist* 47, no. 2 (1984): 111–123.

Friedersdorf, Conor. "Mass Surveillance Is Coming to a City Near You." *Atlantic*, June 21, 2019. https://www.the atlantic.com/ideas/archive/2019/06/mass-surveillance-tech/592117.

Gallup-Healthways Well-Being Index. *State of American Well-Being: 2013 State, Community, and Congressional District Analysis.* Washington, DC: Gallup, 2014. http://cdn2.hubspot.net/hub/162029/file-610480715-pdf/WBI2013/Gallup-Healthways_State_of_American_Well-Being_Full_Report_2013.pdf.

Garlock, Peter D. "'Wayward' Children and the Law, 1820–1900: The Genesis of the Status Offense Jurisdiction of the Juvenile Court." *Georgia Law Review* 13, no. 2 (Winter 1979): 341–447.

Gay Games VII: Chicago 2006. "Los Angeles Police Department Sponsors Gay Games." Press release, December 23, 2005. https://web.archive.org/web/20110404074544/http://www.gaygameschicago.org/media/article.php?aid=123.

Gelman, Andrew, Jeffrey Fagan, and Alex Kiss. "An Analysis of the New York City Police Department's 'Stop-and-Frisk' Policy in the Context of Claims of Racial Bias." *Journal of the American Statistical Association* 102, no. 479 (2007): 813–823.

Georgia General Assembly. *Report of the Committee Appointed by the General Assembly to Investigate the Convict Lease System.* Montgomery, 1897.

Gibson, G., K. Yung, L. Chisholm, and H. Quinn with Lake Babine Nation and Nak'azdli Whut'en. *Indigenous Communities and Industrial Camps: Promoting Healthy Communities in Settings of Industrial Change.* Victoria, BC: Firelight Group, 2017.

Gikandi, Simon. *Slavery and the Culture of Taste.* Princeton, NJ: Princeton University Press, 2011.

Gill, Nick, Diedre Conlon, Dominique Moran, and Andrew Burridge. "Carceral Circuitry: New Directions in Carceral Geography." *Progress in Human Geography* 42, no. 2 (2018): 183–204.

Gilmore, Kim. "Slavery and Prison—Understanding the Connections." In "Critical Resistance to the Prison-Industrial Complex," edited by Critical Resistance Publications Collective. Special issue, *Social Justice* 27, no. 3 (Fall 2000): 195–205. History Is a Weapon, http://www.historyisaweapon.com/defcon1/gilmoreprisonslavery.html.

Gilmore, Ruth Wilson. "Forgotten Places and the Seeds of Grassroots Planning." In *Engaging Contradictions: Theory, Politics, and Methods of Activist Scholarship*, edited by Charles R. Hale, 31–62. Berkeley: University of California Press, 2008.

Gilmore, Ruth Wilson. "Globalization and US Prison Growth: From Military Keynesianism to Post-Keynesian Militarism." *Race & Class* 40, nos. 2–3 (March 1999): 171–188.

Gilmore, Ruth Wilson. *Golden Gulag: Prisons, Surplus, Crisis, and Opposition in Globalizing California.* Berkeley: University of California Press, 2007.

Gilmore, Ruth Wilson. "Prisons and-Class Warfare: An Interview with Ruth Wilson Gilmore." By Clément Petitjean. *Verso* (blog), August 2, 2018. https://www.versobooks.com/blogs/3954-prisons-and-class-warfare-an-interview-with-ruth-wilson-gilmore.

Gilmore, Ruth Wilson. "The Worrying State of the Anti-Prison Movement." *Social Justice*, February 23, 2015. http://www.socialjusticejournal.org/the-worrying-state-of-the-anti-prison-movement.

Gilmore, Ruth Wilson, and James Kilgore. "Some Reflections on Prison Labor." *Brooklyn Rail*, June 2019. https://brooklynrail.org/2019/06/field-notes/Some-Reflections-on-Prison-Labor.

Ginwright, Shawn. *Black Youth Rising: Activism and Radical Healing in Urban America.* New York: Teachers College Press, 2010.

Gledhill, John. "'The People's Oil': Nationalism, Globalization, and the Possibility of Another Country in Brazil, Mexico, and Venezuela." In "Toward an Anthropology of Oil and Domination," edited by Stephen Reyna. Special issue, *Focaal*, no. 52 (December 2008): 57–74.

Goeman, Mishuana. *Mark My Words: Native Women Mapping Our Nations.* Minneapolis: University of Minnesota Press, 2013.

Gómez, Alan Eladio. "Resisting Living Death at Marion Federal Penitentiary, 1972." *Radical History Review* no. 96 (Fall 2006): 58–86.

Gonzalez, Juan. "Board Votes to Close Kane School in N. Philadelphia." *Philadelphia Daily News*, June 21, 1983.

Gonzalez, Juan. "School District Regains Balance, Pays Back $8.5M to City." *Philadelphia Daily News*, May 31, 1984.

Goodman, Philip. "Hero *and* Inmate: Work, Prisons, and Punishment in California's Fire Camps." *WorkingUSA* 15, no. 3 (September 2012): 353–376.

Goodwin, Michele. "The Thirteenth Amendment: Modern Slavery, Capitalism, and Mass Incarceration." *Cornell Law Review* 104, no. 899 (2019): 900–975. https://www.lawschool.cornell.edu/research/cornell-law-review/Print-Edition/upload/Goodwin-final.pdf.

Gordon, Avery F. *Ghostly Matters: Haunting and the Sociological Imagination.* Minneapolis: University of Minnesota Press, 2008.

Gordon, Avery F. "Methodologies of Imprisonment." *PMLA* 123, no. 3 (2008): 651–658.

Gordon, Avery F., and Ines Schaber. *Notes for the Breitenau Room of The Workhouse—A Project by Ines Schaber and Avery F. Gordon.* Kessel: documenta (13) and Hatje Cantz, 2011.

Gordon-Reed, Annette. *Thomas Jefferson and Sally Hemings: An American Controversy.* Charlottesville: University Press of Virginia, 1997.

Gottschalk, Marie. *Caught: The Prison State and the Lockdown of American Politics.* Princeton, NJ: Princeton University Press, 2016.

Government of Canada. "Critical Infrastructure." Public Safety Canada. https://

BIBLIOGRAPHY

www.publicsafety.gc.ca/cnt/ntnl-scrt/
crtcl-nfrstrctr/index-en.aspx.

Government of Canada. "Speech from
the Throne to open the Second Session
Forty First Parliament of Canada."
ParlInfo. Parliament of Canada.
October 16, 2013. Transcript. https://lop.
parl.ca/sites/ParlInfo/default/en_CA/
Parliament/procedure/throneSpeech/
speech412.

Graber, Jennifer. *The Furnace of Afflic-
tion: Prisons and Religion in Antebellum
America*. Chapel Hill: University of
North Carolina Press, 2011.

Graham, James. "Making Coal Historical (a Road Trip)." *Avery Review*, no. 35
(December 2018). http://averyreview.
com/issues/35/making-coal-historical.

Grande, Tony. "In Times of Change, a
Constant Purpose." *CoreCivic Magazine*, Winter 2017. https://ccamericastor
age.blob.core.windows.net/media/
Default/documents/InsideCCA/CC
Magazine-2017-Winter-FINAL_Digital.
pdf.

Gray-Garcia, Lisa "Tiny." *Criminal
of Poverty: Growing Up Homeless in
America*. San Francisco: City Lights,
2006.

Gray-Garcia, Lisa "Tiny." "Poverty
Scholarship." *Educating for Equity* 14,
no. 2 (Fall 2007): 61–63. https://www.
reimaginerpe.org/node/1188.

Gray-Garcia, Lisa "Tiny," Dee Garcia,
and the POOR Magazine Family.
*Poverty Scholarship: Poor People-Led
Theory, Art, Words, & Tears Across
Mama Earth*. Oakland, CA: POOR
Press, 2019.

Greener, Glen N. "Pioneers Are Now
Found in Local Jails." *FamilySearch*
(blog), August 26, 2015. https://www.
familysearch.org/blog/en/pioneers-
local-jails.

Grigson, W. Herbert. "Physical and
Health Education in Special Classes:
History, Problems, and Special
Methods." *The Journal of Health and
Physical Education* 2, no. 3 (1931): 3–55.

Grigson, W. Herbert. "Physical and
Health Education in Special Classes:
The Physical Education Program in
Orthogenic, Backward, and Disciplinary
Classes." *The Journal of Health
and Physical Education* 2, no. 4 (1931):
15–57.

Groys, Boris. "The Obligation to
Self-Design." *e-flux Journal*, no. 00 (November 2008).

Guenther, Lisa. *Solitary Confinement:
Social Death and Its Afterlives*.
Minneapolis: University of Minnesota
Press, 2013.

Guenther, Lisa. "Subjects Without a
World? An Husserlian Analysis of
Solitary Confinement." *Human Studies*
34, no. 3 (2011): 257–276.

Gumbs, Alexis Pauline. "Freedom
Seeds: Growing Abolition in Durham,
North Carolina." In *Abolition Now! Ten
Years of Strategy and Struggle against
The Prison Industrial Complex*, edited
by CR10 Publications Collective, 145–
156. Oakland: AK Press, 2008.

Gupta, Akhil. "The Infrastructure
Toolbox: Suspension." Theorizing the
Contemporary. *Fieldsights*, September
24, 2015. https://culanth.org/fieldsights/
722-suspension.

Haley, Sarah. *No Mercy Here: Gender, Punishment, and the Making of Jim Crow Modernity*. Chapel Hill: University of North Carolina Press, 2016.

Hall, Henry, ed. "Edmond Urquhart." In *America's Successful Men of Affairs: An Encyclopedia of Contemporaneous Biography*. Vol. 1, 667–671. New York: The New York Tribute, 1895.

Hall, Lisa Kahaleole. "Navigating Our Own 'Sea of Islands': Remapping a Theoretical Space for Hawaiian Women and Indigenous Feminism." In "Native Feminism," edited by Mishuana R. Goeman and Jennifer Nez Denetdale. Special issue, *Wicazo Sa Review* 24, no. 2 (Fall 2009): 15–38.

Hall, Stuart. "Gramsci's Relevance for the Study of Race and Ethnicity." *Journal of Communication Inquiry* 10, no. 2 (June 1986): 5–27.

Hall, Stuart, and Doreen Massey. "Interpreting the Crisis." *Soundings* 44 (Spring 2010): 57–71. https://www.lwbooks.co.uk/sites/default/files/s44_06hall_massey.pdf.

Hare, Breeanna, and Lisa Rose. "America's Largest Jail: By the Numbers." *CNN*, September 22, 2016. https://www.cnn.com/2016/09/22/us/lisa-ling-this-is-life-la-county-jail-by-the-numbers/index.html.

Harris, Cheryl L. "Whiteness as Property." *Harvard Law Review* 106, no. 8 (June 1993): 1709–1791. https://www.jstor.org/stable/pdf/1341787.pdf.

Hartman, Saidiya V. *Scenes of Subjection: Terror, Slavery, and Self-Making in Nineteenth-Century America*. New York: Oxford University Press, 1997.

Hartman, Saidiya V. "The Time of Slavery." *The South Atlantic Quarterly* 101, no. 4 (2002): 757–777.

Hartman, Saidiya V. *Wayward Lives, Beautiful Experiments: Intimate Histories of Social Upheaval*. New York: W. W. Norton & Company, 2019.

Harvard Prison Divestment Campaign. *The Harvard-to-Prison Pipeline Report*. Cambridge, MA, October 2019. https://harvardprisondivest.org/the-harvard-to-prison-pipeline-report.

Harvey, David. *Social Justice and the City*. Baltimore: Johns Hopkins University Press, 1973.

Harvey, Penny, and Hannah Knox. *Roads: An Anthropology of Infrastructure and Expertise*. Ithaca, NY: Cornell University Press, 2015.

Hawes-Cooper Convict Labor Act, H.R. 7729, 70th Cong. (1929).

Hawkins, Jayson. "Sentenced to Life in Prison—And a Job Making Furniture." *The Marshall Project*, September 8, 2017. https://www.themarshallproject.org/2017/09/07/sentenced-to-life-in-prison-and-a-job-making-furniture.

Hazzard-Gordon, Katrina. *Jookin': The Rise of Social Dance Formations in African-American Culture*. Philadelphia: Temple University Press, 1990.

Hernández, César Cuauhtémoc García. "Creating Crimmigration." *Brigham Young Law Review* 2013, no. 6 (February 2014): 1457–1515. https://digitalcommons.law.byu.edu/lawreview/vol2013/iss6/4.

Hernández, César Cuauhtémoc García.

BIBLIOGRAPHY

Migrating to Prison: America's Obsession with Locking Up Immigrants. New York: New Press, 2019.

Hernández, Kelly Lytle. *City of Inmates: Conquest, Rebellion, and the Rise of Human Caging in Los Angeles, 1771–1965.* Chapel Hill: University of North Carolina Press, 2017.

Hininger, Damon. Remarks during CCA's 2015 Third Quarter Earnings Call, November 5, 2015. https://seeking-alpha.com/article/3659136-corrections-corporation-americas-cxw-ceo-damon-hininger-q3-2015-results-earnings-call.

Hininger, Damon. Remarks prepared for CCA's 2014 Third Quarter Town Hall, CCA Headquarters, Nashville, August 22, 2014. https://ccamericastorage.blob.core.windows.net/media/Default/documents/Social-Responsibility/Providing-Proven-Re-Entry-Programs/Hininger-Reentry-Speech-Transcript.pdf.

Hininger, Damon. "T. Don Hutto—The Mettle of the Man Behind Our Proud Facility." Employee Insights. CCA, January 19, 2010. https://perma.cc/G9ZZ-KVAJ.

Historic Brushy Mountain State Penitentiary. "Brushy's History." https://tourbrushy.com/history.

Holguin, Carlos. "The History of the Flores Settlement and Its Effects on Immigration." *All Things Considered.* NPR, June 22, 2018. MP3 Audio, 7:33. https://www.npr.org/2018/06/22/622678753/the-history-of-the-flores-settlement-and-its-effects-on-immigration.

Holt v. Hutto, 363 F. (1973).

Holt v. Sarver, 300 F. (1969).

Holt v. Sarver, 309 F. (1970).

hooks, bell. "Choosing the Margin as a Space of Radical Openness." *Framework: The Journal of Cinema and Media*, no. 36 (1989): 15–23.

Hoover, Herbert. "Address to the White House Conference on Home Building and Home Ownership, December 2, 1931." In *January 1 to December 1, 1931*, 572–577. Vol. 3 of *Public Papers of the Presidents: Herbert Hoover, 1929–1933.* Washington, DC: Government Publishing Office, 1976.

Hutto v. Finney, 437 US 678 (1978). https://supreme.justia.com/cases/federal/us/437/678.

Ibrahim, Isra. "Woman Throws Ashes of Niece Who Died in Police Custody at LAPD Chief." *The Black Youth Project*, May 11, 2018. http://blackyouthproject.com/woman-throws-ashes-of-niece-who-died-in-police-custody-at-lapd-chief.

In the Public Interest. *An Examination of Private Financing for Correctional and Immigration Detention Facilities.* June 2018. https://www.inthepublicinterest.org/wp-content/uploads/ITPI_PrivatePrisonP3s_June2018FINAL.pdf.

Incarcerated Workers Organizing Committee. "Prison Strike 2018," June 19, 2018. https://incarceratedworkers.org/campaigns/prison-strike-2018.

Irfan, Umair. "California's Wildfires Are Hardly 'Natural'—Humans Made Them Worse at Every Step." *Vox,*

November 19, 2018. https://www.vox.com/2018/8/7/17661096/california-wildfires-2018-camp-woolsey-climate-change.

Isaacs, Caroline. *Treatment Industrial Complex: How For-Profit Prison Corporations are Undermining Efforts to Treat and Rehabilitate Prisoners for Corporate Gain.* Austin: Grassroots Leadership, 2014. https://grassroots leadership.org/sites/default/files/reports/TIC_report_online.pdf.

It's Going Down. "#PrisonStrike." https://itsgoingdown.org/prisonstrike.

Jacobs, Harriet A. *Incidents in the Life of a Slave Girl, Written by Herself,* edited by Jean Fagan Yellin. Cambridge, MA: Harvard University Press, 1987.

James, Joy. "Political Trauma." In *The Bloomsbury Handbook of Twenty-First-Century Feminist Theory,* edited by Robin Truth Goodman, 345–354. New York: Bloomsbury Academic, 2019.

James, Joy. "The Womb of Western Theory: Trauma, Time Theft, and the Captive Maternal." In *Challenging the Punitive Society,* edited by Perry Zurn and Andrew Dilts, 253–296. Vol. 12 of *Carceral Notebooks,* edited by Bernard E. Harcourt. New York: Carceral Notebooks, 2016.

Jefferson, Thomas. Architectural plan for prison, n.d., N488 (verso). Thomas Jefferson Papers: An Electronic Archive, Architectural Drawings, Miscellaneous Buildings, Massachusetts Historical Society, Boston. http://www.masshist.org/thomasjefferson papers/doc?id=arch_N488verso.

Jefferson, Thomas. *Autobiography of*

Thomas Jefferson. Mineola, NY: Dover Publications, 1959.

Jefferson, Thomas. "Query XIV: The Administration of Justice and Description of the Laws?" In *Notes on the State of Virginia.* Paris, 1785. Avalon Project: Documents in Law, History, and Diplomacy, Yale Law School. https://avalon.law.yale.edu/18th_century/jeffvir.asp.

Jensen, Toni. "Women in the Fracklands: On Water, Land, Bodies, and Standing Rock." *Catapult,* January 3, 2017. https://catapult.co/stories/women-in-the-fracklands-on-water-land-bodies-and-standing-rock.

Jimerson, Randall C. *Archives Power: Memory, Accountability, and Social Justice.* Chicago: Society of American Archivists, 2009.

Jobe v. Urquhart, 102 Ark. 470 (1912).

Jordan, Miriam. "A New Surge at the Border Is Forcing Migrant Families into Motel Rooms." *New York Times,* October 18, 2018. https://www.nytimes.com/2018/10/18/us/migrant-families-arizona-ice-motels.html.

Kann, Mark E. *Punishment, Prisons, and Patriarchy: Liberty and Power in the Early American Republic.* New York: New York University Press, 2005.

Kant, Immanuel. "On National Characteristics, So far as They Depend upon the Distinct Feeling of the Beautiful and Sublime." In *Race and the Enlightenment: A Reader,* edited by Emmanuel Chukwudi Eze, 49–57. Cambridge, MA: Blackwell Publishers, 1997.

Kant, Immanuel. "On the Different

BIBLIOGRAPHY

Races of Men" (1777). In *Race and the Enlightenment: A Reader*, edited by Emmanuel Chukwudi Eze, 38–48. Cambridge, MA: Blackwell Publishers, 1997.

Karafin, Harry J. "Penna. Probes Job Abuses, Wage Chiseling, Beatings At City Disciplinary School." *Philadelphia Inquirer*, February 24, 1960.

Karafin, Harry J. "Wetter Praises Boone Principal: Knowledge of Abuses Denied." *Philadelphia Inquirer*, February 25, 1960.

Kassie, Emily. "Detained: How the United States Created the Largest Immigrant Detention System in the World." *Marshall Project*, September 24, 2019. https://www.themarshall project.org/2019/09/24/detained.

Kato, Daniel. "Carceral State 2.0?: From Enclosure to Control and Punishment to Surveillance." *New Political Science* 39, no. 2 (2017): 198–217.

Katz, Ellen D. "African-American Freedom in Antebellum Cumberland County, Virginia—Freedom: Personal Liberty and Private Law." *Chicago Kent Law Review* 70, no. 3 (April 1995): 952–953.

Kelkar, Kamala. "Incarcerated Women Risk Their Lives Fighting California Fires—Part of a Long History of Prison Labor." *San Francisco Bay View*, October 25, 2017. https://sfbayview.com/2017/10/incarcerated-women-risk-their-lives-fighting-california-fires-part-of-a-long-history-of-prison-labor.

Kelly, Brian. *Race, Class, and Power in the Alabama Coalfields, 1908–1921.* Urbana: University of Illinois Press, 2001.

Ketelaar, Eric. "Archival Temples, Archival Prisons: Modes of Power and Protection." *Archival Science* 2, nos. 3–4 (September 2002): 221–238.

Kilgore, James. "Challenging E-Carceration." https://www.challenging ecarceration.org.

Kilgore, James. "The Myth of Prison Slave Labor Camps in the US." *CounterPunch*, August 9, 2013. https://www.counterpunch.org/2013/08/09/the-myth-of-prison-slave-labor-camps-in-the-u-s.

King, Shannon. *Whose Harlem Is This, Anyway?: Community Politics and Grassroots Activism during the New Negro Era*. New York: New York University Press, 2015.

King, Tiffany Lethabo. *The Black Shoals: Offshore Formations of Black and Native Studies*. Durham, NC: Duke University Press, 2019.

King, Tiffany Lethabo. "The Labor of (Re)reading Plantation Landscapes Fungible(ly)." *Antipode* 48, no. 4 (2016): 1022–1039.

King, Wayne. "Contracts for Detention Raise Legal Questions." *New York Times*, March 6, 1984. https://www.ny times.com/1984/03/06/us/contracts-for-detention-raise-legal-questions.html.

Kino-nda-niimi Collective. *The Winter We Danced: Voices from the Past, the Future, and the Idle No More Movement*. Winnipeg, MB: ARP Books, 2014.

Kirby, Holly, et al. *The Dirty Thirty: Nothing to Celebrate about 30 Years of Corrections Corporation of America*. Austin: Grassroots Leadership, 2013.

Kirk, Michael, dir. *Frontline*. Season 19, episode 10. "LAPD Blues." Aired May 15, 2001, on PBS.

Knowlton, Winthrop. *Corrections Corporation of America*. Cambridge, MA: Harvard Kennedy School of Government Case Program, 1985.

Komisaruk, Katya. "They Are Searching." In *Hauling Up the Morning: Writings and Art by Political Prisoners and Prisoners of War in the US*, edited by Tim Blunk and Raymond Luc Levasseur, 32–33. Trenton, NJ: The Red Sea Press, 1990.

Kopytoff, Igor. "The Cultural Biography of Things: Commoditization as Process." In *The Social Life of Things: Commodities in Cultural Perspective*, edited by Arjun Appadurai, 64–92. Cambridge, UK: Cambridge University Press, 1986.

Korn, Richard. "The Effects of Confinement in the High Security Unit at Lexington." *Social Justice* 15, no. 1 (1988): 8–19.

Korn, Richard. "Follow-Up Report on the Effects of Confinement in the High Security Unit at Lexington." *Social Justice* 15, no. 1 (1988): 20–29.

Kovach, Bill. "Convict Coal Mining Is Holdover From Nineteenth Century." *Tennessean*, June 27, 1965.

Kovach, Bill. "Spreadeagled Men Feel Bite of a Heavy Leather Strap: Bars Shut Public Out, Convicts In." *Tennessean*, July 4, 1965.

Kun, Josh, and Laura Pulido, eds. *Black and Brown in Los Angeles: Beyond Conflict and Coalition*. Berkeley: University of California Press, 2014.

Kurashige, Scott. *The Shifting Grounds of Race: Black and Japanese Americans in the Making of Multiethnic Los Angeles*. Princeton, NJ: Princeton University Press, 2008.

Kyllo v. United States, 533 US 27 (2001).

Laird, Lorelei. "Meet the Father of the Landmark Lawsuit that Secured Basic Rights for Immigrant Minors." *ABA Journal*, February 1, 2016. http://www.abajournal.com/magazine/article/meet_the_father_of_the_land mark_lawsuit_that_secured_basic_rights_for_immig.

Larkin, Brian. "The Politics and Poetics of Infrastructure." *Annual Review of Anthropology* 42 (October 2013): 327–343.

Larsen, Erik. "Captive Company." *Inc.*, June 1, 1988. https://www.inc.com/magazine/19880601/803.html.

Lawrence, David Todd. "The Rural Black Nowhere: Invisibility, Urbannormativity, and the Geography of Indifference." *The Journal of the Midwest Modern Language Association* 48, no. 1 (2015): 221–244.

Lea, Tess, and Paul Pholeros. "This Is Not a Pipe: The Treacheries of Indigenous Housing." *Public Culture* 22, no. 1 (Winter 2010): 187–209.

Lefebvre, Henri. *The Production of Space*. Translated by Donald Nicholson-Smith. Oxford: Blackwell, 1991.

LeFlouria, Talitha L. *Chained in Silence: Black Women and Convict Labor in*

BIBLIOGRAPHY

the New South. Chapel Hill: University of North Carolina Press, 2015.

Lerman, Amy E., and Vesla M. Weaver. *Arresting Citizenship: The Democratic Consequences of American Crime Control*. Chicago: University of Chicago Press, 2014.

Levin, Sam. "Hundreds Dead, No One Charged: The Uphill Battle against Los Angeles Police Killings." *The Guardian*, August 24, 2018. https://www.theguardian.com/us-news/2018/aug/24/los-angeles-police-violence-shootings-african-american.

Lichtenstein, Alexander C. *Twice the Work of Free Labor: The Political Economy of Convict Labor in the New South*. London and New York: Verso, 1996.

Liebelson, Dana. "In Prison, and Fighting to Vote." *The Atlantic*, September 6, 2019. https://www.theatlantic.com/politics/archive/2019/09/when-prisoners-demand-voting-rights/597190.

Lim, Nelson, Carl Matthies, Greg Ridgeway, and Brian Gifford. *To Protect and to Serve: Enhancing the Efficiency of LAPD Recruiting*. Santa Monica, CA: RAND Center on Quality Policing, 2009.

Lipman, Pauline. *The New Political Economy of Urban Education: Neoliberalism, Race, and the Right to the City*. New York: Routledge, 2011.

Logsdon, Alexis. "Ethical Digital Libraries and Prison Labor?" Paper presented at the Digital Library Forum, Tampa, FL, October 15, 2019. https://osf.io/w7xe3.

Lopez, Sarah. "From Penal to 'Civil': A Legacy of Private Prison Policy in a Landscape of Migrant Detention." *American Quarterly* 71, no. 1 (March 2019): 105–134.

Los Angeles Almanac. "Los Angeles County Jail System by the Numbers." http://www.laalmanac.com/crime/cr25b.php.

Los Angeles Law Enforcement Gays and Lesbians (LEGAL). "'Beyond Tolerance': The 10th Annual International Criminal Justice Diversity Symposium," archived March 29, 2009. https://web.archive.org/web/2009-0329113605/http://www.losangeleslegal.org/pages/symposium/symposium1-cover.shtml.

Loury, Glenn C. *Race, Incarceration, and American Values*. Cambridge, MA: MIT Press, 2008.

Lukács, György. "Reification and the Consciousness of the Proletariat." In *History and Class Consciousness; Studies in Marxist Dialectics*, translated by Rodney Livingstone. Cambridge, MA: MIT Press, 1971.

Madden, David J., and Peter Marcuse. *In Defense of Housing: The Politics of Crisis*. London and New York: Verso, 2016.

Mancini, Matthew J. *One Dies, Get Another: Convict Leasing in the American South, 1866–1928*. Columbia: University of South Carolina Press, 1996.

Manion, Jen. *Liberty's Prisoners: Carceral Culture in Early America*. Philadelphia: University of Pennsylvania Press, 2015.

Massachusetts Department of Correction. *Department of Correction Annual Report 2017.* Boston, 2018. https://www.mass.gov/doc/doc-annual-report-2017.

Massey, Doreen B. *Space, Place, and Gender.* Minneapolis: University of Minnesota Press, 1994.

Mather, Kate. "LA Agrees to Pay Nearly $300,000 to Settle Case of Woman Who Died in LAPD Jail Cell." *Los Angeles Times*, December 13, 2017. https://www.latimes.com/local/lanow/la-me-ln-lapd-settlements-20171213-story.html.

Mazer, Katie, and Martin Danyluk. *Mapping a Many Headed Hydra: The Struggle Over the Dakota Access Pipeline.* Toronto: Infrastructure Otherwise, 2017. http://infrastructureotherwise.org/DAPL_Report_2017 0921_FINAL.pdf.

McCloskey, Sharon, and Bruce Orenstein, eds. *The Plunder of Black Wealth in Chicago: New Findings on the Lasting Toll of Predatory Housing Contracts.* Durham, NC: The Samuel Du Bois Cook Center on Social Equity at Duke University, 2019. https://socialequity.duke.edu/wp-content/uploads/2019/10/Plunder-of-Black-Wealth-in-Chicago.pdf.

McKelvey, Blake. "A Half a Century of Southern Penal Exploitation." *Social Forces* 13, no. 1 (October 1934–May 1935): 112–123.

McKittrick, Katherine. *Demonic Grounds: Black Women and the Cartographies of Struggle.* Minneapolis: University of Minnesota Press, 2006.

McKittrick, Katherine. "On Plantations,

Prisons, and a Black Sense of Place." *Social & Cultural Geography* 12, no. 8 (December 2011): 947–963.

McKittrick, Katherine. "Plantation Futures." *Small Axe* 17, no. 3 (November 2013): 1–15.

McKittrick, Katherine, and Sylvia Wynter. "Unparalleled Catastrophe for Our Species? Or, to Give Humanness a Different Future: Conversations." In *Sylvia Wynter: On Being Human as Praxis*, edited by Katherine McKittrick, 9–89. Durham, NC: Duke University Press, 2015.

McNeill, Fergus, and Kristel Beyens. "Introduction: Studying Mass Supervision." In *Offender Supervision in Europe*, edited by Fergus McNeill and Kristel Beyens, 1–18. New York: Palgrave Macmillan, 2013.

Mendieta, Eduardo. "Edge City: Reflections on the Urbanocene and the Plantatiocene." *Critical Philosophy of Race* 7, no. 1 (2019): 81–106.

Miller, Martin B. "At Hard Labor: Rediscovering the Nineteenth-Century Prison." *Issues in Criminology* 9, no. 1 (Spring 1974): 91–114.

Miller, Reuben Jonathan, and Amanda Alexander. "The Price of Carceral Citizenship: Punishment, Surveillance, and Social Welfare Policy in an Age of Carceral Expansion." *Michigan Journal of Race and Law* 21, no. 2 (2016): 291–314.

Miller, Todd. *Empire of Borders: The Expansion of the US Border around the World.* London and New York: Verso, 2019.

BIBLIOGRAPHY

Mitchell, Morgan. "Madawaska School History Goes Digital." *Fiddlehead Focus*. April 13, 2019. https://fiddlehead focus.com/2019/04/13/news/community/top-stories/madawaska-school-history-goes-digital.

Mitchell, Nicole. "Georgia Penitentiary at Milledgeville." In *New Georgia Encyclopedia*. Georgia Humanities, December 8, 2003. https://www.georgia encyclopedia.org/articles/history-archaeology/georgia-penitentiary-milledgeville.

Mitchell, Timothy. *Carbon Democracy: Political Power in the Age of Oil*. London and New York: Verso, 2011.

Montoya, Teresa. "Violence on the Ground, Violence below the Ground." Hot Spots. *Fieldsights*, December 22, 2016. https://culanth.org/fieldsights/1018-violence-on-the-ground-violence-below-the-ground.

Moran, Dominique, Jennifer Turner, and Anna K. Schliehe. "Conceptualizing the Carceral in Carceral Geography." *Progress in Human Geography* 42, no. 5 (2018): 666–686.

Morgan, Rod. "Report for Amnesty International, International Secretariat RE: High Security Unit (HSU) for Women at Lexington Federal Prison, Kentucky, USA." Appendix to Amnesty International, International Secretariat, *United States of America: The High Security Unit, Lexington Federal Prison, Kentucky*. London: Amnesty International, 1988.

Moroz, Jordan. "Inmates Find Purpose Indexing Vital Records." *Daily Universe*, February 6, 2015. https://universe.byu.edu/2015/02/06/being-set-free-through-indexing-the-positive-change-its-had-on-prison-systems1.

Moten, Fred. *Stolen Life*. Durham, NC: Duke University Press, 2018.

Moten, Fred, and Stefano Harney. *The Undercommons: Fugitive Planning and Black Study*. New York: Minor Compositions, 2013.

Mrazek, Rudolf. *Engineers of Happy Land: Technology and Nationalism in a Colony*. Princeton, NJ: Princeton University Press, 2002.

Muhammad, Khalil Gibran. *The Condemnation of Blackness: Race, Crime, and the Making of Modern Urban America*. Cambridge, MA: Harvard University Press, 2011.

Muhlstein, Julie. "Oklahoma Prisoners' Project Digitizes Everett High Yearbooks." *Daily Herald* (blog), June 7, 2016. https://www.heraldnet.com/news/oklahoma-prisoners-project-digitizes-everett-high-yearbooks.

Muller, Christopher. "Freedom and Convict Leasing in the Postbellum South." *The American Journal of Sociology* 124, no. 2 (September 2018): 367–405.

Murakawa, Naomi. *The First Civil Right: How Liberals Built Prison America*. Oxford: Oxford University Press, 2014.

Murphy, Michelle. *The Economization of Life*. Durham, NC: Duke University Press, 2017.

Murton, Thomas O. "The Arkansas Effect." *New York Times*, February 17, 1978. https://www.nytimes.com/1978/

02/17/archives/the-arkansas-effect.html.

Murton, Thomas O., and Joseph Hyams. *Accomplices to the Crime: The Arkansas Prison Scandal*. New York: Grove Press, 1969.

Naison, Mark D. *Communists in Harlem during the Depression*. New York: Grove Press, 1985.

Naison, Mark D. "From Eviction Resistance to Rent Control: Tenant Activism in the Great Depression." In *The Tenant Movement in New York City, 1904–1984*, edited by Ronald Lawson and Mark D. Naison, chap. 3. New Brunswick, NJ: Rutgers University Press, 1986. TenantNet. http://www.tenant.net/Community/history/histtoc.html.

Najmabadi, Shannon. "Across the Country, Basements, Offices, and Hotels Play Short-Term Host to People in ICE Custody." *Texas Tribune*, August 29, 2018. https://www.texastribune.org/2018/08/29/heres-ice-network-basements-offices-and-hotels-hold-immigrants.

Nareit. "Summary of the REIT Modernization Proposal." https://www.reit.com/nareit/advocacy/policy/federal-tax-legislation/reit-modernization-act-rma/summary-reit-modernization.

National Commission on Excellence in Education. *A Nation at Risk: The Imperative for Educational Reform, A Report to the Nation and the Secretary of Education*. Washington, DC: United States Department of Education, 1983.

National Oceanic and Atmospheric Administration. "2018 Was 4th Hottest Year on Record for the Globe." Press release, February 6, 2019. https://www.noaa.gov/news/2018-was-4th-hottest-year-on-record-for-globe.

National Prison Project of the ACLU Foundation. "Report on the High Security Unit for Women, Federal Correctional Institution, Lexington, Kentucky." *Social Justice* 15, no. 1 (1988): 1–7.

Nelson, Scott Reynolds. *Steel Drivin' Man: John Henry, the Untold Story of an American Legend*. New York: Oxford University Press, 2006.

New York Advisory Committee to the US Commission on Civil Rights. *The Solitary Confinement of Youth in New York: A Civil Rights Violation*. Washington, DC: US Commission on Civil Rights, 2014. https://www1.nyc.gov/assets/boc/downloads/pdf/NYSAC%20to%20U.S.%20Commission%20on%20Civil%20Rights.pdf.

O'Connor, Matt. "Firms, Prisons Join to Unlock Labor Pool: Use of Inmates Becomes Big Business." *Chicago Tribune*, December 13, 1987.

O'Melveny, Mary. "Portrait of a US Political Prison—The Lexington High Security Unit for Women." In *Cages of Steel: The Politics of Imprisonment in the United States*, edited by Ward Churchill and J.J. Vander Wall. Washington, DC: Maisonneuve Press, 1992.

Obama, Barack. "Directive on Critical Infrastructure Security and Resilience, February 12, 2013." Presidential Policy Directive No. 21. In *January 1 to June 1, 2013*, 106–115. Vol. 9 of *Public Papers of the Presidents: Barack Obama, 2009–2017*. Washington, DC: Government Printing Office, 2018.

BIBLIOGRAPHY

Office of Energy Policy. *Kentucky Quarterly Coal Report: January to March 2019.* Frankfort: Kentucky Energy and Environment Cabinet, 2019. https://eec.ky.gov/Energy/NewsPublications/Quarterly%20Coal%20Reports/2019-Q1.pdf.

Oklahoma Correctional Industries Sales. "Non-Destructive Scanning Yearbook Project." http://www.ocisales.com/non-destructive-scanning.

Ong, Paul M., ed. *Impacts of Affirmative Action: Policies and Consequences in California.* Walnut Creek: AltaMira Press, 1999.

Parenti, Christian. *Lockdown America: Police and Prisons in the Age of Crisis.* London and New York: Verso, 2000.

Parenti, Christian. "Making Prison Pay." *The Nation,* January 29, 1996.

Paris, Francesca. "Motel 6 to Pay $12 Million After Improperly Giving Guest Lists to ICE." *NPR,* April 5, 2019. https://www.npr.org/2019/04/05/710137783/motel-6-to-pay-12-million-after-improperly-giving-guest-lists-to-ice.

Pasternak, Shiri. "Jurisdiction and Settler Colonialism: Where Laws Meet." In "Law and Decolonization," edited by Stacy Douglas and Suzanne Lenon. Special issue, *Canadian Journal of Law and Society* 29, no. 2 (August 2014): 145–161.

Pasternak, Shiri, and Tia Dafnos. "How Does a Settler State Secure the Circuitry of Capital?" *Environment and Planning D: Society and Space* 36, no. 4 (2018): 739–757.

Patterson, William L., ed. *We Charge Genocide: The Historic Petition to the United Nations for Relief from a Crime of the United States Government against the Negro People.* New York: Civil Rights Congress, 1951.

Peart, Karen N. "Yale and FBI Launch Future Law Enforcement Youth Academy." *YaleNews,* May 10, 2016. https://news.yale.edu/2016/05/10/yale-and-fbi-launch-future-law-enforcement-youth-academy.

Pedroni, Tom C. *Market Movements: African American Involvement in School Voucher Reform.* New York: Routledge, 2007.

Pennsylvania State Department of Public Instruction. *Types of Schools, Teachers, Vocational Education.* Vol. 3 of *Report of the Survey of the Public Schools of Philadelphia.* Philadelphia: The Public Education and Child Labor Association of Pennsylvania, 1922.

Perdue, Robert Todd, and Kenneth Sanchagrin. "Imprisoning Appalachia: The Socio-Economic Impacts of Prison Development." *Journal of Appalachian Studies* 22, no. 2 (2016): 210–223.

Perry, Tekla S. "New Wearable Sensor Detects Stress Hormone in Sweat." *IEEE Spectrum,* July 20, 2018. https://spectrum.ieee.org/view-from-the-valley/biomedical/diagnostics/new-wearable-sensor-detects-stress-hormone-in-sweat.

Petteruti, Amanda, and Nastassia Walsh. *Jailing Communities: The Impact of Jail Expansion and Effective Public Safety Strategies.* Washington, DC: Justice Policy Institute, 2008.

Pfaff, John F. *Locked In: The True Causes of Mass Incarceration—and How* to Achieve Real Reform. New York: Basic Books, 2017.

Phelps, Noah Amherst. A History of the Copper Mines and Newgate Prison, at Granby, Connecticut: Also, of the Captivity of Daniel Hayes, of Granby, by the Indians, in 1707. Hartford: Case, Tiffany & Burnham, 1845.

Phelps, Richard H. A History of Newgate of Connecticut, at Simsbury, Now East Granby: Its Insurrections and Massacres, the Imprisonment of the Tories in the Revolution, and the Working of Its Mines. Also, Some Account of the State Prison at Wethersfield. Albany: J. Munsell, 1860.

Phillips, Kristine. "'That's Wakiesha!' A Woman Said as She Threw Her Niece's Ashes at the Los Angeles Police Chief." Washington Post, May 9, 2018. https://www.washingtonpost.com/news/post-nation/wp/2018/05/09/thats-wakiesha-a-woman-said-as-she-threw-her-nieces-ashes-at-the-los-angeles-police-chief.

Pierce, Bradford K. A Half Century with Juvenile Delinquents; Or, the New York House of Refuge and Its Times. New York: D. Appleton & Co., 1869.
Pierson, Paul. "The Study of Policy Development." In "New Directions in Policy History," edited by Julian E. Zelizer. Special issue, Journal of Policy Development 17, no. 1 (2005): 34–51.

Prison Industry Programs: Effects on Inmates, Law-Abiding Workers, and Business: Hearing before the Subcommittee on Oversight and Investigations of the Committee on Education and the Workforce. 105th Cong., 2nd Session (1998). http://hdl.handle.net/2027/pst.000043016037.

Prison Policy Initiative. "State and Federal Prison Wage Policies and Sourcing Information," April 10, 2017. https://www.prisonpolicy.org/reports/wage_policies.html.

Puar, Jasbir K. Terrorist Assemblages: Homonationalism in Queer Times. Durham, NC: Duke University Press, 2007.

Public Safety Canada. National Strategy for Critical Infrastructure. Ottawa: Government of Canada, 2009.

Pulido, Laura. Black, Brown, Yellow, and Left: Radical Activism in Southern California. Berkeley: University of California Press, 2006.

Pulido, Laura, Laura Barraclough, and Wendy Cheng. A People's Guide to Los Angeles. Berkeley: University of California Press, 2012.

Quinlan, J. Michael. "Letter to Ian Martin, June 12, 1987." In Amnesty International, International Secretariat, United States of America: The High Security Unit, Lexington Federal Prison, Kentucky. London: Amnesty International, 1988.

Rankine, Claudia. The White Card: A Play. Minneapolis: Graywolf Press, 2019.

Raspberry, William. "Control Data Chief: Prison Productivity Matters." Port Arthur News, June 24, 1984.

Reid, Ira D. "Mrs. Bailey Pays the Rent." In Ebony and Topaz: A Collectanea, edited by Charles Spurgeon Johnson, 144–148. New York: Opportunity and National Urban League, 1927.

Rice, Howard C., Jr. "A French Source

BIBLIOGRAPHY

of Jefferson's Plan for the Prison at Richmond." *Journal of Society of Architectural Historians* 12, no. 4 (December 1953): 28–30.

Rikard, Marlene Hunt. "Russell M. Cunningham." In *Encyclopedia of Alabama*. Alabama Humanities Foundation, September 30, 2014. http://www.encyclopediaofalabama.org/article/h-1620.

Robertson, Stephen, Shane White, Stephen Garton, and Graham White. "Disorderly Houses: Residences, Privacy, and the Surveillance of Sexuality in 1920s Harlem." *Journal of the History of Sexuality* 21, no. 3 (2012): 443–466.

Rodríguez, Dylan. "Abolition as Praxis of Human Being: A Foreword." *Harvard Law Review* 132, no. 6 (April 2019): 1575–1612.

Rodríguez, Dylan. *Forced Passages: Imprisoned Radical Intellectuals and the US Prison Regime*. Minneapolis: University of Minnesota Press, 2006.

Rodríguez, Dylan. *White Reconstruction*. New York: Fordham University Press, 2020 (forthcoming).

Rodriguez, Sal. *Fact Sheet: The High Cost of Solitary Confinement*. Washington, DC: Solitary Watch, 2011. https://solitarywatch.org/wp-content/uploads/2011/06/FACT-SHEET-The-High-Cost-of-Solitary-Confinement2.pdf.

Rogers, Douglas. "Oil and Anthropology." *Annual Review of Anthropology* 44 (2015): 365–380.

Rondinone, Nicholas. "Woman Shot in New Haven after Hamden, Yale Police Open Fire on Man Suspected in Armed Robbery." *Hartford Courant*, April 16, 2019. https://www.courant.com/breaking-news/hc-br-new-haven-officer-involved-shooting-20190416h7q7ldqenzg67pr7dtj72hdwfq-story.html.

Rosenberg, Susan. *An American Radical: Political Prisoner in My Own Country*. New York: Citadel Press, 2011.

Rosenberg, Susan. "Reflections on Being Buried Alive." In *Cages of Steel: The Politics of Imprisonment in the United States*, edited by Ward Churchill and J.J. Vander Wall. Washington, DC: Maisonneuve Press, 1992.

Rosenblum, Nina, dir. *Through the Wire*. New York: Daedalus Productions and London: Amnesty International, 1989.

Rowland, Cameron. *91020000*. Exhibition Booklet. Artists Space, New York, 2016. https://texts.artistsspace.org/uwcc1tpk.

Rowland, Cameron. *D37*. Pamphlet. Museum of Contemporary Art, Los Angeles, 2018. https://www.moca.org/storage/app/media/Cameron Rowland_D37_Pamphlet.pdf.

Royal Canadian Mounted Police. *Criminal Threats to the Canadian Petroleum Industry*. Ottawa: Critical Infrastructure Intelligence Assessments, 2014.

Rubin, Joel. "15 Officers Face Melee Discipline." *Los Angeles Times*, September 17, 2008. https://www.latimes.com/archives/la-xpm-2008-sep-17-me-mayday17-story.html.

Ruffin v. Commonwealth, 62 Va. 790 (1871).

Russ, Valeria M. "A Tough Class of Kids." *Philadelphia Daily News*, February 10, 1986.

Ryerson, Sylvia. "Speak Your Piece: Prison Progress?" *Daily Yonder*, February 20, 2013. https://www.daily yonder.com/speak-your-piece-prison-progress/2013/02/20.

Samuels, Liz. "Improvising on Reality." In *The Hidden 1970s: Histories of Radicalism*, edited by Dan Berger, 21–38. New Brunswick, NJ: Rutgers University Press, 2010.

Sander, Richard Henry. *Moving toward Integration: The Past and Future of Fair Housing*. Cambridge, MA: Harvard University Press, 2018.

Sawyer, Wendy, and Peter Wagner. "Mass Incarceration: The Whole Pie 2020." Prison Policy Initiative. Press release, March 24, 2020. https:// www.prisonpolicy.org/reports/pie 2020.html.

Schept, Judah. *Progressive Punishment: Job Loss, Jail Growth, and the Neoliberal Logic of Carceral Expansion*. New York: New York University Press, 2015.

Schept, Judah. "(Un)Seeing like a Prison: Counter-Visual Ethnography of the Carceral State." *Theoretical Criminology* 18, no. 2 (May 2014): 198–223.

Schept, Judah, and Jordan E. Mazurek. "Layers of Violence: Coal Mining, Convict Leasing, and Carceral Tourism in Central Appalachia." In Wilson et al., *The Palgrave Handbook of Prison Tourism*, 171–190.

School District of Philadelphia. "District Enrollment Open Data." June 1, 2019. https://www.philasd.org/ performance/programsservices/open-data/school-information/#district_ enrollment.

School District of Philadelphia. *Facility Condition Assessment Summary Report*. 2018. https://www.philasd.org/capital programs/wp-content/uploads/ sites/18/2017/06/Camelot-Academy-Boone.pdf.

Segura, Liliana. "The First Step Act Could be a Big Gift to Core Civic and the Private Prison Industry." *The Intercept*, December 22, 2018. https:// theintercept.com/2018/12/22/first-step-act-corecivic-private-prisons.

Selbst, Andrew D. "Disparate Impact in Big Data Policing." *Georgia Law Review* 52, no. 1 (2017): 109–185.

Shabazz, Rashad. *Spatializing Blackness: Architectures of Confinement and Black Masculinity in Chicago*. Urbana: University of Illinois Press, 2015.

Shapiro, Karin A. *A New South Rebellion: The Battle against Convict Labor in the Tennessee Coalfields, 1871–1896*. Chapel Hill: University of North Carolina Press, 1998.

Sharpe, Christina E. *In the Wake: On Blackness and Being*. Durham, NC: Duke University Press, 2016.

Sheller, Mimi. *Citizenship from Below: Erotic Agency and Caribbean Freedom*. Durham, NC: Duke University Press, 2012.

Sherman, Christopher, Martha Mendoza, and Garance Burke. "US Held Record Number of Migrant Children in Custody in 2019." *Assoc-*

BIBLIOGRAPHY

iated Press, November 12, 2019. https://apnews.com/015702afdb4d4fbf85cf5070cd2c6824.

Silary, Ted. "A Boon for Boone: Woman Coach Earns Respect of Tough Guys." *Philadelphia Daily News*, January 8, 1988.

Silver, Jonathan D. Letter no. 201320007 to Company A (believed to be CCA), May 17, 2013. https://www.irs.gov/pub/irs-wd/1320007.pdf.

Simmons, Kami Chavis. "The Legacy of Stop and Frisk: Addressing the Vestiges of a Violent Police Culture." *Wake Forest Law Review* 49, no. 3 (Fall 2014): 849–872.

Simmons, Kristen. "Settler Atmospherics." Dispatches. *Fieldsights*, November 20, 2017. https://culanth.org/fieldsights/1221-settler-atmospherics.

Simon, Jonathan. "Refugees in a Carceral Age: The Rebirth of Immigration Prisons in the United States." *Public Culture* 10, no. 3 (Spring 1998): 577–607.

Simone, AbdouMaliq. "People as Infrastructure: Intersecting Fragments in Johannesburg." *Public Culture* 16, no. 3 (Fall 2004): 407–429.

Simpson, Audra. *Mohawk Interruptus: Political Life across the Borders of Settler States*. Durham, NC: Duke University Press, 2014.

Simpson, Audra. "The State is a Man: Theresa Spence, Loretta Saunders, and the Gender of Settler Sovereignty." In "On Colonial Unknowing," edited by Alyosha Goldstein, Juliana Hu Pegues, and Manu Vimalassery. Special issue, *Theory & Event* 19, no. 4 (2016).

Singh, Nikhil Pal. "On Race, Violence, and So-Called Primitive Accumulation." *Social Text* 34, no. 3 (September 2016): 27–50.

Singh, Nikhil Pal. *Race and America's Long War*. Berkeley: University of California Press, 2019.

Smith, Caleb. "Harry Hawser's Fate: Eastern State Penitentiary and the Birth of Prison Literature." In *Buried Lives: Incarcerated in Early America*, edited by Michele Lise Tarter and Richard Bell, 231–258. Athens: University of Georgia Press, 2012.

Smith, Valerie. *Self-Discovery and Authority in Afro-American Narrative*. Cambridge, MA: Harvard University Press, 1987.

Soja, Edward W. "The Socio-Spatial Dialectic." *Annals of the Association of American Geographers* 70, no. 2 (1980): 207–225.

Sojoyner, Damien M. *First Strike: Educational Enclosures in Black Los Angeles*. Minneapolis: University of Minnesota Press, 2016.

Spice, Anne. "Interrupting Industrial and Academic Extraction on Native Land." Hot Spots. *Fieldsights*, December 22, 2016. https://culanth.org/fieldsights/1021-interrupting-industrial-and-academic-extraction-on-native-land.

Star, Susan Leigh. "The Ethnography of Infrastructure." *American Behavioral Scientist* 43, no. 3 (November/December 1999): 377–391.

State of Tennessee. *Report of the*

Warden, Superintendent, and Other Officers of the Tennessee Penitentiary. Nashville, 1893.

State of Washington v. Motel 6 Operating LP et al., King County Sup. Ct. No. 18-2-00283-4 SEA (2019). http://agportal-s3bucket.s3.amazonaws.com/uploadedfiles/Another/News/Press_Releases/Complaint.Scan2.pdf.

Stevenson, Bryan. "Why American Prisons Owe Their Cruelty to Slavery." In "The 1619 Project." Special issue, New York Times Magazine, August 14, 2019. https://www.nytimes.com/interactive/2019/08/14/magazine/prison-industrial-complex-slavery-racism.html.

Story, Brett. Prison Land: Mapping Carceral Power across Neoliberal America. Minneapolis: University of Minnesota Press, 2019.

Story, Brett, dir. The Prison in Twelve Landscapes. Documentary. New York: Grasshopper Film, 2016.

Story, Brett, Jack Norton, Jordan T. Camp, Annie Spencer, Christina Heatherton, and Kanishka Goonewardena. "Brett Story, The Prison in Twelve Landscapes (documentary, 87 Min., 2016)." In "Neoliberal Confinements: Social Suffering in the Carceral State," edited by Alessandro De Giorgi and Benjamin Fleury-Steiner. Special Issue, Social Justice 44, nos. 2–3 (2017): 163–176.

Summers, Martin Anthony. Manliness and Its Discontents: The Black Middle Class and the Transformation of Masculinity, 1900–1930. Chapel Hill: University of North Carolina Press, 2004.

Susler, Jan. "The Women's High Security Unit in Lexington, KY." Yale Journal of Law and Liberation 1, no. 1 (1989): 31–41.

Sutherland, Tonia. "The Carceral Archive: Documentary Records, Narrative Construction, and Predictive Risk Assessment." Journal of Cultural Analytics, June 4, 2019. https://culturalanalytics.org/article/11047.

Syedullah, Jasmine. "What the World Needs Now." In Radical Dharma: Talking Race, Love, and Liberation. Edited by angel Kyodo williams, Lama Rod Owens, and Jasmine Syedullah, 184. Berkeley, CA: North Atlantic Books, 2016.

TallBear, Kim. "Badass (Indigenous) Women Caretake Relations: #NoDAPL, #IdleNoMore, #BlackLivesMatter." Hot Spots. Fieldsights, December 22, 2016. https://culanth.org/fieldsights/1019-badass-indigenous-women-caretake-relations-nodapl-idlenomore-blacklivesmatter.

Tasker, John Paul. "Trudeau Cabinet Approves Trans Mountain, Line 3 Pipelines, Rejects Northern Gateway." CBC News, November 29, 2016. http://www.cbc.ca/news/politics/federal-cabinet-trudeau-pipeline-decisions-1.3872828.

Telmate Guardian. "Getting Started with Guardian." http://guardianmonitor.com/faq/getting-started-with-guardian.

Texas Correctional Industries. "Geographic Information System (GIS) Data Conversion Services." April 2018. https://tci.tdcj.texas.gov/services/gis.aspx.

Texas v. Brown, 460 US 730 (1983).

BIBLIOGRAPHY

Thomas, Robert A. "6 New City Schools: All Will Open Their Doors by Early Next Year to Meet Record 273,900 Enrollment." *Philadelphia Inquirer*, September 8, 1963.

Thompson, Heather Ann. *Blood in the Water: The Attica Prison Uprising of 1971 and Its Legacy*. New York: Pantheon Books, 2016.

Thuma, Emily L. *All Our Trials: Prisons, Policing, and the Feminist Fight to End Violence*. Urbana: University of Illinois Press, 2019.

TransCanada Corporation. "The Benefits." In *Coastal GasLink Pipeline Project*. Calgary: TransCanada, 2017. https://www.tcenergy.com/siteassets/pdfs/natural-gas/coastal-gaslink/transcanada-2017-coastal-gaslink-project-overview.pdf.

Travis, Jeremy. "Reducing Mass Incarceration: Exploring the Values of Values." Opening address presented at the 2015 National Forum on Criminal Justice, Atlanta, Georgia, August 3, 2015.

Trotter, Joe William. *Coal, Class, and Color: Blacks in Southern West Virginia, 1915–1932*. Urbana: University of Illinois Press, 1990.

Trudeau, Justin. "Statement by the Prime Minister of Canada on National Aboriginal Day." Press release, June 21, 2016. https://pm.gc.ca/eng/news/2016/06/21/statement-prime-minister-canada-national-aboriginal-day.

Truong, Erik. "Products of Prison Labor on Campus." *George Mason University Fourth Estate*, February 25, 2018. http://gmufourthestate.com/2018/02/25/products-of-prison-labor-on-campus.

Turner, Jennifer, and Kimberley Peters. "Unlocking Carceral Atmospheres: Designing Visual/Material Encounters at the Prison Museum." In "Designing Atmospheres," edited by Tim Edensor and Shanti Sumartojo. Special issue, *Visual Communication* 14, no. 3 (August 2015): 309–330.

UNICOR. *Factories with Fences: 85 Years Building Brighter Futures*. Petersburg, VA: UNICOR Print Plant, Federal Correctional Institute, 2018. https://www.unicor.gov/publications/corporate/CATMC1101_C.pdf.

United Nations General Assembly. Resolution 61/295. United Nations Declaration on the Rights of Indigenous Peoples. A/RES/61/295, September 13, 2007. http://www.un.org/esa/socdev/unpfii/documents/DRIPS_en.pdf.

United States Bureau of Labor Statistics. "Labor Force Statistics from the Current Population Survey." http://www.bls.gov/cps/cpsaat11.htm.

United States Bureau of the Census. "Population—Pennsylvania, Table 13: Composition and Characteristics of the Population for Wards of Cities of 50,000 or More, Philadelphia." In *Population, 1920: Composition and Characteristics of the Population by States*, 887–906. Vol. 3 of *Fourteenth Census of the United States*. Washington, DC: Government Printing Office, 1922.

United States Federal Bureau of Investigation. "FBI and Marquette University Police Department to Host 2019 Future Law Enforcement Youth Academy." Press release, February 20, 2019. https://www.fbi.gov/contact-us/field-offices/milwaukee/news/press-releases/fbi-and-marquette-university-police-department-host-2019-future-law-enforcement-youth-academy.

United States Federal Bureau of Investigation. "Now Accepting Applications for FBI/Yale Future Law Enforcement Youth Academy Program." Press release, May 6, 2016. https://www.fbi.gov/contact-us/field-offices/newhaven/news/press-releases/now-accepting-applications-for-fbi-yale-future-law-enforcement-youth-academy-program.

United States General Accounting Office. *Immigration Control: Immigration Policies Affect INS Detention Efforts.* Report to the Chairman of the United States Senate Committee on Judiciary Subcommittee on International Law, Immigration, and Refugees. Washington, DC, 1992.

United States Prison Industries Reorganization Administration. *The Prison Labor Problem in Tennessee.* Washington, DC, 1937.

United States v. City of Los Angeles, 2:00-cv-11769-GAF-RC (C.D. Cal. June 15, 2001). Consent decree. https://www.justice.gov/crt/file/826956/download.

United States v. Jones, 565 US 400 (2012).

Upton, Dell. "Lancasterian Schools, Republican Citizenship, and the Spatial Imagination in Early Nineteenth-Century America." *Journal of the Society of Architectural Historians* 55, no. 3 (1996): 238–253.

Utah Department of Administrative Services, Division of Purchasing and General Services. "Contract No. UCI1869: Data Entry, Scanning, and Micrographic Services." With Utah Correctional Industries, September 19, 2016. https://purchasing.utah.gov/wp-content/uploads/UCI1869.pdf.

Valentino-DeVries, Jennifer. "Tracking Phones, Google Is a Dragnet for the Police." *New York Times*, April 13, 2019. https://www.nytimes.com/interactive/2019/04/13/us/google-location-tracking-police.html.

Vimalassery, Manu. "The Prose of Counter-Sovereignty." In *Formations of United States Colonialism*, edited by Alyosha Goldstein, 87–109. Durham, NC: Duke University Press, 2014.

Vogel, Shane. "The Sensuous Harlem Renaissance: Sexuality and Queer Culture." In *A Companion to the Harlem Renaissance*, edited by Cherene Sherrard-Johnson, 267–283. Chicester: Wiley-Blackwell, 2015.

Voices: Indigenous Women on the Frontlines Speak. http://voicesbook.tumblr.com/about.

Wacquant, Loïc. "From Slavery to Mass Incarceration." *New Left Review*, no. 13 (January–February 2002): 41–60. https://newleftreview.org/issues/II13/articles/loic-wacquant-from-slavery-to-mass-incarceration.

Walcott, Rinaldo. *Writing Black Canada*. 2nd rev. ed. Toronto: Insomniac Press, 2003.

Wang, Jackie. *Carceral Capitalism*. South Pasadena: Semiotext(e), 2018.

Warren, Calvin L. *Ontological Terror: Blackness, Nihilism, and Emancipation*. Durham, NC: Duke University Press, 2018.

BIBLIOGRAPHY

Watts, Michael. "Securing Oil: Frontiers, Risk, and Spaces of Accumulated Insecurity." In *Subterranean Estates: Life Worlds of Oil and Gas*, edited by Hannah Appel, Arthur Mason, and Michael Watts, 211–236. Ithaca, NY: Cornell University Press, 2015.

We Charge Genocide. *Police Violence Against Chicago's Youth of Color.* Report prepared for the United Nations Committee against Torture on the occasion of its Review of the United States of America's Third Periodic Report to the Committee against Torture. Chicago, 2014. http://report.we chargegenocide.org/index.html.

We Charge Genocide, and Black Lives Matter—Chicago. "An Open Letter to the ACLU of Illinois Regarding Stop & Frisk." We Charge Genocide, August 12, 2015. http://wechargegeno cide.org/an-open-letter-to-the-aclu-of-illinois-regarding-stop-frisk.

Weheliye, Alexander G. *Phonographies: Grooves in Sonic Afro-Modernity.* Durham, NC: Duke University Press, 2005.

Welch, Michael. "The Immigration Crisis: Detention as an Emerging Mechanism of Social Control." In "Immigration: A Civil Rights Issue for the Americas in the 21st Century," edited by Susanne Jonas and Suzie Dod Thomas. Special issue, *Social Justice* 23, no. 3 (Fall 1996): 169–184.

Wells-Barnett, Ida B. "Southern Horrors: Lynch Law in All Its Phases." In *Selected Works of Ida B. Wells-Barnett*, edited by Trudier Harris, 14–45. New York: Oxford University Press, 1991.

White, Michael D., and Henry F. Fradella. *Stop and Frisk: The Use and Abuse of a Controversial Policing Tactic.* New York: New York University Press, 2016.

Wicker, Tom. *A Time to Die: The Attica Prison Revolt.* Chicago: Haymarket Books, 2011.

Widener, Daniel. *Black Arts West: Culture and Struggle in Postwar Los Angeles.* Durham, NC: Duke University Press, 2010.

Williams, Eric. *Capitalism and Slavery.* Chapel Hill: University of North Carolina Press, 1994.

Williams, Kristian. *Our Enemies in Blue: Police and Power in America.* Boston: South End Press, 2007.

Willse, Craig. *The Value of Homelessness: Managing Surplus Life in the United States.* Minneapolis: University of Minnesota Press, 2015.

Wilson, Francille Rusan. "Mapping the Great Migration." In *The Segregated Scholars: Black Social Scientists and the Creation of Black Labor Studies, 1890–1950*, 115–172. Charlottesville: University of Virginia Press, 2006.

Wilson, Jacqueline Z., Sarah Hodgkinson, Justin Piché, and Kevin Walby, eds. *The Palgrave Handbook of Prison Tourism.* Palgrave Studies in Prisons and Penology. London: Palgrave Macmillan, 2017.

Wilson, James F. *Bulldaggers, Pansies, and Chocolate Babies: Performance, Race, and Sexuality in the Harlem Renaissance.* Ann Arbor: University of Michigan Press, 2010.

Wilson, Mabel O. "Carceral Architectures." Superhumanity. *e-flux architecture*, October 4, 2016. https://www.e-flux.com/architecture/superhumanity/68676/carceral-architectures.

Wilt, James. "How the Spectre of Oil Trains is Deceptively Used to Push Pipelines." *The Narwhal* (formerly *Desmog Canada*), January 6, 2017. https://thenarwhal.ca/how-spectre-oil-trains-deceptively-used-push-pipelines.

Witmer, Lightner. "The Clinical Study and Treatment of Normal and Abnormal Development: A Psychological Clinic." In "Race Improvement in the United States," special issue, *The Annals of the American Academy of Political and Social Science* 34, no. 1 (July 1909): 141–162.

Witmer, Lightner. "The Restoration of Children of the Slums." *Psychological Clinic* 3, no. 9 (1910): 266–280.

Witmer, Lightner. *The Special Class for Backward Children; An Educational Experiment Conducted for the Instruction of Teachers and Other Students of Child Welfare by the Psychological Laboratory and Clinic of the University of Pennsylvania*. Philadelphia: The Psychological Clinic Press, 1911.

Wolfe, Patrick. "Settler Colonialism and the Elimination of the Native." *Journal of Genocide Research* 8, no. 4 (2006): 387–409.

Women's Earth Alliance and Native Youth Sexual Health Network. *Violence on the Land, Violence on Our Bodies: Building an Indigenous Response to Environmental Violence*. Report and Toolkit, 2016.

Wood, Lee, and Barbara Esposito. *Prison Slavery in the Thirteenth Amendment*. Washington, DC: Committee to Abolish Prison Slavery, 1978.

Woods, Clyde Adrian. *Development Arrested: The Blues and Plantation Power in the Mississippi Delta*. London and New York: Verso, 2017.

Wright, Wendy L. "Finding a Home in the Stop-and-Frisk Regime." *Social Justice* 43, no. 3 (2016): 25–45.

Wrigley, Heather Whittle. "Prisoners Rescuing Prisoners: Indexing at Utah State Prison." The Church of Jesus Christ of Latter-Day Saints, October 28, 2011. https://www.churchofjesuschrist.org/church/news/prisoners-rescuing-prisoners-indexing-at-utah-state-prison.

Wynter, Sylvia. "The Re-Enchantment of Humanism: An Interview with Sylvia Wynter." By David Scott, *Small Axe* 8 (September 2000): 119–207.

Yarbrough, Willard. "Reopening of 'New' Brushy Mountain Prison Perks Up Economic Outlook in Petros Area." *Knoxville News-Sentinel*, August 29, 1976.

Young, David W. "'You Feel So Out of Place': Germantown's J. Gordon Baugh and the 1913 Commemoration of the Emancipation Proclamation." *The Pennsylvania Magazine of History and Biography* 137, no. 1 (2013): 79–93.

Youth United for Change, Advancement Project, and the Education Law Center. *Zero Tolerance in Philadelphia: Denying Educational Opportunities and Creating a Pathway to Prison*. Philadelphia: Youth United for Change,

BIBLIOGRAPHY

2011. https://www.atlanticphilanthropies.org/wp-content/uploads/2015/09/Zero-Tolerance-in-Philadelphia-2.pdf.

Yusoff, Kathryn. *A Billion Black Anthropocenes or None.* Minneapolis: University of Minnesota Press, 2018.

Zimmerman, Jane. "The Convict Lease System in Arkansas and the Fight for Abolition." *The Arkansas Historical Quarterly* 8, no. 3 (Autumn 1949): 171–188.

Zuboff, Shoshana. *The Age of Surveillance Capitalism: The Fight for a Human Future at the New Frontier of Power.* London: Profile Books, 2019.

Zwerman, Gilda. "Special Incapacitation: The Emergence of a New Correctional Facility for Women Political Prisoners." *Social Justice* 15, no. 1 (1988): 31–47.

Columbia Books on Architecture and the City
An imprint of the Graduate School of Architecture, Planning, and Preservation

Columbia University
1172 Amsterdam Ave
407 Avery Hall
New York, NY 10027
arch.columbia.edu/books

Distributed by Columbia University Press
cup.columbia.edu

Paths to Prison: On the Architectures of Carcerality

Editor: Isabelle Kirkham-Lewitt
Contributors: Adrienne Brown, Stephen Dillon, Jarrett M. Drake,
Sable Elyse Smith, James Graham, Leslie Lodwick, Dylan Rodríguez, Anne Spice,
Brett Story, Jasmine Syedullah, Mabel O. Wilson, and Wendy L. Wright.

ISBN 978-1-941332-66-5
Library of Congress Control Number: 2020940607

Copyediting: Grace Sparapani
Graphic Design: Laura Coombs
Lithography: Marjeta Morinc
Printing: DZA Druckerei zu Altenburg GmbH
Paper: Peydur Feinleinen, Munken Print Cream 15
Typefaces: LC Schoolbook, Century Schoolbook, Times Ten

Director of Publications: Isabelle Kirkham-Lewitt
Associate Editor: Joanna Joseph

This project was supported by a generous grant from The Graham Foundation for
Advanced Studies in the Fine Arts.

**Graham
Foundation**